I couldn't go cherry blossom viewing...
...for two years in a row!!
Who cares?

Kazunari Kakei

It seems like just the other day that snow was falling, but cherry blossom season is already upon us. (By the time this book comes it, it'll be early summer.) I was feeling melancholy about how time seems to pass more quickly as you grow older...but then I realized I just didn't notice the seasons changing outside because I've been stuck indoors drawing this manga.

NORA: The Last Chronicle of Devildom is Kazunari Kakei's first manga series. It debuted in the April 2004 issue of *Monthly Shonen Jump* and eventually spawned a second series, *SUREBREC: NORA the 2nd*, which premiered in *Monthly Shonen Jump*'s March 2007 issue.

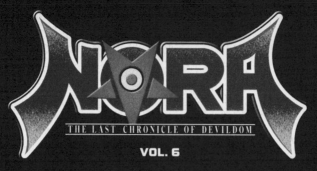

NORA

THE LAST CHRONICLE OF DEVILDOM

VOL. 6

STORY AND ART BY
KAZUNARI KAKEI

English Adaptation/Park Cooper & Barb Lien-Cooper
Translation/Nori Minami
Touch-up Art & Lettering/Annaliese Christman
Design/Sam Elzway
Editor/Shaenon K. Garrity

VP, Production/Alvin Lu
VP, Sales & Product Marketing/Gonzalo Ferreyra
VP, Creative/Linda Espinosa
Publisher/Hyoe Narita

Printed in the U.S.A.

Published by VIZ Media, LLC
P.O. Box 77010
San Francisco, CA 94107

10 9 8 7 6 5 4 3 2
First printing, August 2009
Second printing, September 2009

THE WORLD'S MOST
CUTTING-EDGE MANGA

SHONEN JUMP
ADVANCED

www.shonenjump.com

VIZ
media

www.viz.com

SHONEN JUMP ADVANCED
Manga Edition

NORA
THE LAST CHRONICLE OF DEVILDOM

Volume 6:
Cerberus and the Dark Liege

Kazunari Kakei

R OF THE DEVILDOM A

OUR DEVILISH CAST

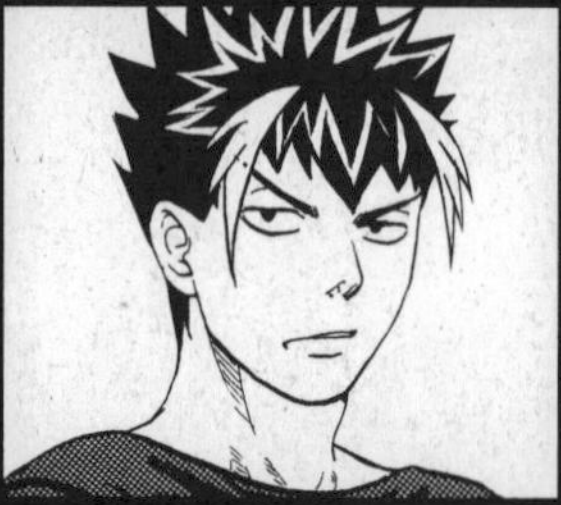

KAZUMA

KAZUMA SEEMS TO HAVE IT ALL. HE'S THE PRESIDENT OF THE STUDENT COUNCIL AS WELL AS A CLEVER GUY WHO'S GOOD AT SPORTS. HE'S ALSO NORA'S MASTER. DESPITE SEEMING CALM AND COMPOSED, KAZUMA'S GOT QUITE A TEMPER. AS A RESULT, OTHER STUDENTS FEAR HIM. VERDICT: HE'S MORE DEVILISH THAN ANY DEMON.

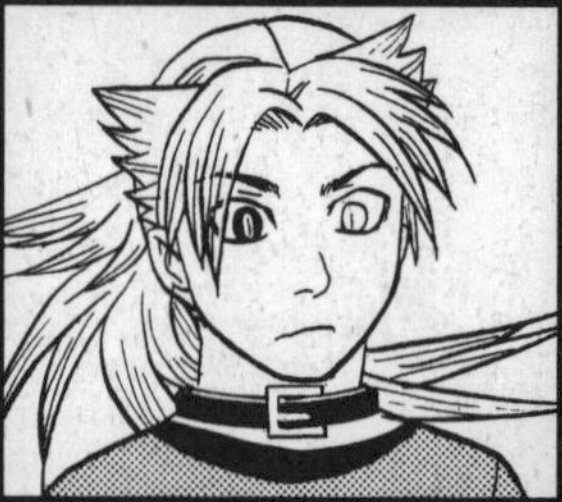

NORA

THE DEMON WORLD'S PROBLEM CHILD, NORA'S FOUL TEMPER IS SURPASSED ONLY BY HIS STUPIDITY. NORA IS BETTER KNOWN AS THE VICIOUS DOG OF DISASTER, THE LEGENDARY DEMON CERBERUS. HIS POWER IS SAID TO SURPASS THAT OF THE DARK LIEGE HERSELF.

DARK LIEGE ARMY

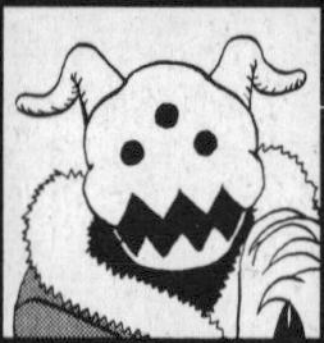

HER INFERNAL MAJESTY, THE DARK LIEGE

THE COMMANDER-IN-CHIEF OF THE DARK LIEGE ARMY AND THE ONE WHO EXILED NORA TO THE HUMAN WORLD. WHEN SHE WEARS HER GLAMOUR SPELL, SHE'S ONE SMOKIN' HOTTIE. ALTHOUGH EVIL KEEPS HER BUSY, SHE NEVER NEGLECTS HER BEAUTY REGIMEN!

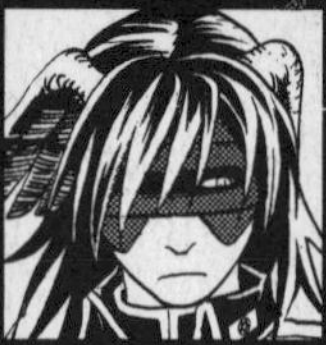

KAIN

A GOVERNOR-GENERAL AIDE AND RIGHT-HAND MAN TO THE DARK LIEGE. IN ADDITION TO BEING A COMMANDER, HE'S THE DARK LIEGE'S MOST TRUSTED CONFIDANTE.

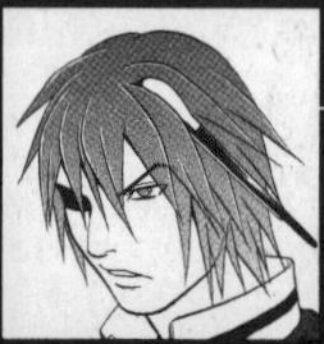

RIVAN

LAID BACK AND SEEMINGLY LAZY, ONCE RIVAN SNAPS, NOBODY CAN HOLD HIM DOWN. HE'S INTO FISHING.

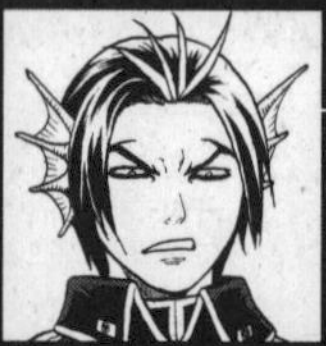

BARIK

BARIK IS SURLY, INFLEXIBLE AND NOT REMOTELY FOND OF NORA. BAD LUCK SEEMS TO PLAGUE HIM WHEREVER HE GOES.

TENRYO ACADEMY MIDDLE SCHOOL, STUDENT COUNCIL

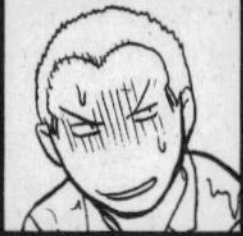

FUJIMOTO

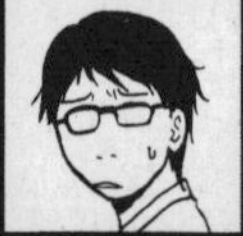

YANO

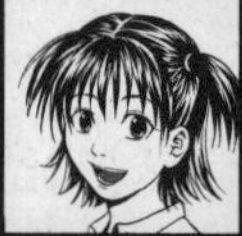

KOYUKI HIRASAKA

N THE LAST CHRONICLE O

THE RESISTANCE

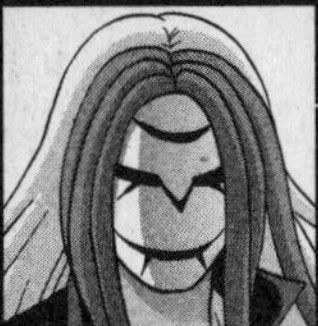

THE MASTERMIND IN THE MASK

THE MYSTERIOUS HEAD OF THE RESISTANCE. RUMOR HAS IT HE KNOWS ALL THE SECRETS OF THE DEMON WORLD. IT'S CURRENTLY UNKNOWN WHY HE OPPOSES THE DARK LIEGE ARMY.

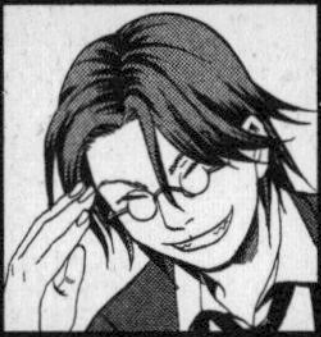

KNELL

A MEMBER OF THE DEMON RESISTANCE WHO MAY HAVE HIS OWN SECRET AGENDA. OR MAYBE HE'D JUST RATHER PICK UP GIRLS. IGUNISU MAGIA HAS NO EFFECT ON HIM—INSTEAD, THE *LADIES* SEEM TO BE HIS WEAKNESS.

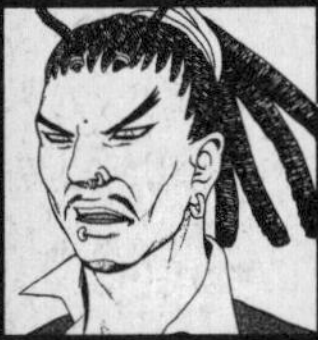

TYRON

A POWERFUL DEMON CAPABLE OF CRACKING THE GROUND WITH EARTH-TYPE MAGIC AND SLICING THROUGH AN OPPONENT'S MAGICAL ATTACK WITH A SWORD.

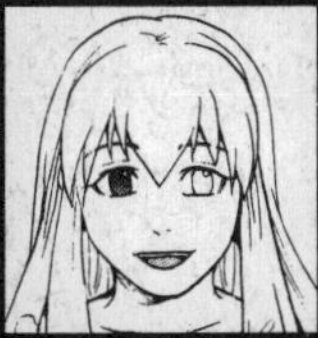

DAHLIA

A GIRL WHO GREW UP WITH NORA IN A RESTRICTED AREA OF THE DEMON WORLD. SHE HAS THE ABILITY TO IDENTIFY DARK LIEGE SOUL FRAGMENTS AND HAS BEEN DOING SO FOR THE RESISTANCE...FOR PERSONAL REASONS.

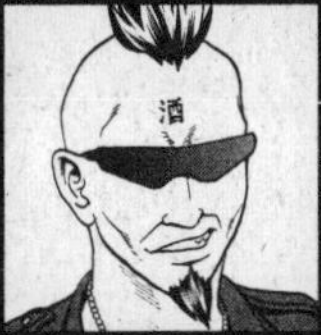
酒

THE SNITCH

HE'S GOT ALL THE ANSWERS CONCERNING BOTH THE DARK LIEGE AND THE RESISTANCE. WHEN NOT SNITCHING, HE MANAGES A CAFÉ.

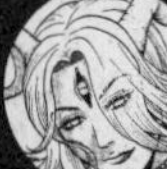

LISTEN TO TEACHER! ♥
THE DARK LIEGE EXPLAINS IT ALL

HELLO, SWEETUMS, DARK LIEGE HERE. MISS ME?♥

FOR THOSE WHO'VE JUST ARRIVED...GOSH, MY LITTLE DEMON PUP NORA HAS BEEN A BOTHER! DON'T I HAVE ENOUGH TROUBLE WITH THE RESISTANCE AND OUTLAW DEMONS REBELLING AGAINST MY DARK LIEGE ARMY WITHOUT NORA CAUSING ME PROBLEMS?

THAT'S WHY I SENT MY STRAY DOGGIE TO THE HUMAN WORLD, TELLING HIM HE SIMPLY MUST LEARN TO BEHAVE.♥

OH, I'M SO WICKED! THE HUMAN I CHOSE TO HOUSEBREAK MY LITTLE CUR IS KAZUMA MAGARI.

BY ENTERING INTO A MASTER AND SERVANT CONTRACT WITH KAZUMA, NORA BECAME KAZUMA'S "FAMILIAR SPIRIT." AS SUCH, NORA CAN'T USE HIS MAGIC OR RELEASE HIS SEAL SPELL TO RETURN TO HIS REGULAR APPEARANCE WITHOUT HIS MASTER'S "APPROVAL."

KAZUMA DOESN'T EXACTLY HAVE MAGICAL ABILITIES...OR RATHER, HE DIDN'T. THE CLEVER BOY RECENTLY MADE A DEAL WITH A DEMONIC "INFORMATION SOURCE" (A.K.A. A SNITCH). IN EXCHANGE FOR FIVE YEARS OF HIS LIFE, HE LEARNED HOW TO CONTROL THE MAGIC THAT SEEPS INTO HIS SYSTEM AS A RESULT OF BEING NORA'S MASTER. USUALLY IT'S IMPOSSIBLE FOR MAGICAL POWER TO PERMEATE A HUMAN BODY. BUT KAZUMA ISN'T YOUR AVERAGE HUMAN.♥

AFTER THAT MY LOVELY LADS TOOK ON THE BOSS OF THE RESISTANCE. HOW GALLANT OF THEM! THE MEANIE IN THE MASK TOLD MY POOR PUPPY THAT A CERBERUS IS FATED TO DIE WHEN HE REACHES MAXIMUM POWER, AND BY TRAINING HIM UP I'VE AS GOOD AS KILLED HIM!! NO WONDER MY LITTLE CUR CAN'T TELL HIS HEAD FROM HIS WAGGLY TAIL!

NORA
THE LAST CHRONICLE OF DEVILDOM

CONTENTS

Volume 6:
Cerberus and
the Dark Liege

Story 21: Cerberus and the Dark Liege

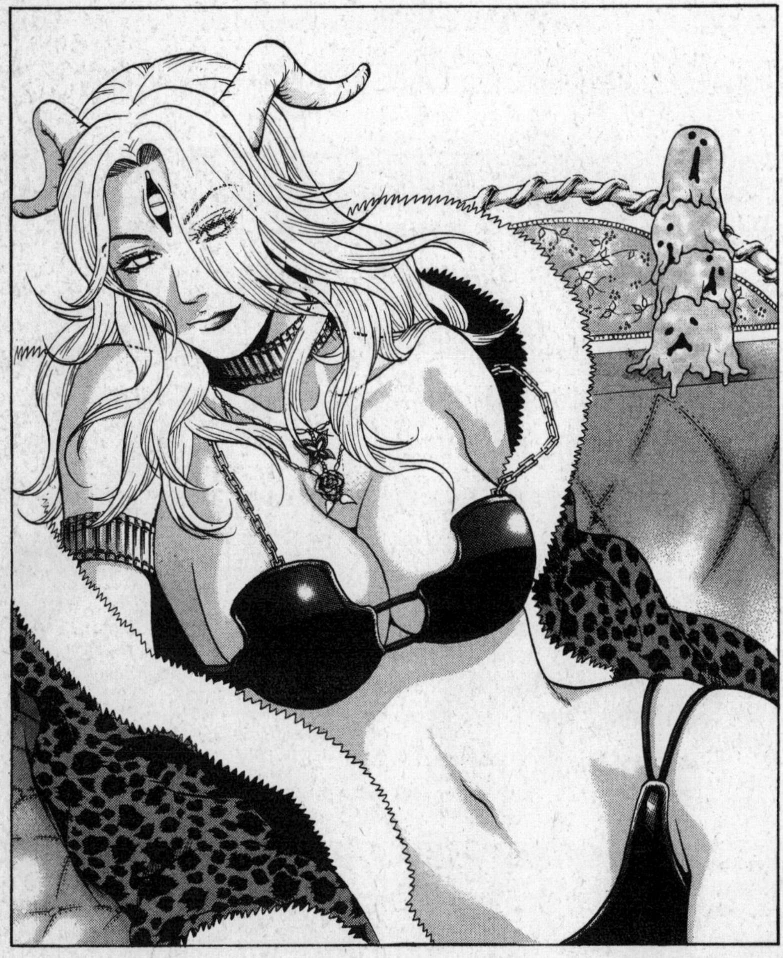

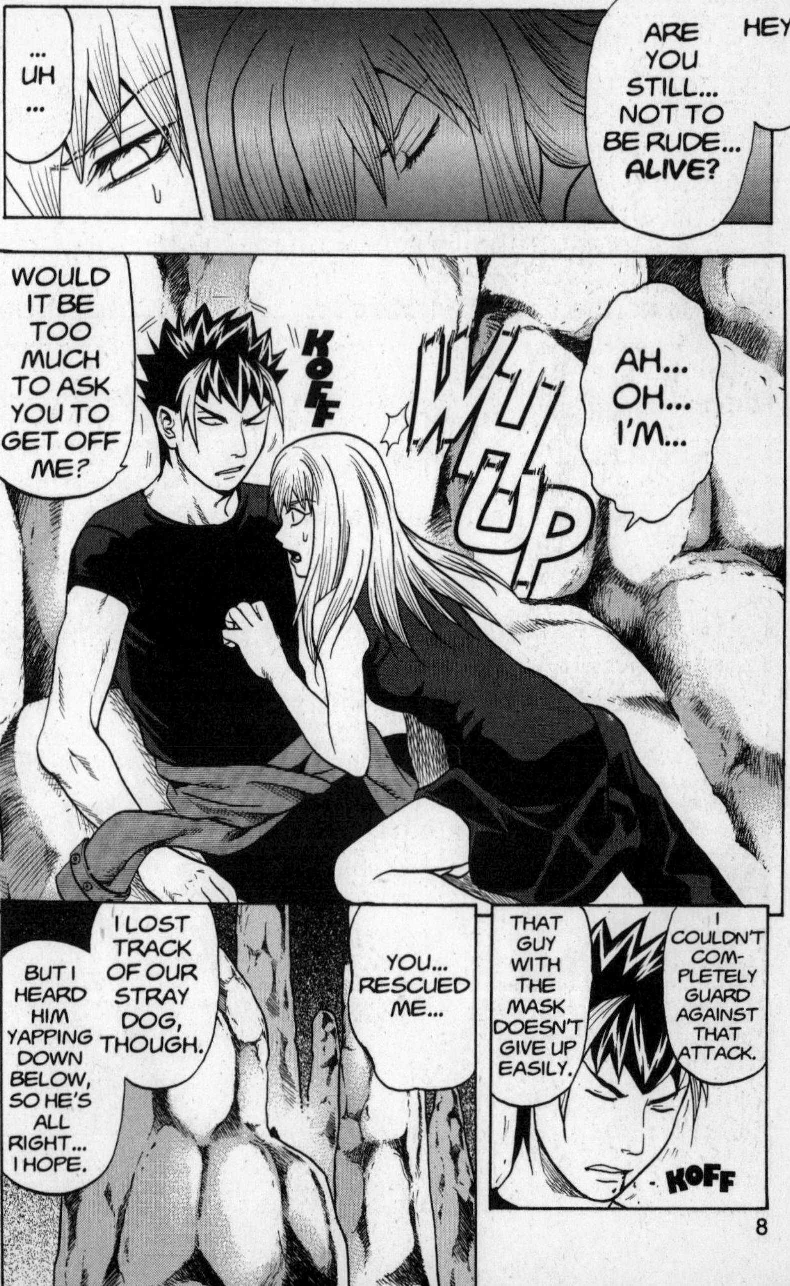
HEY...
ARE YOU STILL... NOT TO BE RUDE... ALIVE?
... UH ...
AH... OH... I'M...
WHUP
KOFF
WOULD IT BE TOO MUCH TO ASK YOU TO GET OFF ME?
I COULDN'T COMPLETELY GUARD AGAINST THAT ATTACK.
THAT GUY WITH THE MASK DOESN'T GIVE UP EASILY.
KOFF
YOU... RESCUED ME...
I LOST TRACK OF OUR STRAY DOG, THOUGH.
BUT I HEARD HIM YAPPING DOWN BELOW, SO HE'S ALL RIGHT... I HOPE.

READ THIS WAY

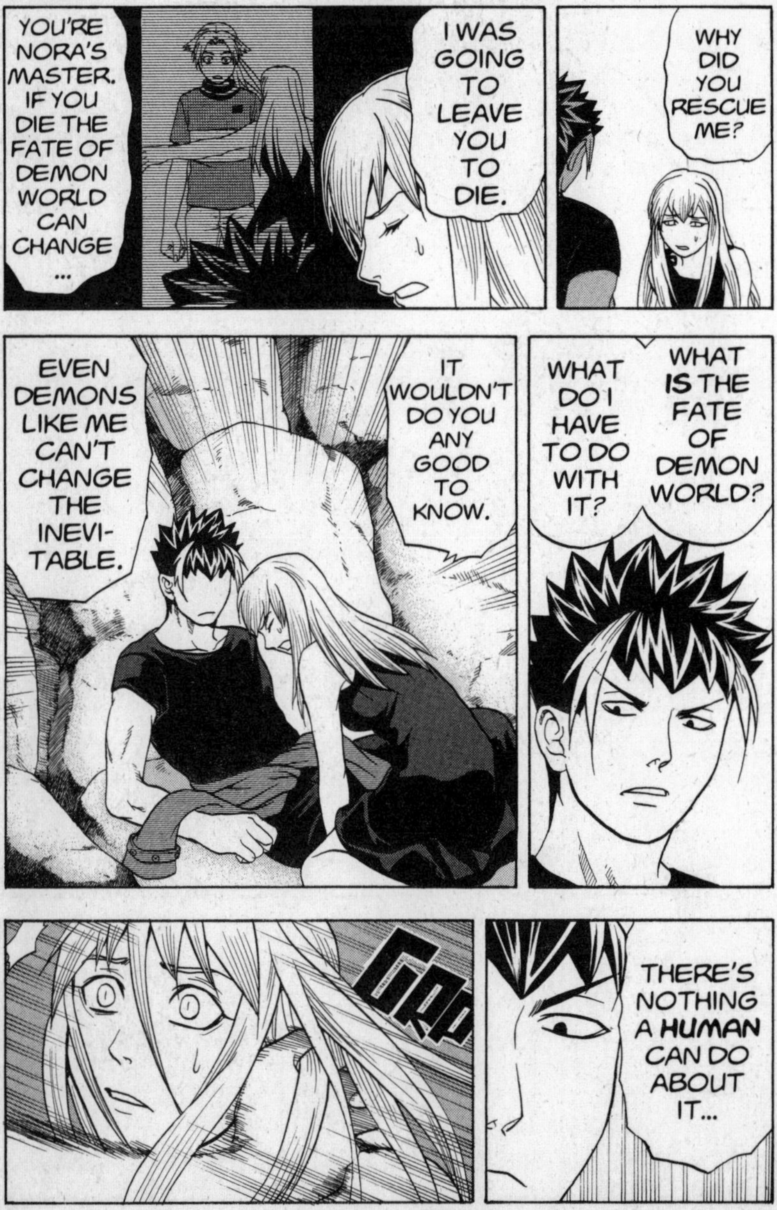
WHY DID YOU RESCUE ME?
I WAS GOING TO LEAVE YOU TO DIE.
YOU'RE NORA'S MASTER. IF YOU DIE THE FATE OF DEMON WORLD CAN CHANGE ...
WHAT IS THE FATE OF DEMON WORLD?
WHAT DO I HAVE TO DO WITH IT?
IT WOULDN'T DO YOU ANY GOOD TO KNOW.
EVEN DEMONS LIKE ME CAN'T CHANGE THE INEVITABLE.
THERE'S NOTHING A HUMAN CAN DO ABOUT IT...

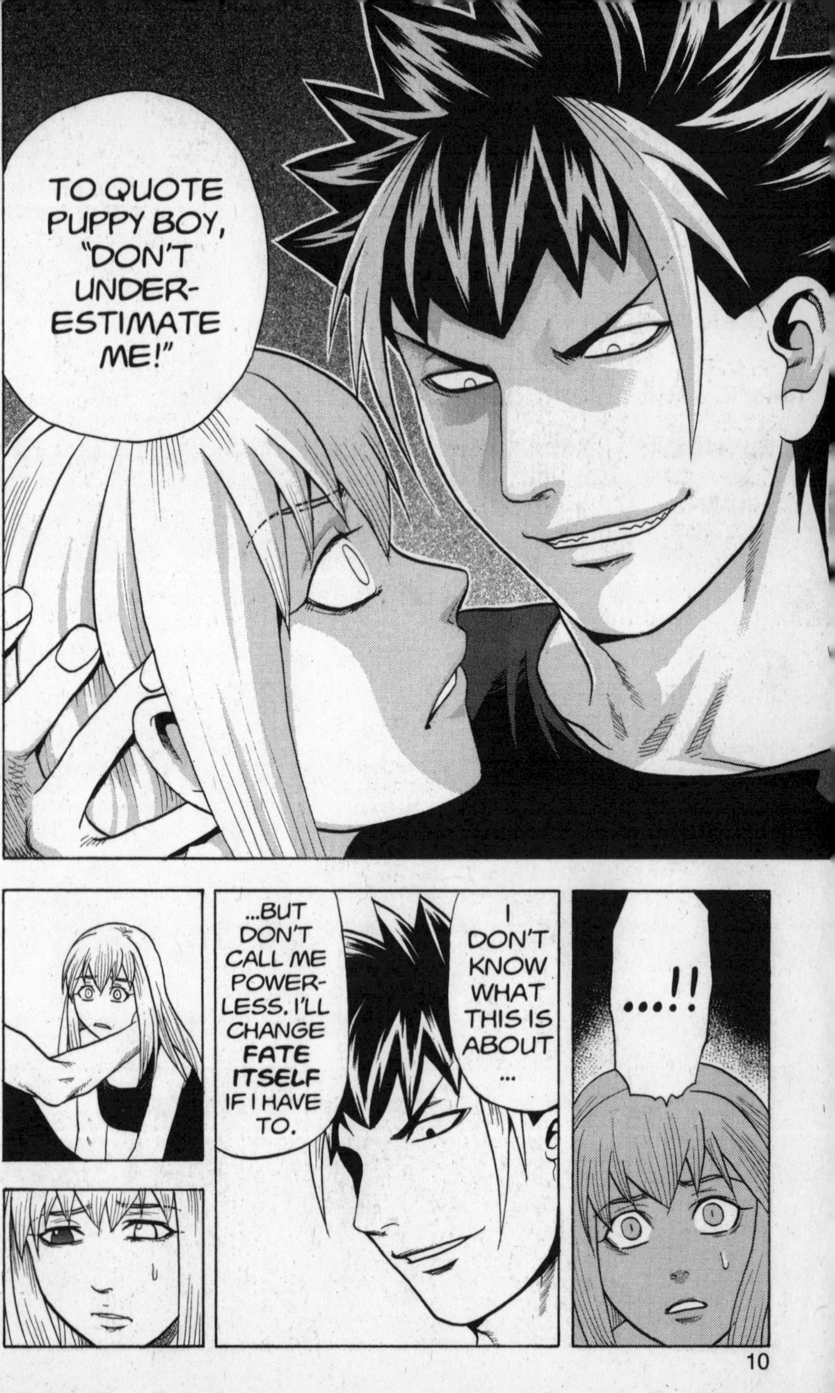
TO QUOTE PUPPY BOY, "DON'T UNDER-ESTIMATE ME!"
...!!
I DON'T KNOW WHAT THIS IS ABOUT...
...BUT DON'T CALL ME POWER-LESS. I'LL CHANGE **FATE ITSELF** IF I HAVE TO.

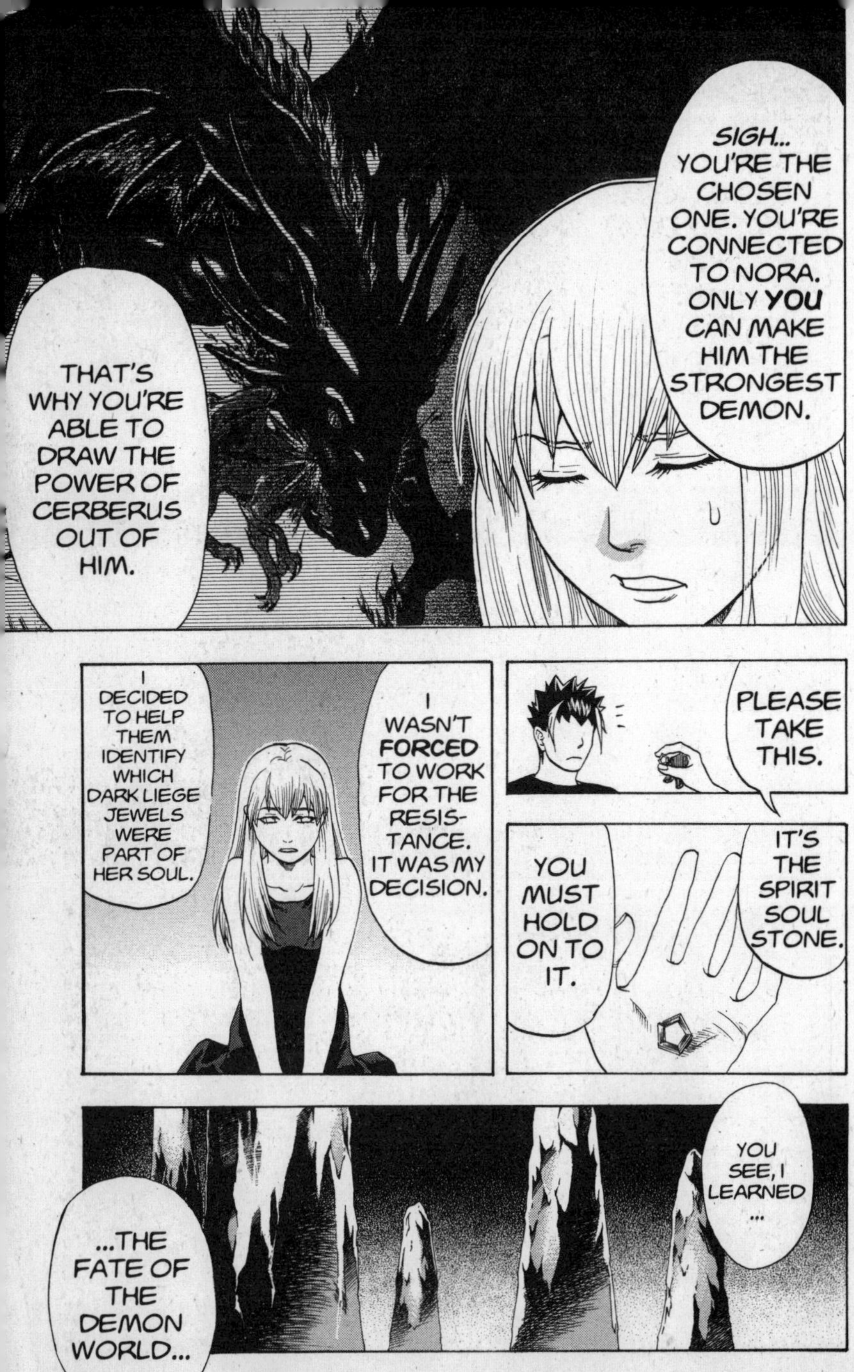
SIGH... YOU'RE THE CHOSEN ONE. YOU'RE CONNECTED TO NORA. ONLY YOU CAN MAKE HIM THE STRONGEST DEMON.
THAT'S WHY YOU'RE ABLE TO DRAW THE POWER OF CERBERUS OUT OF HIM.
PLEASE TAKE THIS.
IT'S THE SPIRIT SOUL STONE.
YOU MUST HOLD ON TO IT.
I WASN'T FORCED TO WORK FOR THE RESISTANCE. IT WAS MY DECISION.
I DECIDED TO HELP THEM IDENTIFY WHICH DARK LIEGE JEWELS WERE PART OF HER SOUL.
YOU SEE, I LEARNED ...
...THE FATE OF THE DEMON WORLD...

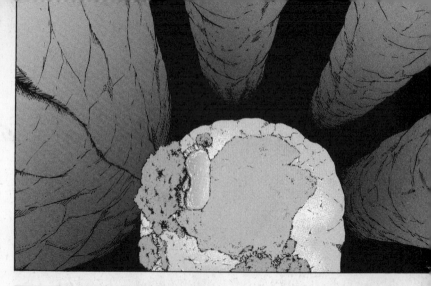

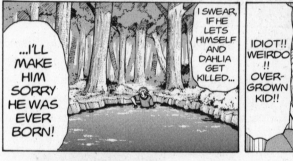

HEY, YOU! CAN YOU HEAR ME NOW?
IDIOT!! WEIRDO!! OVER-GROWN KID!!
I SWEAR, IF HE LETS HIMSELF AND DAHLIA GET KILLED...
...I'LL MAKE HIM SORRY HE WAS EVER BORN!
WHY'S DAHLIA WORKING FOR THE RESIS-TANCE ANYWAY?
I DON'T GET **ANYTHING** THAT'S GOIN' ON ANY-MORE.
TRY TO BECOME THE STRON-GEST AND YOU'LL DIE.
...
I'M TIRED.
I'M IN PAIN.
WORST OF ALL, MY **BRAIN HURTS** FROM HAVING TO THINK SO MUCH.
BLUP
BLUP

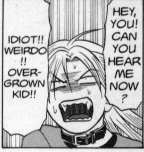

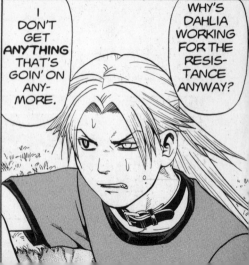

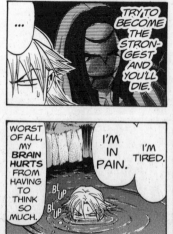

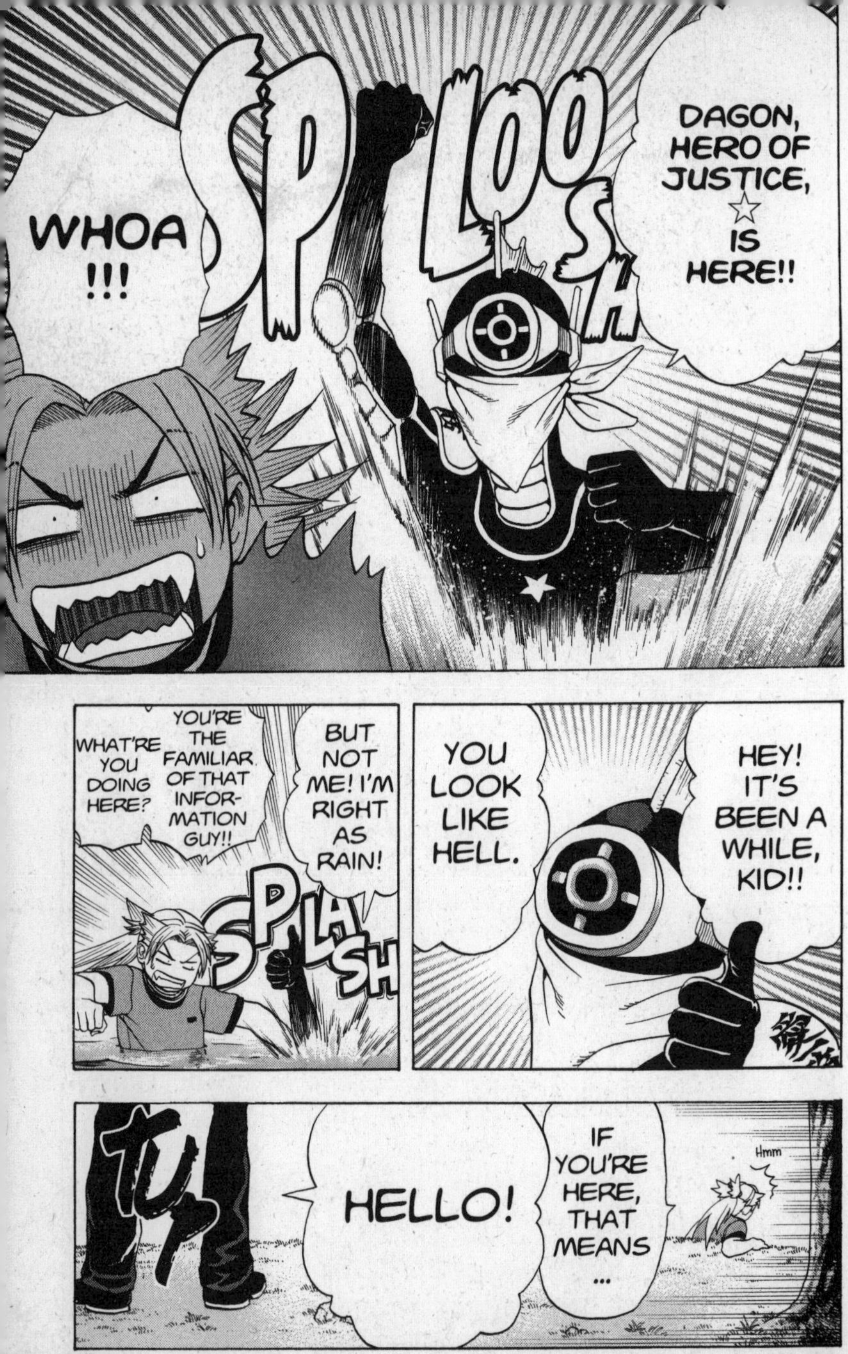
DAGON, HERO OF JUSTICE, ☆ IS HERE!!
SPLOOSH
WHOA!!!
HEY! IT'S BEEN A WHILE, KID!!
YOU LOOK LIKE HELL.
BUT NOT ME! I'M RIGHT AS RAIN!
YOU'RE THE FAMILIAR OF THAT INFORMATION GUY!!
WHAT'RE YOU DOING HERE?
SPLASH
Hmm
IF YOU'RE HERE, THAT MEANS ...
HELLO!

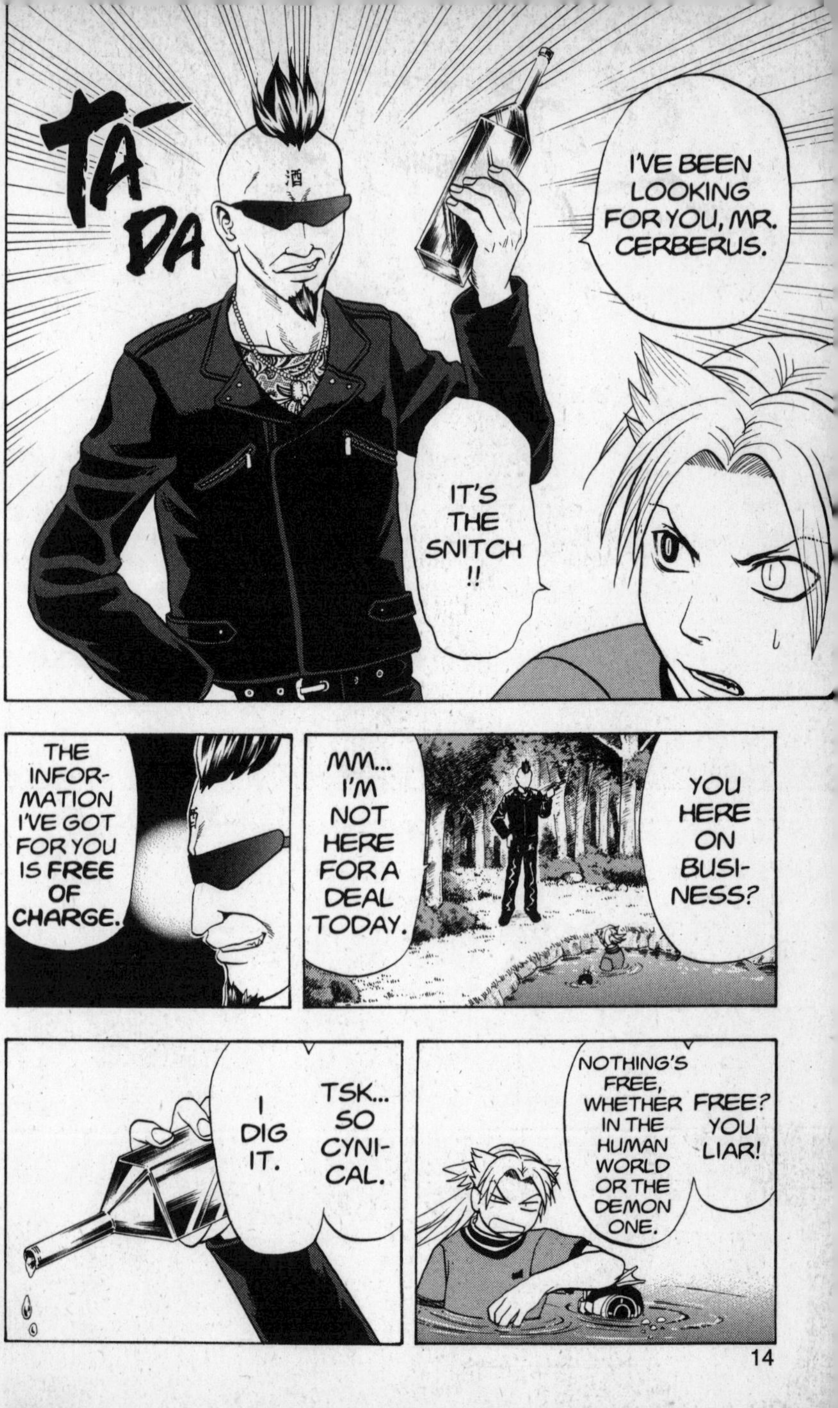
I'VE BEEN LOOKING FOR YOU, MR. CERBERUS.
TA-DA
IT'S THE SNITCH!!
YOU HERE ON BUSINESS?
MM... I'M NOT HERE FOR A DEAL TODAY.
THE INFORMATION I'VE GOT FOR YOU IS FREE OF CHARGE.
FREE? YOU LIAR!
NOTHING'S FREE, WHETHER IN THE HUMAN WORLD OR THE DEMON ONE.
TSK... SO CYNICAL.
I DIG IT.

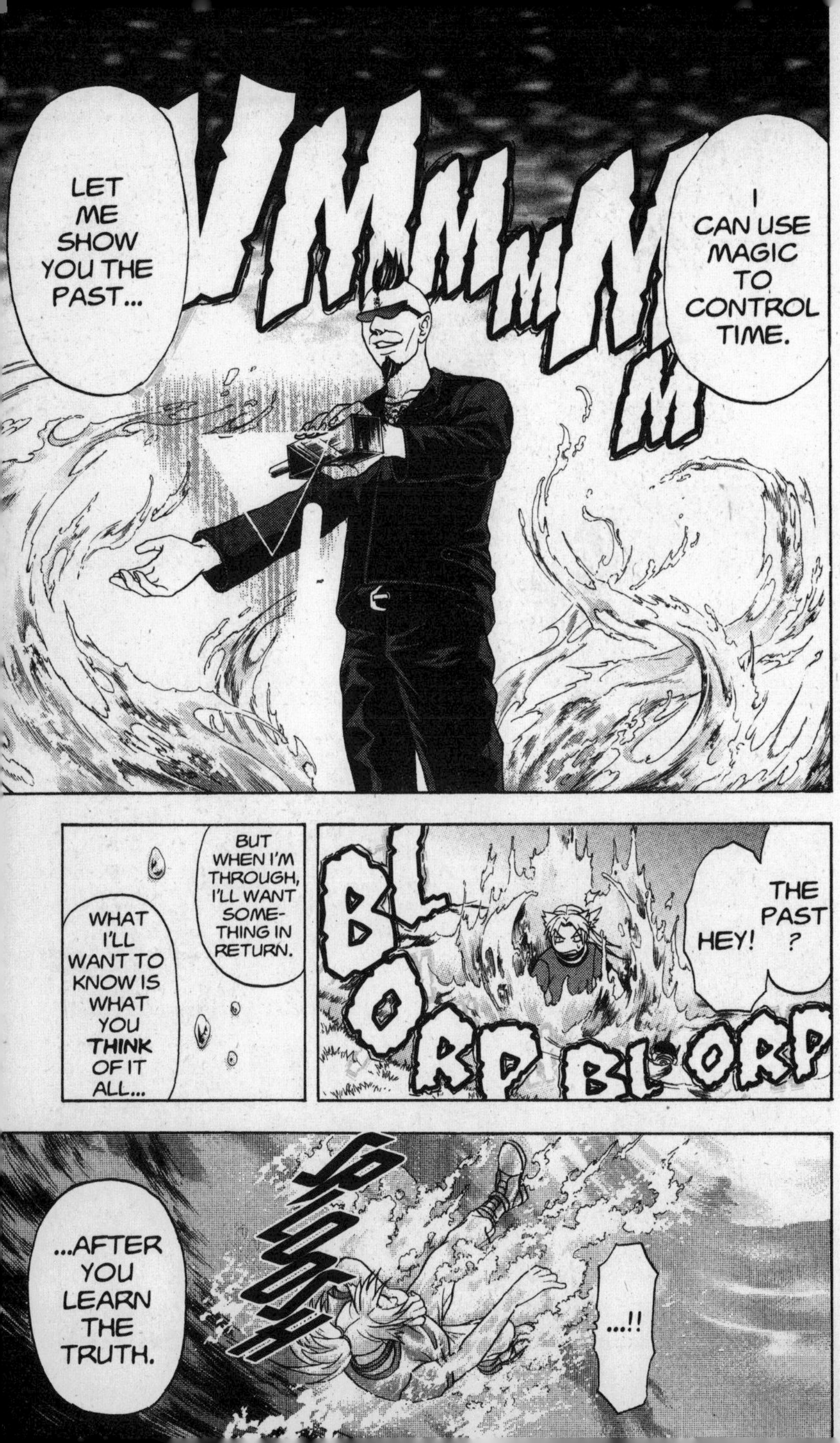
I CAN USE MAGIC TO CONTROL TIME.
VMMMMM
LET ME SHOW YOU THE PAST...
THE PAST?
HEY!
BLORP BLORP
BUT WHEN I'M THROUGH, I'LL WANT SOME-THING IN RETURN.
WHAT I'LL WANT TO KNOW IS WHAT YOU THINK OF IT ALL...
...!!
SPLOOSH!!
...AFTER YOU LEARN THE TRUTH.

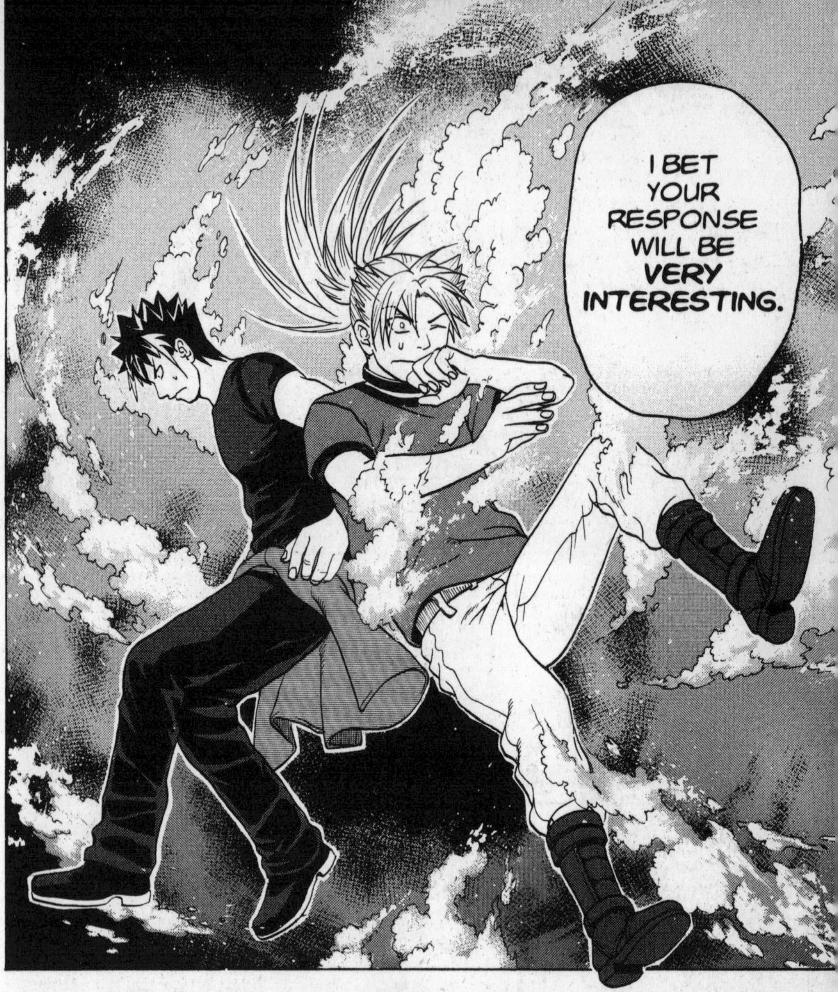
I BET YOUR RESPONSE WILL BE **VERY INTERESTING.**

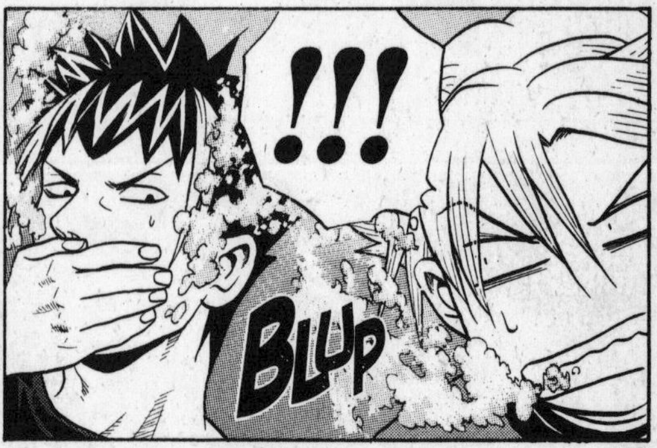
!!!
BLUP

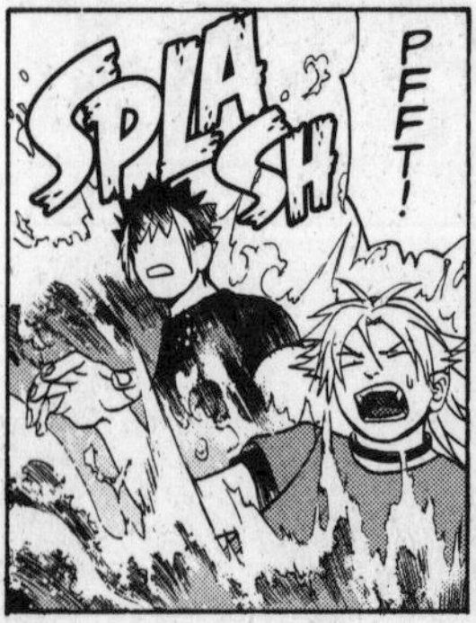
SPLASH
PFFT!

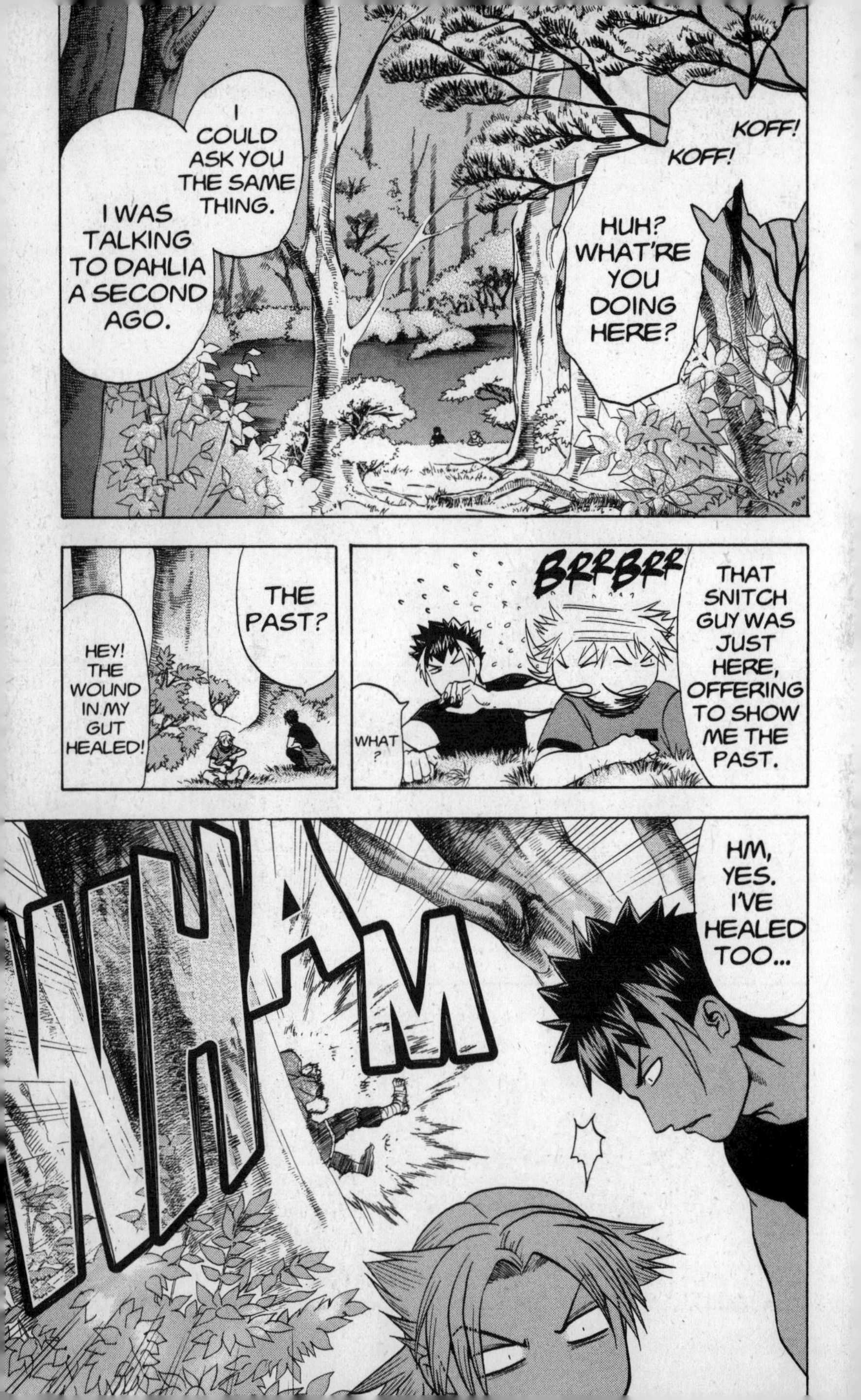
KOFF!
KOFF!
HUH? WHAT'RE YOU DOING HERE?
I COULD ASK YOU THE SAME THING.
I WAS TALKING TO DAHLIA A SECOND AGO.
BRRBRR
THAT SNITCH GUY WAS JUST HERE, OFFERING TO SHOW ME THE PAST.
WHAT?
THE PAST?
HEY! THE WOUND IN MY GUT HEALED!
HM, YES. I'VE HEALED TOO...
WHAM

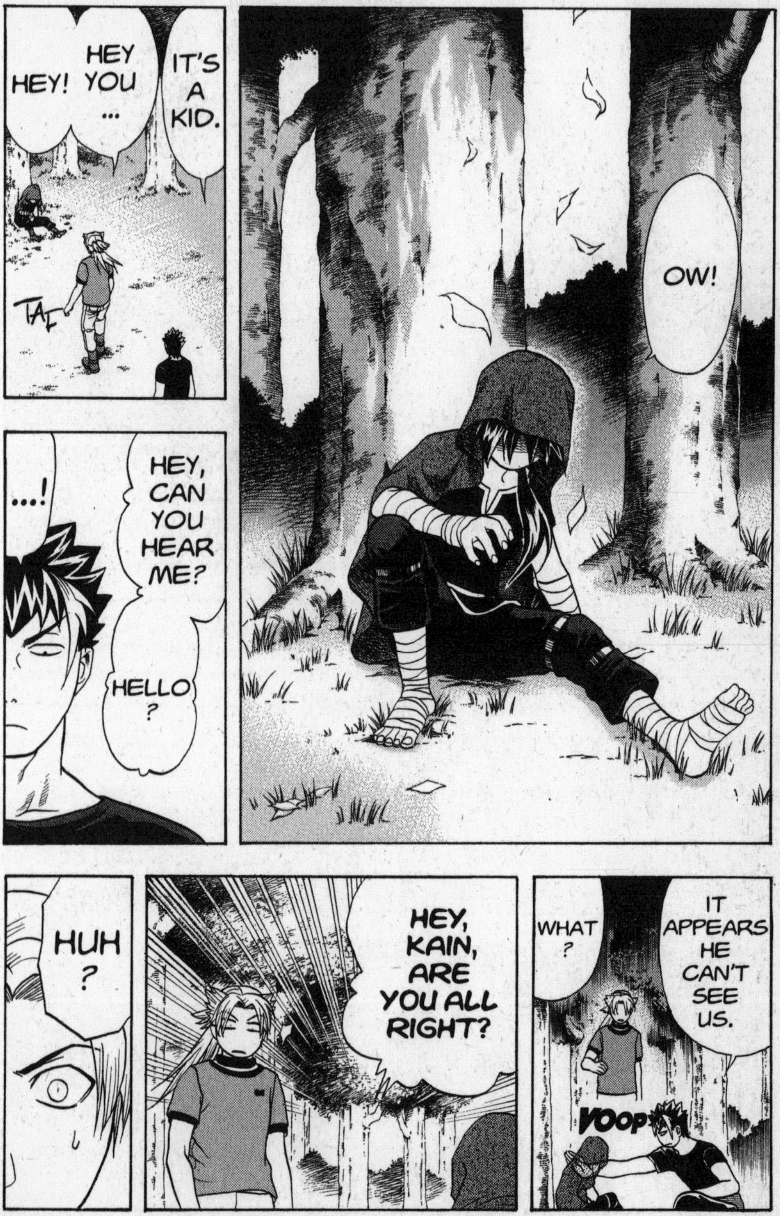
OW!
IT'S A KID.
HEY YOU ...
HEY!
HEY, CAN YOU HEAR ME?
HELLO?
...!
IT APPEARS HE CAN'T SEE US.
WHAT?
VOOP
HEY, KAIN, ARE YOU ALL RIGHT?
HUH?

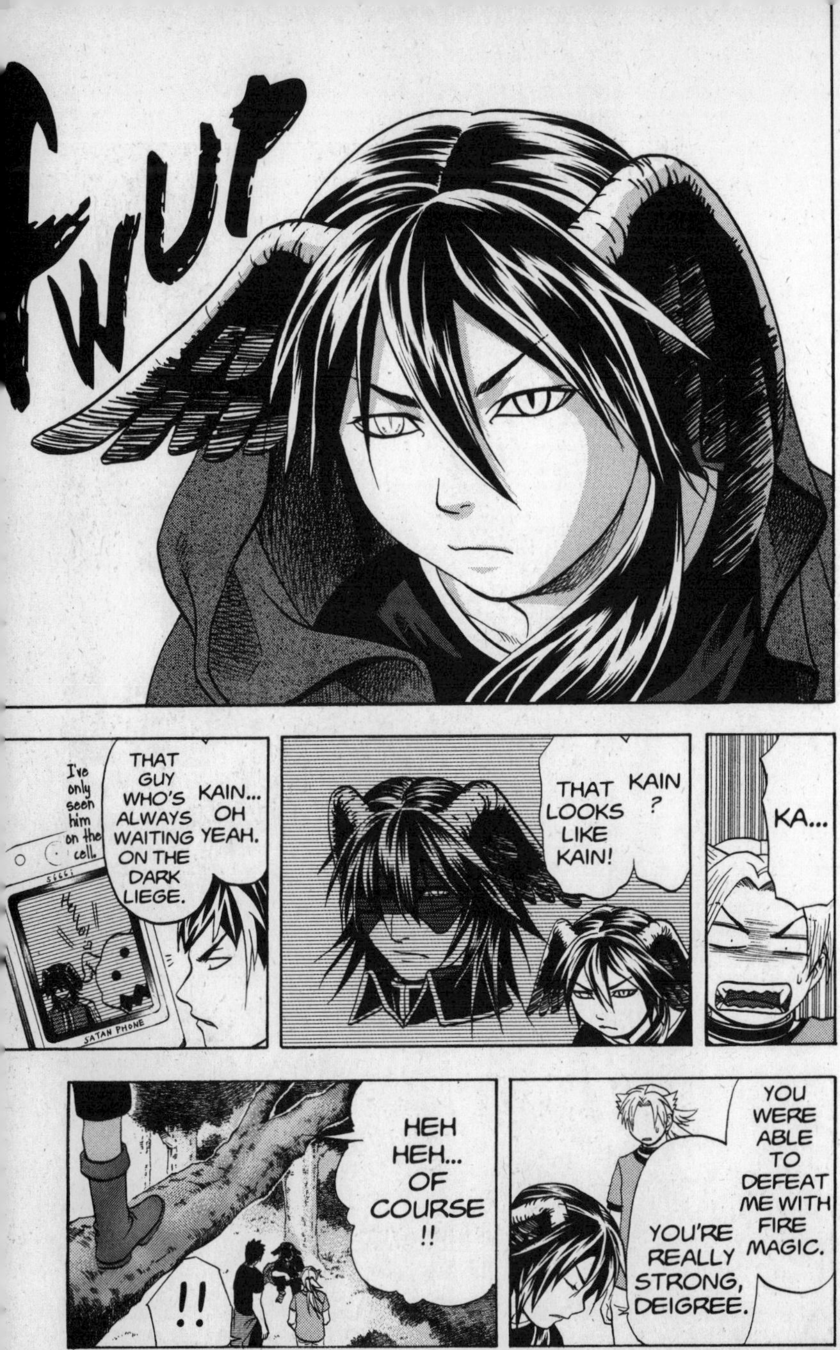
FWUP
KA...
KAIN ?
THAT LOOKS LIKE KAIN!
KAIN... OH YEAH.
THAT GUY WHO'S ALWAYS WAITING ON THE DARK LIEGE.
I've only seen him on the cell.
SATAN PHONE
YOU WERE ABLE TO DEFEAT ME WITH FIRE MAGIC.
YOU'RE REALLY STRONG, DEIGREE.
HEH HEH... OF COURSE !!
!!

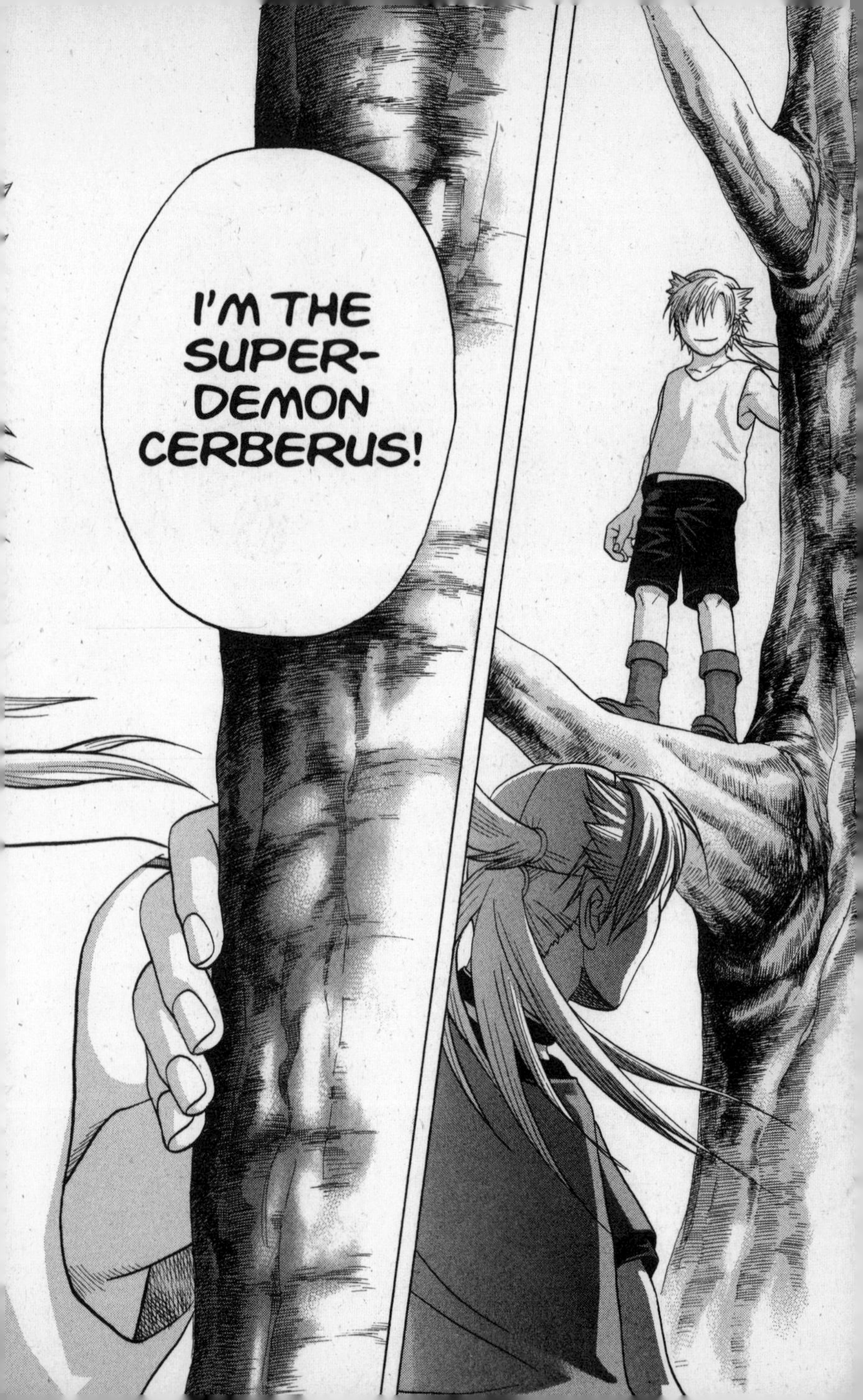
I'M THE SUPER-DEMON CERBERUS!

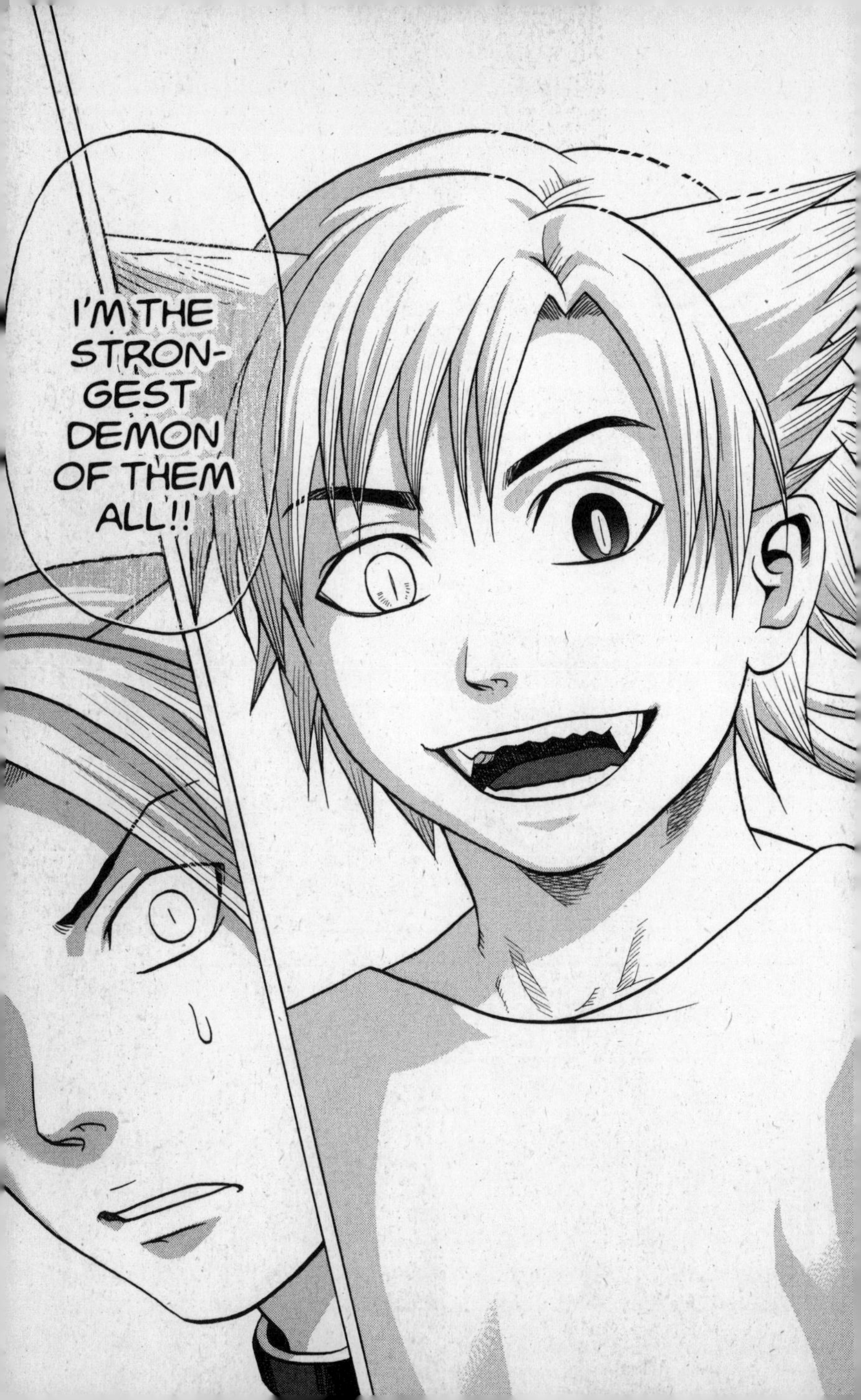
I'M THE STRON-GEST DEMON OF THEM ALL!!

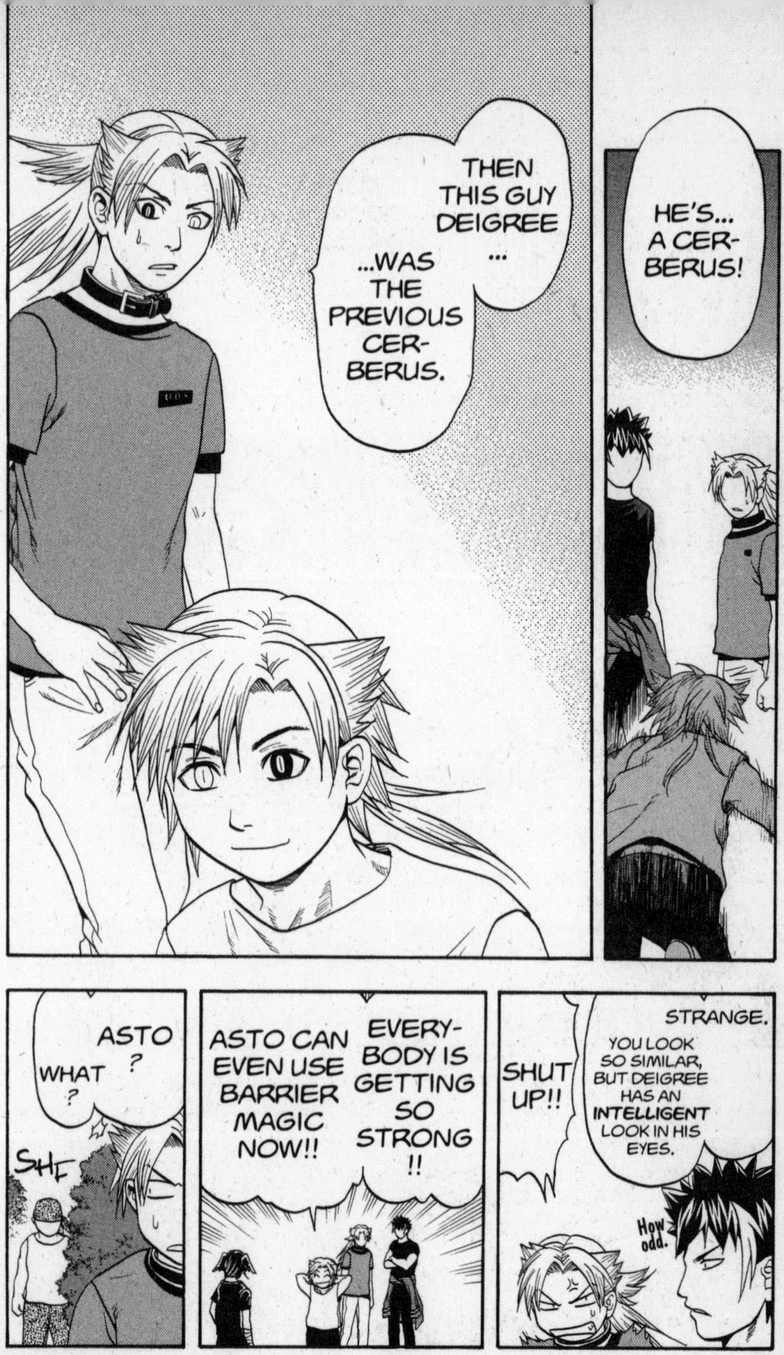
HE'S... A CER-BERUS!
THEN THIS GUY DEIGREE ...
...WAS THE PREVIOUS CER-BERUS.
STRANGE.
YOU LOOK SO SIMILAR, BUT DEIGREE HAS AN **INTELLIGENT** LOOK IN HIS EYES.
SHUT UP!!
How odd.
EVERY-BODY IS GETTING SO STRONG!!
ASTO CAN EVEN USE BARRIER MAGIC NOW!!
ASTO?
WHAT?

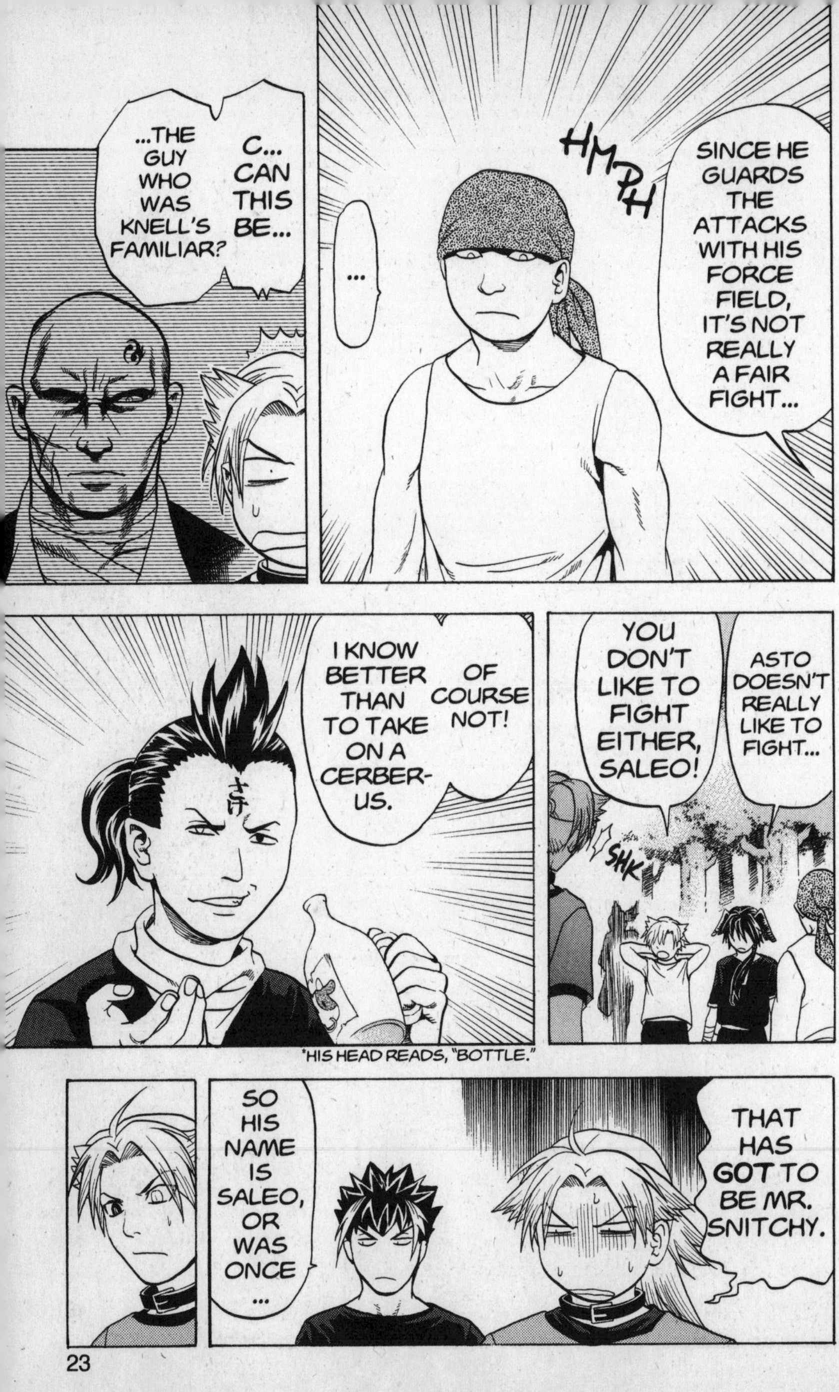
SINCE HE GUARDS THE ATTACKS WITH HIS FORCE FIELD, IT'S NOT REALLY A FAIR FIGHT...
HMPH
...
C... CAN THIS BE...
...THE GUY WHO WAS KNELL'S FAMILIAR?
ASTO DOESN'T REALLY LIKE TO FIGHT...
YOU DON'T LIKE TO FIGHT EITHER, SALEO!
SHK
OF COURSE NOT!
I KNOW BETTER THAN TO TAKE ON A CERBERUS.
さけ
THAT HAS GOT TO BE MR. SNITCHY.
SO HIS NAME IS SALEO, OR WAS ONCE...
*HIS HEAD READS, "BOTTLE."

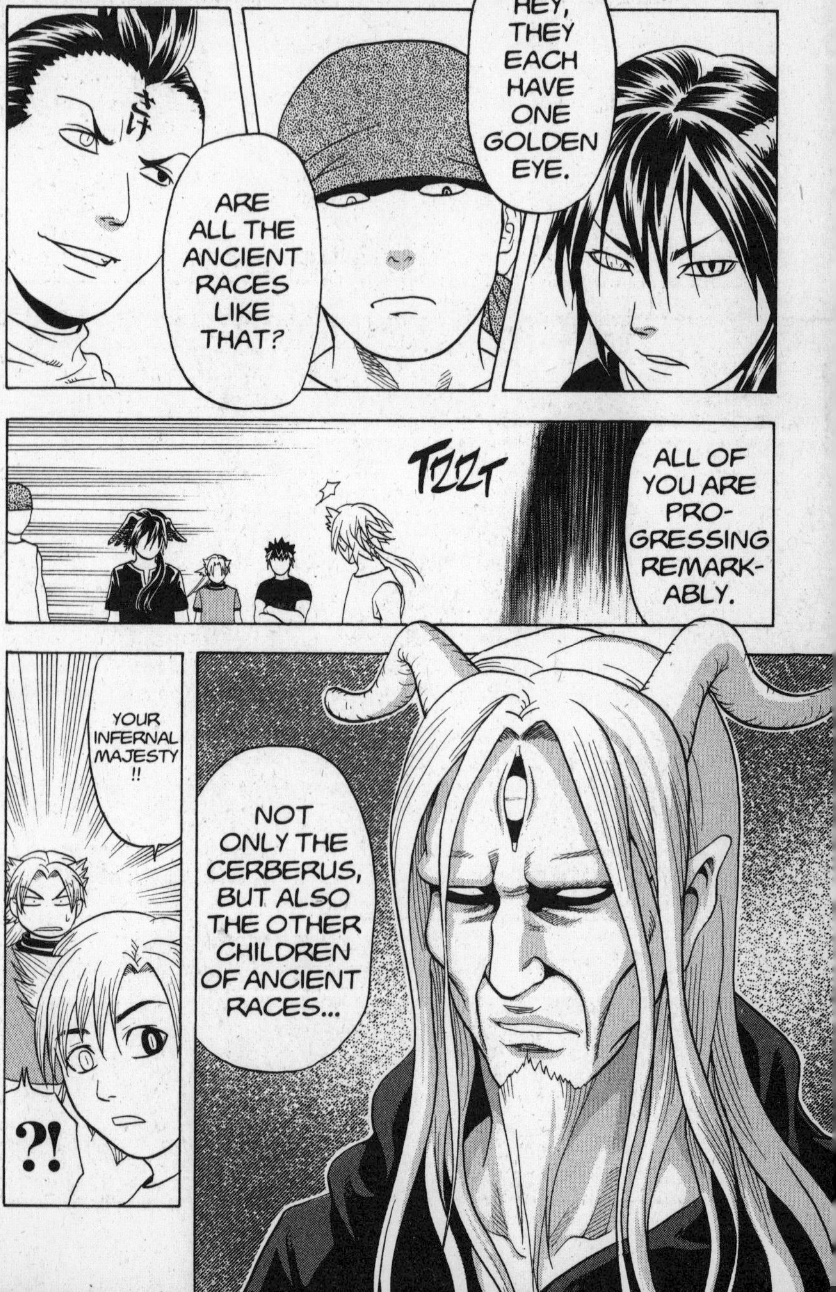
HEY, THEY EACH HAVE ONE GOLDEN EYE.
ARE ALL THE ANCIENT RACES LIKE THAT?
ALL OF YOU ARE PRO-GRESSING REMARK-ABLY.
TZZT
NOT ONLY THE CERBERUS, BUT ALSO THE OTHER CHILDREN OF ANCIENT RACES...
YOUR INFERNAL MAJESTY !!
?!

READ THIS WAY

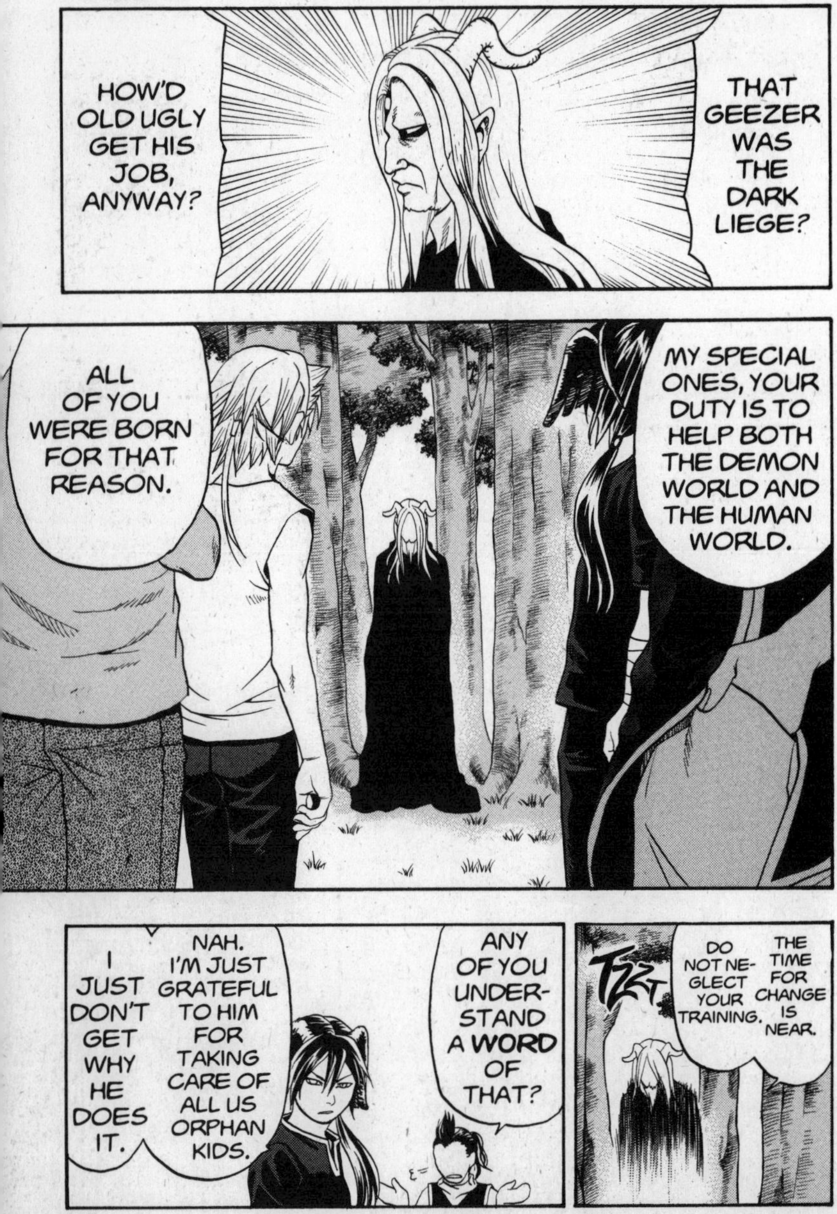

THAT GEEZER WAS THE DARK LIEGE?
HOW'D OLD UGLY GET HIS JOB, ANYWAY?
MY SPECIAL ONES, YOUR DUTY IS TO HELP BOTH THE DEMON WORLD AND THE HUMAN WORLD.
ALL OF YOU WERE BORN FOR THAT REASON.
TZZT
THE TIME FOR CHANGE IS NEAR.
DO NOT NEGLECT YOUR TRAINING.
ANY OF YOU UNDERSTAND A **WORD** OF THAT?
NAH. I'M JUST GRATEFUL TO HIM FOR TAKING CARE OF ALL US ORPHAN KIDS.
I JUST DON'T GET WHY HE DOES IT.

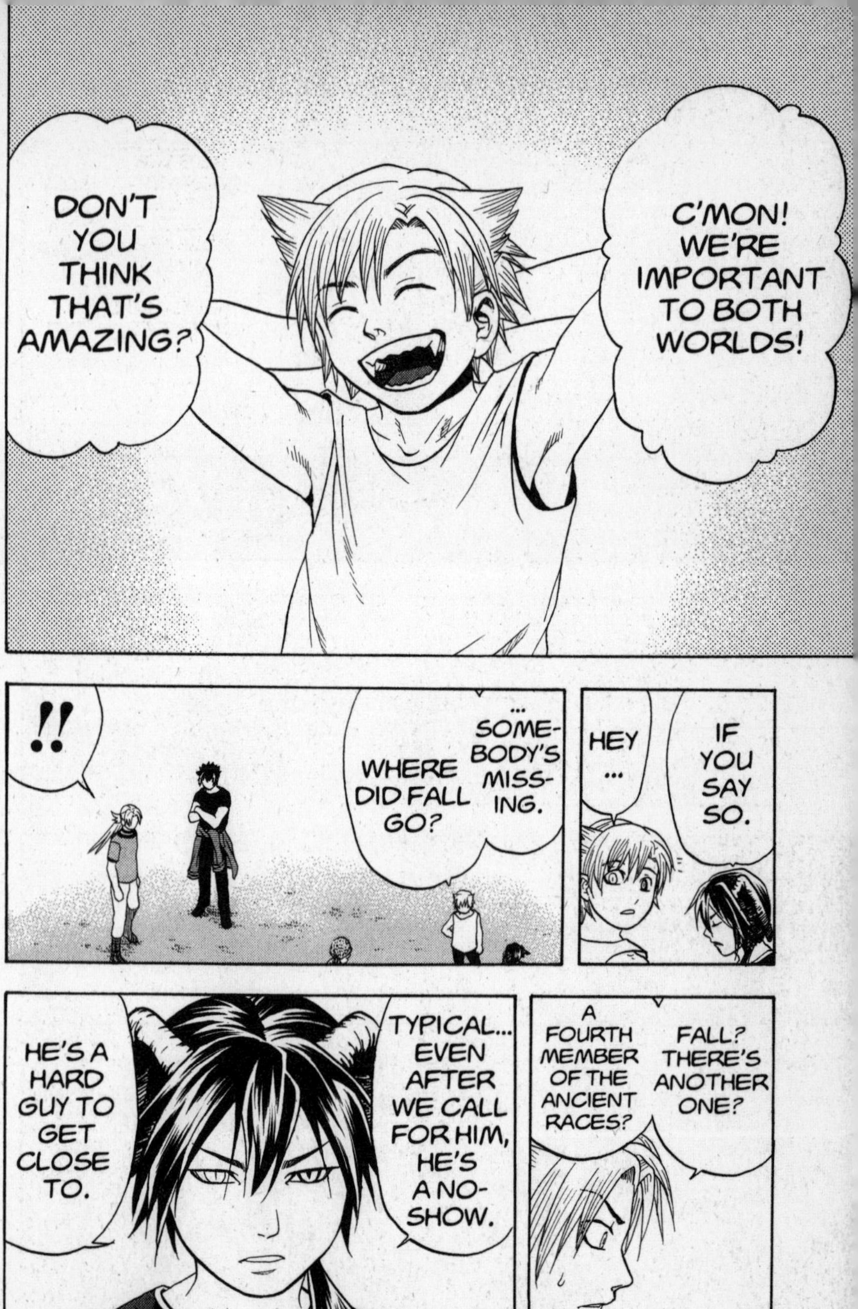
C'MON! WE'RE IMPORTANT TO BOTH WORLDS!
DON'T YOU THINK THAT'S AMAZING?
IF YOU SAY SO.
HEY ...
... SOMEBODY'S MISSING.
WHERE DID FALL GO?
!!
FALL? THERE'S ANOTHER ONE?
A FOURTH MEMBER OF THE ANCIENT RACES?
TYPICAL... EVEN AFTER WE CALL FOR HIM, HE'S A NO-SHOW.
HE'S A HARD GUY TO GET CLOSE TO.

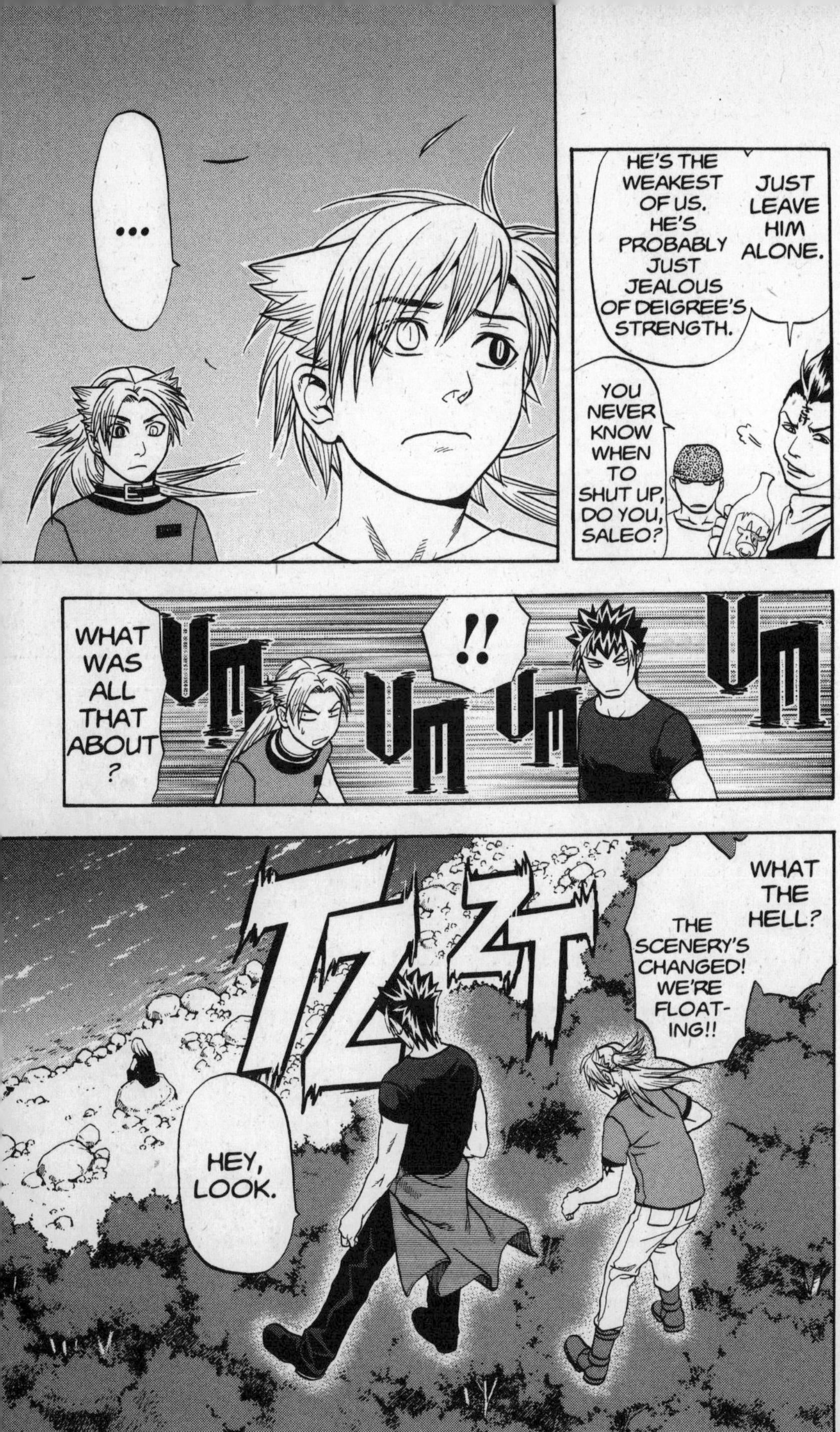
HE'S THE WEAKEST OF US. HE'S PROBABLY JUST JEALOUS OF DEIGREE'S STRENGTH.
JUST LEAVE HIM ALONE.
YOU NEVER KNOW WHEN TO SHUT UP, DO YOU, SALEO?
...
VM
!!
VM
VM
VM
WHAT WAS ALL THAT ABOUT?
WHAT THE HELL?
THE SCENERY'S CHANGED! WE'RE FLOATING!!
TZZT
HEY, LOOK.

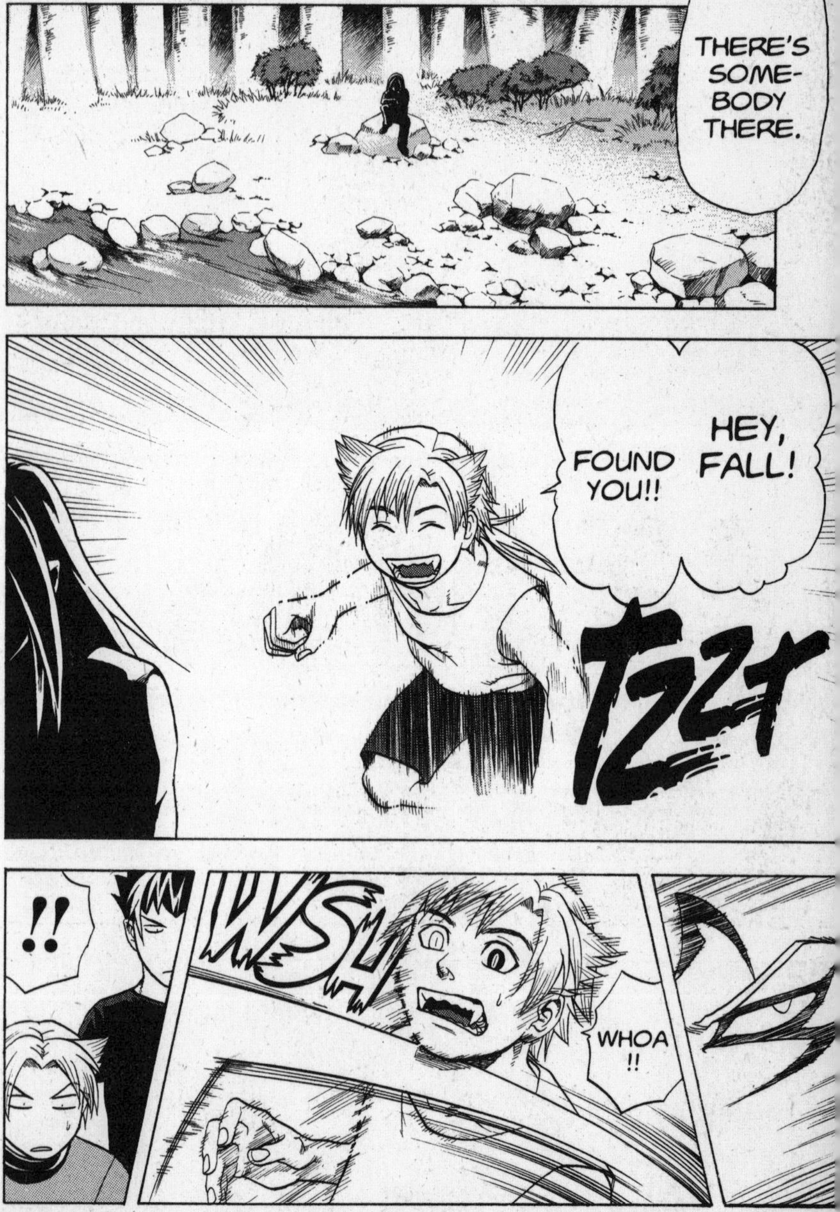
THERE'S SOME-BODY THERE.
HEY, FALL!
FOUND YOU!!
TZZT
!!
WSH
WHOA !!

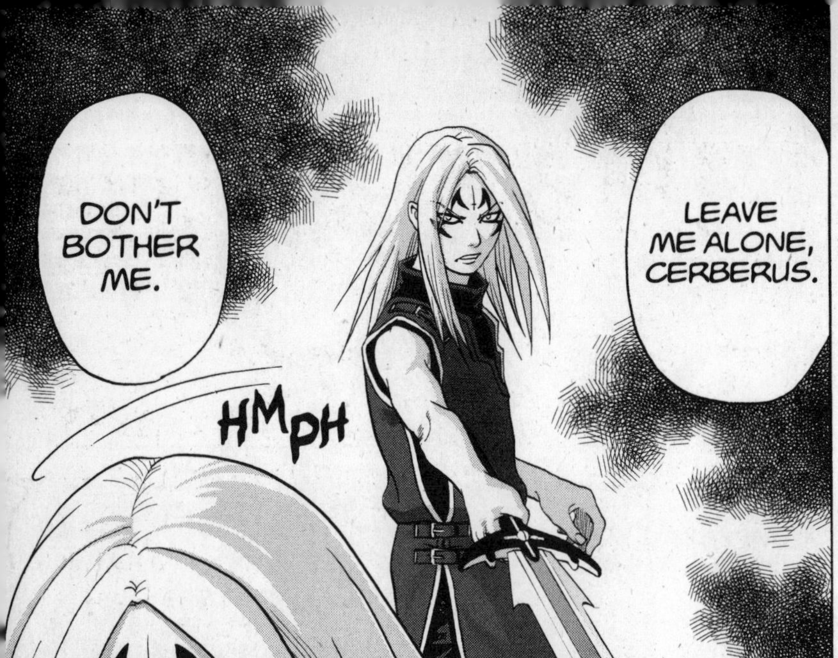
LEAVE ME ALONE, CERBERUS.
DON'T BOTHER ME.
HMPH

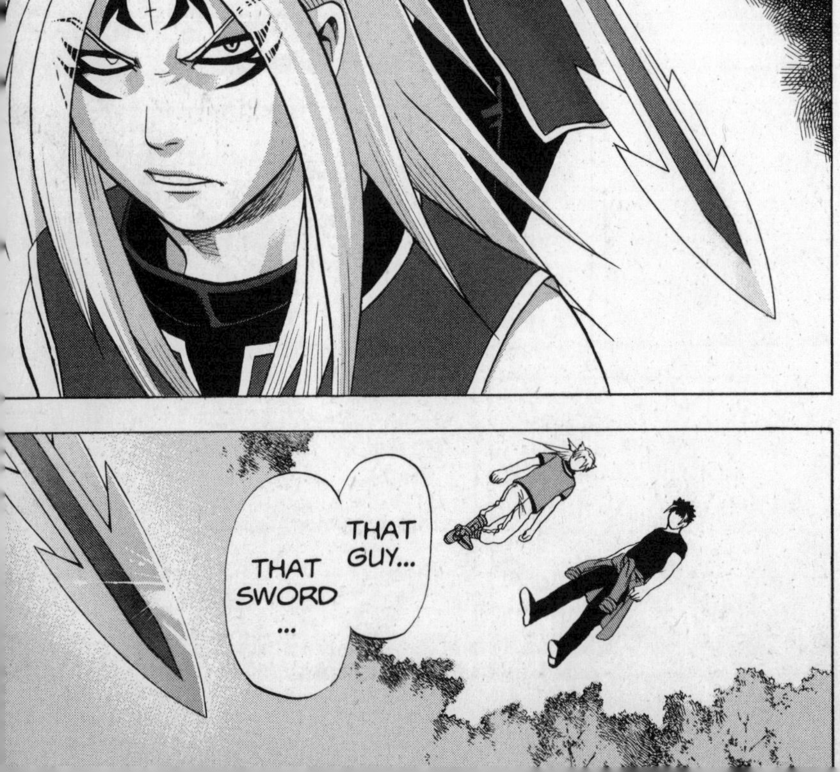
THAT GUY...
THAT SWORD ...

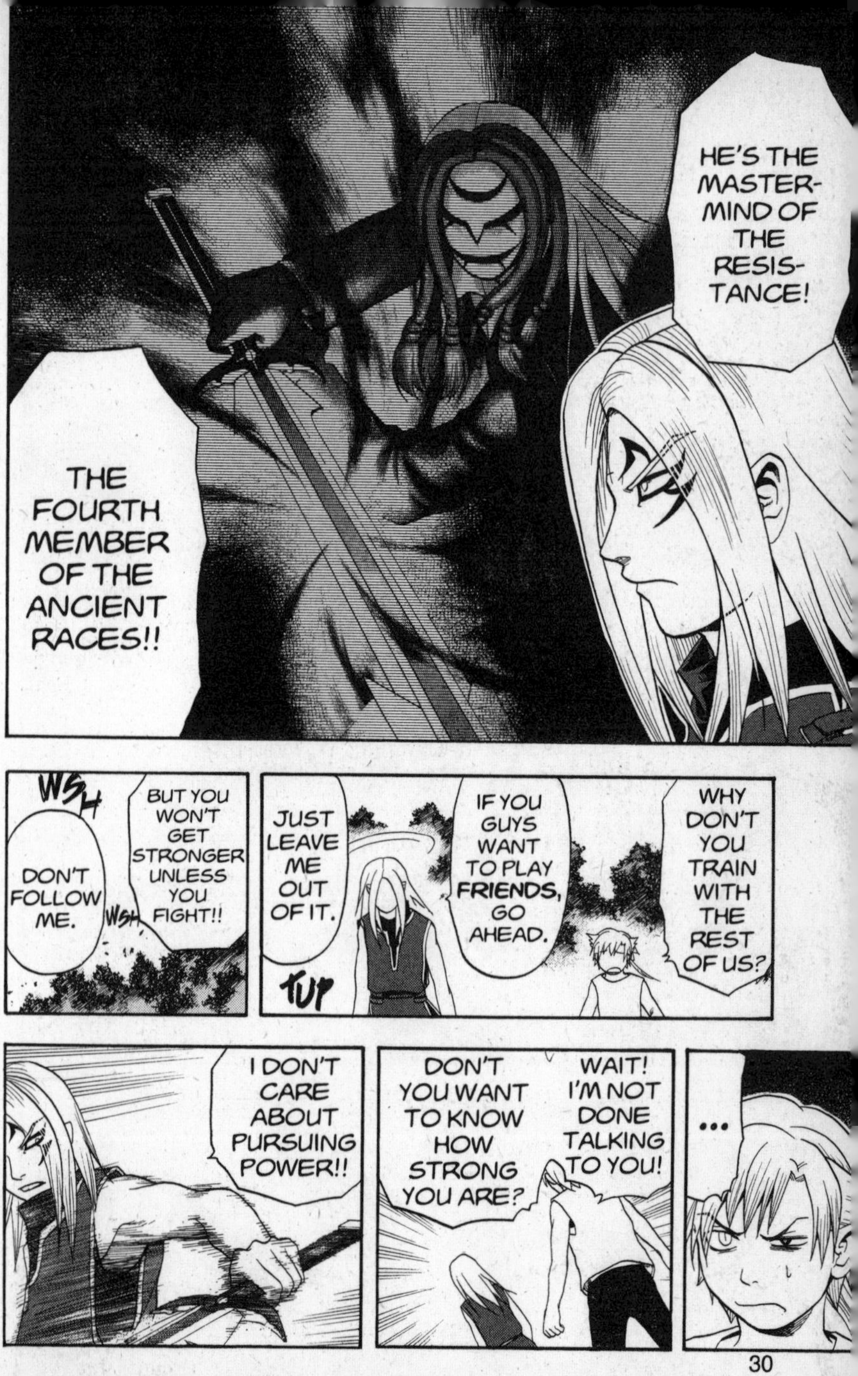
HE'S THE MASTER-MIND OF THE RESIS-TANCE!
THE FOURTH MEMBER OF THE ANCIENT RACES!!
WHY DON'T YOU TRAIN WITH THE REST OF US?
IF YOU GUYS WANT TO PLAY **FRIENDS**, GO AHEAD.
JUST LEAVE ME OUT OF IT.
TUP
BUT YOU WON'T GET STRONGER UNLESS YOU FIGHT!!
WSH
DON'T FOLLOW ME.
WSH
...
WAIT! I'M NOT DONE TALKING TO YOU!
DON'T YOU WANT TO KNOW HOW STRONG YOU ARE?
I DON'T CARE ABOUT PURSUING POWER!!

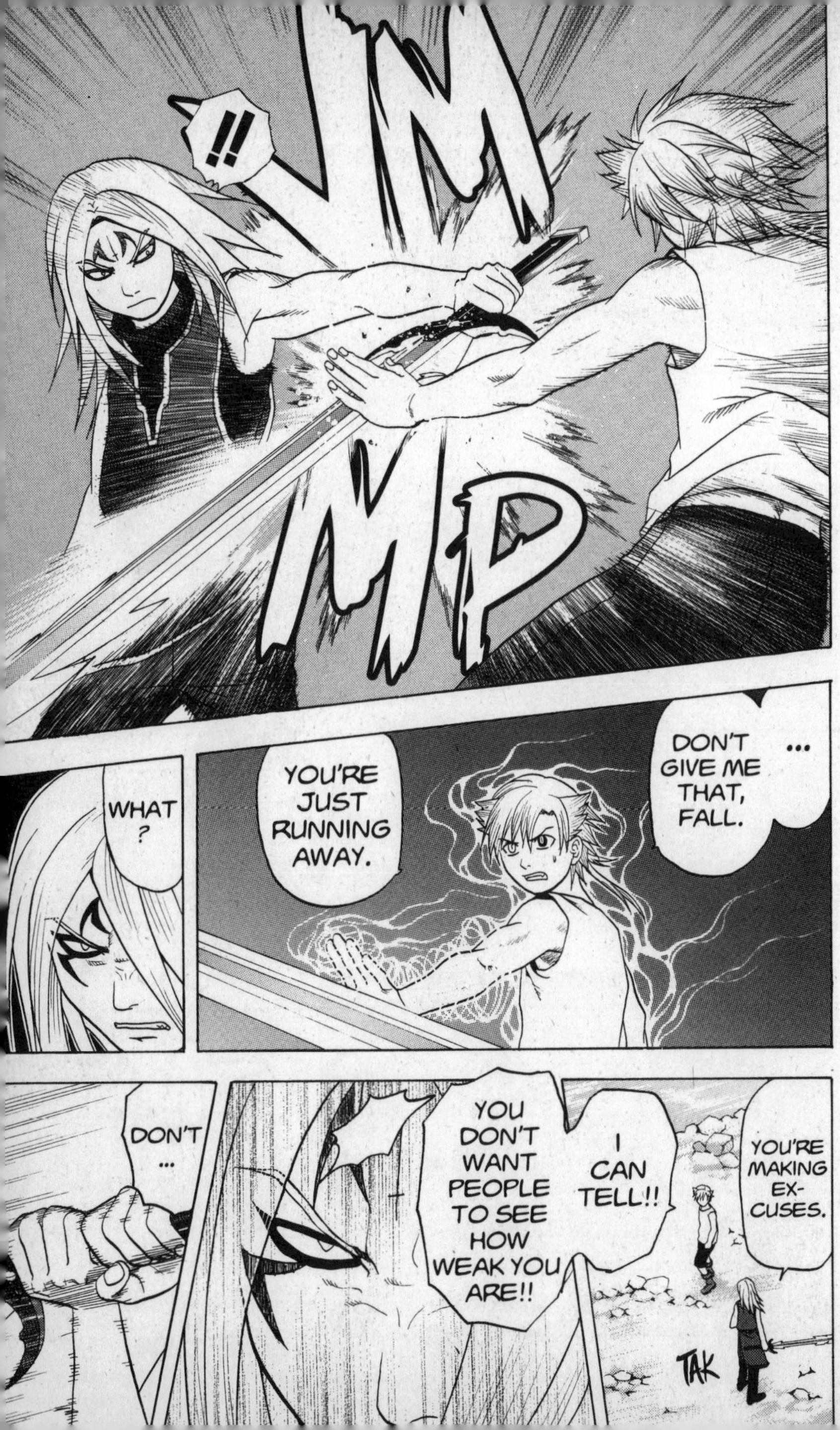
!!
...
DON'T GIVE ME THAT, FALL.
YOU'RE JUST RUNNING AWAY.
WHAT?
YOU'RE MAKING EX-CUSES.
TAK
I CAN TELL!!
YOU DON'T WANT PEOPLE TO SEE HOW WEAK YOU ARE!!
DON'T ...

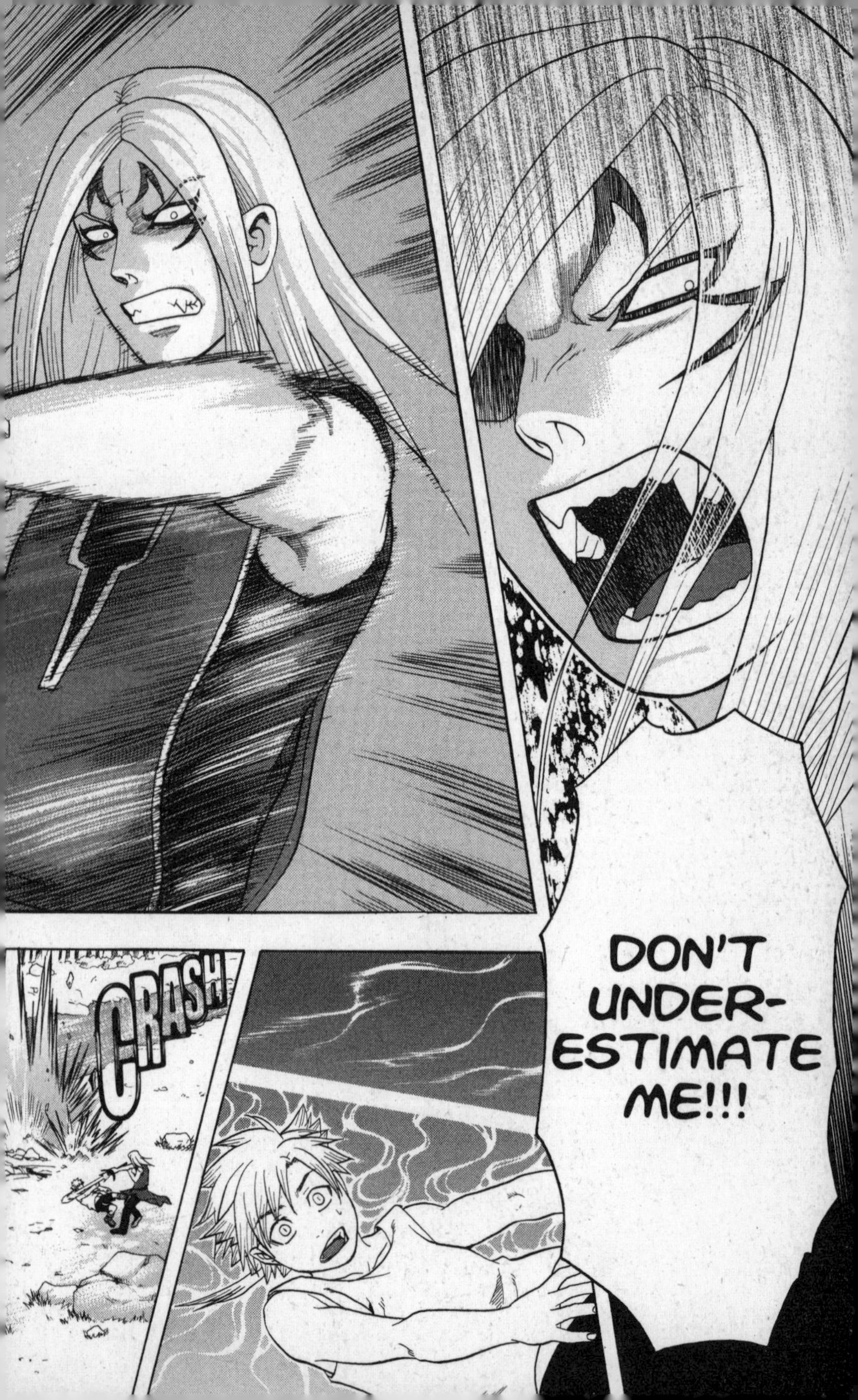
DON'T UNDER-ESTIMATE ME!!!
CRASH

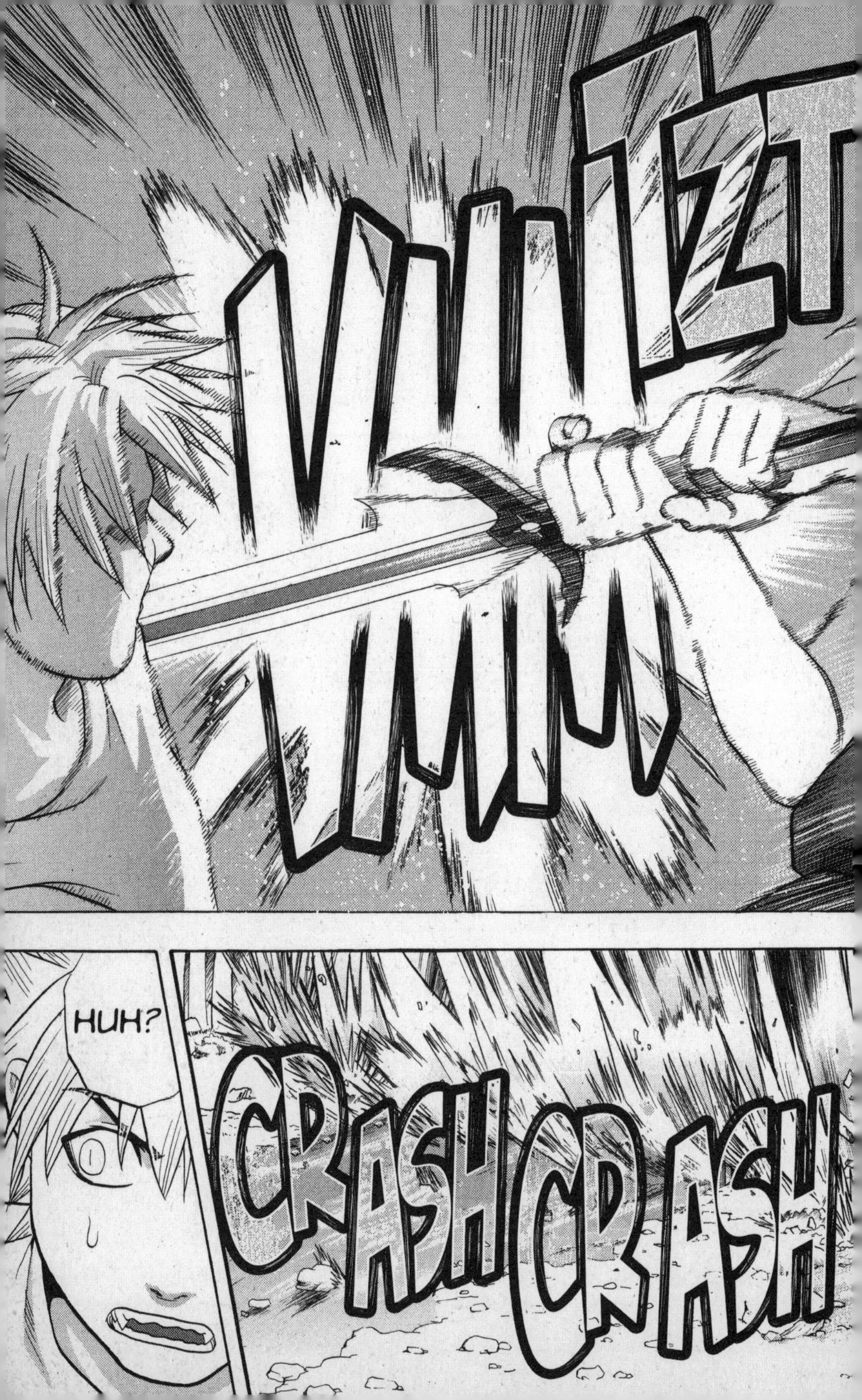
CRASH CRASH
HUH?

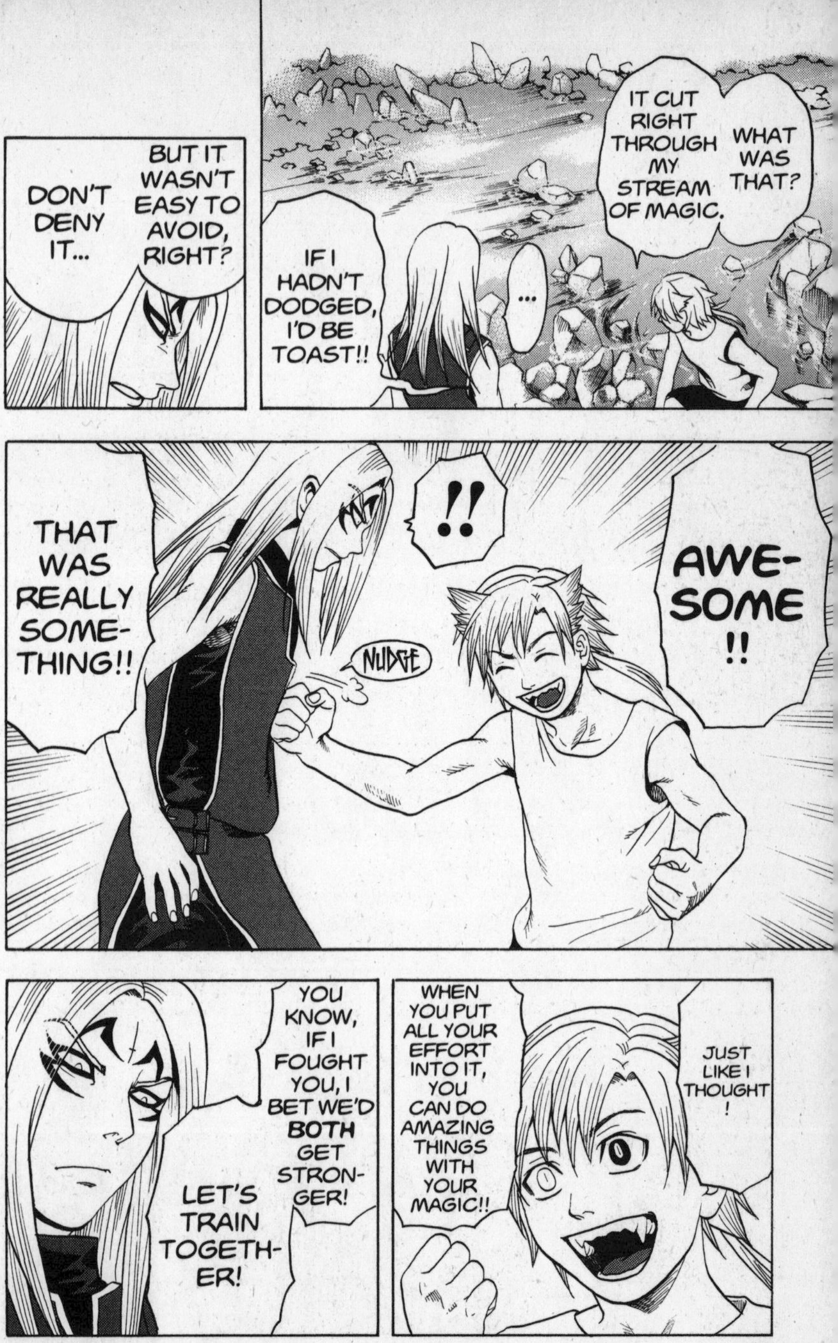
WHAT WAS THAT?
IT CUT RIGHT THROUGH MY STREAM OF MAGIC.
...
IF I HADN'T DODGED, I'D BE TOAST!!
BUT IT WASN'T EASY TO AVOID, RIGHT?
DON'T DENY IT...
AWE-SOME!!
!!
NUDGE
THAT WAS REALLY SOME-THING!!
JUST LIKE I THOUGHT!
WHEN YOU PUT ALL YOUR EFFORT INTO IT, YOU CAN DO AMAZING THINGS WITH YOUR MAGIC!!
YOU KNOW, IF I FOUGHT YOU, I BET WE'D **BOTH** GET STRON-GER!
LET'S TRAIN TOGETH-ER!

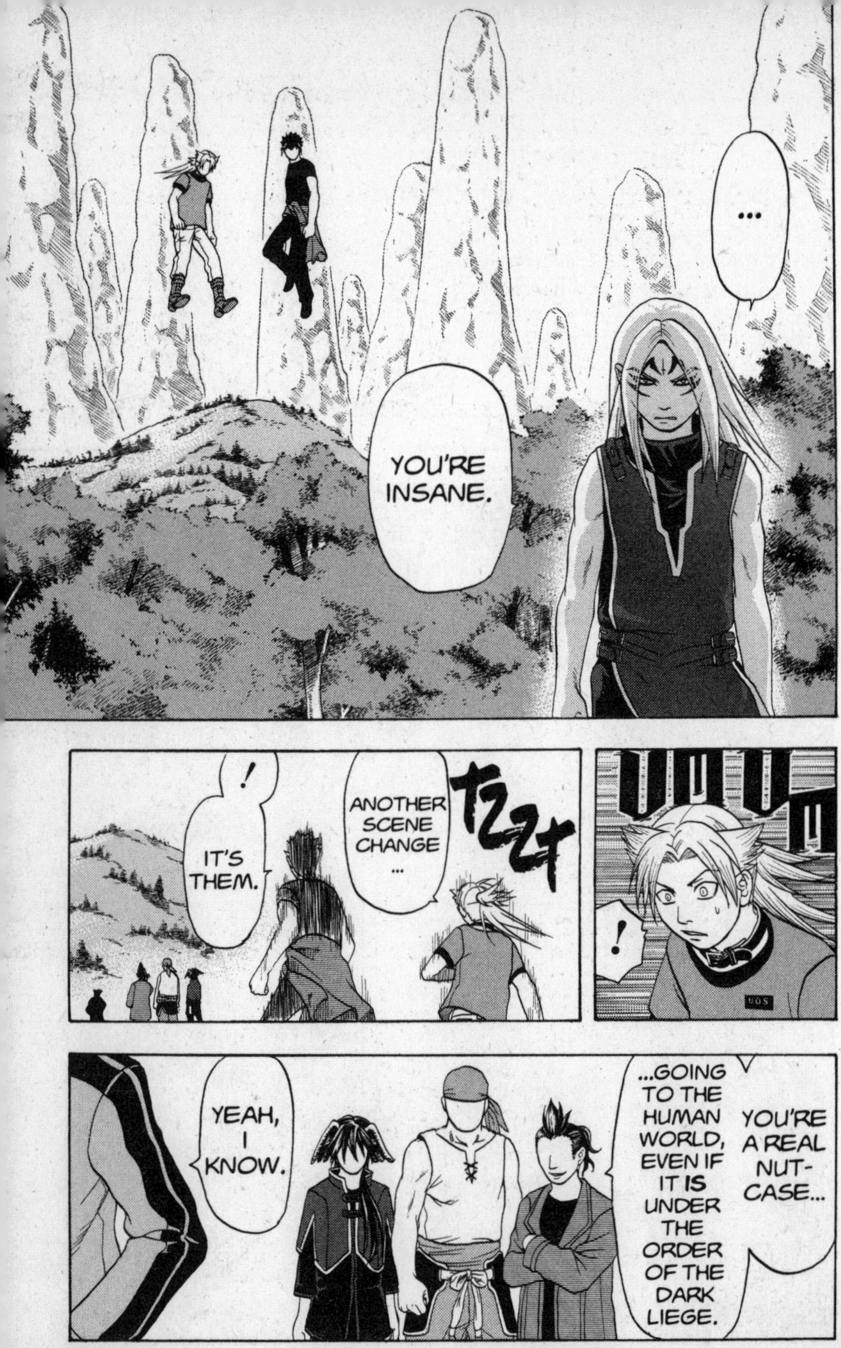
...
YOU'RE INSANE.
!
TZZT
ANOTHER SCENE CHANGE ...
! IT'S THEM.
YOU'RE A REAL NUT-CASE...
...GOING TO THE HUMAN WORLD, EVEN IF IT IS UNDER THE ORDER OF THE DARK LIEGE.
YEAH, I KNOW.

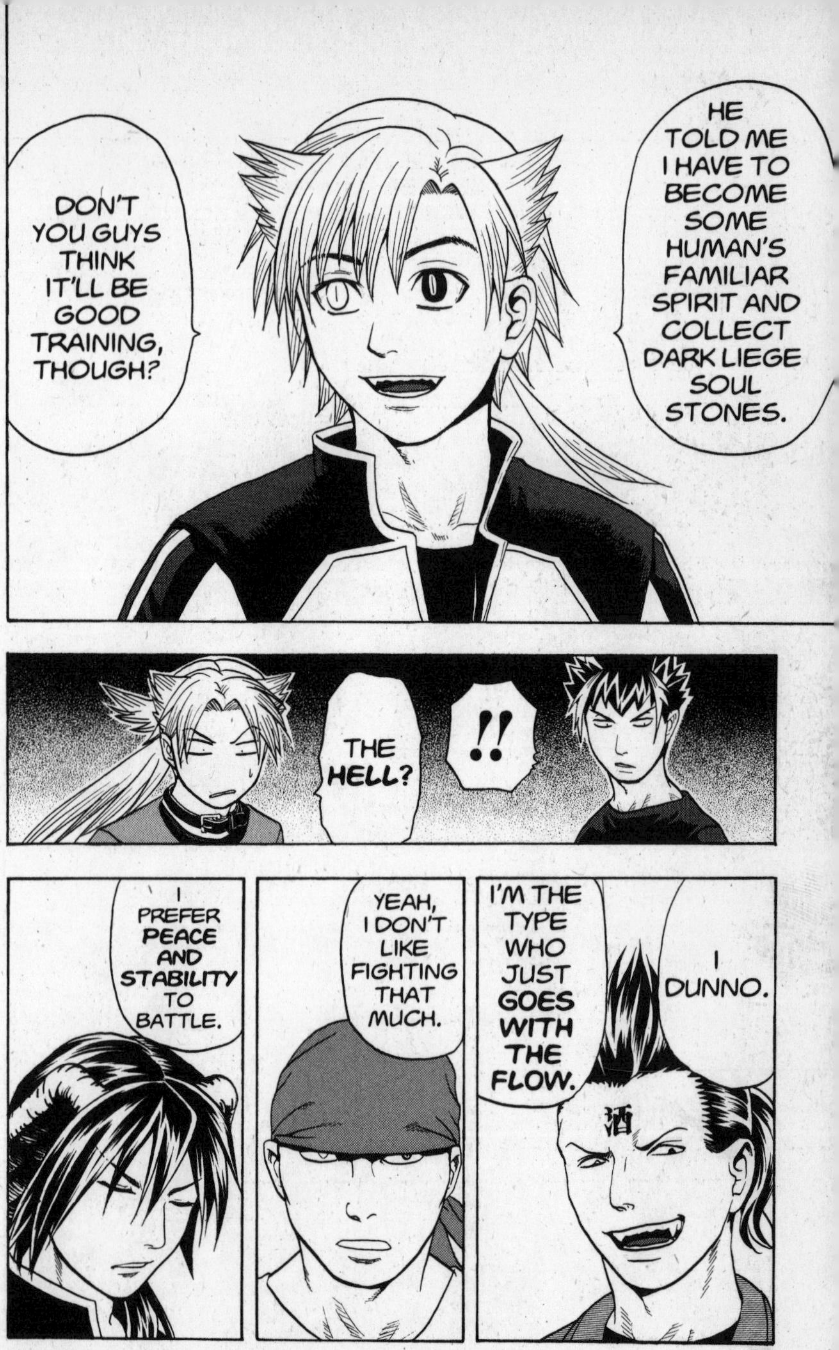
HE TOLD ME I HAVE TO BECOME SOME HUMAN'S FAMILIAR SPIRIT AND COLLECT DARK LIEGE SOUL STONES.
DON'T YOU GUYS THINK IT'LL BE GOOD TRAINING, THOUGH?
!!
THE **HELL?**
I DUNNO.
I'M THE TYPE WHO JUST **GOES WITH THE FLOW.**
酒
YEAH, I DON'T LIKE FIGHTING THAT MUCH.
I PREFER **PEACE AND STABILITY** TO BATTLE.

READ THIS WAY

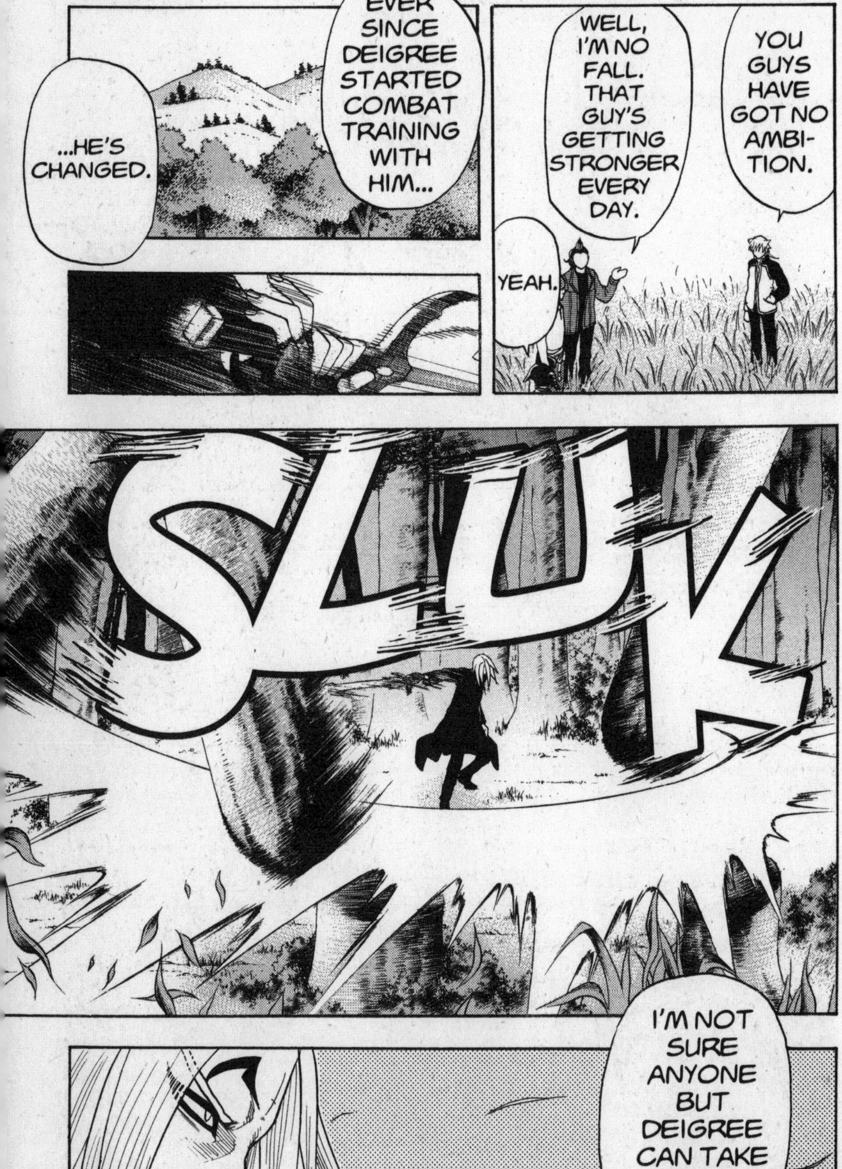
YOU GUYS HAVE GOT NO AMBITION.
WELL, I'M NO FALL. THAT GUY'S GETTING STRONGER EVERY DAY.
YEAH.
EVER SINCE DEIGREE STARTED COMBAT TRAINING WITH HIM...
...HE'S CHANGED.
SLUK
I'M NOT SURE ANYONE BUT DEIGREE CAN TAKE HIM ON NOW...

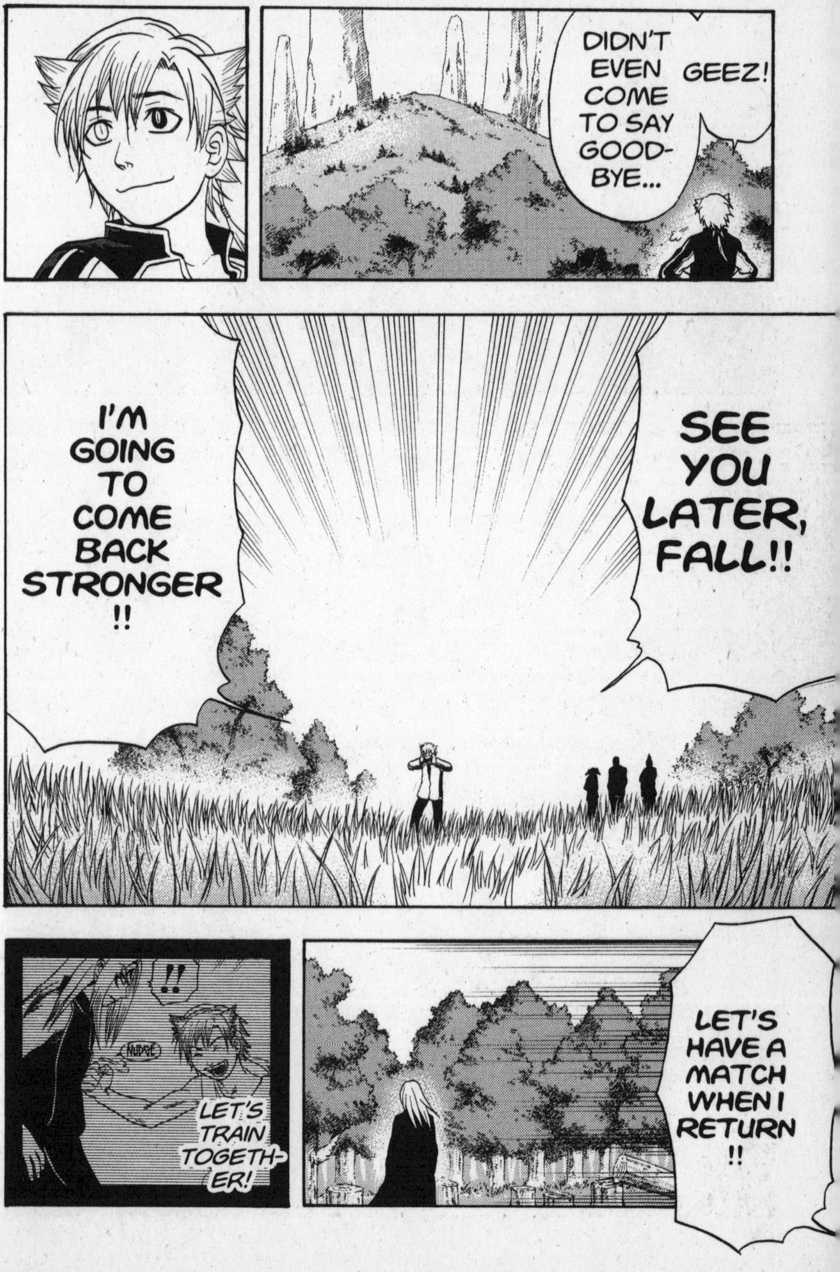
GEEZ!
DIDN'T EVEN COME TO SAY GOOD-BYE...
SEE YOU LATER, FALL!!
I'M GOING TO COME BACK STRONGER!!
LET'S HAVE A MATCH WHEN I RETURN!!
!!
NUDGE
LET'S TRAIN TOGETH-ER!

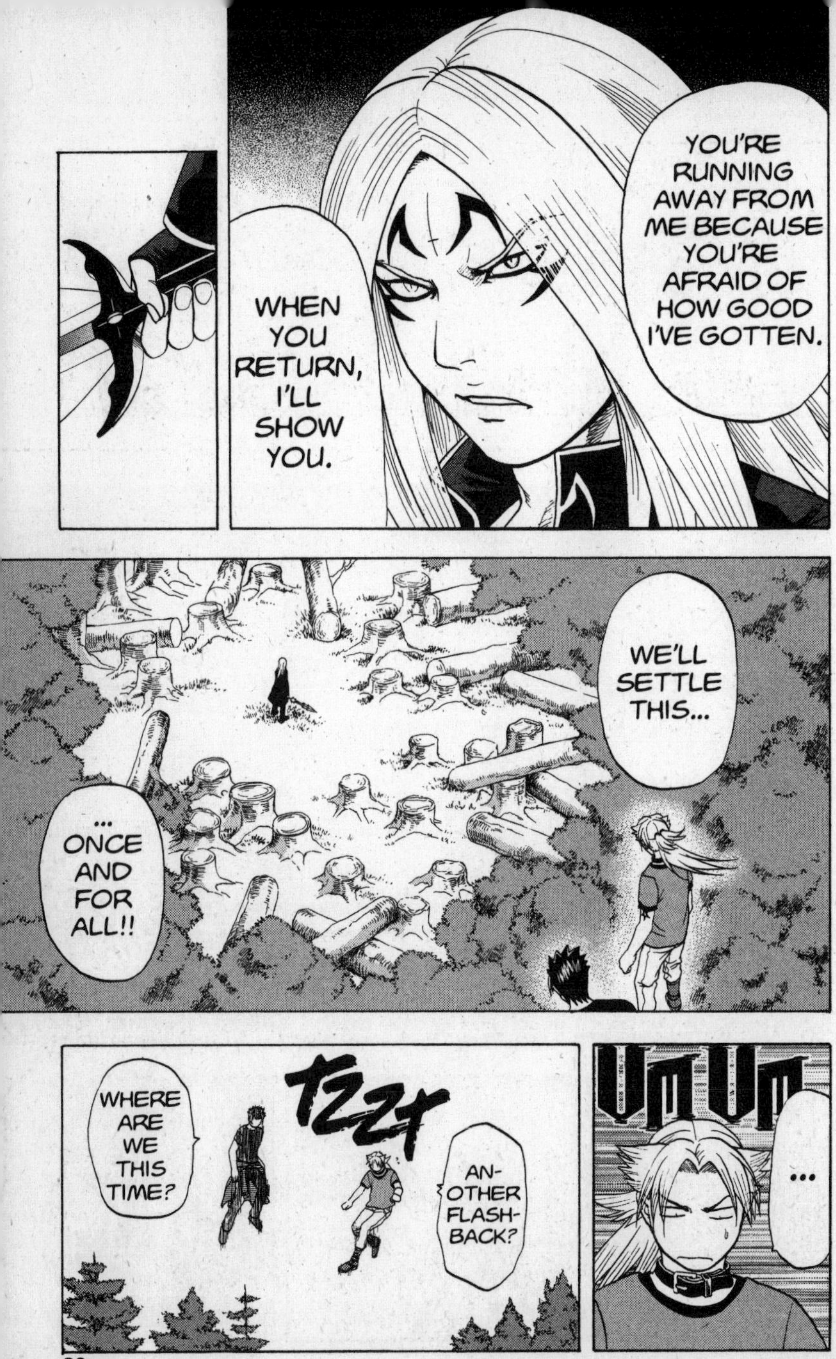
YOU'RE RUNNING AWAY FROM ME BECAUSE YOU'RE AFRAID OF HOW GOOD I'VE GOTTEN.
WHEN YOU RETURN, I'LL SHOW YOU.
WE'LL SETTLE THIS...
...ONCE AND FOR ALL!!
VMVM
...
TZZT
AN-OTHER FLASH-BACK?
WHERE ARE WE THIS TIME?

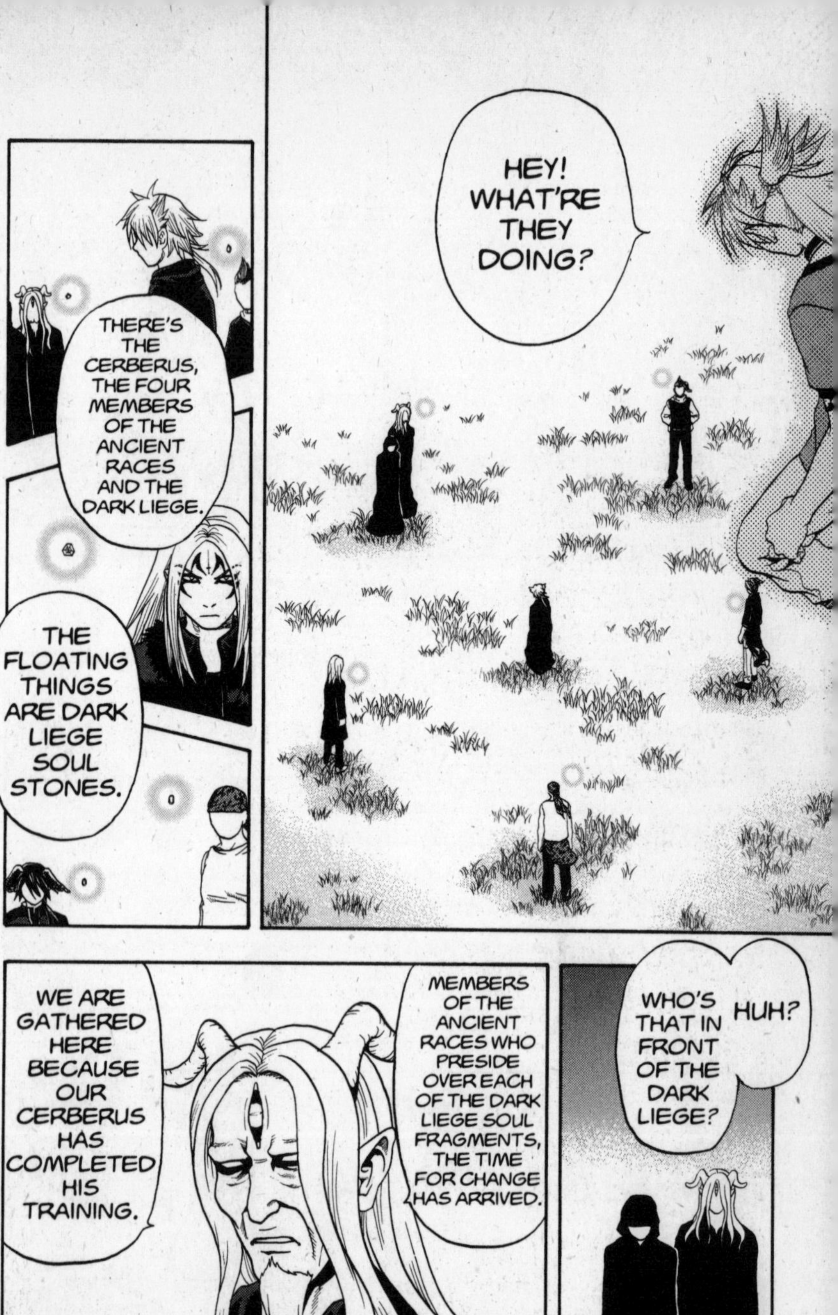
HEY! WHAT'RE THEY DOING?
THERE'S THE CERBERUS, THE FOUR MEMBERS OF THE ANCIENT RACES AND THE DARK LIEGE.
THE FLOATING THINGS ARE DARK LIEGE SOUL STONES.
HUH?
WHO'S THAT IN FRONT OF THE DARK LIEGE?
MEMBERS OF THE ANCIENT RACES WHO PRESIDE OVER EACH OF THE DARK LIEGE SOUL FRAGMENTS, THE TIME FOR CHANGE HAS ARRIVED.
WE ARE GATHERED HERE BECAUSE OUR CERBERUS HAS COMPLETED HIS TRAINING.

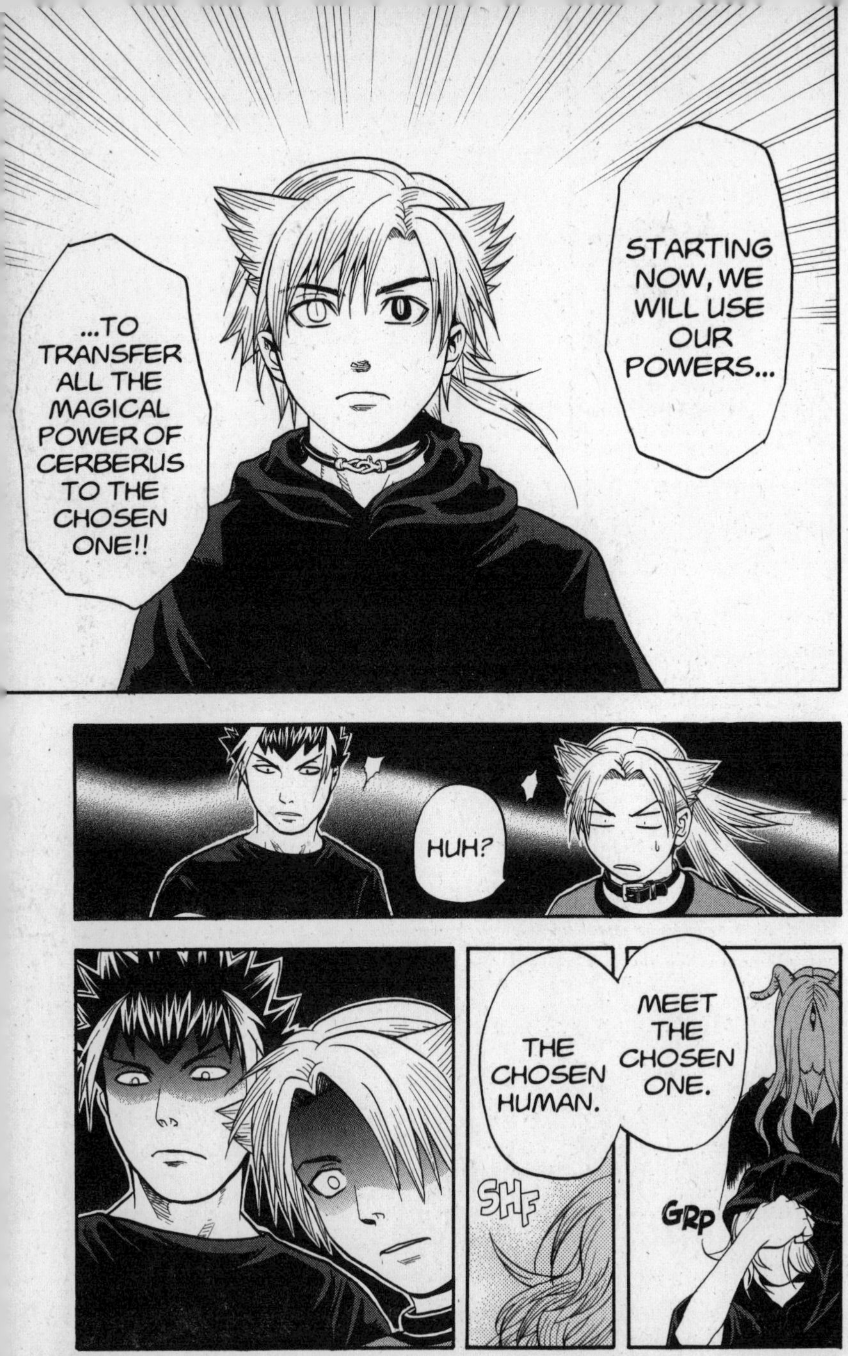
STARTING NOW, WE WILL USE OUR POWERS...
...TO TRANSFER ALL THE MAGICAL POWER OF CERBERUS TO THE CHOSEN ONE!!
HUH?
MEET THE CHOSEN ONE.
GRP
THE CHOSEN HUMAN.
SHF

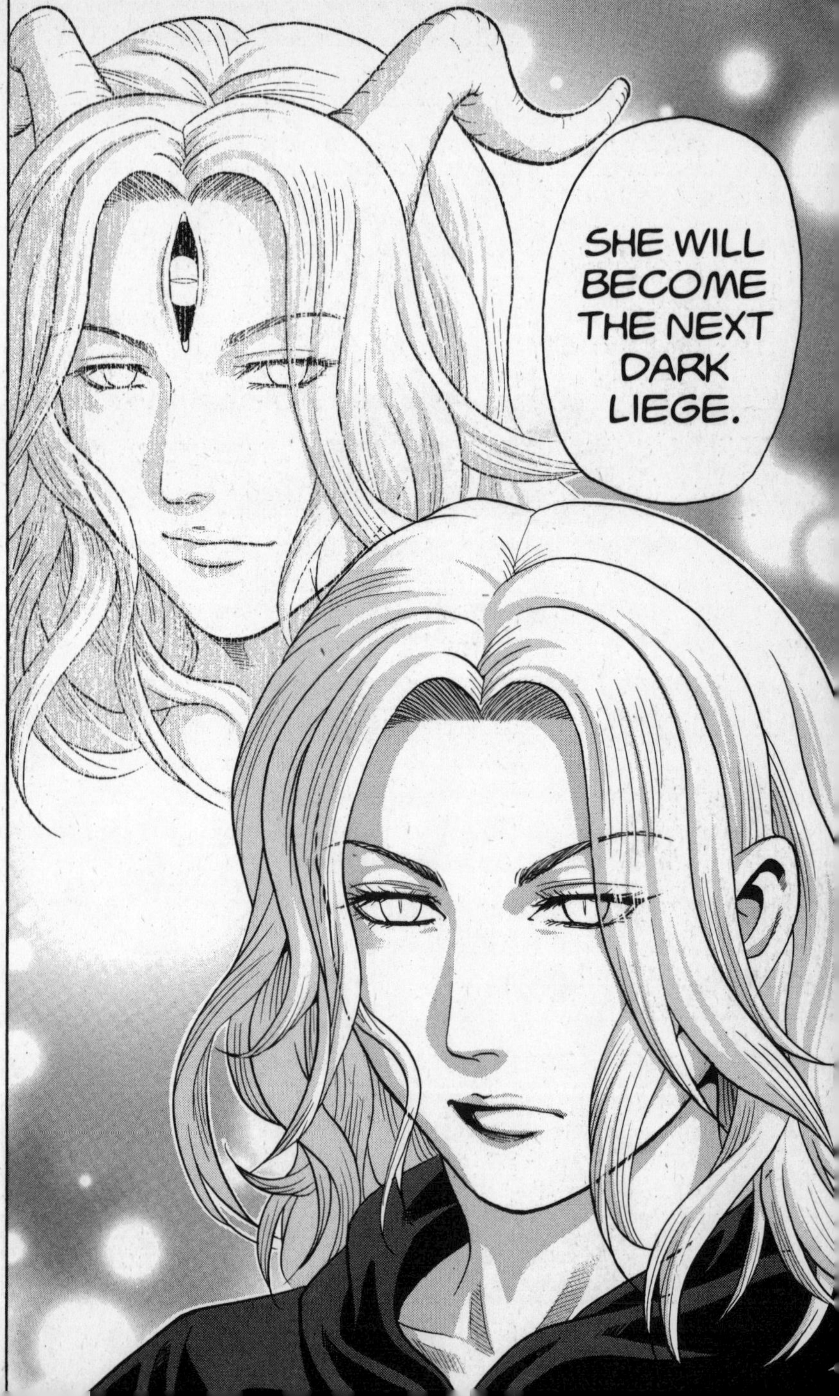
SHE WILL BECOME THE NEXT DARK LIEGE.

READ THIS WAY

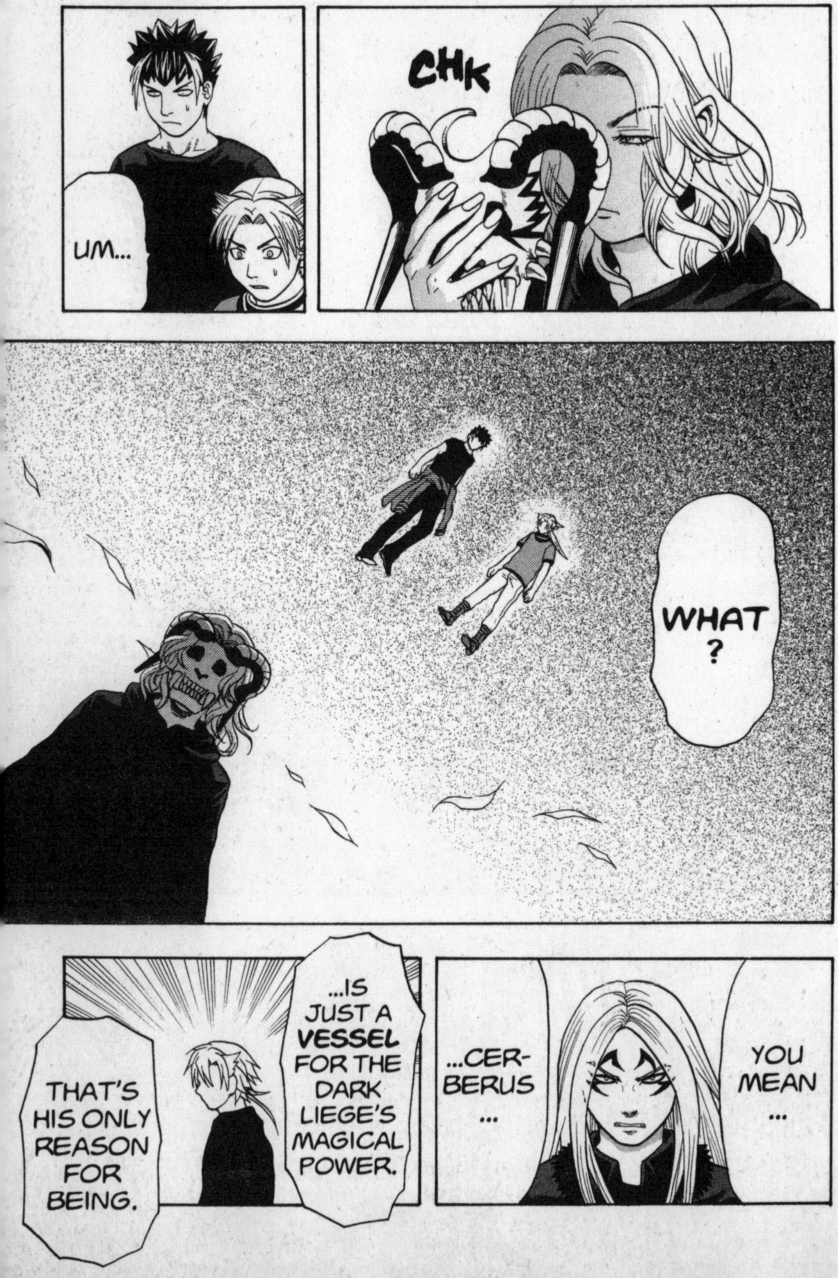
CHK
UM...
WHAT ?
YOU MEAN ...
...CER-BERUS ...
...IS JUST A **VESSEL** FOR THE DARK LIEGE'S MAGICAL POWER.
THAT'S HIS ONLY REASON FOR BEING.

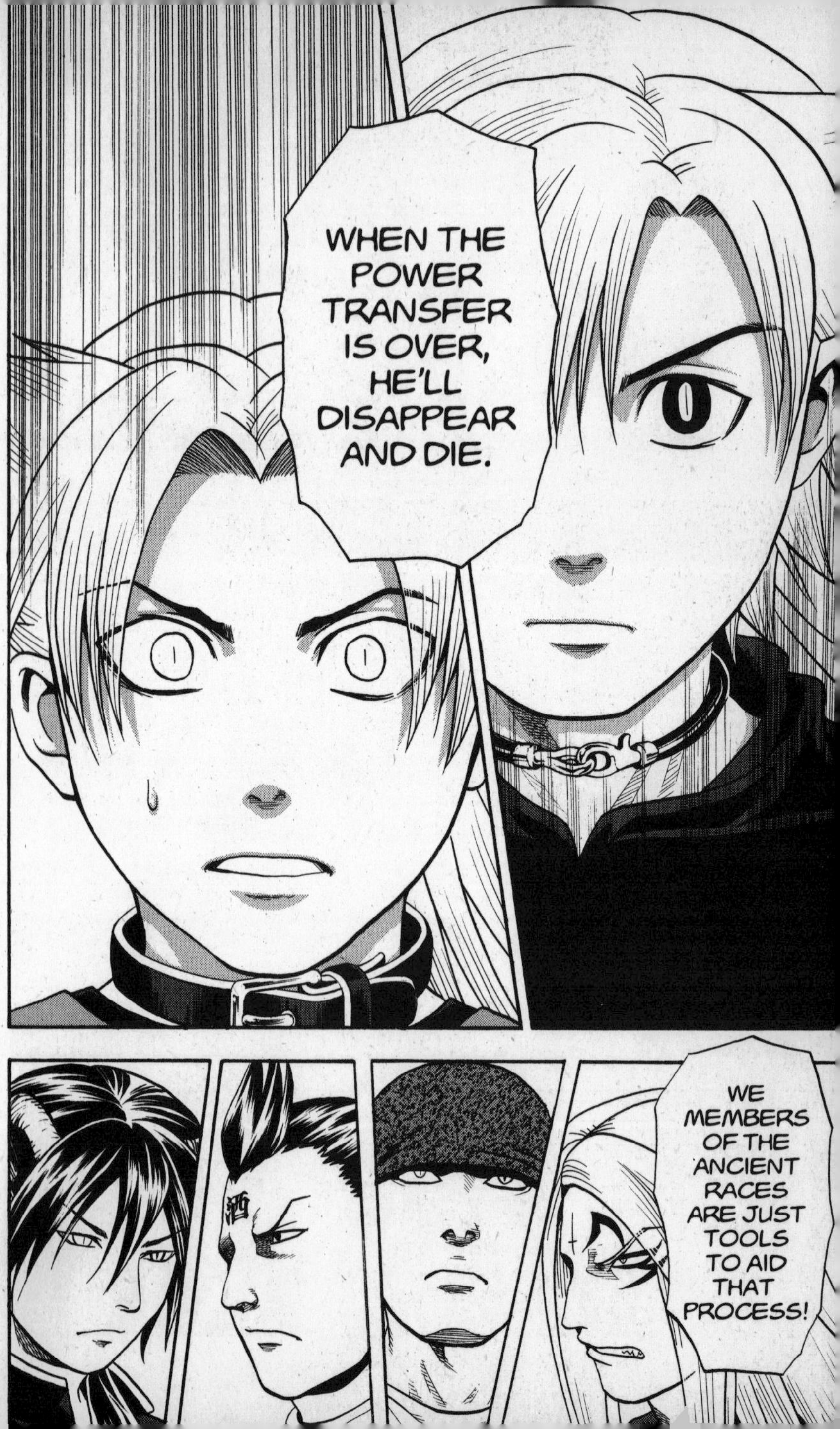
WHEN THE POWER TRANSFER IS OVER, HE'LL DISAPPEAR AND DIE.
WE MEMBERS OF THE ANCIENT RACES ARE JUST TOOLS TO AID THAT PROCESS!
酒

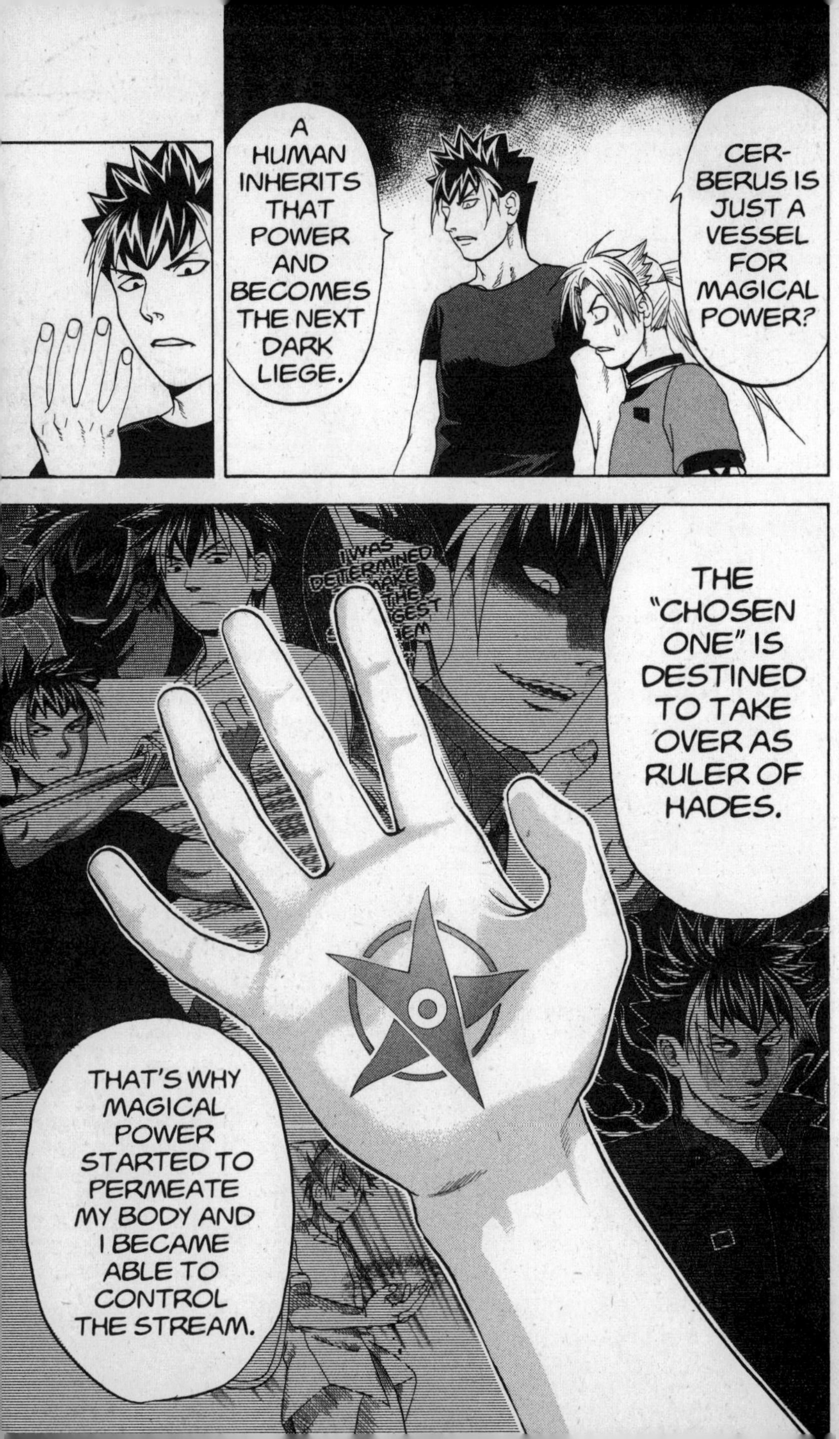
CER-BERUS IS JUST A VESSEL FOR MAGICAL POWER?
A HUMAN INHERITS THAT POWER AND BECOMES THE NEXT DARK LIEGE.
THE "CHOSEN ONE" IS DESTINED TO TAKE OVER AS RULER OF HADES.
THAT'S WHY MAGICAL POWER STARTED TO PERMEATE MY BODY AND I BECAME ABLE TO CONTROL THE STREAM.

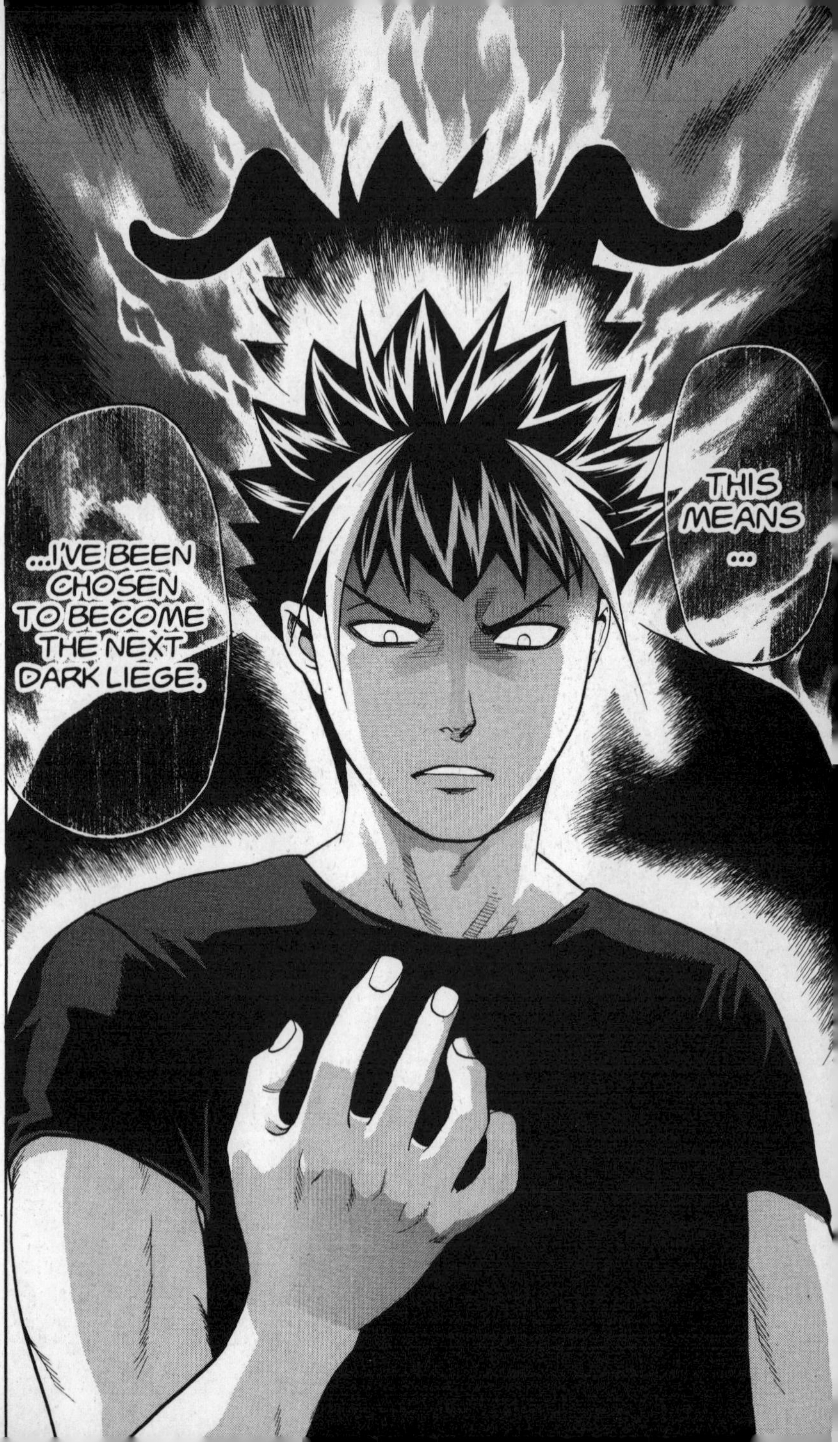
THIS MEANS ...
...I'VE BEEN CHOSEN TO BECOME THE NEXT DARK LIEGE.

READ THIS WAY

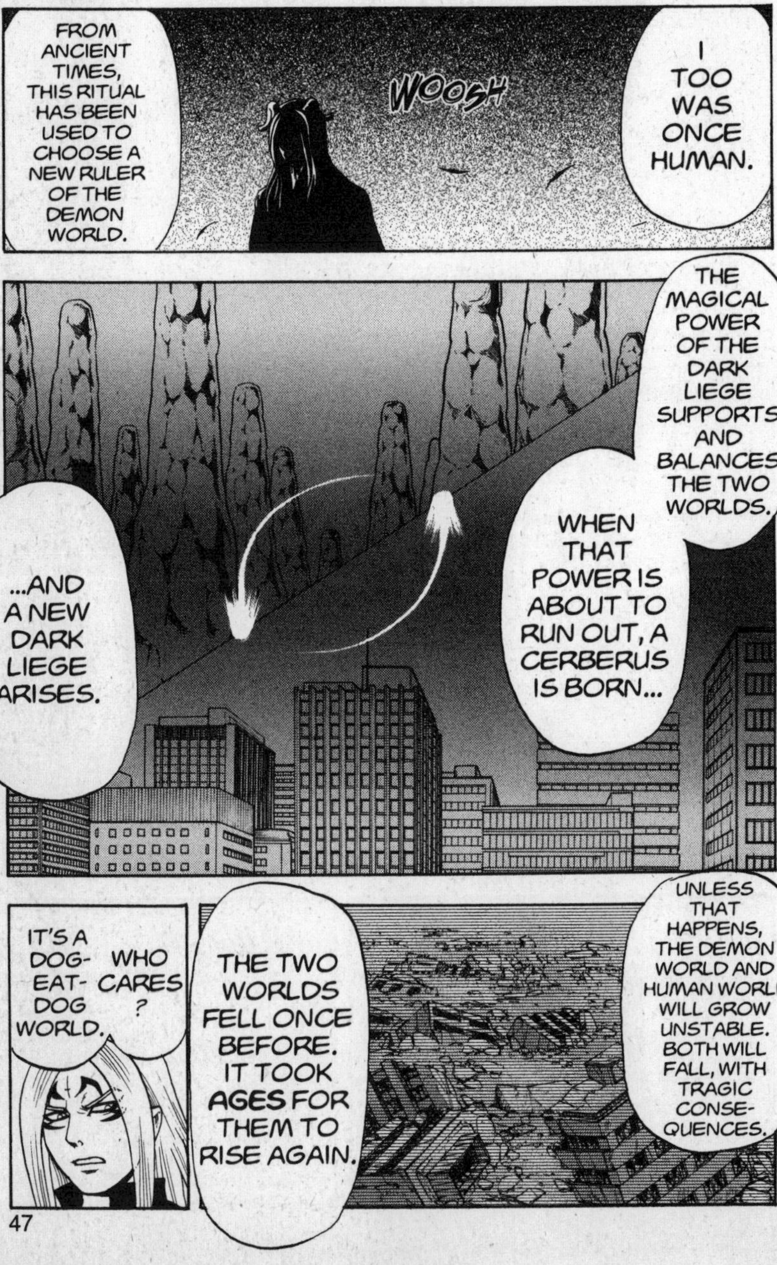
I TOO WAS ONCE HUMAN.
WOOSH
FROM ANCIENT TIMES, THIS RITUAL HAS BEEN USED TO CHOOSE A NEW RULER OF THE DEMON WORLD.
THE MAGICAL POWER OF THE DARK LIEGE SUPPORTS AND BALANCES THE TWO WORLDS.
WHEN THAT POWER IS ABOUT TO RUN OUT, A CERBERUS IS BORN...
...AND A NEW DARK LIEGE ARISES.
UNLESS THAT HAPPENS, THE DEMON WORLD AND HUMAN WORLD WILL GROW UNSTABLE. BOTH WILL FALL, WITH TRAGIC CONSE-QUENCES.
THE TWO WORLDS FELL ONCE BEFORE. IT TOOK AGES FOR THEM TO RISE AGAIN.
WHO CARES?
IT'S A DOG-EAT-DOG WORLD.

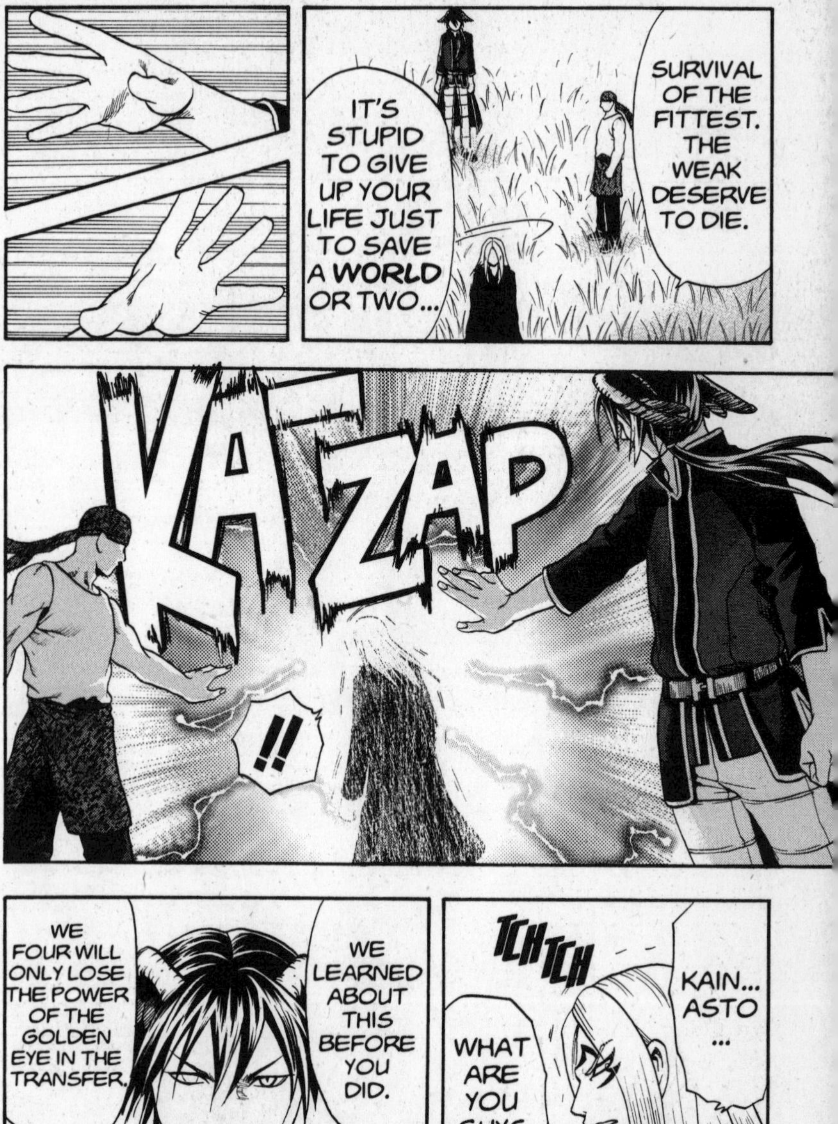
SURVIVAL OF THE FITTEST. THE WEAK DESERVE TO DIE.
IT'S STUPID TO GIVE UP YOUR LIFE JUST TO SAVE A **WORLD** OR TWO...
KAZAP
!!
KAIN... ASTO ...
TCHTCH
WHAT ARE YOU GUYS DOING?
WE LEARNED ABOUT THIS BEFORE YOU DID.
WE FOUR WILL ONLY LOSE THE POWER OF THE GOLDEN EYE IN THE TRANSFER.

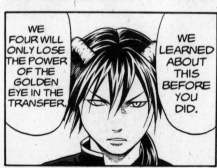

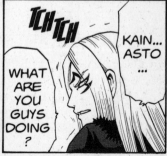

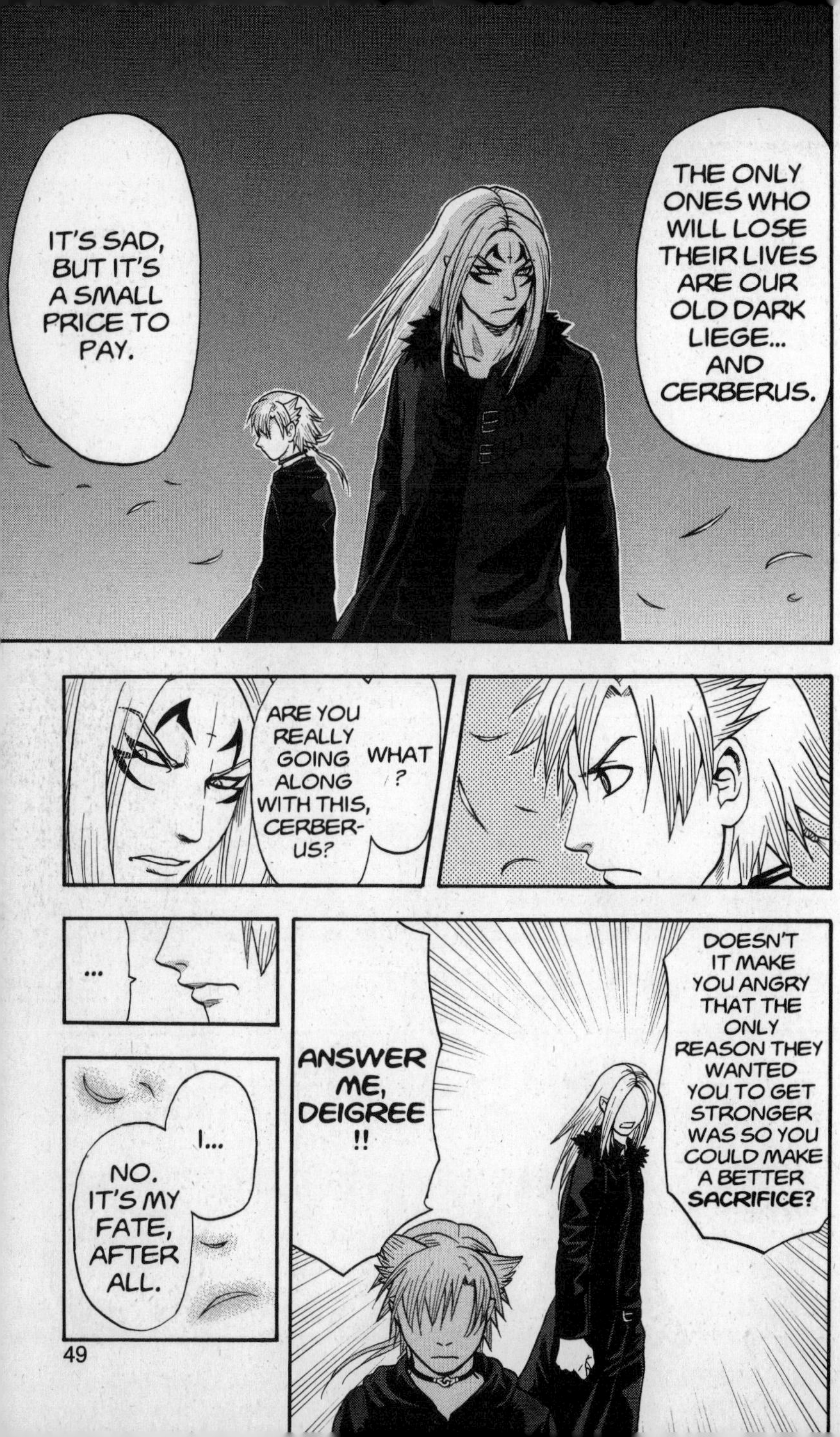
THE ONLY ONES WHO WILL LOSE THEIR LIVES ARE OUR OLD DARK LIEGE... AND CERBERUS.
IT'S SAD, BUT IT'S A SMALL PRICE TO PAY.
ARE YOU REALLY GOING ALONG WITH THIS, CERBERUS?
WHAT?
DOESN'T IT MAKE YOU ANGRY THAT THE ONLY REASON THEY WANTED YOU TO GET STRONGER WAS SO YOU COULD MAKE A BETTER SACRIFICE?
ANSWER ME, DEIGREE!!
...
I...
NO. IT'S MY FATE, AFTER ALL.

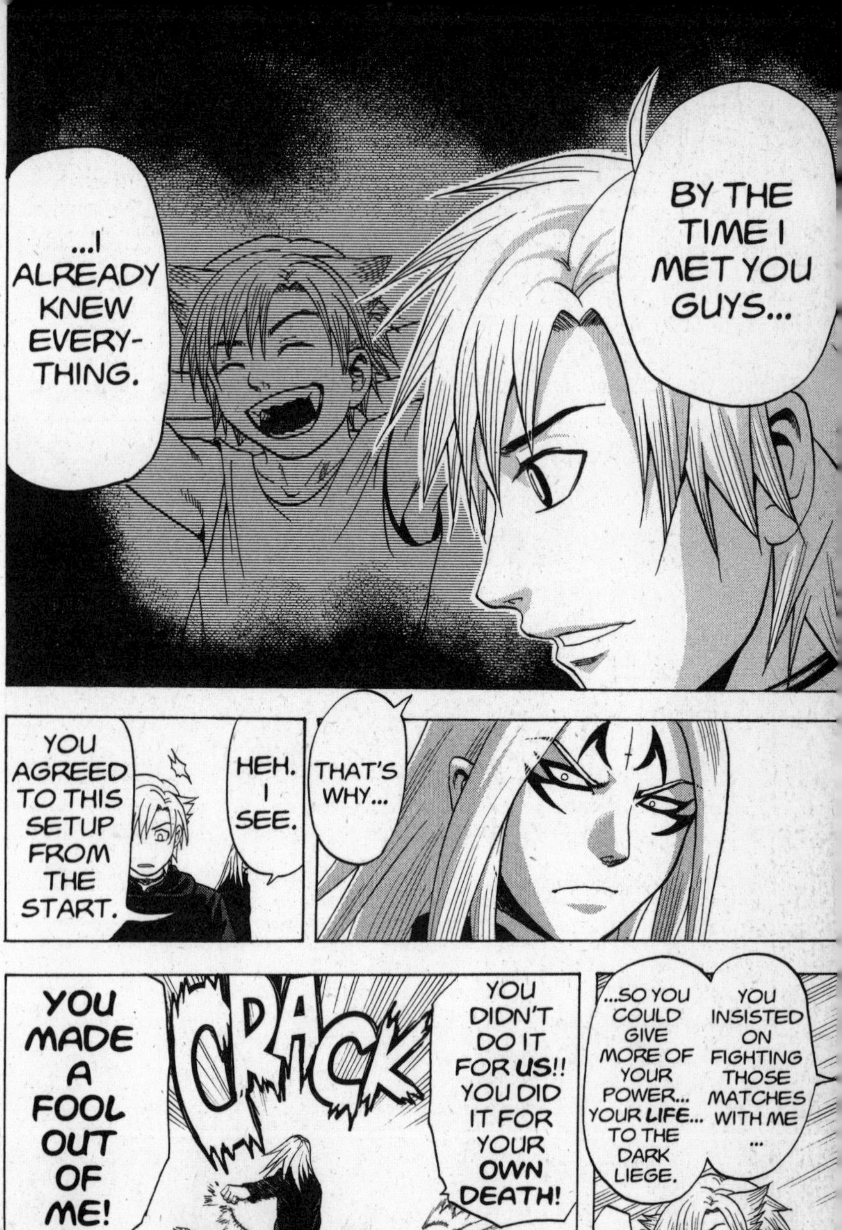
BY THE TIME I MET YOU GUYS...
...I ALREADY KNEW EVERYTHING.
THAT'S WHY...
HEH. I SEE.
YOU AGREED TO THIS SETUP FROM THE START.
YOU INSISTED ON FIGHTING THOSE MATCHES WITH ME...
...SO YOU COULD GIVE MORE OF YOUR POWER... YOUR **LIFE**... TO THE DARK LIEGE.
...!
YOU DIDN'T DO IT FOR **US**!! YOU DID IT FOR YOUR **OWN** DEATH!
CRACK
YOU MADE A FOOL OUT OF ME!

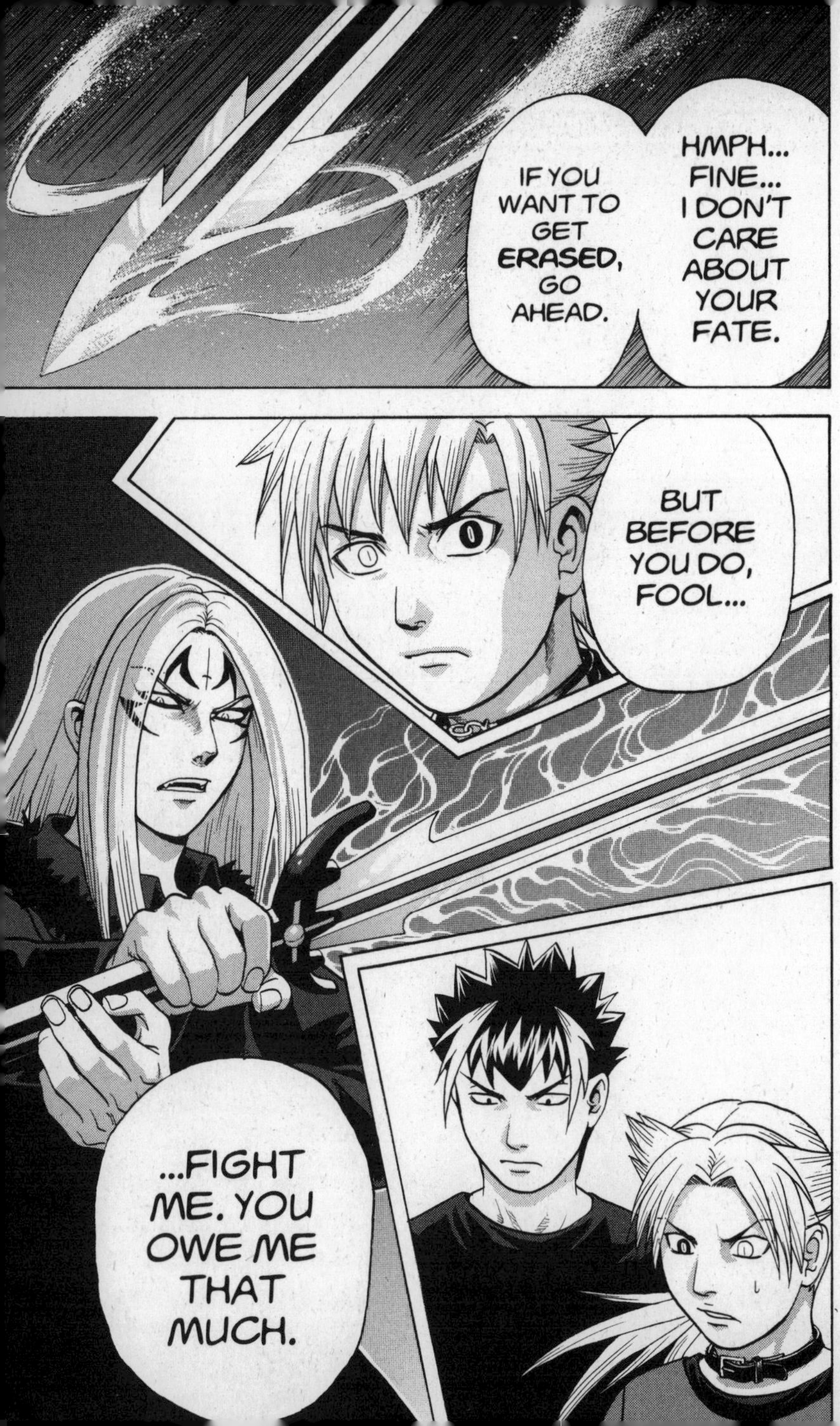
HMPH... FINE... I DON'T CARE ABOUT YOUR FATE.
IF YOU WANT TO GET **ERASED**, GO AHEAD.
BUT BEFORE YOU DO, FOOL...
...FIGHT ME. YOU OWE ME THAT MUCH.

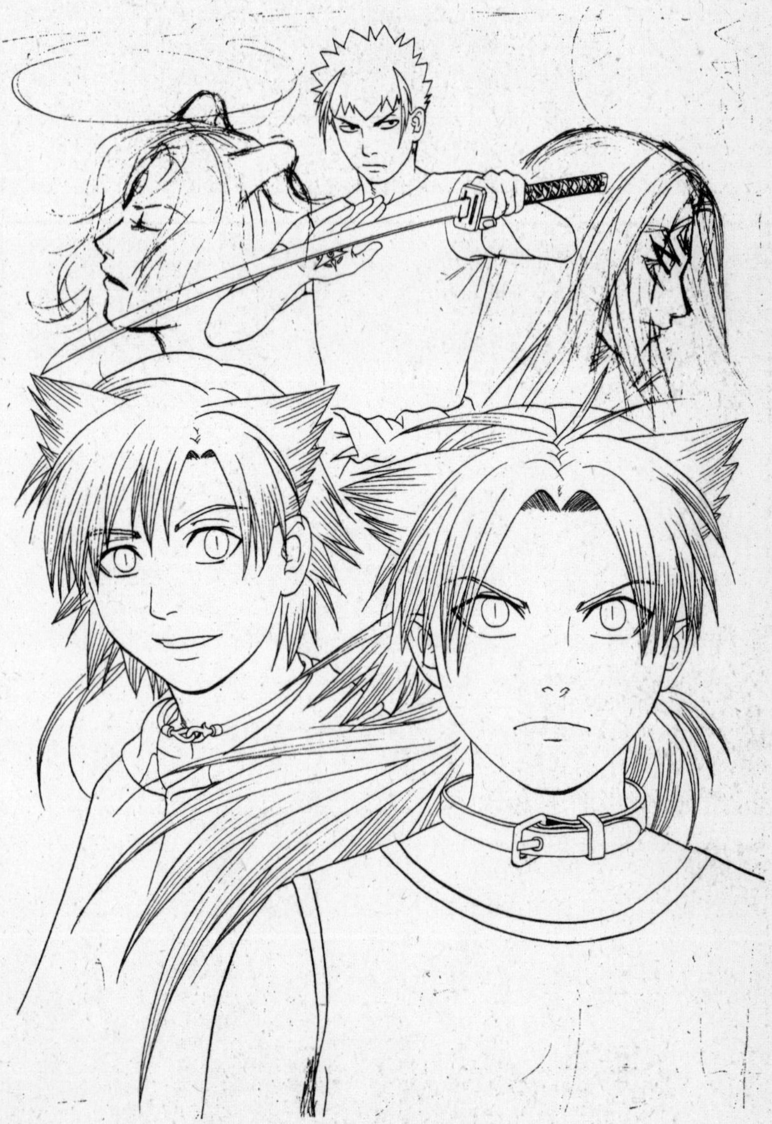

Story 22: The Decision

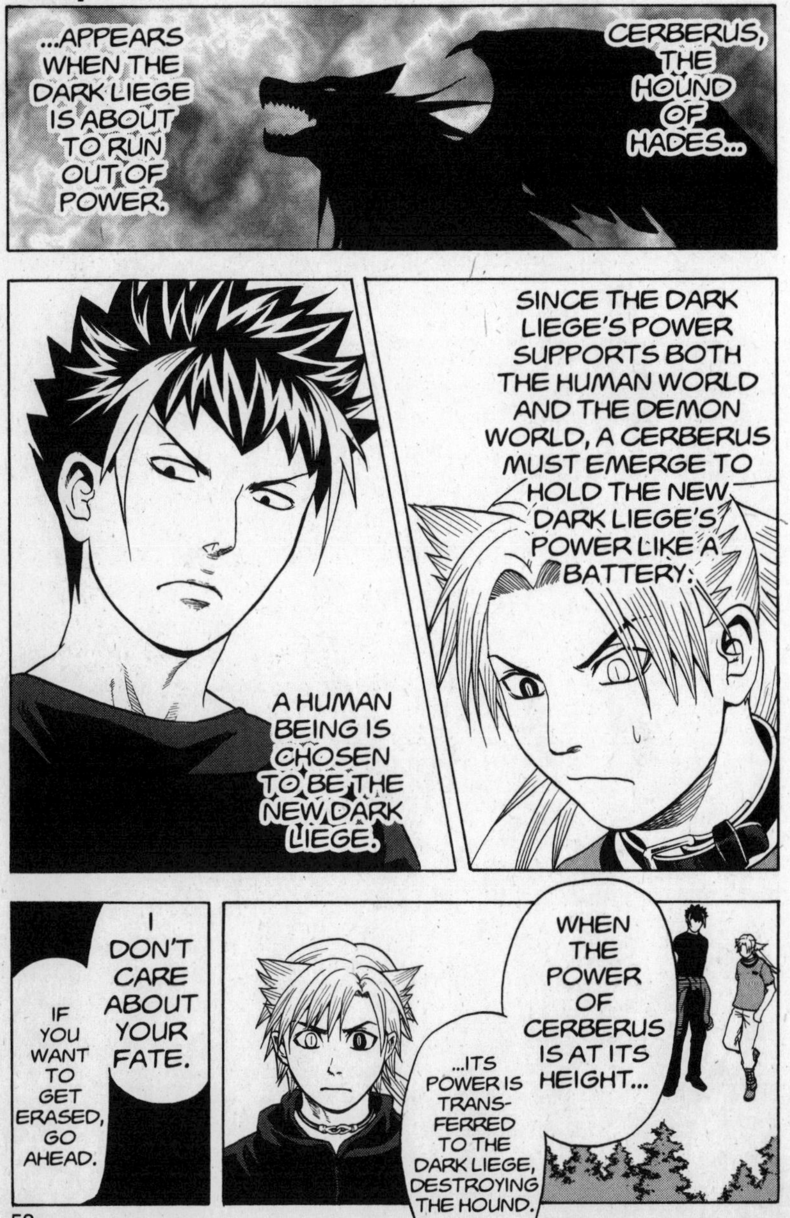
CERBERUS, THE HOUND OF HADES...
...APPEARS WHEN THE DARK LIEGE IS ABOUT TO RUN OUT OF POWER.
SINCE THE DARK LIEGE'S POWER SUPPORTS BOTH THE HUMAN WORLD AND THE DEMON WORLD, A CERBERUS MUST EMERGE TO HOLD THE NEW DARK LIEGE'S POWER LIKE A BATTERY.
A HUMAN BEING IS CHOSEN TO BE THE NEW DARK LIEGE.
WHEN THE POWER OF CERBERUS IS AT ITS HEIGHT...
...ITS POWER IS TRANS-FERRED TO THE DARK LIEGE, DESTROYING THE HOUND.
I DON'T CARE ABOUT YOUR FATE.
IF YOU WANT TO GET ERASED, GO AHEAD.

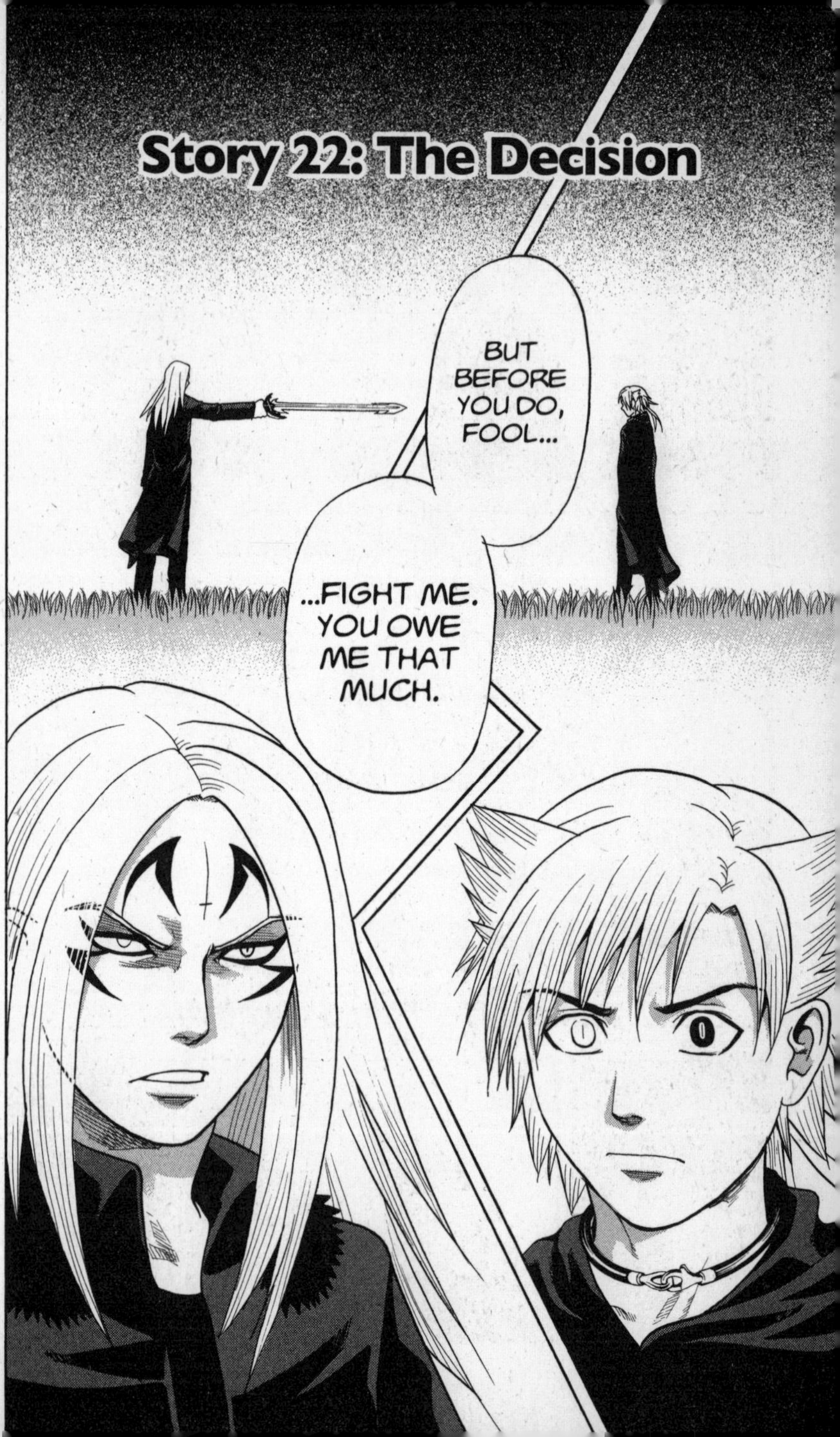
Story 22: The Decision
BUT BEFORE YOU DO, FOOL...
...FIGHT ME. YOU OWE ME THAT MUCH.

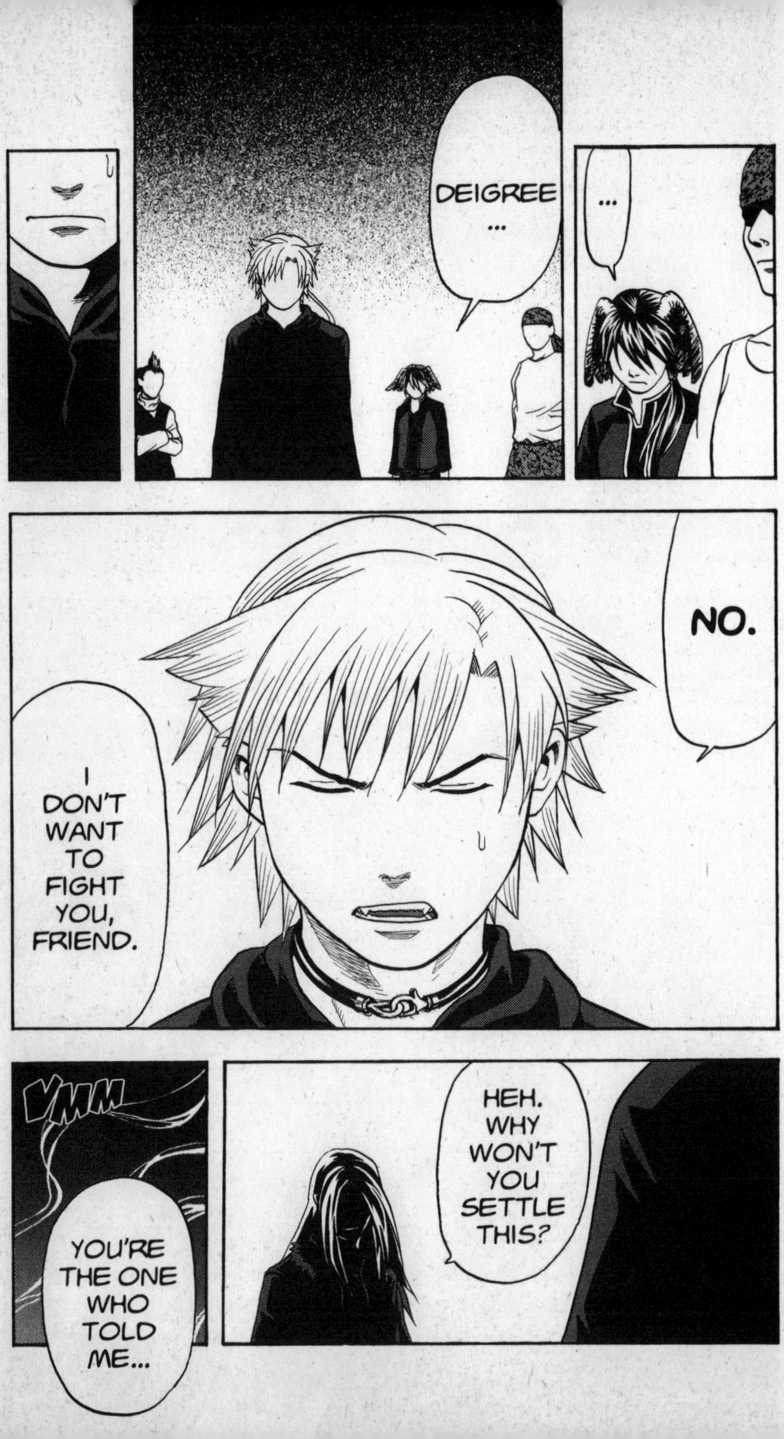
...
DEIGREE ...
NO.
I DON'T WANT TO FIGHT YOU, FRIEND.
HEH. WHY WON'T YOU SETTLE THIS?
VMM
YOU'RE THE ONE WHO TOLD ME...

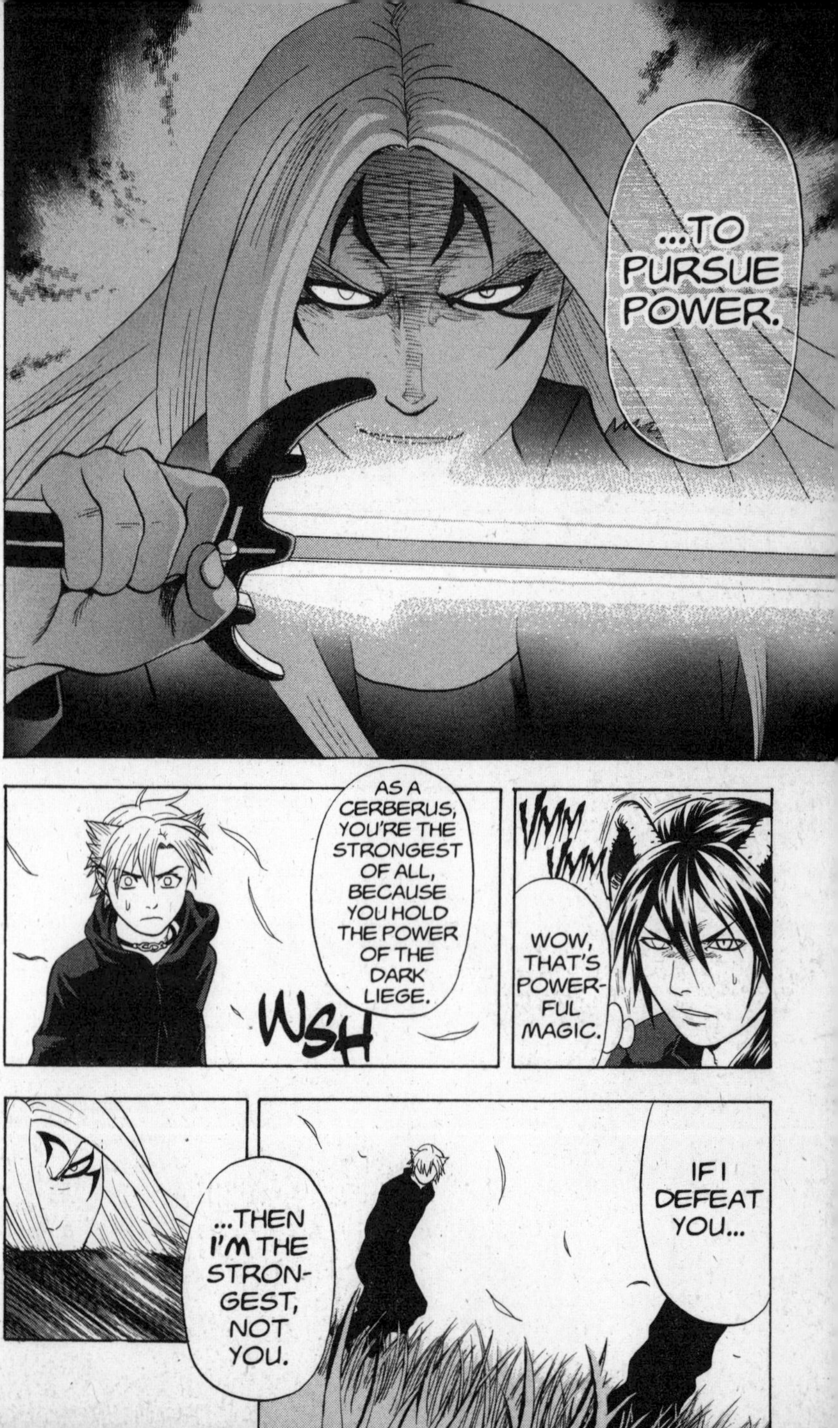
...TO PURSUE POWER.
VMM VMM
WOW, THAT'S POWER-FUL MAGIC.
AS A CERBERUS, YOU'RE THE STRONGEST OF ALL, BECAUSE YOU HOLD THE POWER OF THE DARK LIEGE.
WSH
IF I DEFEAT YOU...
...THEN I'M THE STRON-GEST, NOT YOU.

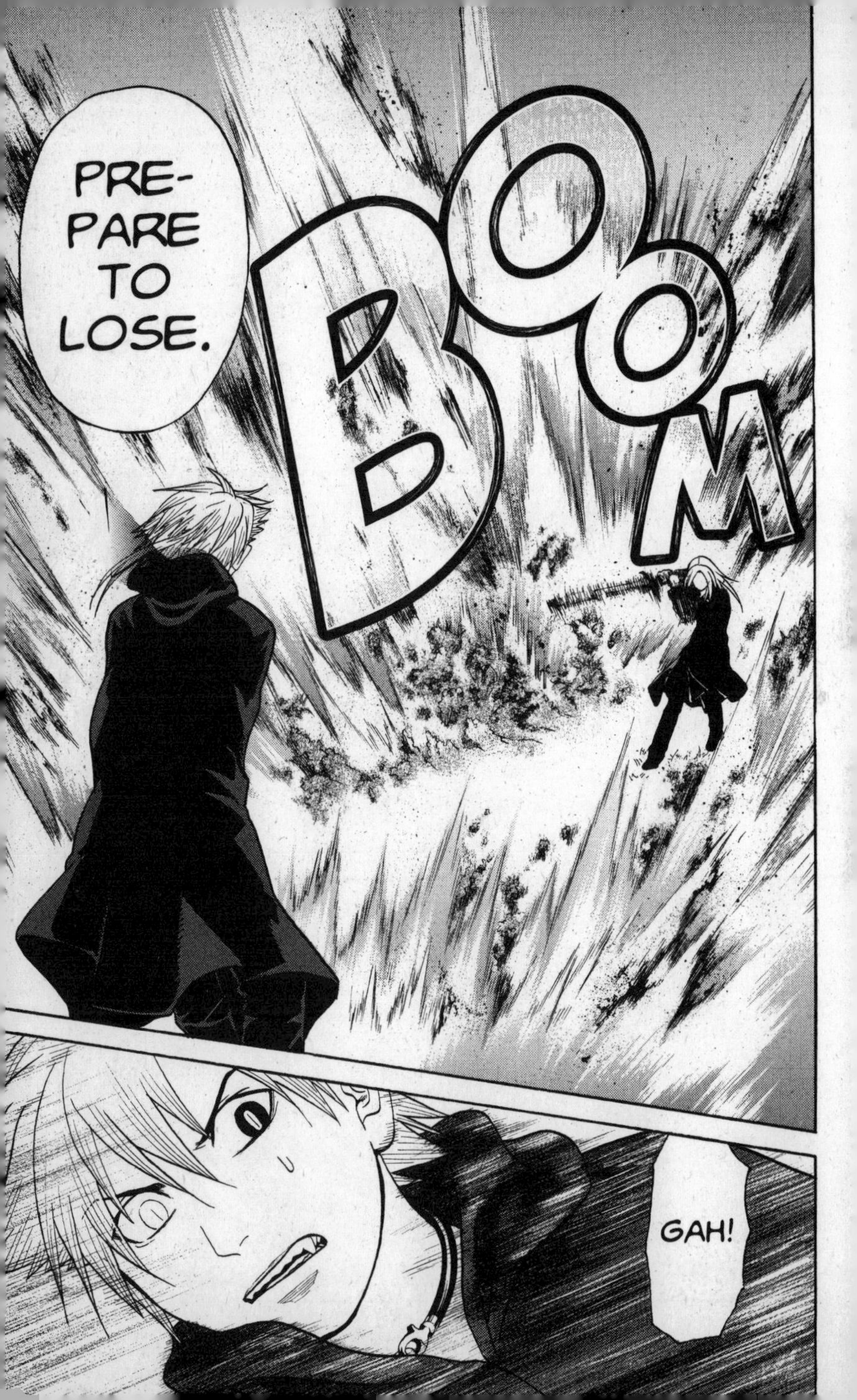
PRE-
PARE
TO
LOSE.
BOOOM
GAH!

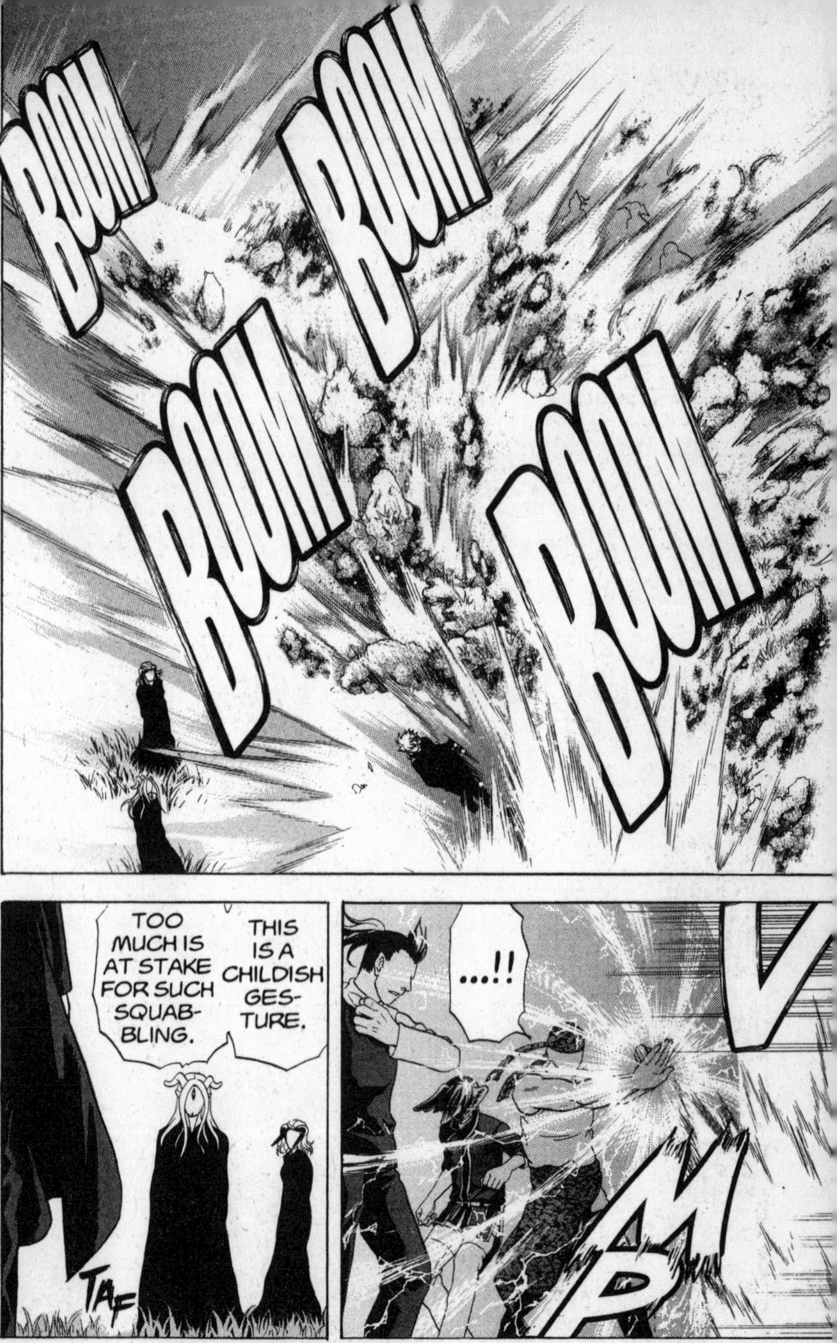
BOOM
BOOM
BOOM
BOOM
...!!
VMP
THIS IS A CHILDISH GES-TURE.
TOO MUCH IS AT STAKE FOR SUCH SQUAB-BLING.
TAF

READ THIS WAY

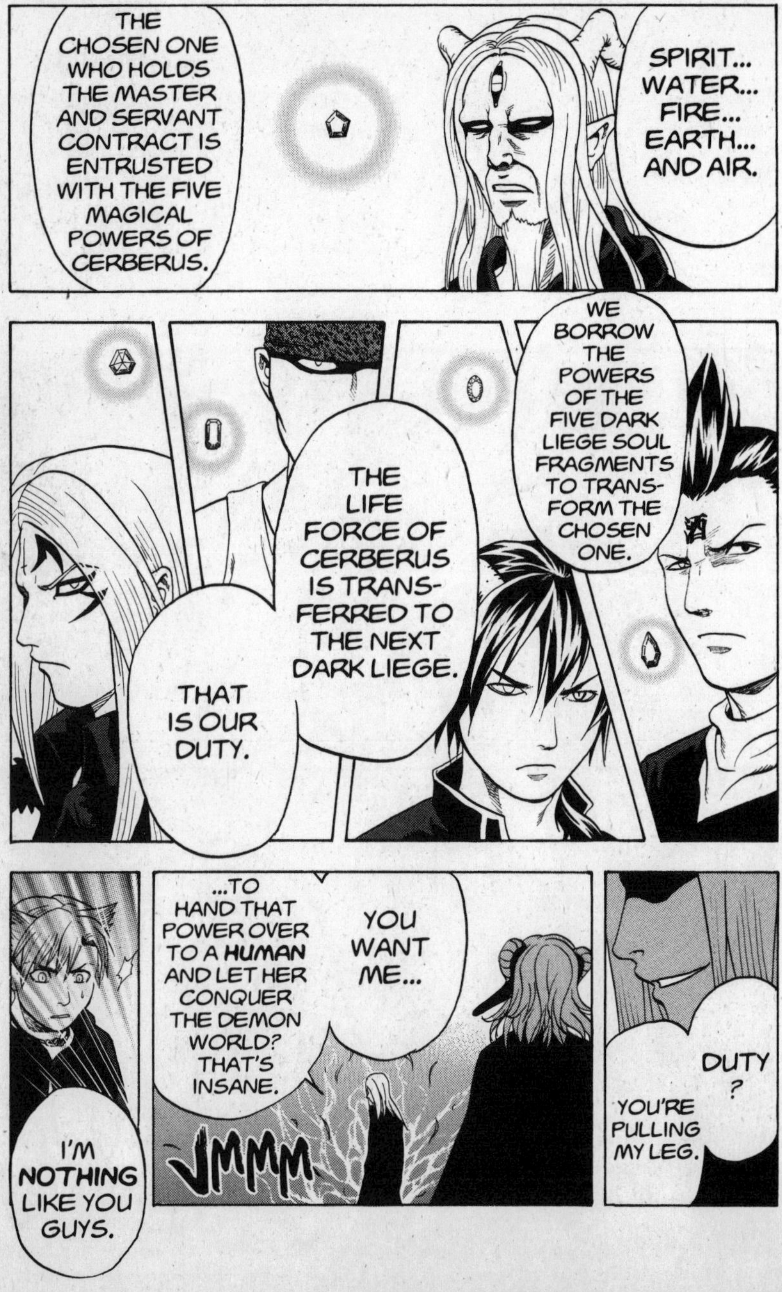
SPIRIT... WATER... FIRE... EARTH... AND AIR.
THE CHOSEN ONE WHO HOLDS THE MASTER AND SERVANT CONTRACT IS ENTRUSTED WITH THE FIVE MAGICAL POWERS OF CERBERUS.
WE BORROW THE POWERS OF THE FIVE DARK LIEGE SOUL FRAGMENTS TO TRANSFORM THE CHOSEN ONE.
THE LIFE FORCE OF CERBERUS IS TRANSFERRED TO THE NEXT DARK LIEGE.
THAT IS OUR DUTY.
DUTY?
YOU'RE PULLING MY LEG.
YOU WANT ME...
...TO HAND THAT POWER OVER TO A HUMAN AND LET HER CONQUER THE DEMON WORLD? THAT'S INSANE.
JMMM
I'M NOTHING LIKE YOU GUYS.

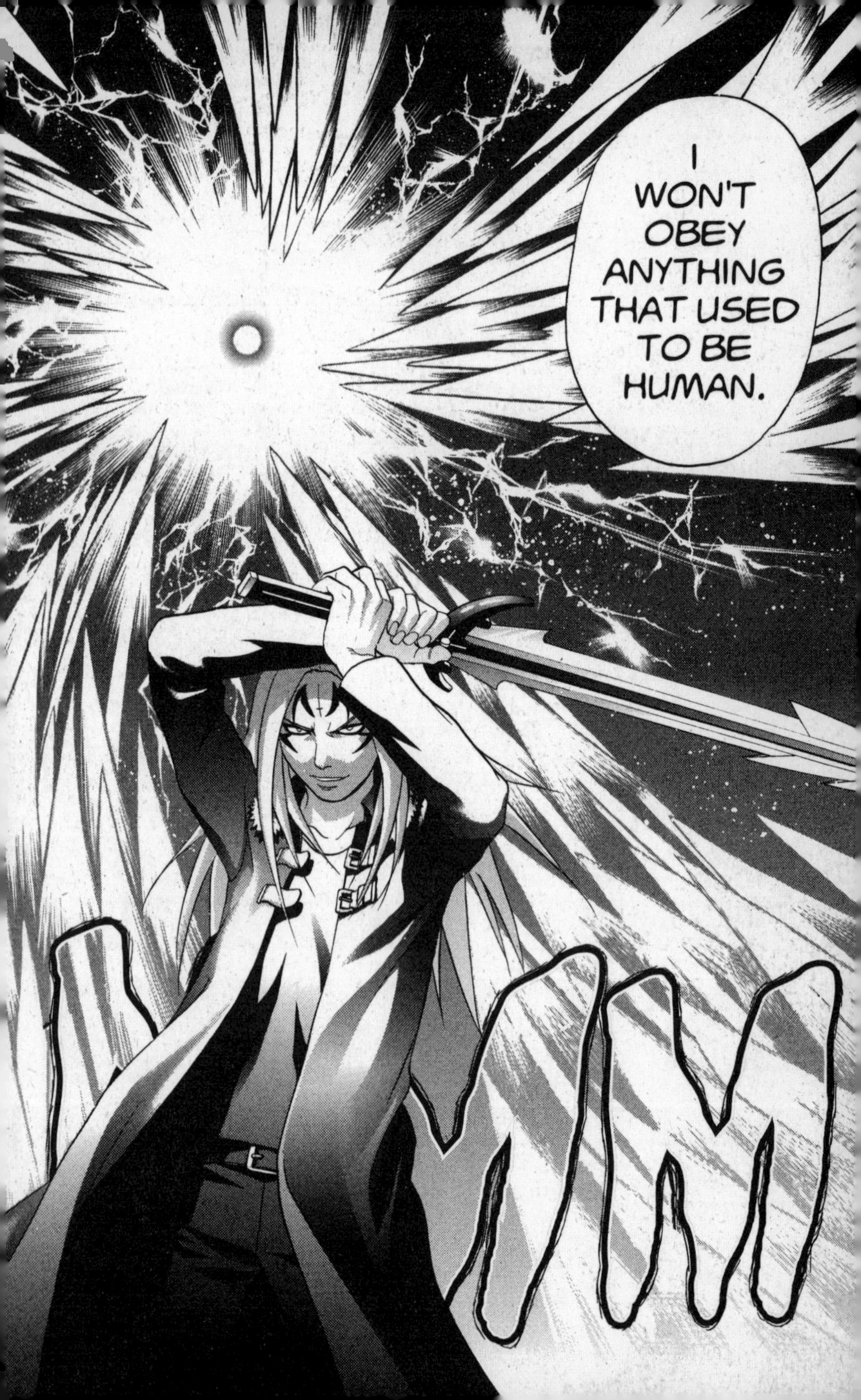
I WON'T OBEY ANYTHING THAT USED TO BE HUMAN.
VMM

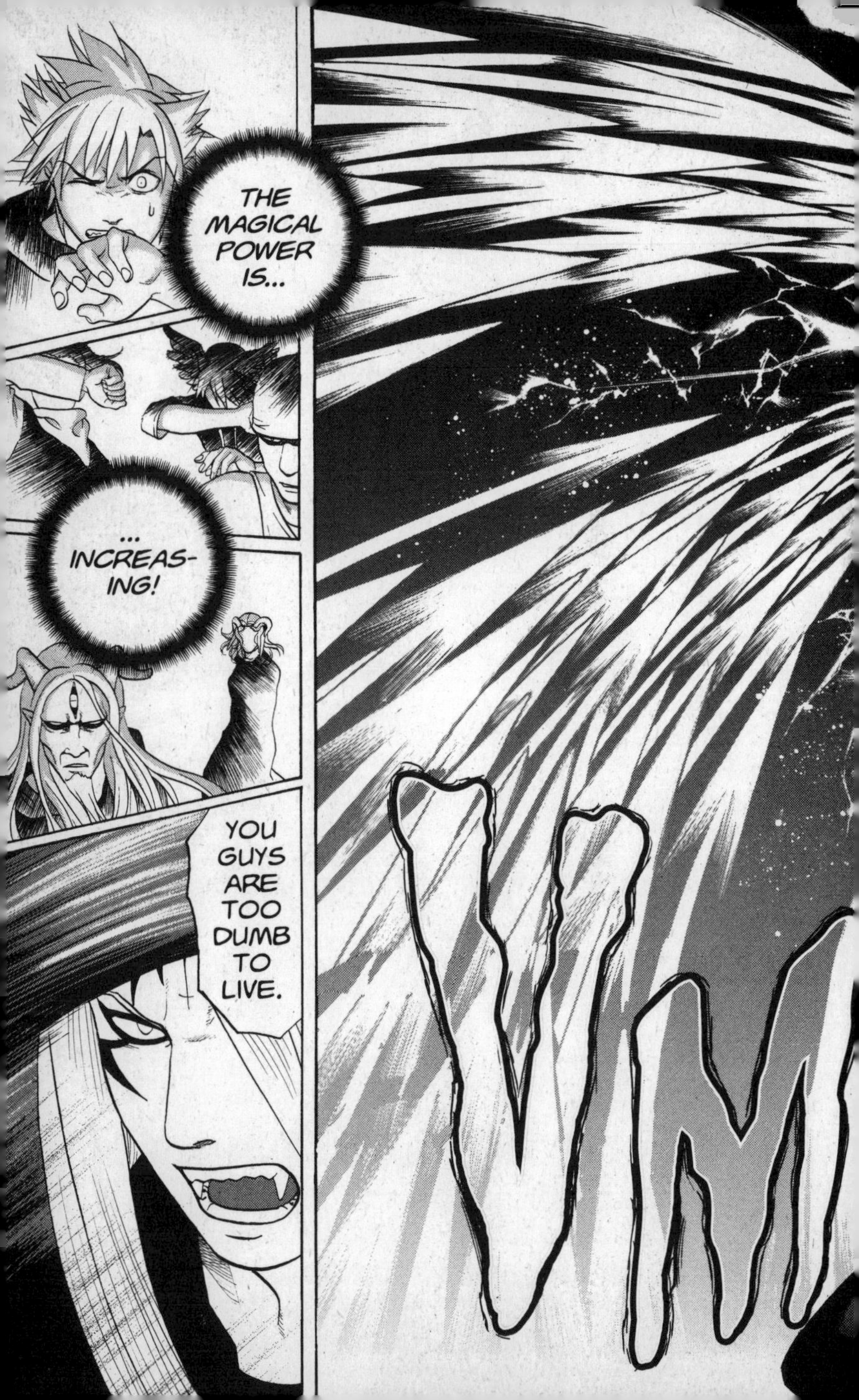
THE MAGICAL POWER IS...
...INCREASING!
YOU GUYS ARE TOO DUMB TO LIVE.

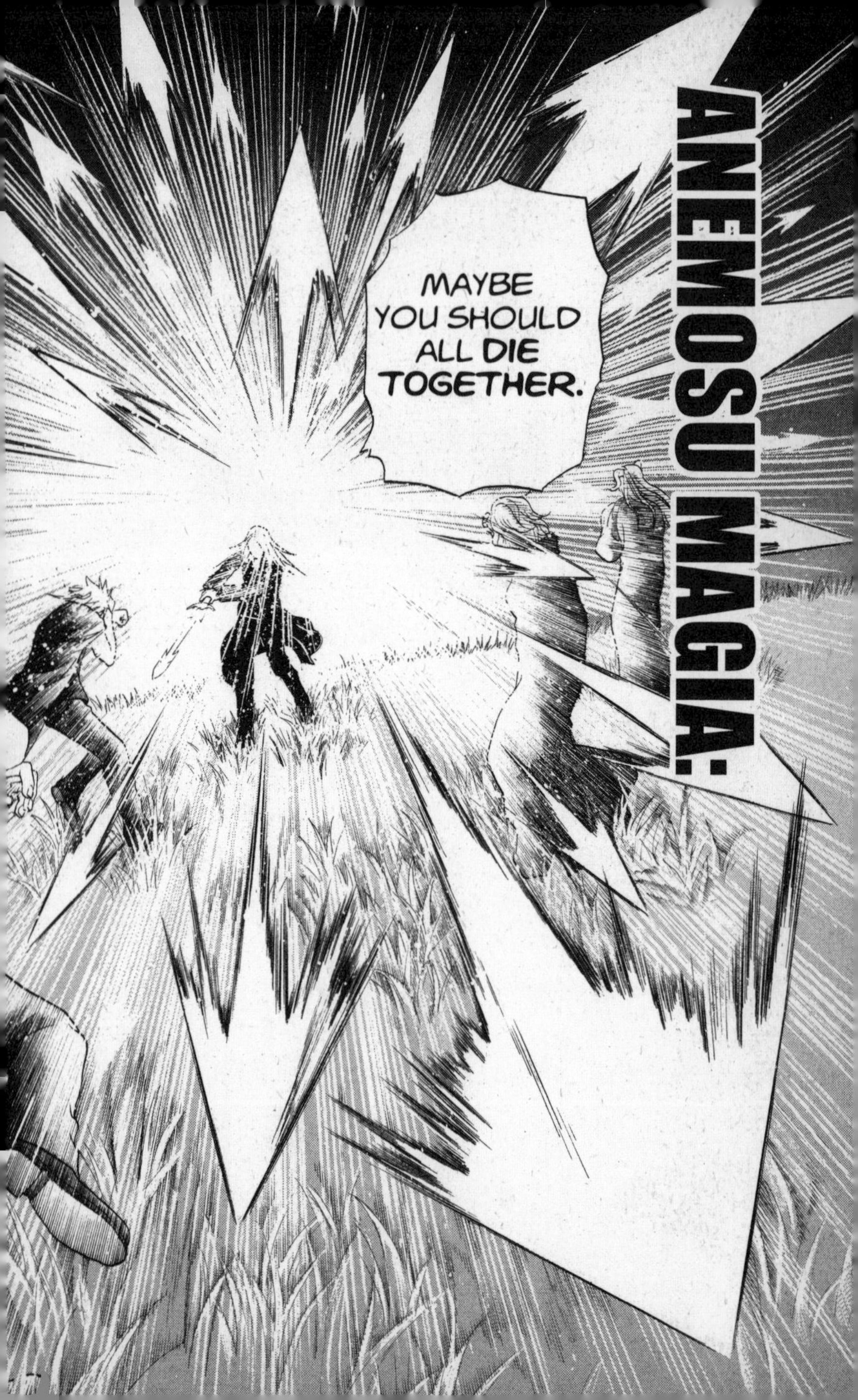
ANEMOSU MAGIA:
MAYBE YOU SHOULD ALL DIE TOGETHER.

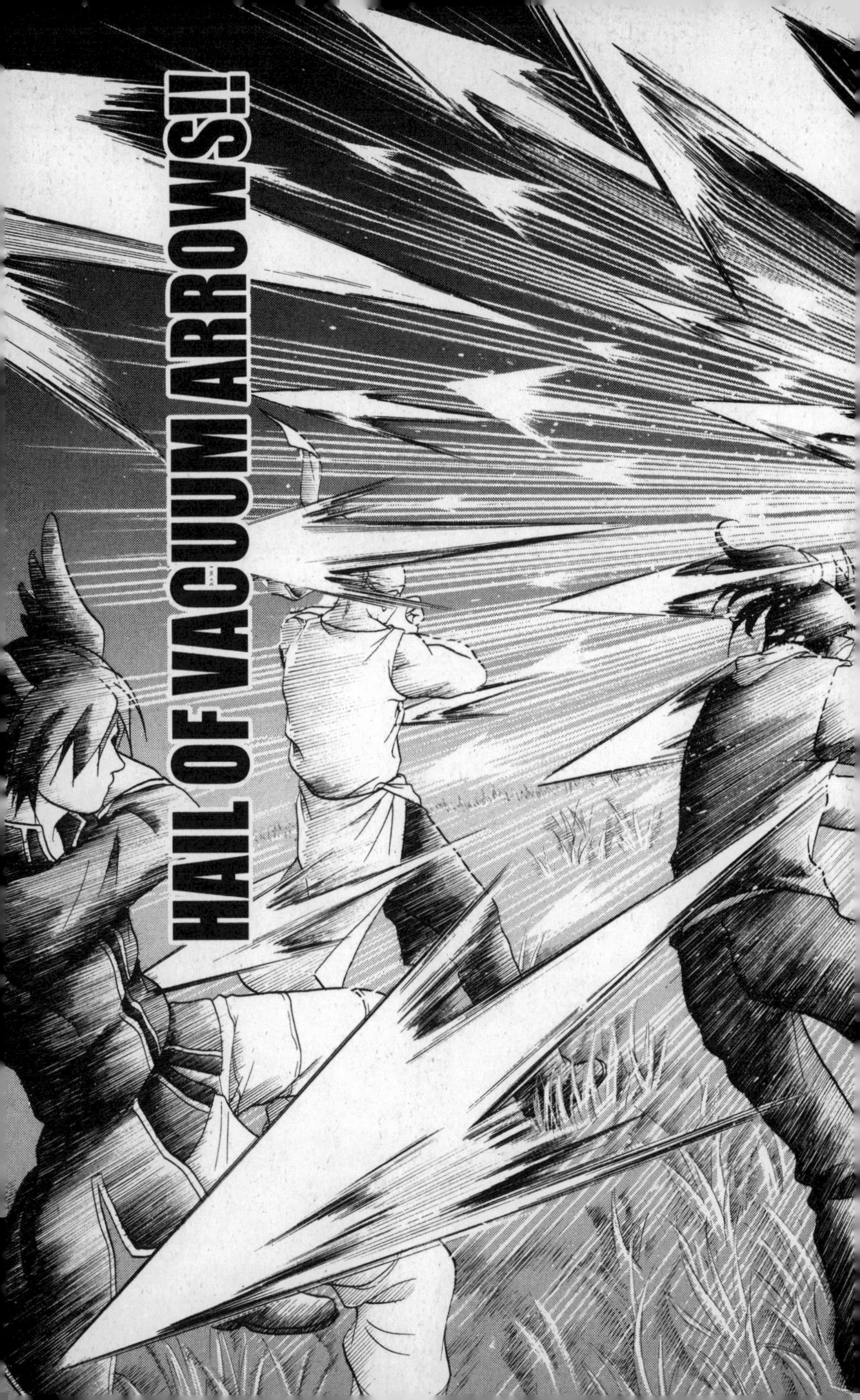
HAIL OF VACUUM ARROWS!!

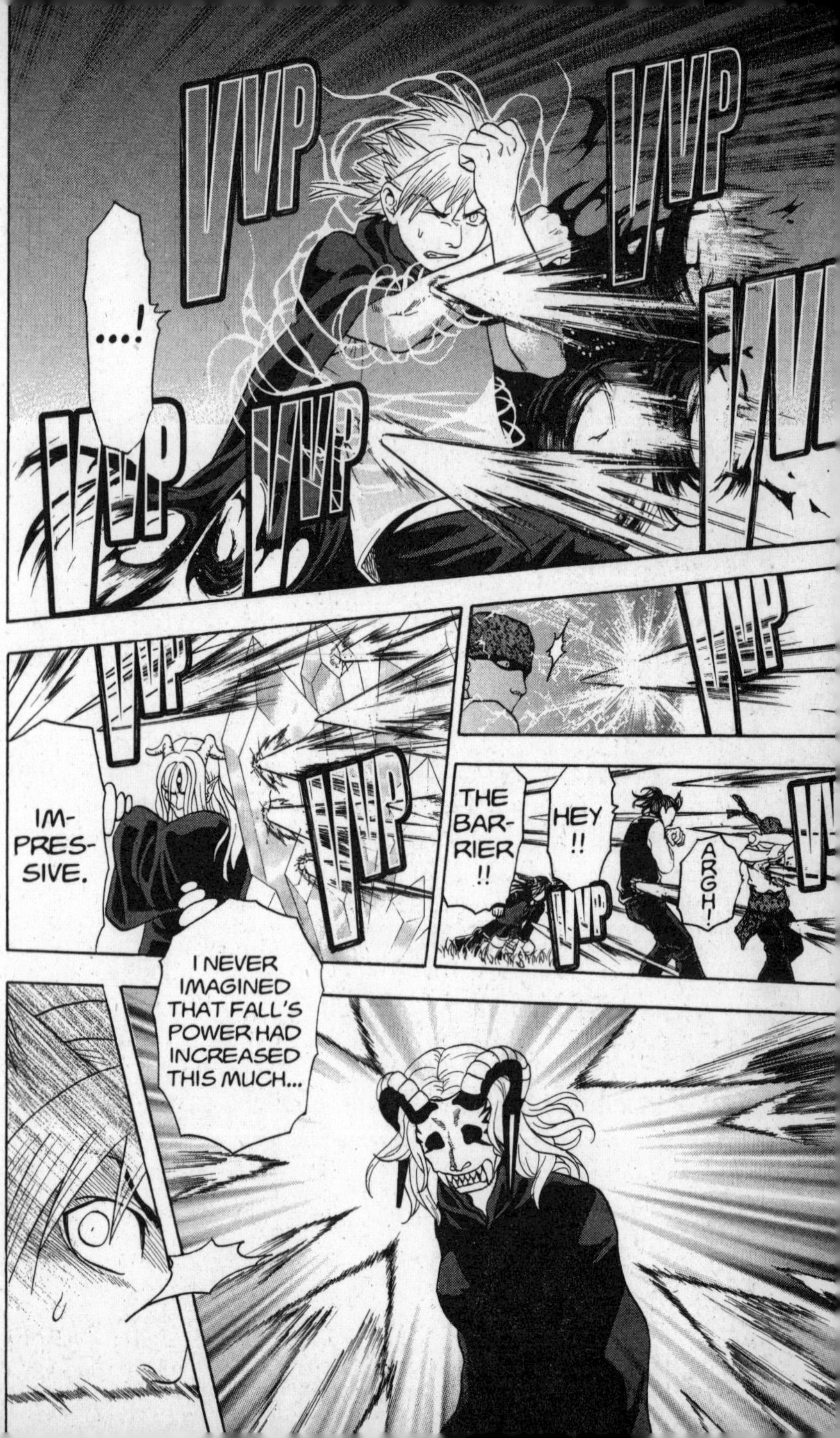
VVP
VVP
...!
VVP
VVP
VVP
HEY !!
THE BAR-RIER !!
ARGH!
VVP
VVP
VVP
IM-PRES-SIVE.
I NEVER IMAGINED THAT FALL'S POWER HAD INCREASED THIS MUCH...

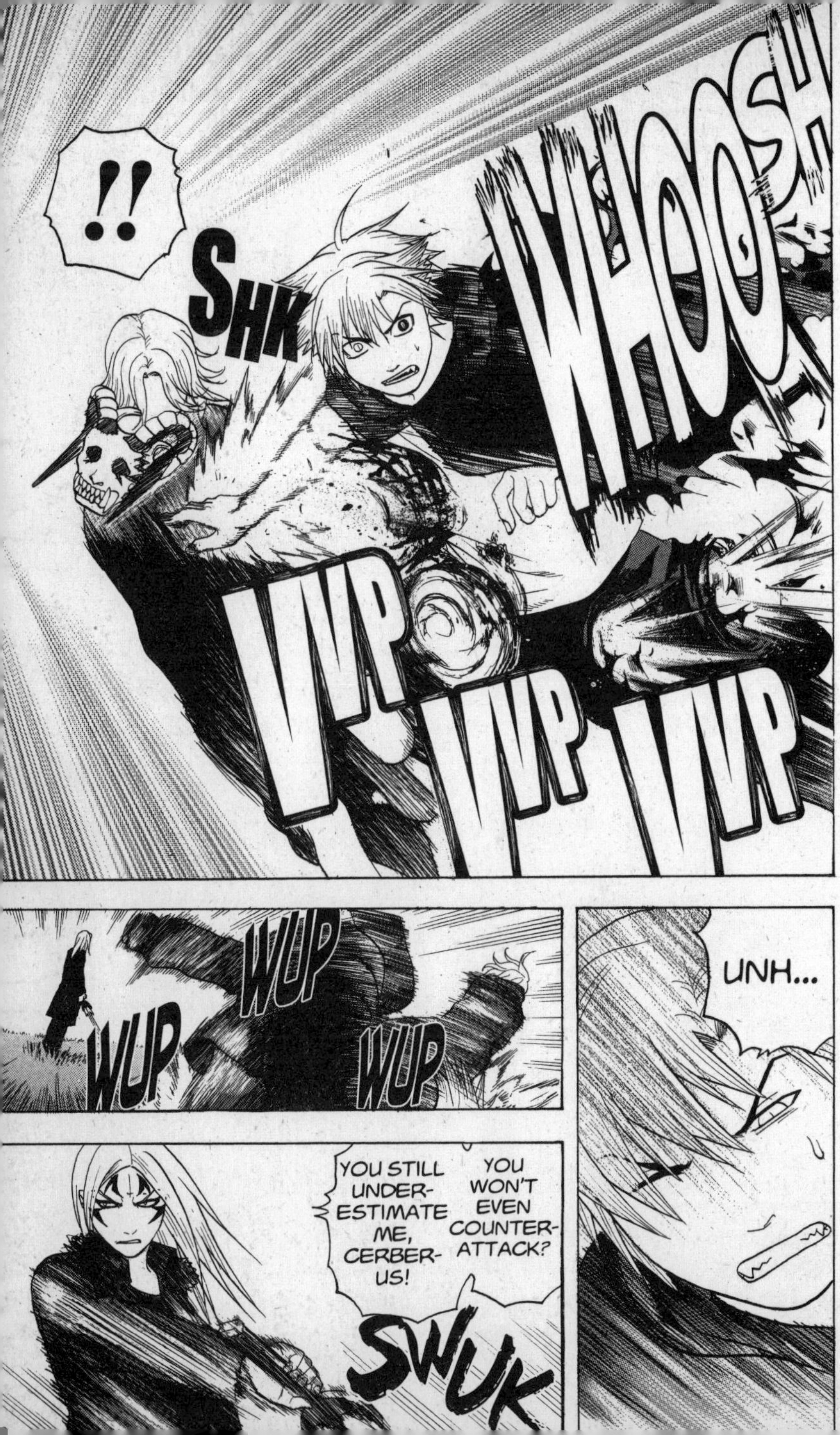
WHOOSH
!!
SHK
VVP VVP VVP
UNH...
WUP WUP WUP
YOU WON'T EVEN COUNTER-ATTACK?
YOU STILL UNDER-ESTIMATE ME, CERBER-US!
SWUK

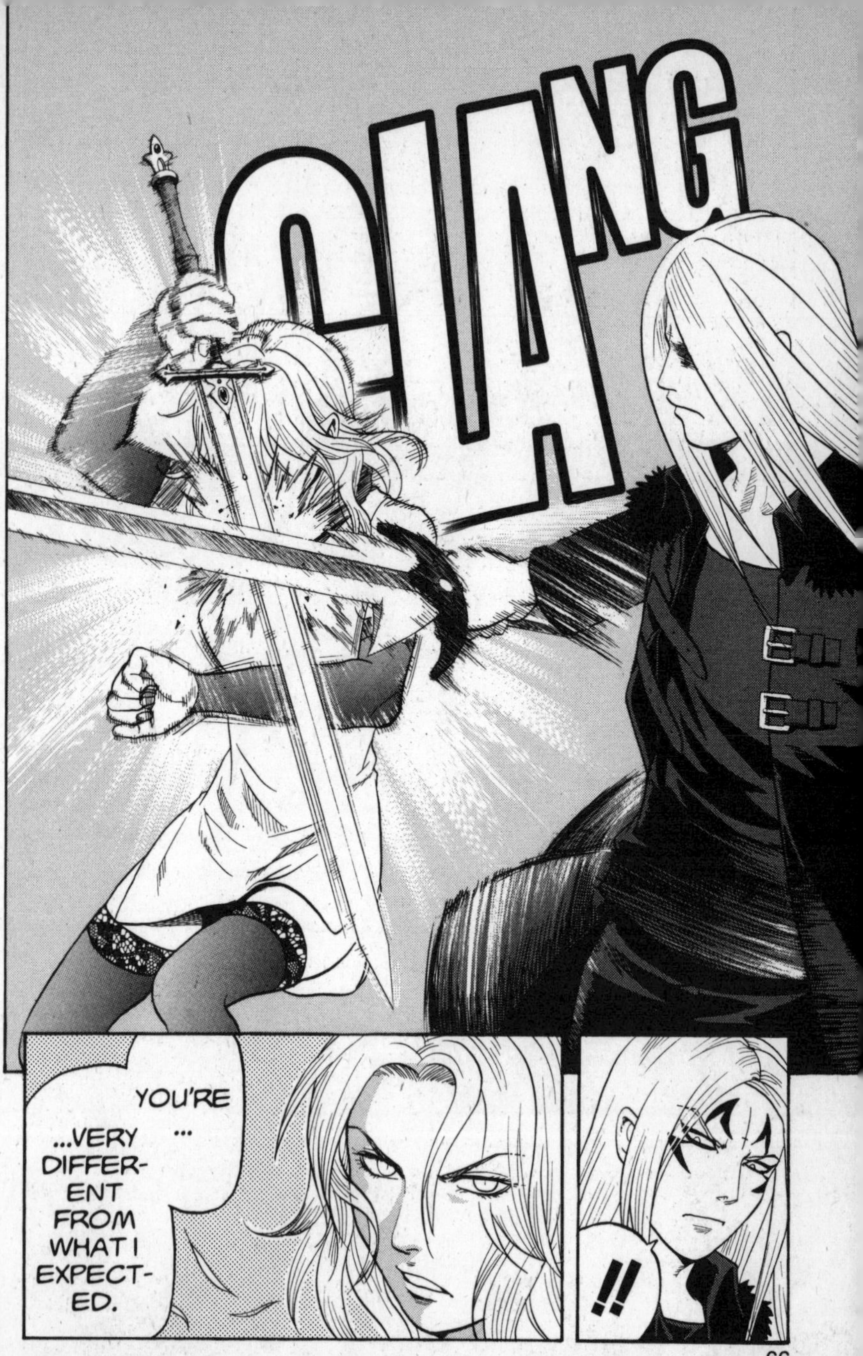
CLANG
!!
YOU'RE ...
...VERY DIFFERENT FROM WHAT I EXPECTED.

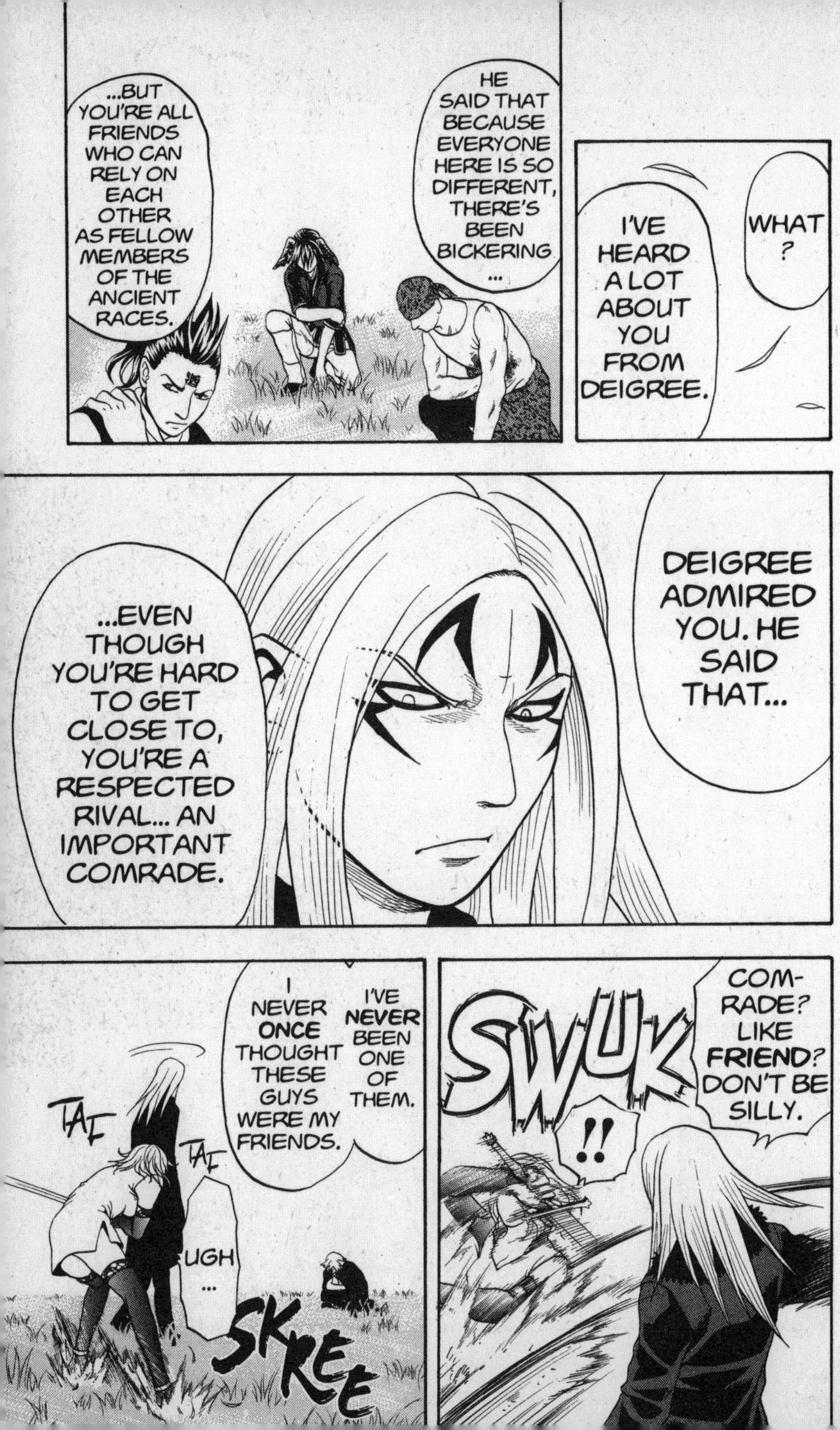
WHAT?
I'VE HEARD A LOT ABOUT YOU FROM DEIGREE.
HE SAID THAT BECAUSE EVERYONE HERE IS SO DIFFERENT, THERE'S BEEN BICKERING...
...BUT YOU'RE ALL FRIENDS WHO CAN RELY ON EACH OTHER AS FELLOW MEMBERS OF THE ANCIENT RACES.
DEIGREE ADMIRED YOU. HE SAID THAT...
...EVEN THOUGH YOU'RE HARD TO GET CLOSE TO, YOU'RE A RESPECTED RIVAL... AN IMPORTANT COMRADE.
COM-RADE? LIKE **FRIEND**? DON'T BE SILLY.
SWUK
!!
I'VE **NEVER** BEEN ONE OF THEM.
I NEVER **ONCE** THOUGHT THESE GUYS WERE MY FRIENDS.
TAF
TAF
UGH...
SKREE

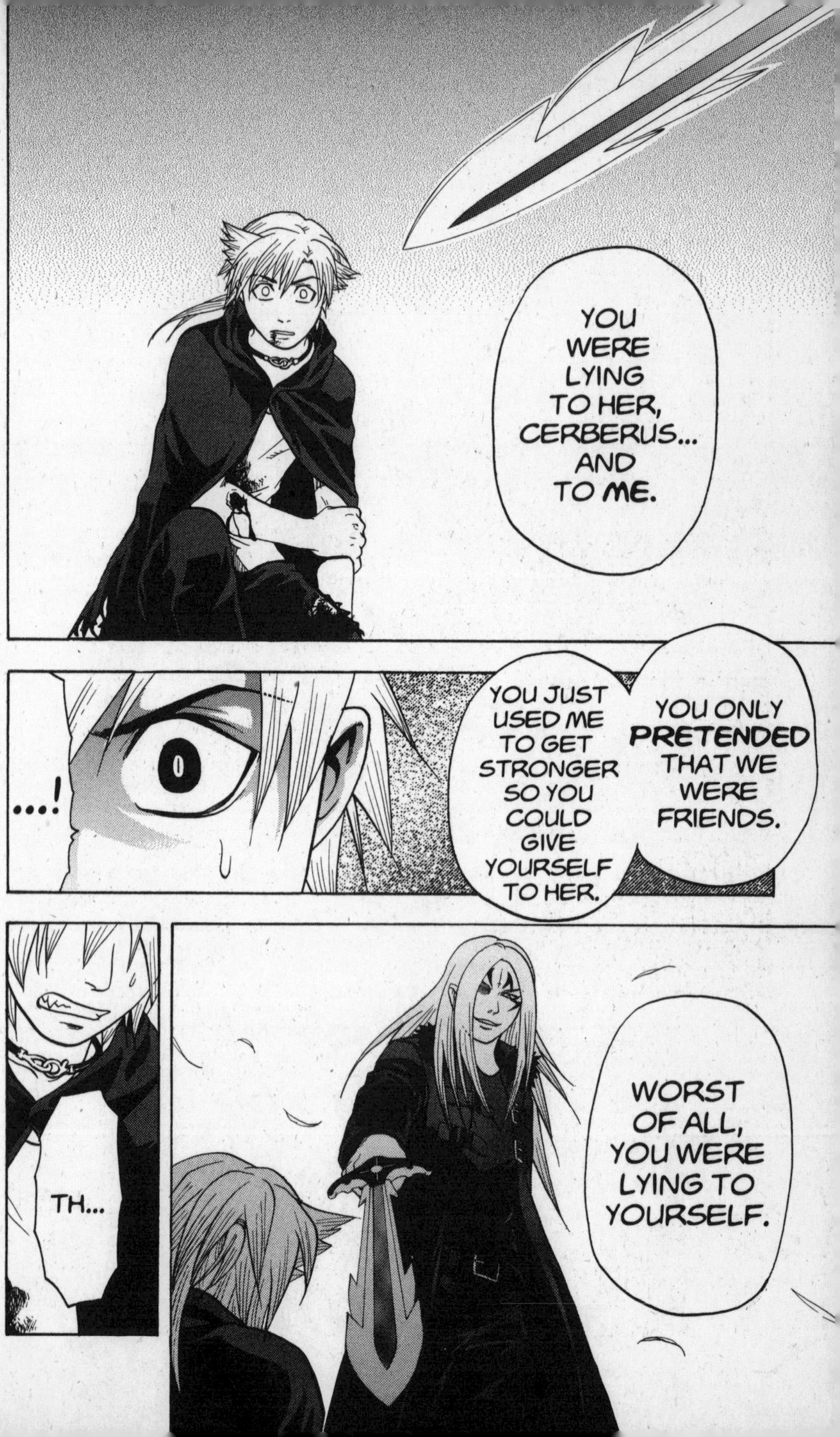
YOU WERE LYING TO HER, CERBERUS... AND TO ME.
YOU ONLY PRETENDED THAT WE WERE FRIENDS.
YOU JUST USED ME TO GET STRONGER SO YOU COULD GIVE YOURSELF TO HER.
...!
WORST OF ALL, YOU WERE LYING TO YOURSELF.
TH...

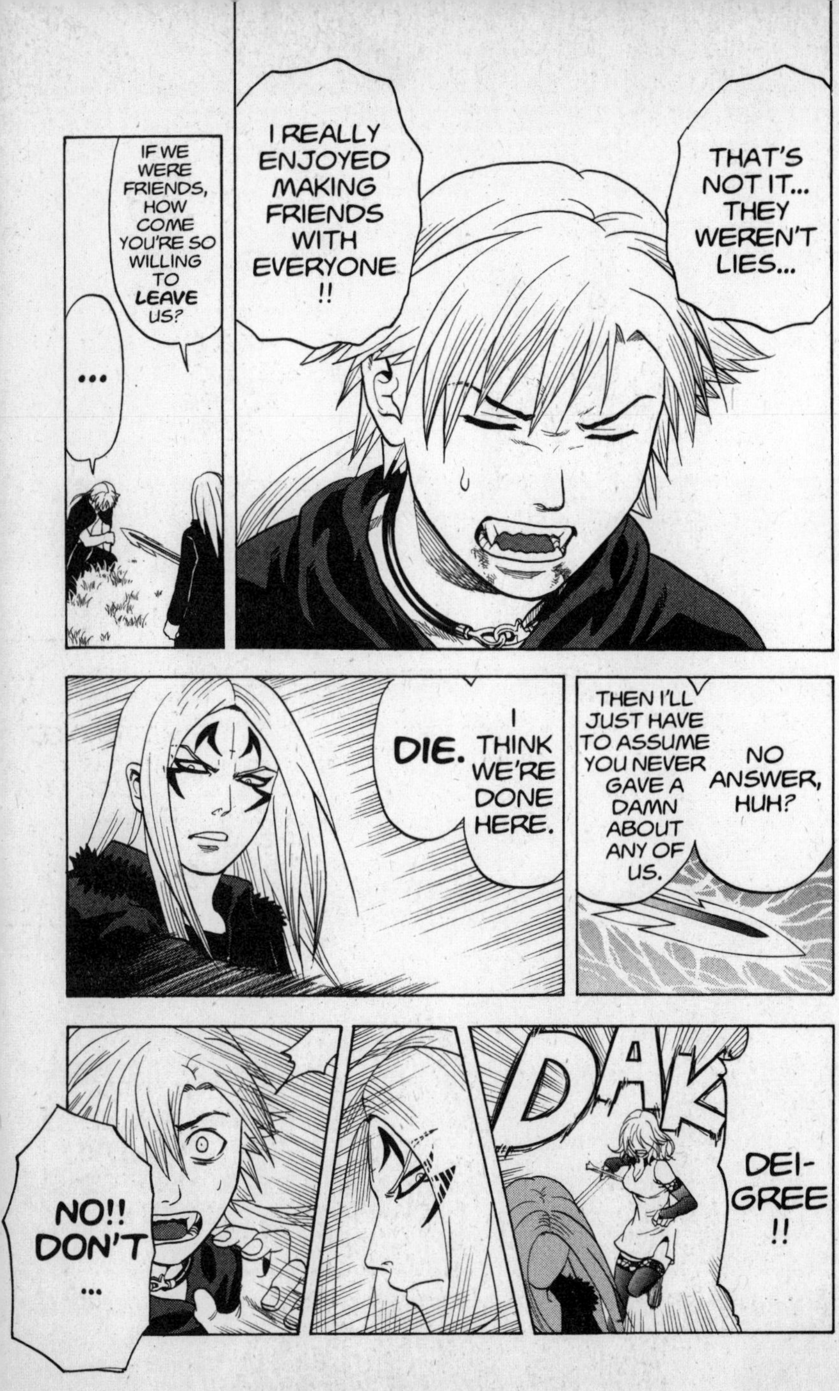
THAT'S NOT IT... THEY WEREN'T LIES...
I REALLY ENJOYED MAKING FRIENDS WITH EVERYONE !!
IF WE WERE FRIENDS, HOW COME YOU'RE SO WILLING TO LEAVE US?
...
NO ANSWER, HUH?
THEN I'LL JUST HAVE TO ASSUME YOU NEVER GAVE A DAMN ABOUT ANY OF US.
I THINK WE'RE DONE HERE.
DIE.
DAK
DEI-GREE !!
NO!! DON'T ...

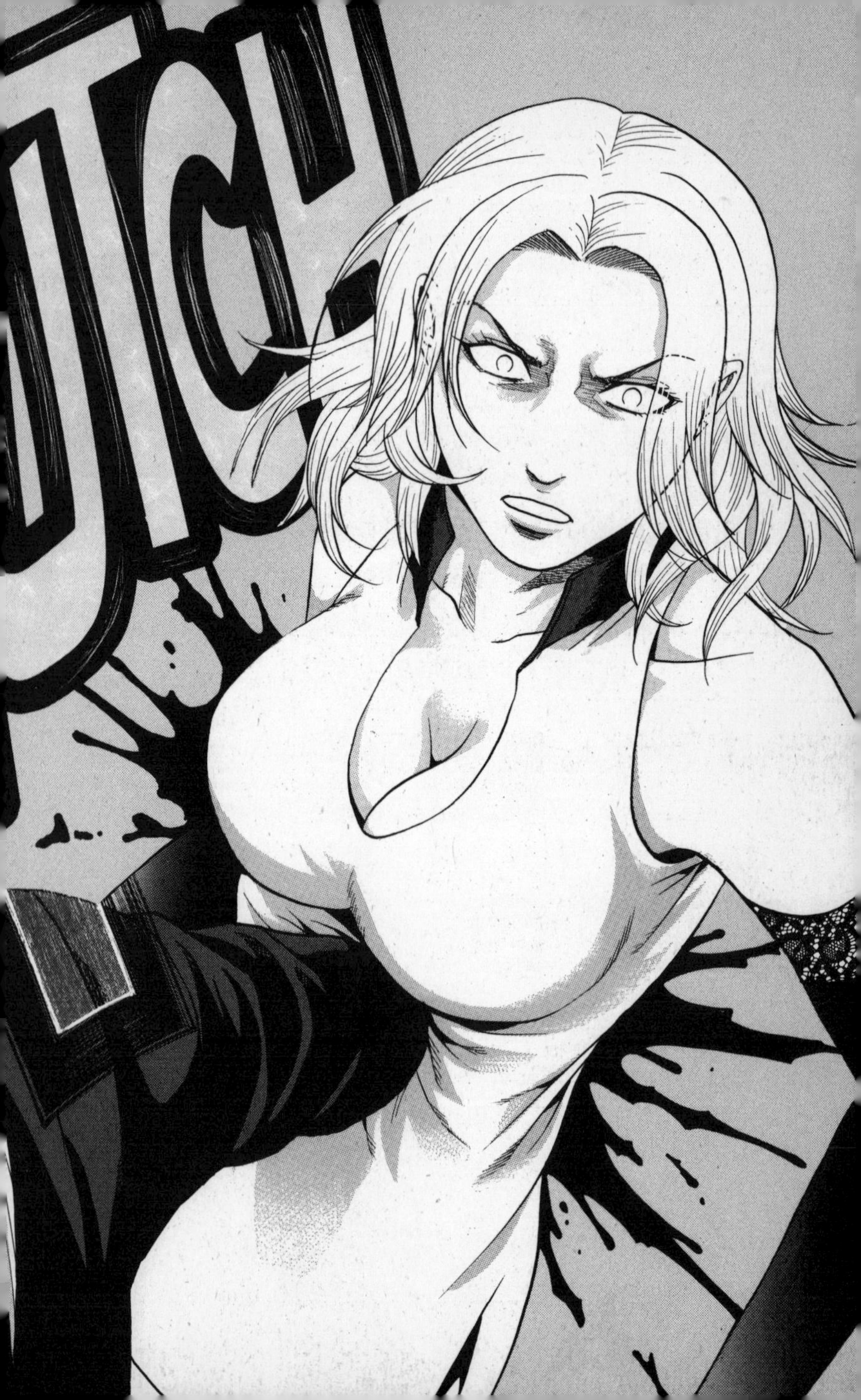

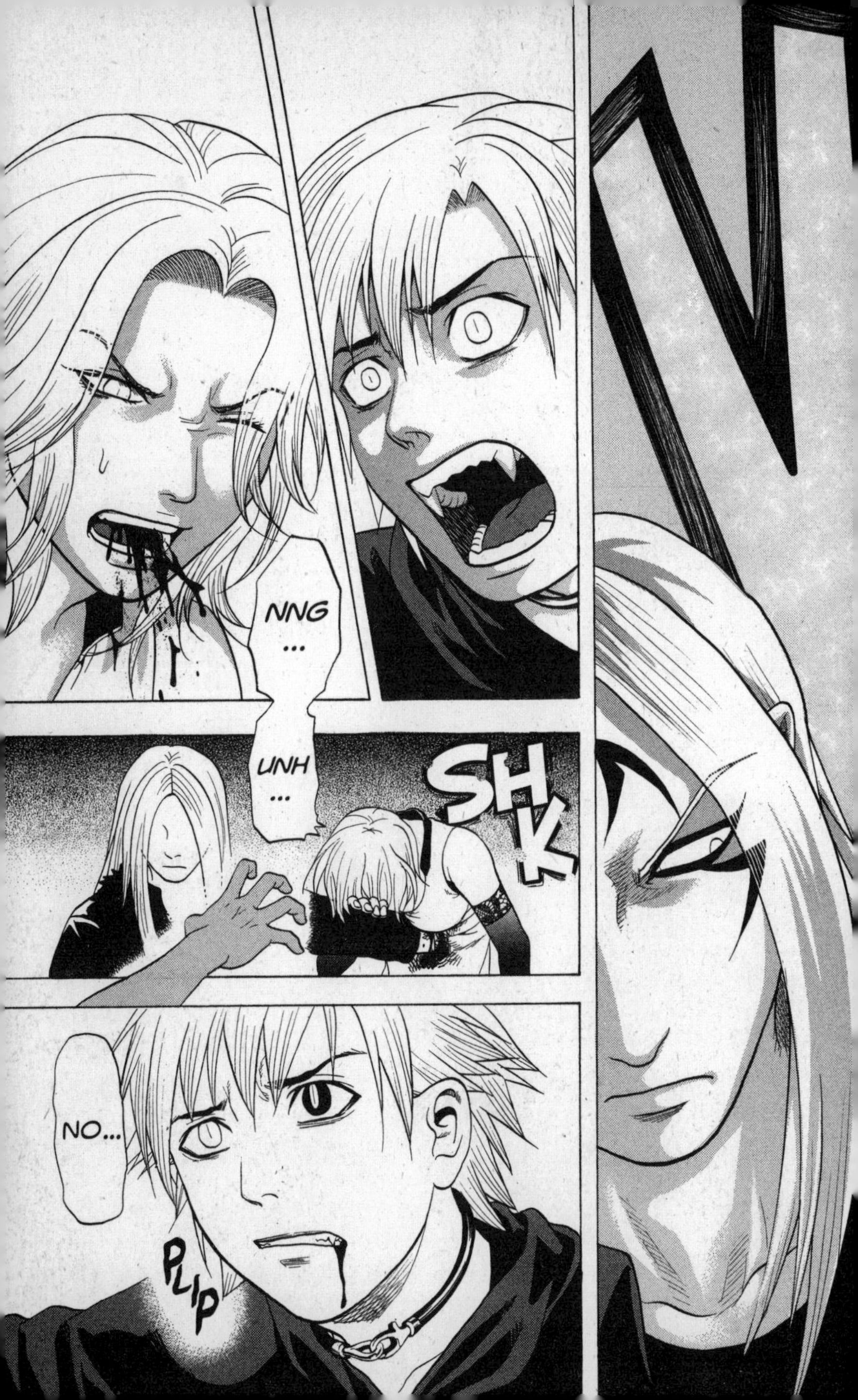

NNG...
SHK
UNH...
NO...
PLIP

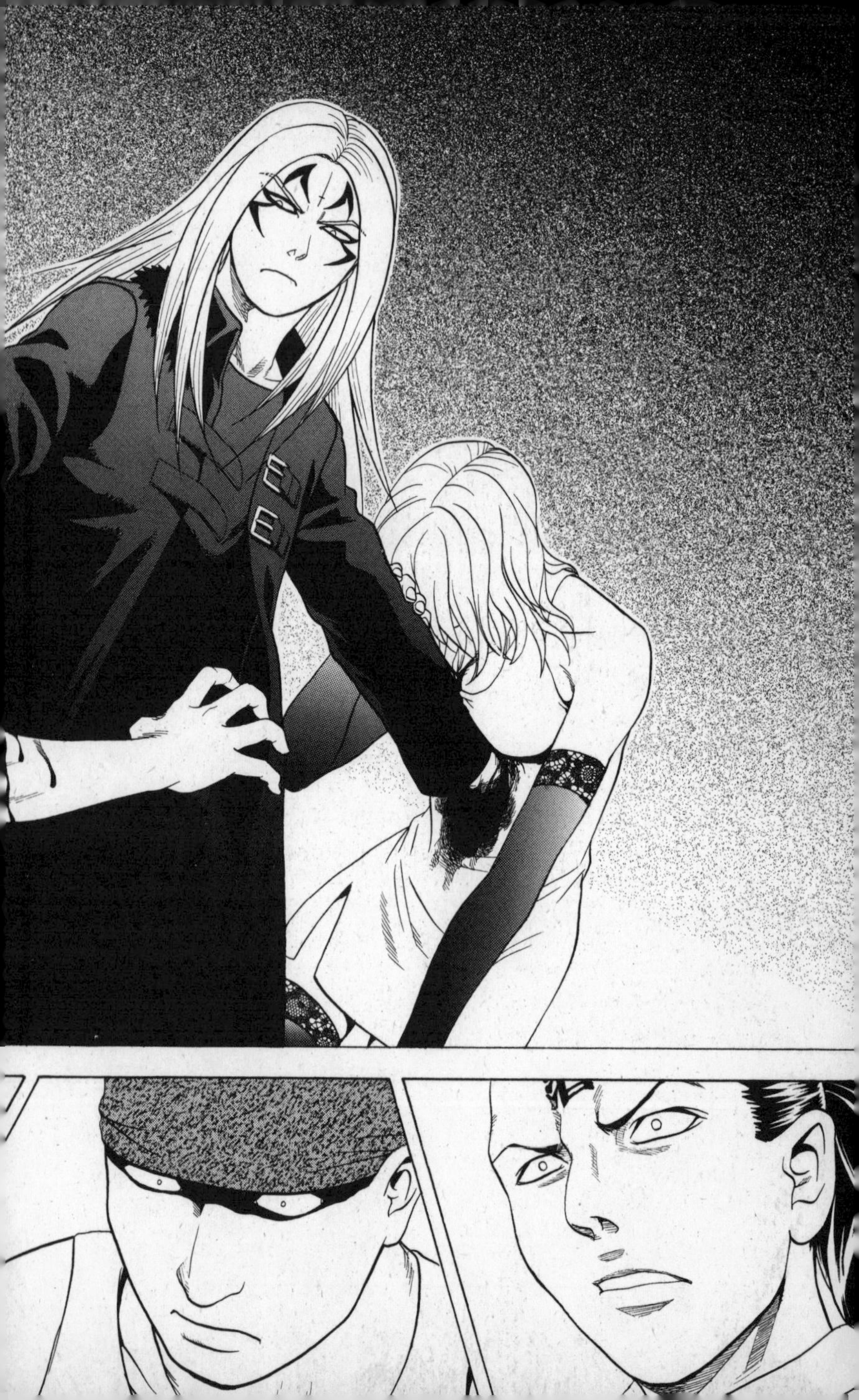

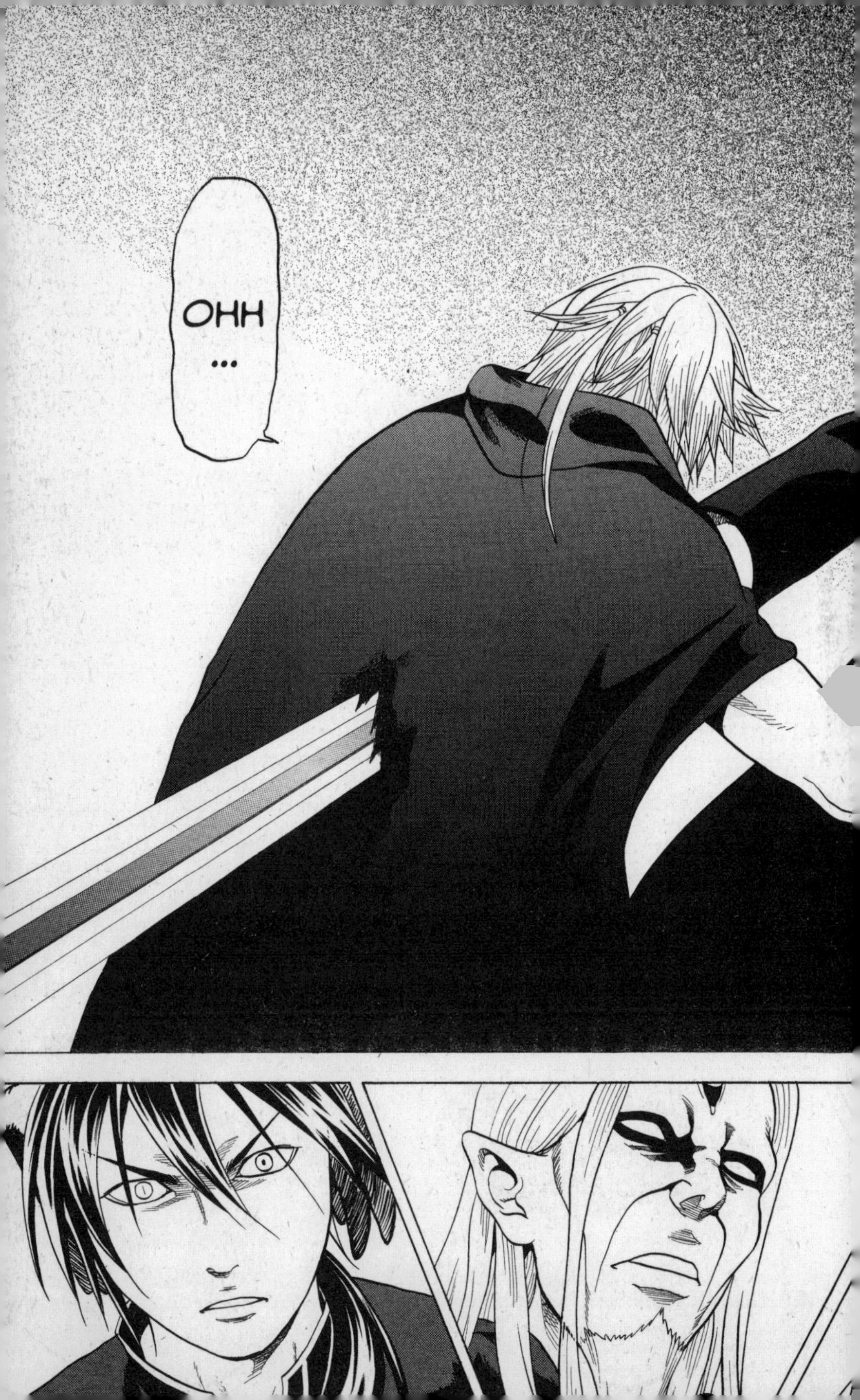
OHH
...

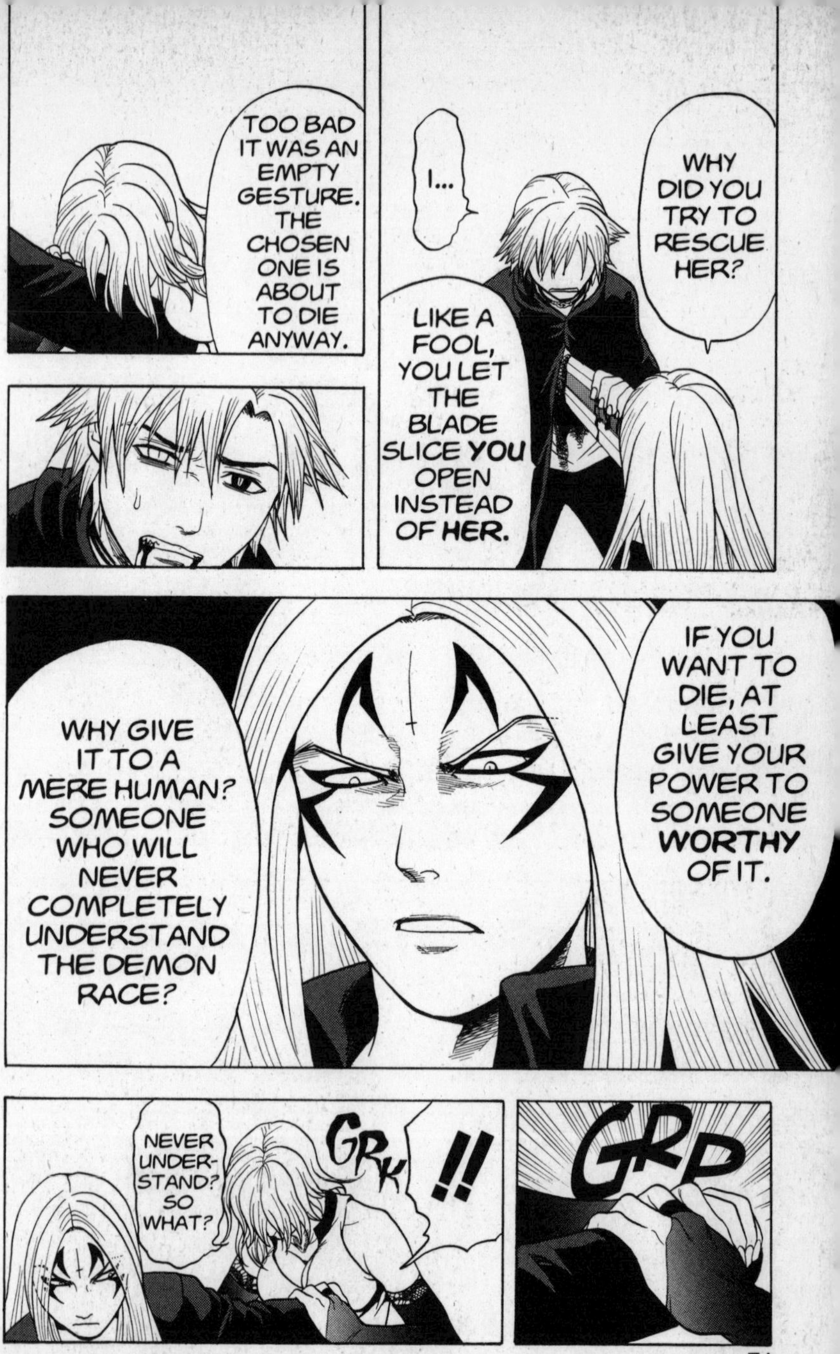
WHY DID YOU TRY TO RESCUE HER?
I...
LIKE A FOOL, YOU LET THE BLADE SLICE YOU OPEN INSTEAD OF HER.
TOO BAD IT WAS AN EMPTY GESTURE. THE CHOSEN ONE IS ABOUT TO DIE ANYWAY.
IF YOU WANT TO DIE, AT LEAST GIVE YOUR POWER TO SOMEONE WORTHY OF IT.
WHY GIVE IT TO A MERE HUMAN? SOMEONE WHO WILL NEVER COMPLETELY UNDERSTAND THE DEMON RACE?
GRP
GRK!!
NEVER UNDER-STAND? SO WHAT?

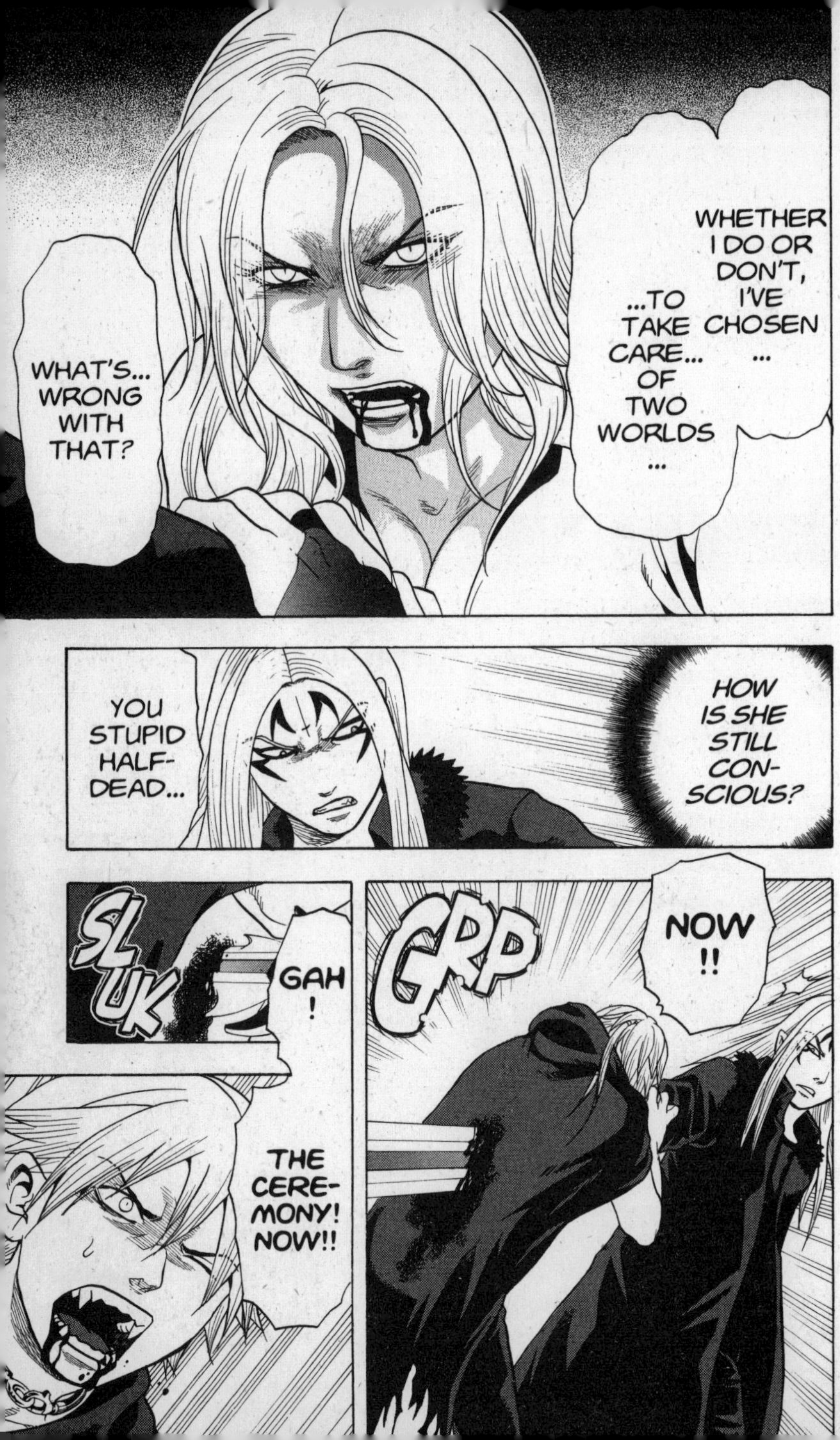
WHETHER I DO OR DON'T, I'VE CHOSEN...
...TO TAKE CARE... OF TWO WORLDS...
WHAT'S... WRONG WITH THAT?
HOW IS SHE STILL CON-SCIOUS?
YOU STUPID HALF-DEAD...
NOW !!
GRP
GAH !
SLUK
THE CERE-MONY! NOW!!

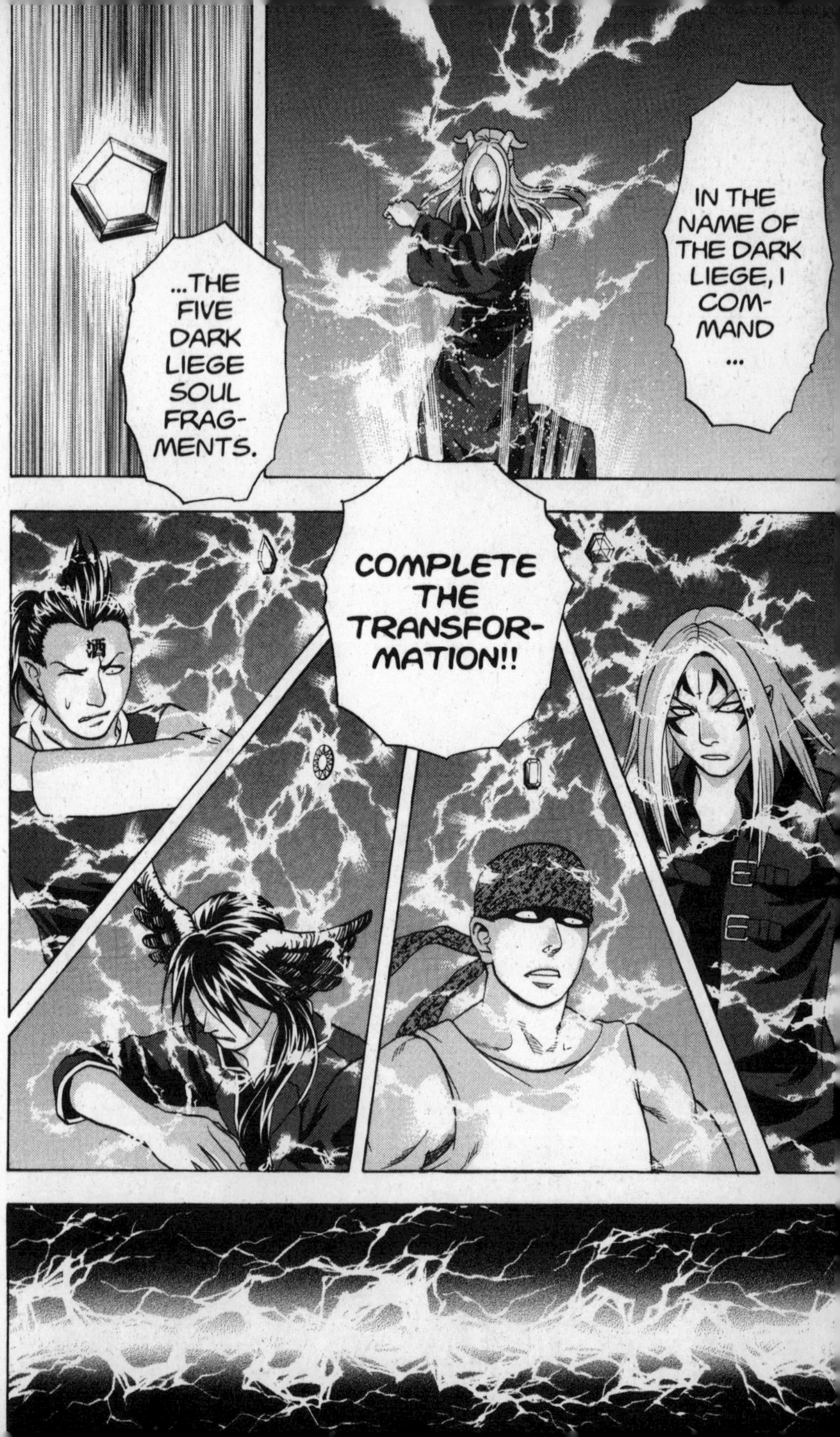
IN THE NAME OF THE DARK LIEGE, I COMMAND ...
...THE FIVE DARK LIEGE SOUL FRAGMENTS.
COMPLETE THE TRANSFORMATION!!

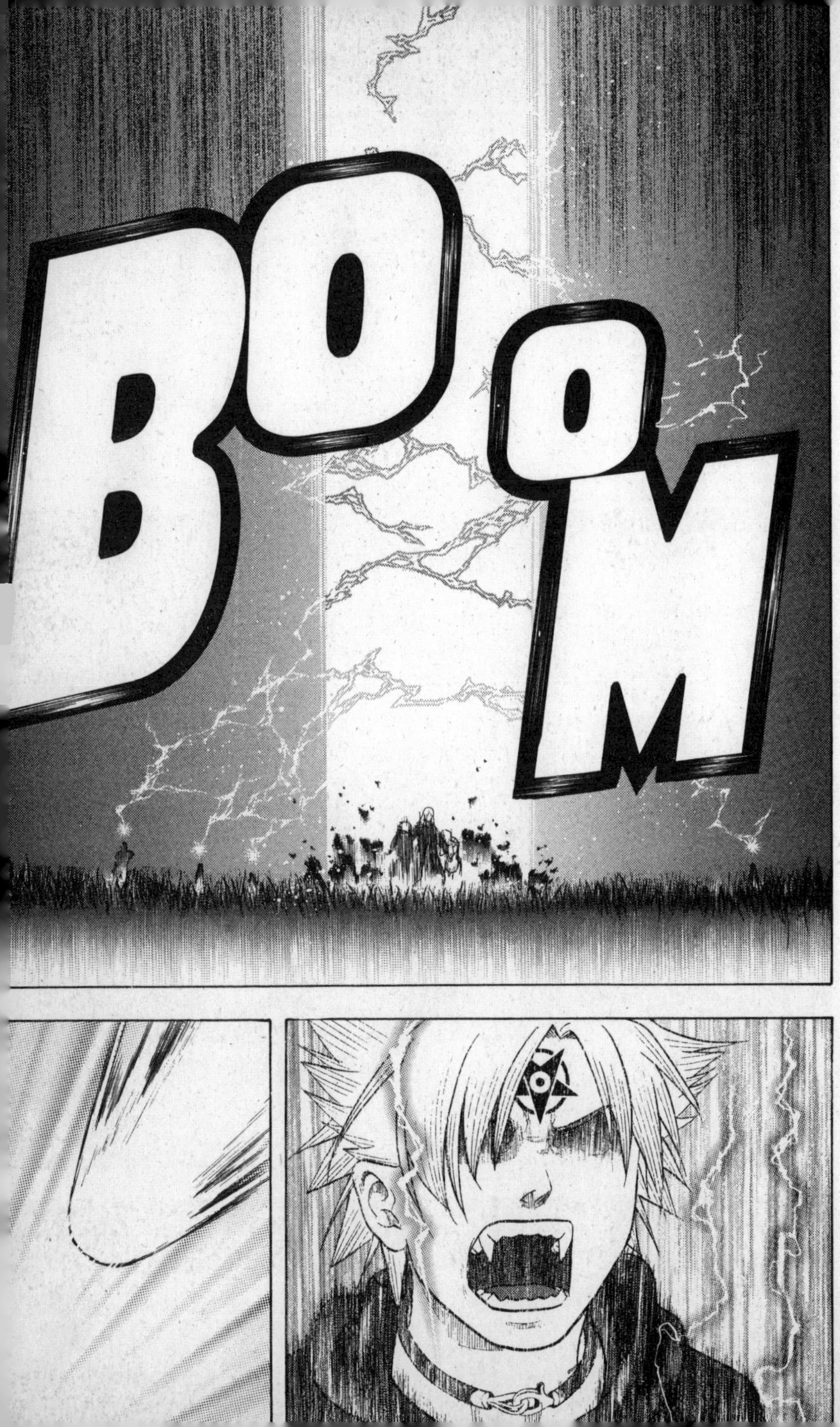
BOOM

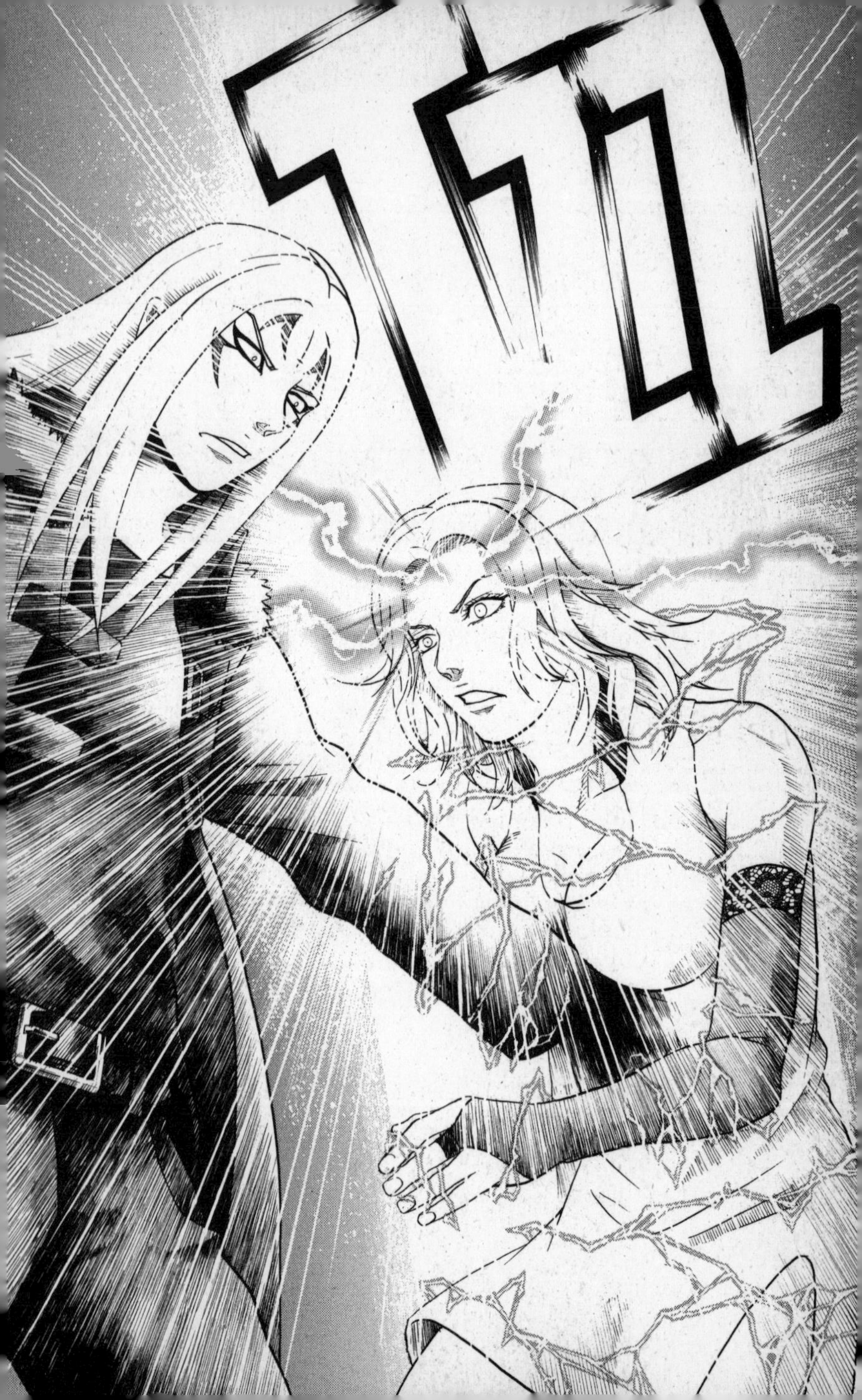

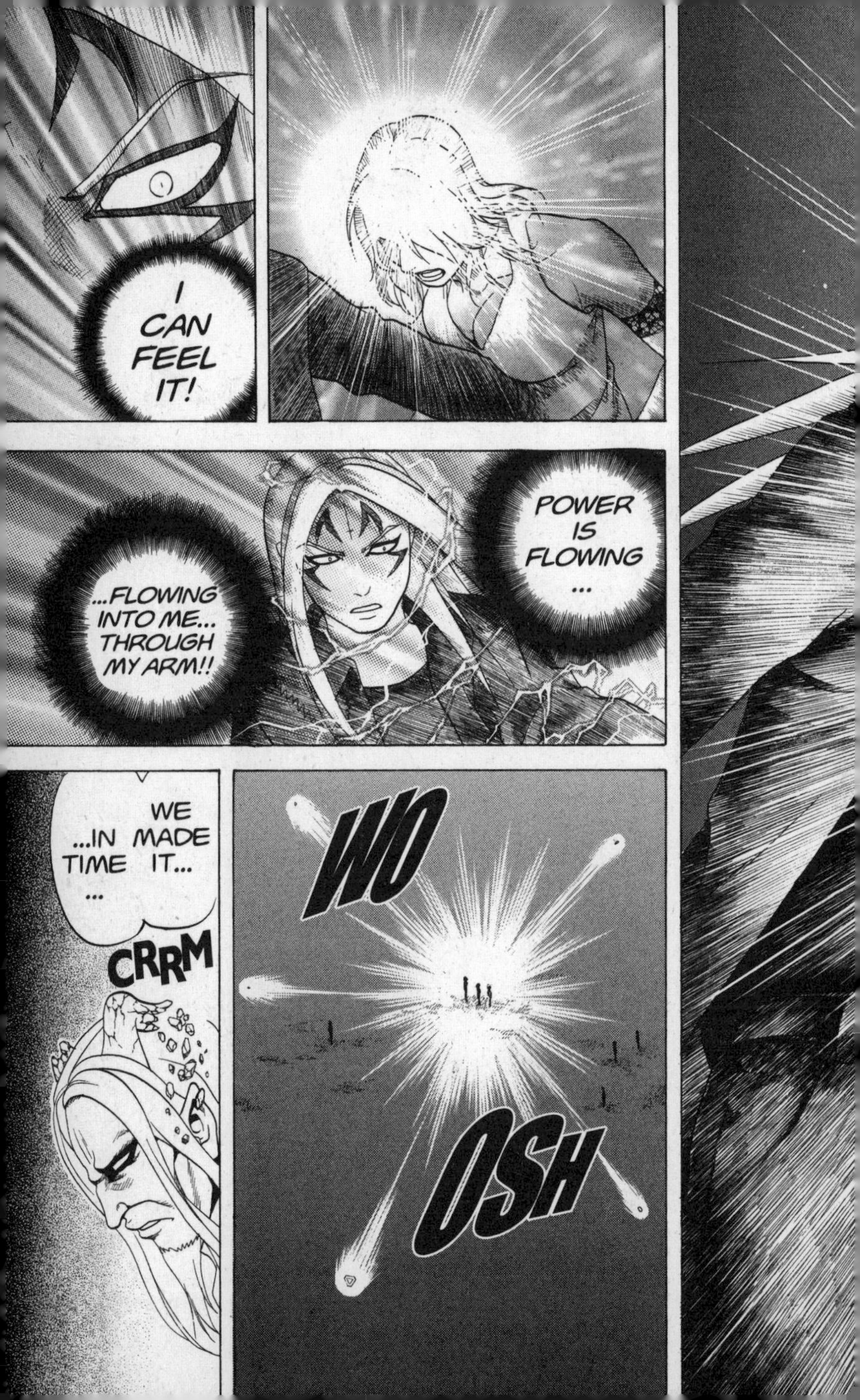
I CAN FEEL IT!
POWER IS FLOWING...
...FLOWING INTO ME... THROUGH MY ARM!!
WOOSH
WE MADE IT... ...IN TIME...
CRRM

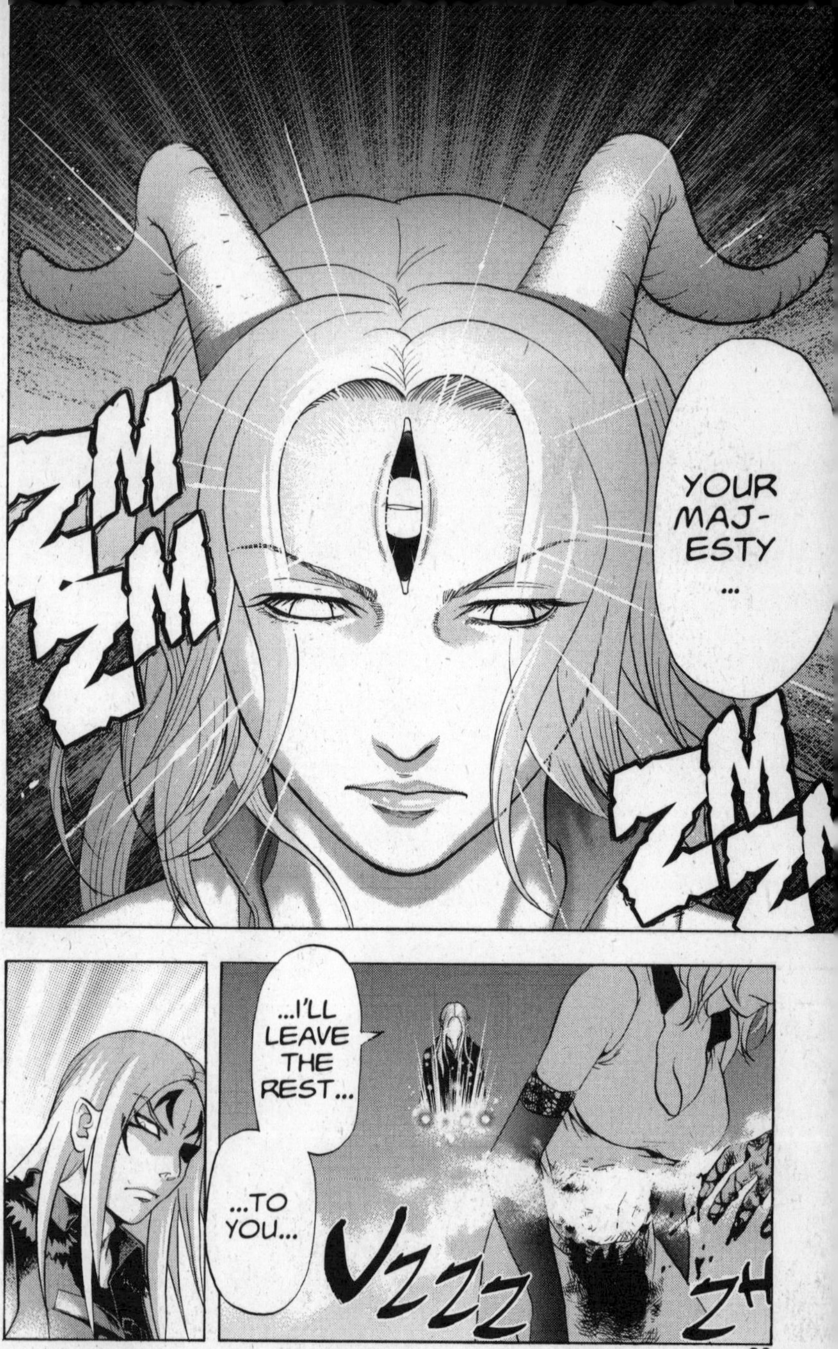
YOUR MAJ- ESTY ...
ZM ZM
ZM ZM
...I'LL LEAVE THE REST...
...TO YOU...
VZZZ

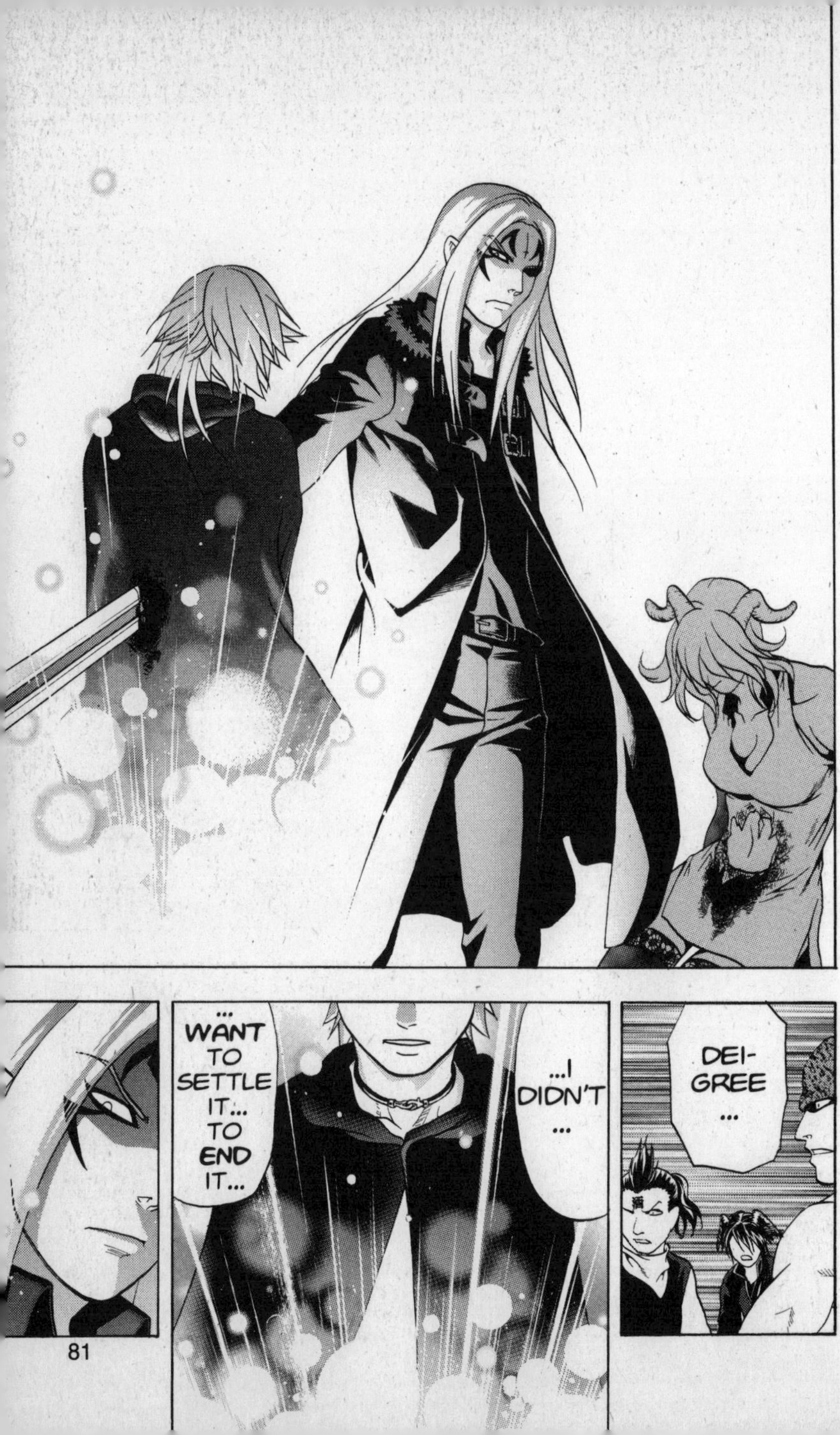
DEI-GREE ...
...I DIDN'T ...
... WANT TO SETTLE IT... TO END IT...

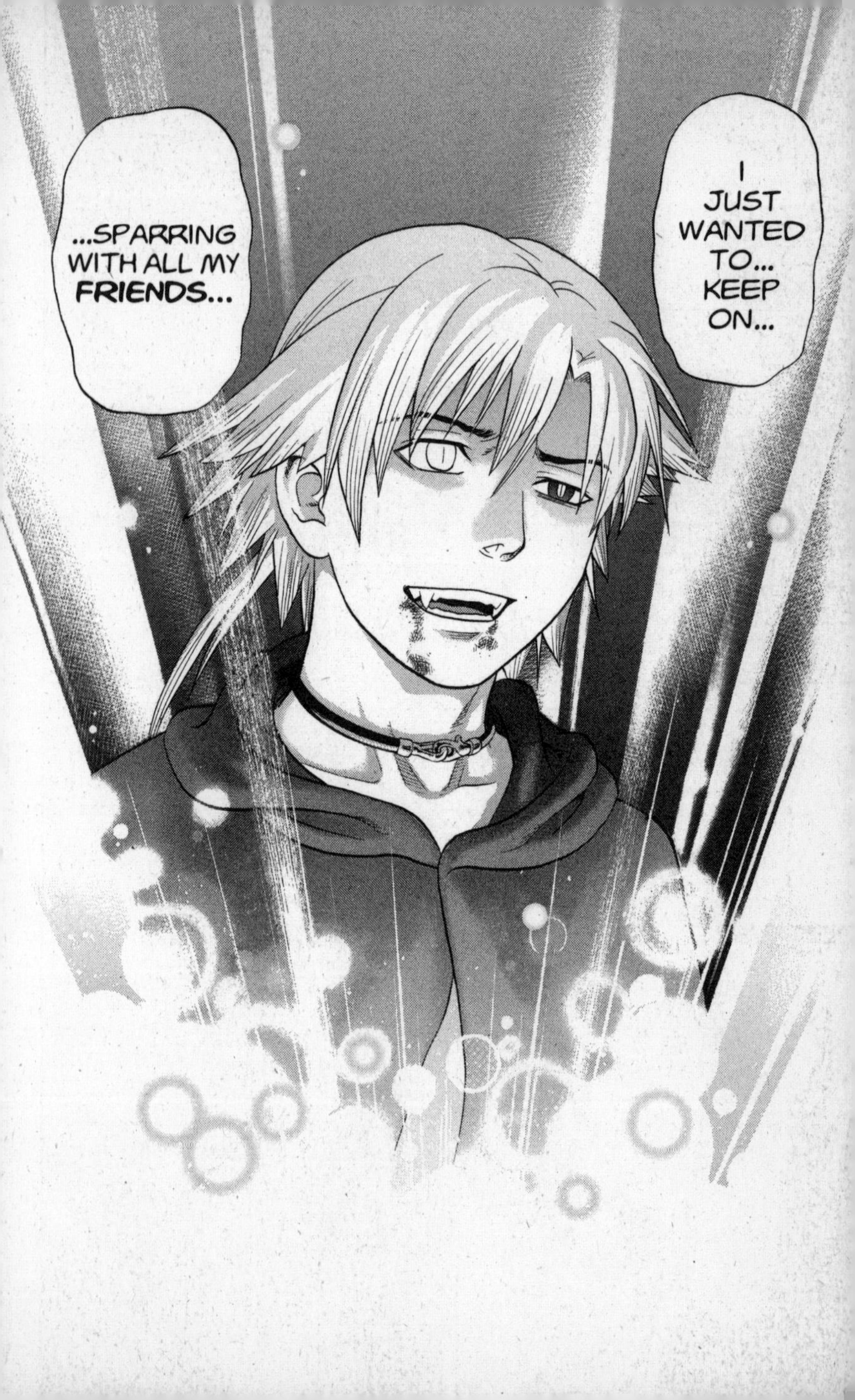
I JUST WANTED TO... KEEP ON...
...SPARRING WITH ALL MY FRIENDS...

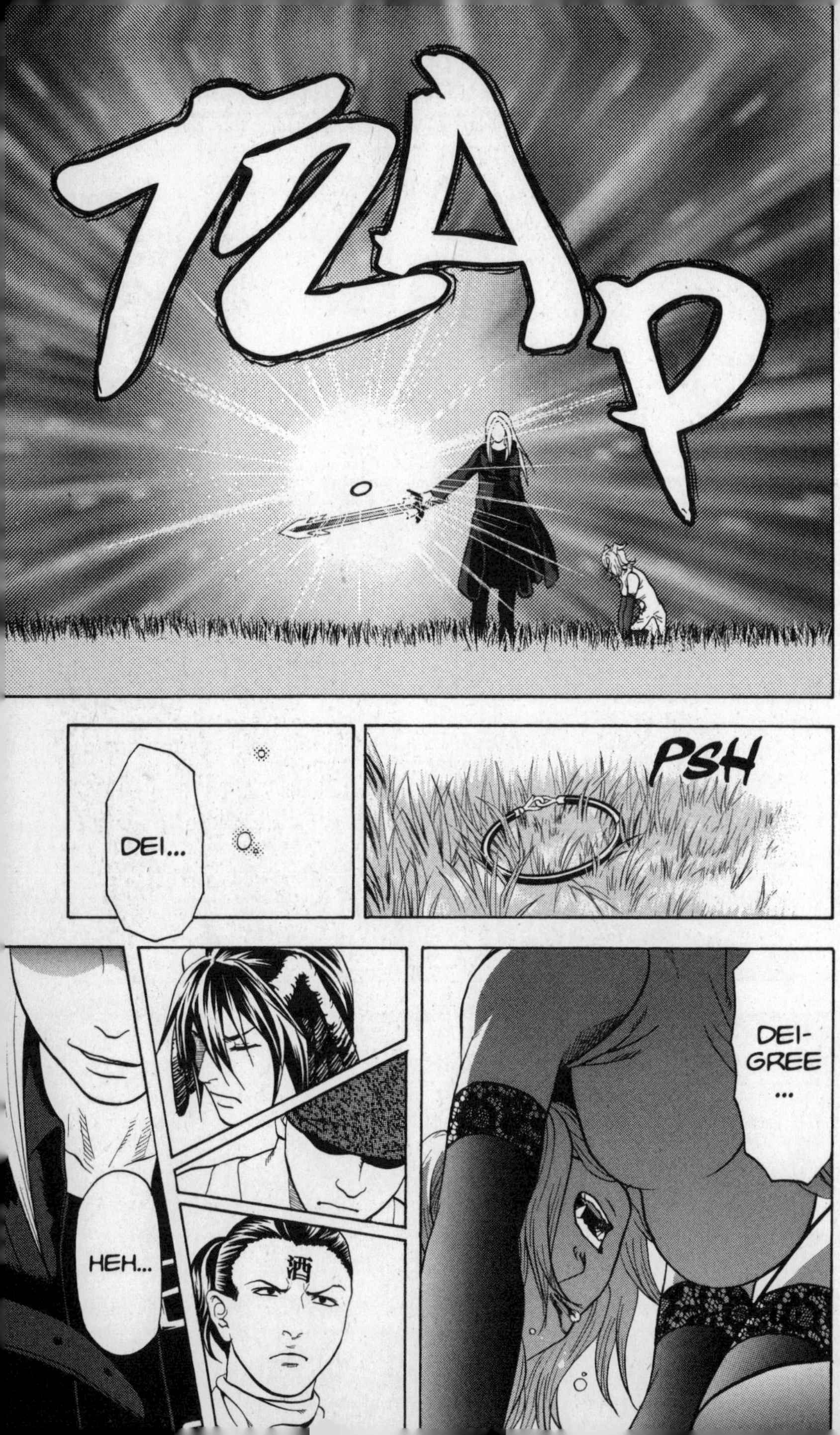
ZZAP
PSH
DEI...
DEI-GREE ...
HEH...

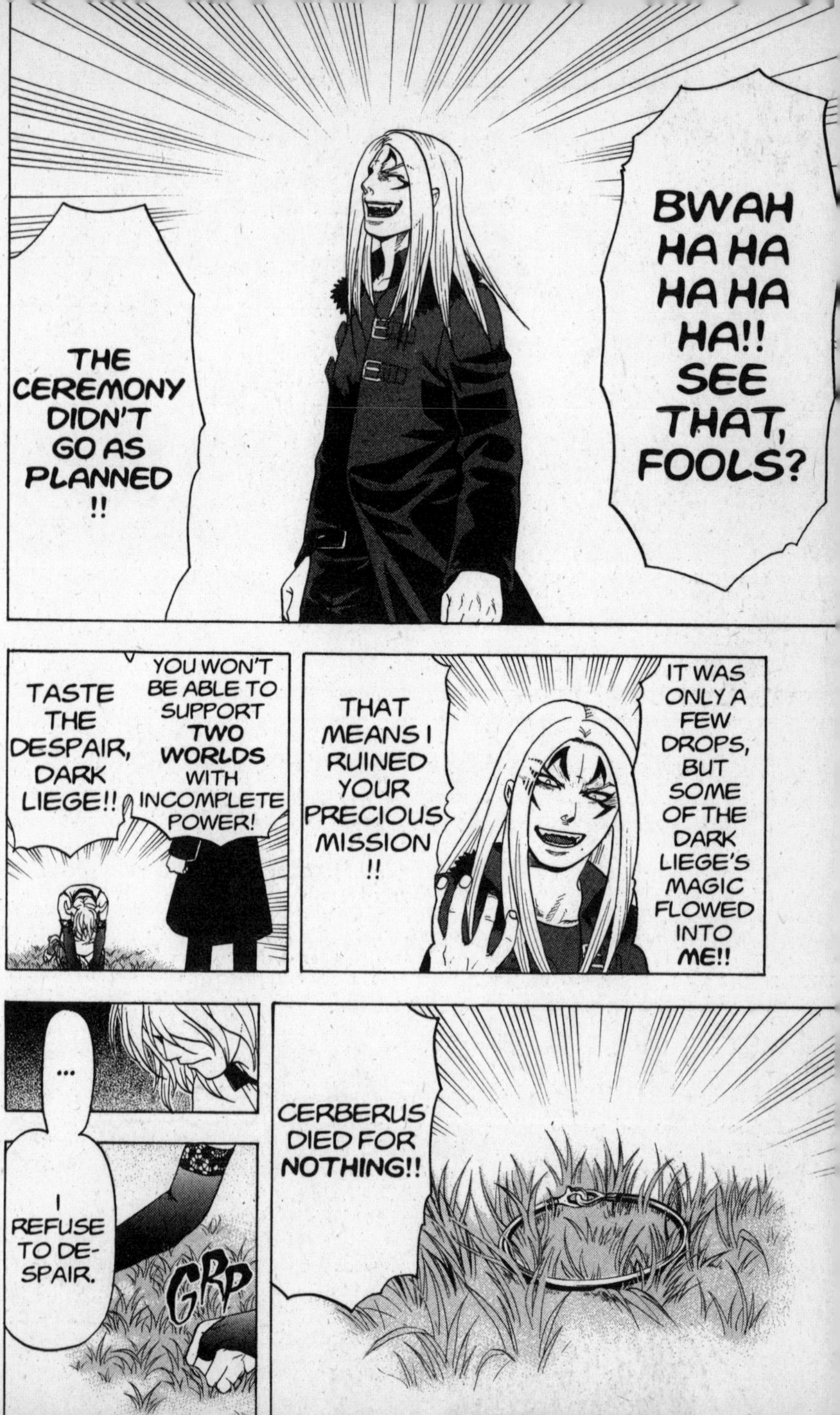
BWAH HA HA HA HA HA!! SEE THAT, FOOLS?
THE CEREMONY DIDN'T GO AS PLANNED!!
IT WAS ONLY A FEW DROPS, BUT SOME OF THE DARK LIEGE'S MAGIC FLOWED INTO ME!!
THAT MEANS I RUINED YOUR PRECIOUS MISSION!!
YOU WON'T BE ABLE TO SUPPORT TWO WORLDS WITH INCOMPLETE POWER!
TASTE THE DESPAIR, DARK LIEGE!!
CERBERUS DIED FOR NOTHING!!
...
I REFUSE TO DE-SPAIR.
GRP

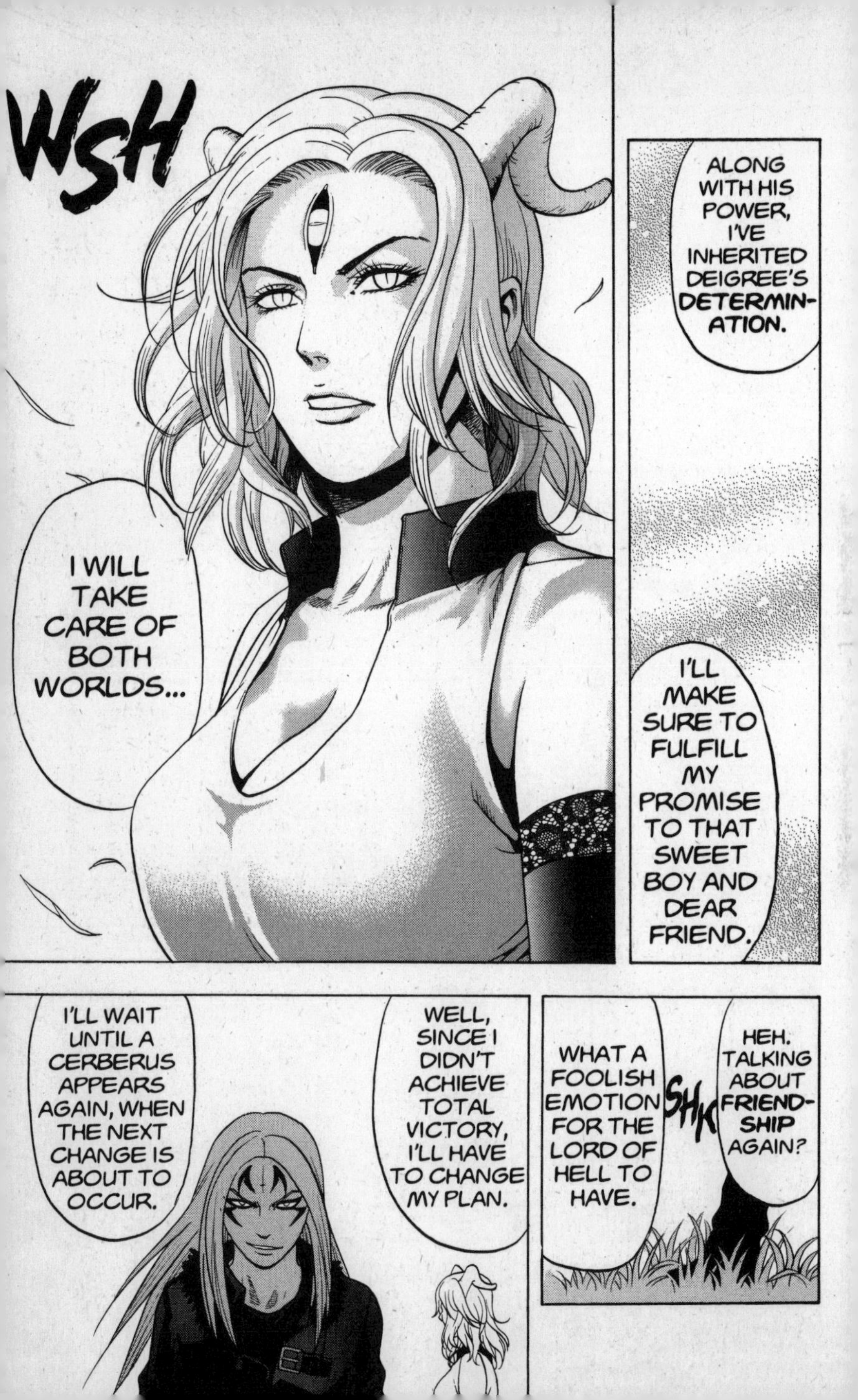
ALONG WITH HIS POWER, I'VE INHERITED DEIGREE'S **DETERMINATION.**
I'LL MAKE SURE TO FULFILL MY PROMISE TO THAT SWEET BOY AND DEAR FRIEND.
WSH
I WILL TAKE CARE OF BOTH WORLDS...
HEH. TALKING ABOUT **FRIENDSHIP** AGAIN?
SHK
WHAT A FOOLISH EMOTION FOR THE LORD OF HELL TO HAVE.
WELL, SINCE I DIDN'T ACHIEVE TOTAL VICTORY, I'LL HAVE TO CHANGE MY PLAN.
I'LL WAIT UNTIL A CERBERUS APPEARS AGAIN, WHEN THE NEXT CHANGE IS ABOUT TO OCCUR.

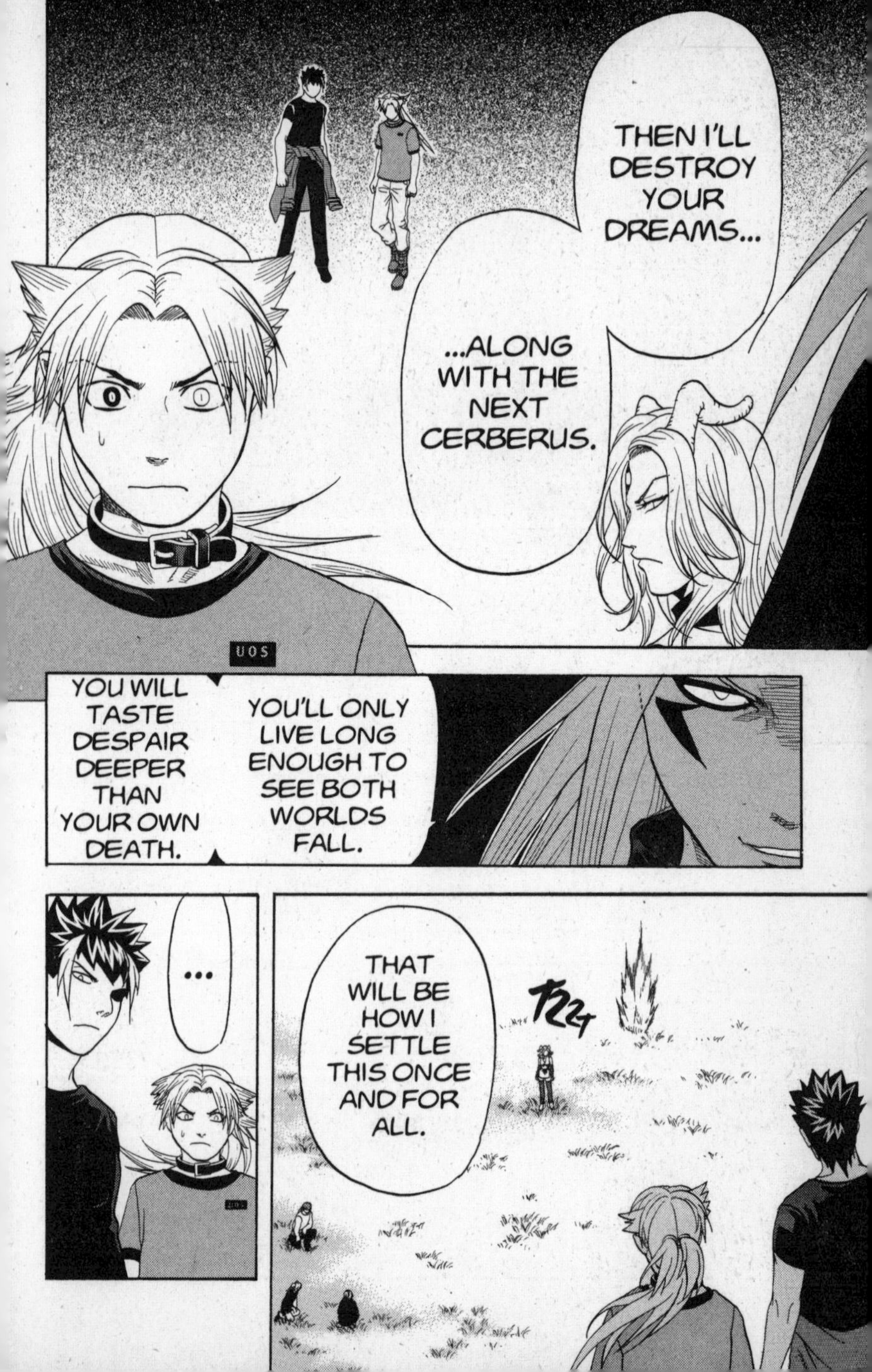
THEN I'LL DESTROY YOUR DREAMS...
...ALONG WITH THE NEXT CERBERUS.
YOU'LL ONLY LIVE LONG ENOUGH TO SEE BOTH WORLDS FALL.
YOU WILL TASTE DESPAIR DEEPER THAN YOUR OWN DEATH.
THAT WILL BE HOW I SETTLE THIS ONCE AND FOR ALL.
...

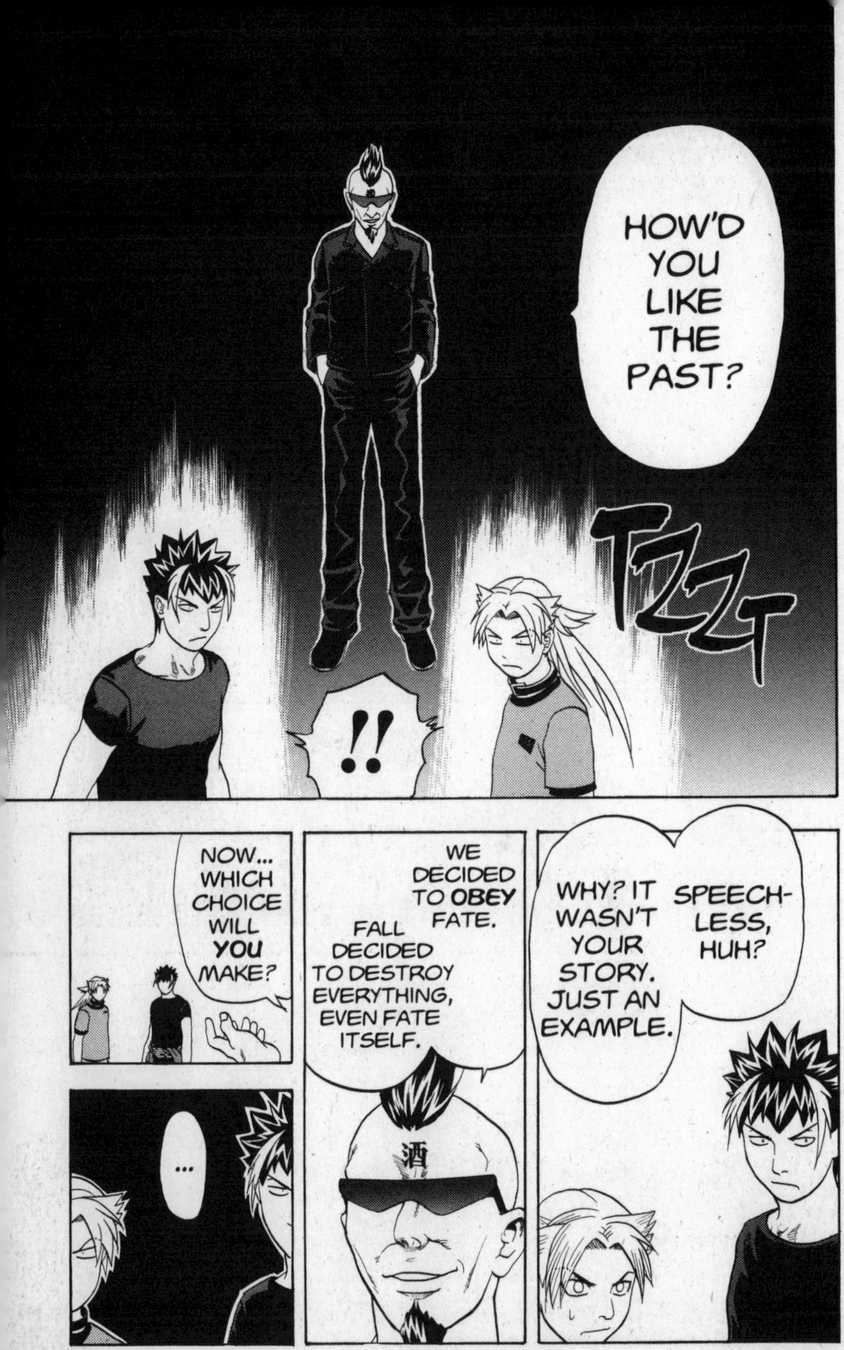

HOW'D YOU LIKE THE PAST?
TZZT
!!
SPEECHLESS, HUH?
WHY? IT WASN'T YOUR STORY. JUST AN EXAMPLE.
WE DECIDED TO OBEY FATE.
FALL DECIDED TO DESTROY EVERYTHING, EVEN FATE ITSELF.
NOW... WHICH CHOICE WILL YOU MAKE?
...

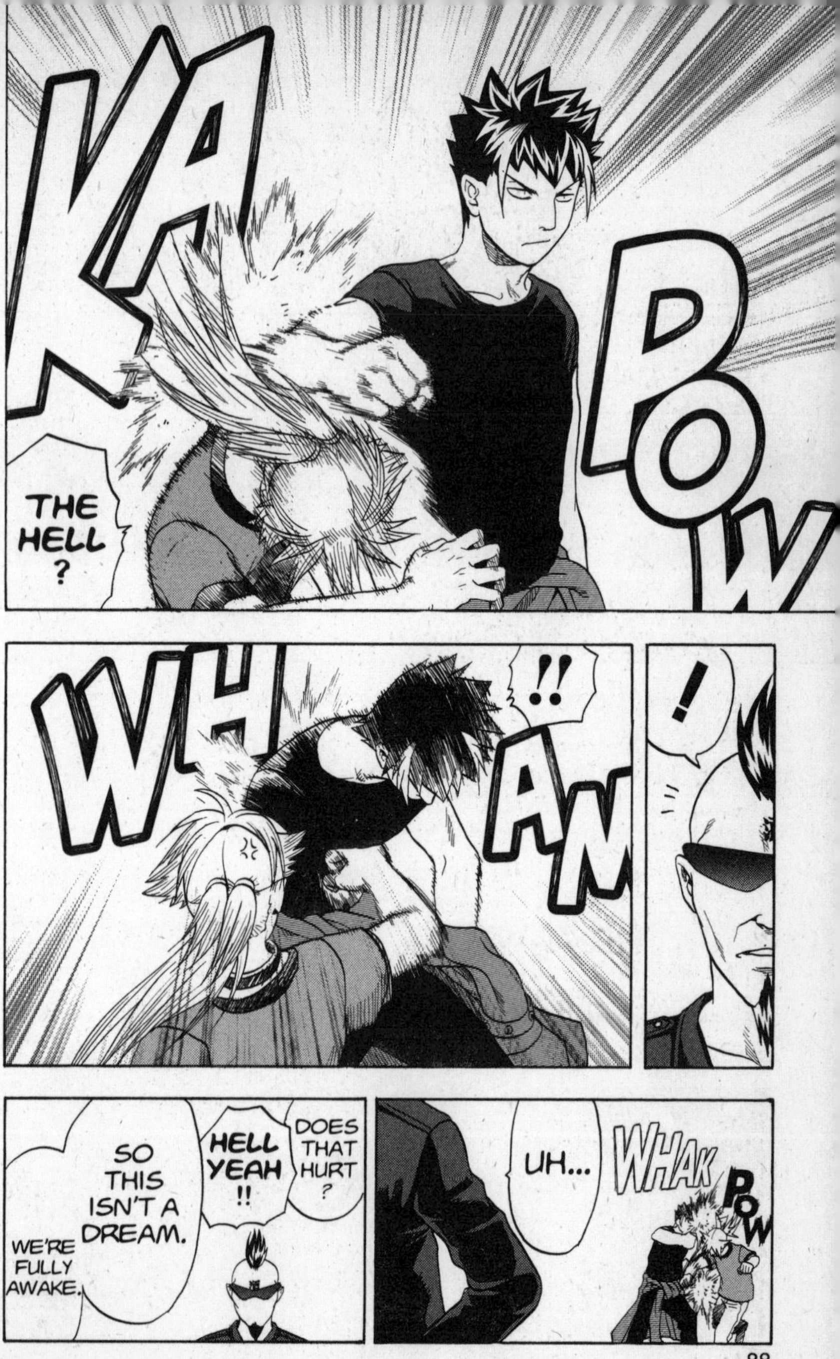
KA POW
THE HELL?
!
WHAM
!!
UH...
WHAK POW
DOES THAT HURT?
HELL YEAH!!
SO THIS ISN'T A DREAM.
WE'RE FULLY AWAKE.

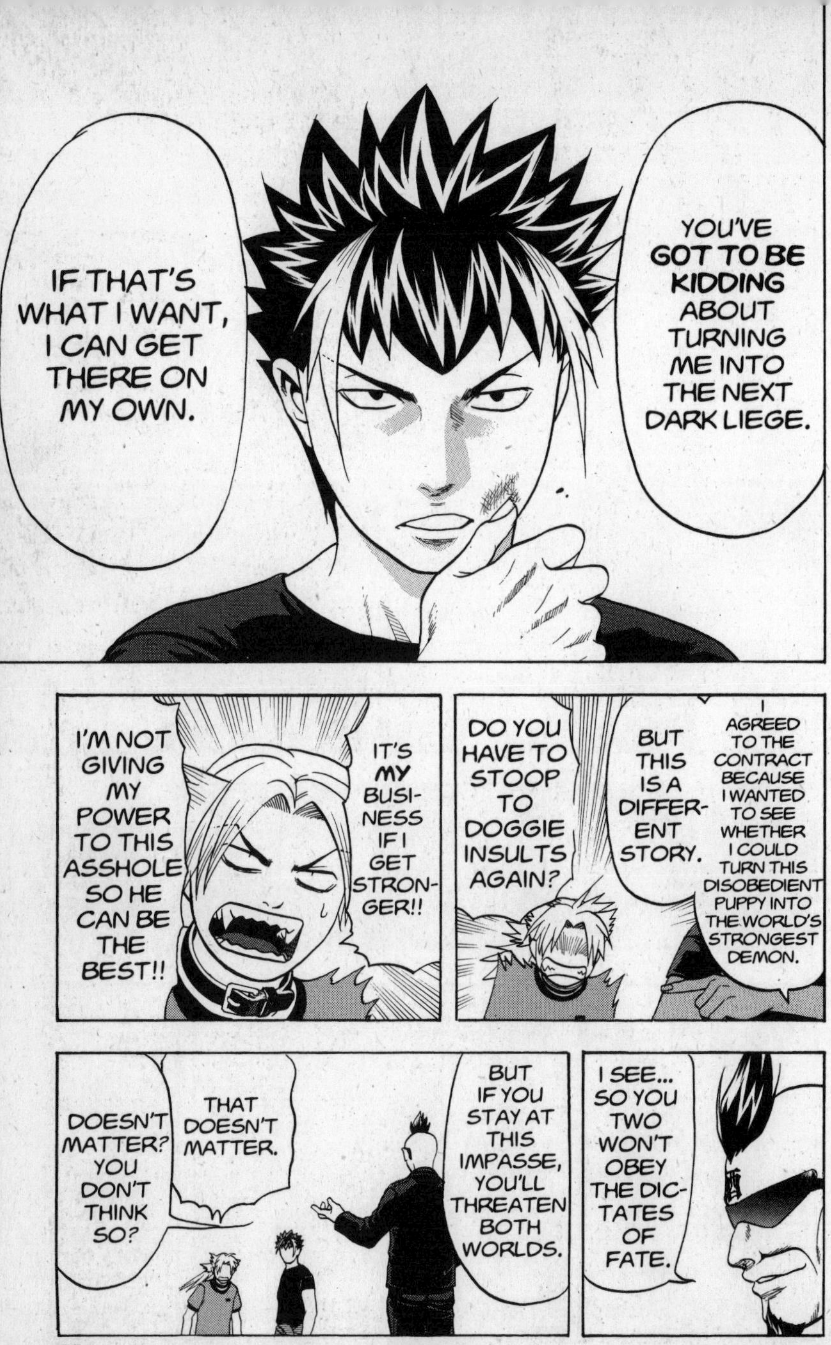
YOU'VE GOT TO BE KIDDING ABOUT TURNING ME INTO THE NEXT DARK LIEGE.
IF THAT'S WHAT I WANT, I CAN GET THERE ON MY OWN.
I AGREED TO THE CONTRACT BECAUSE I WANTED TO SEE WHETHER I COULD TURN THIS DISOBEDIENT PUPPY INTO THE WORLD'S STRONGEST DEMON.
BUT THIS IS A DIFFERENT STORY.
DO YOU HAVE TO STOOP TO DOGGIE INSULTS AGAIN?
IT'S MY BUSINESS IF I GET STRONGER!!
I'M NOT GIVING MY POWER TO THIS ASSHOLE SO HE CAN BE THE BEST!!
I SEE... SO YOU TWO WON'T OBEY THE DICTATES OF FATE.
BUT IF YOU STAY AT THIS IMPASSE, YOU'LL THREATEN BOTH WORLDS.
THAT DOESN'T MATTER.
DOESN'T MATTER? YOU DON'T THINK SO?

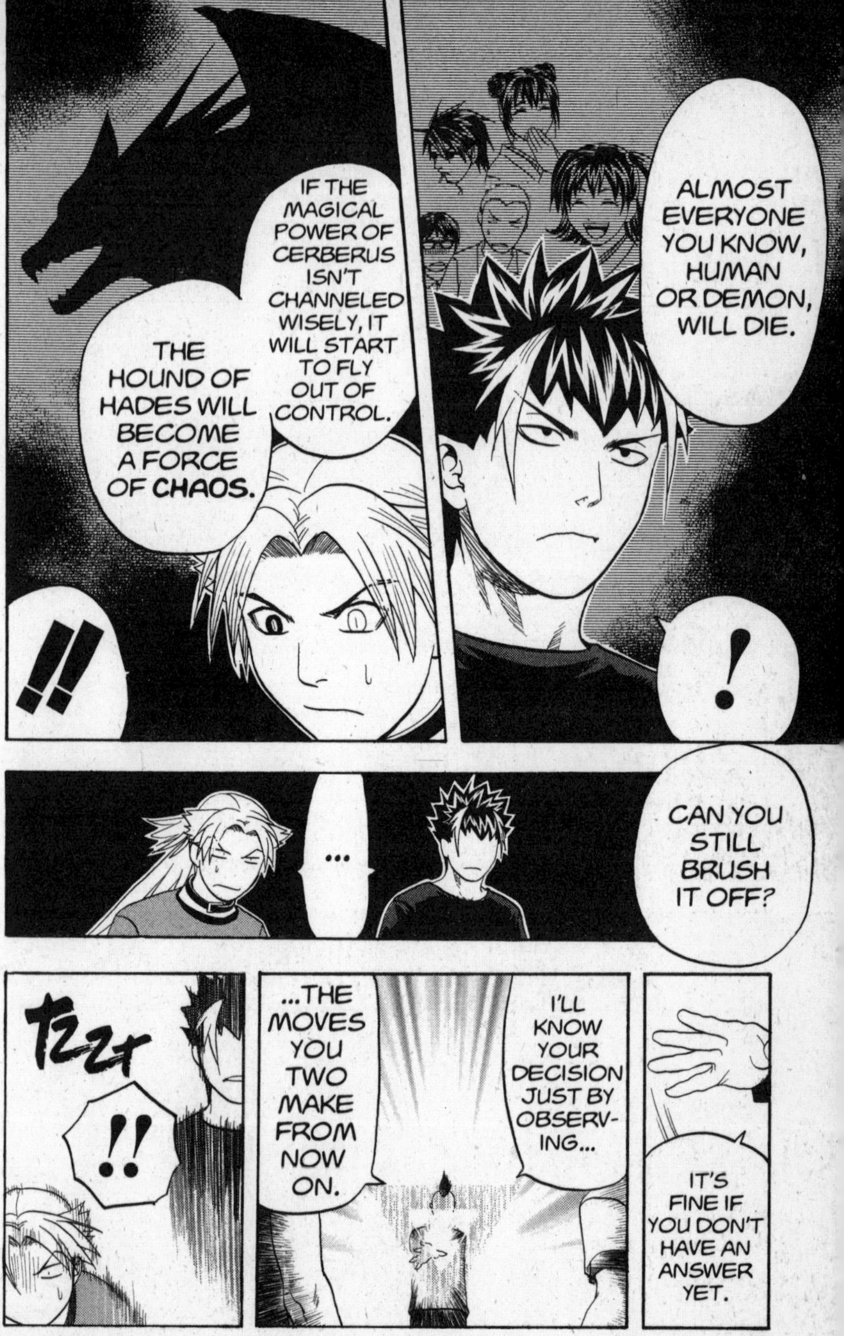
ALMOST EVERYONE YOU KNOW, HUMAN OR DEMON, WILL DIE.
!
IF THE MAGICAL POWER OF CERBERUS ISN'T CHANNELED WISELY, IT WILL START TO FLY OUT OF CONTROL.
THE HOUND OF HADES WILL BECOME A FORCE OF **CHAOS.**
!!
CAN YOU STILL BRUSH IT OFF?
...
IT'S FINE IF YOU DON'T HAVE AN ANSWER YET.
I'LL KNOW YOUR DECISION JUST BY OBSERV-ING...
...THE MOVES YOU TWO MAKE FROM NOW ON.
TZZT
!!

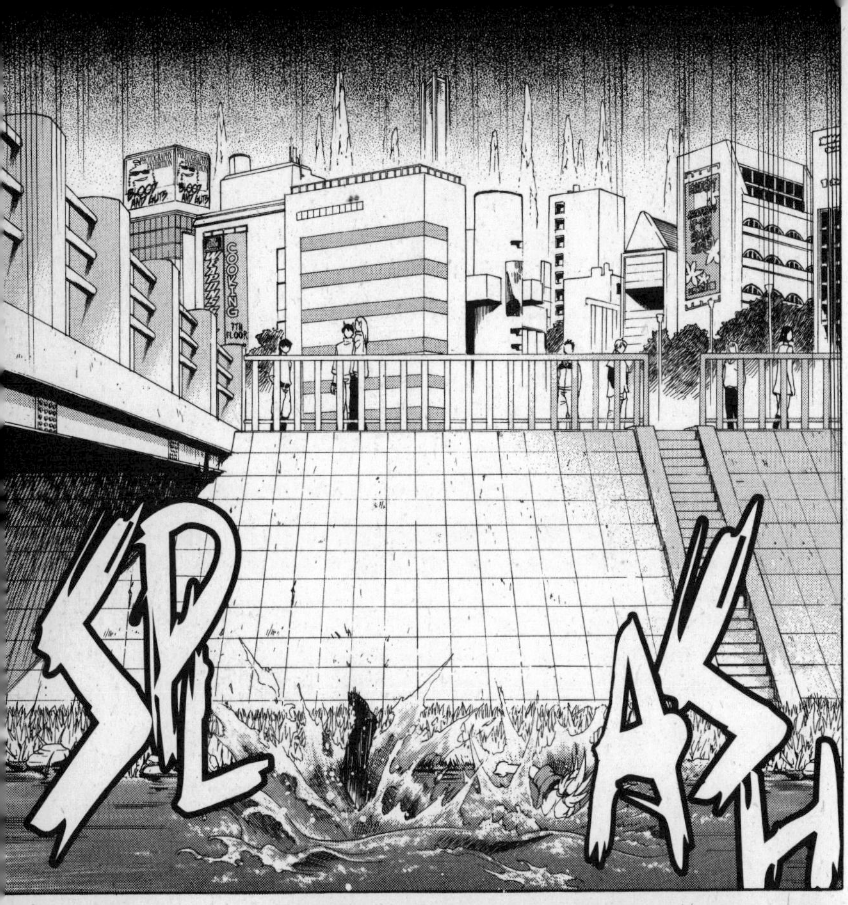
COOKING
7TH FLOOR
SPLASH

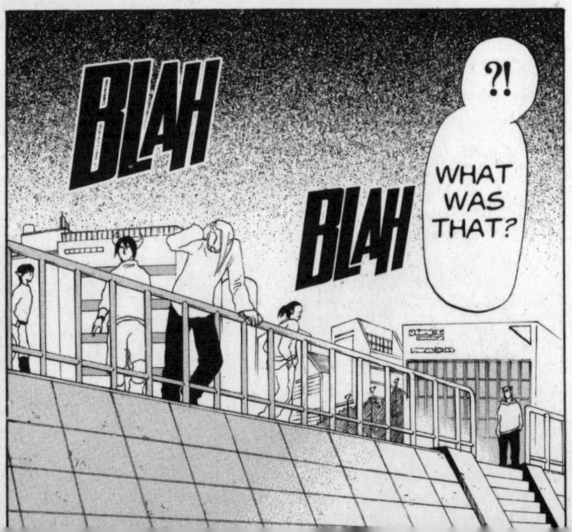
?!
WHAT WAS THAT?
BLAH
BLAH

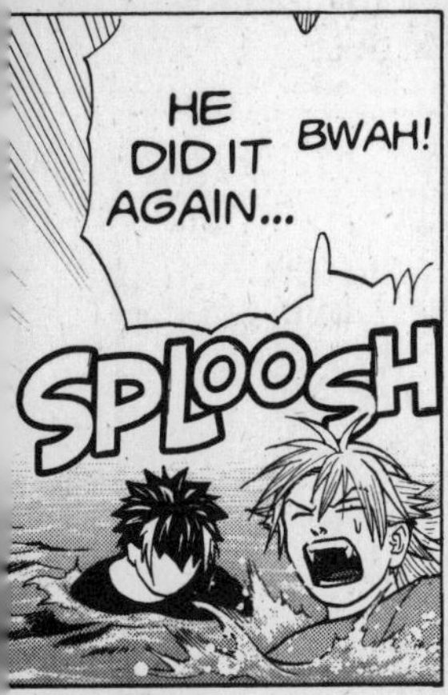
BWAH!
HE DID IT AGAIN...
SPLOOSH

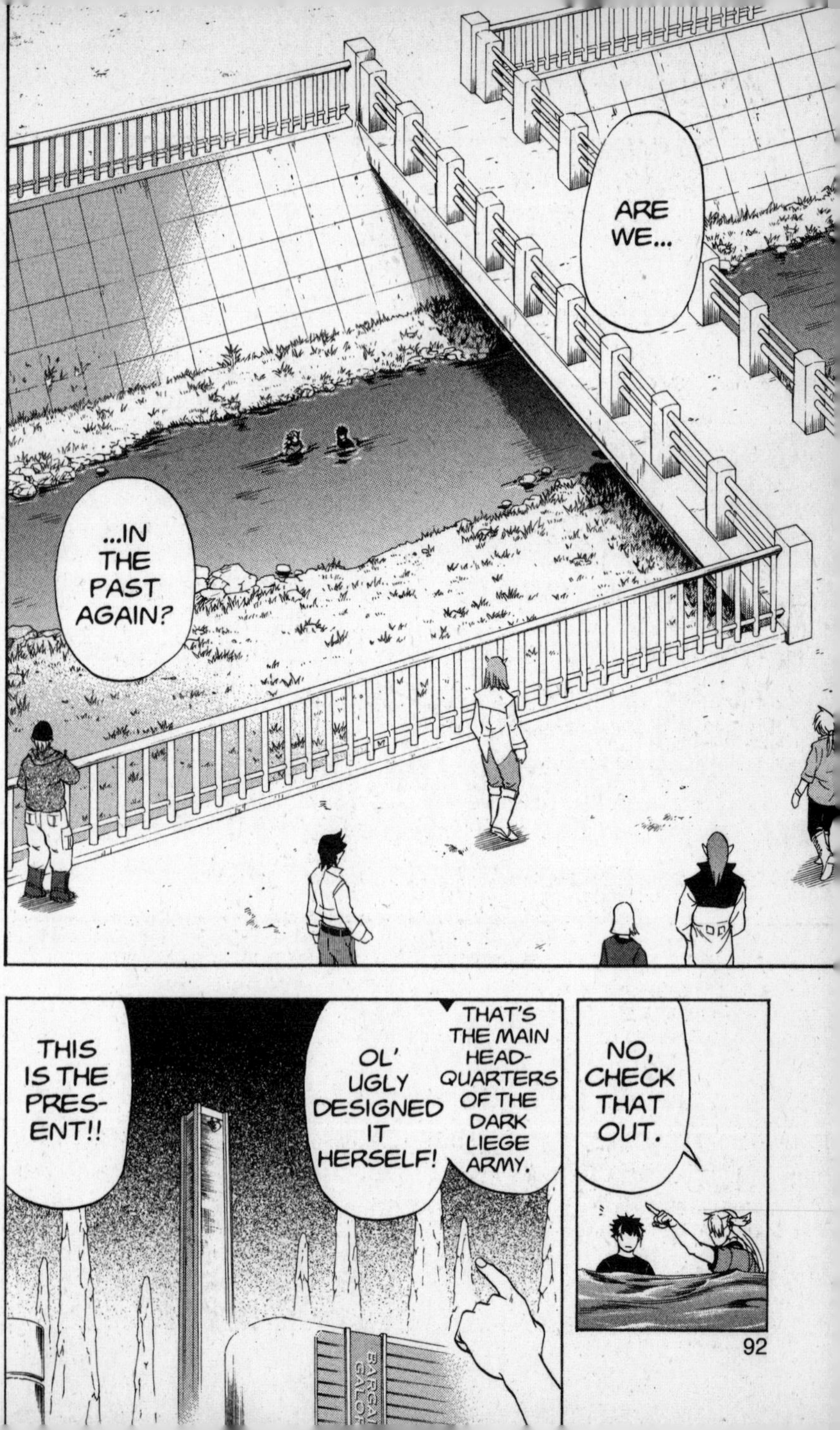
ARE WE...
...IN THE PAST AGAIN?
NO, CHECK THAT OUT.
THAT'S THE MAIN HEAD-QUARTERS OF THE DARK LIEGE ARMY.
OL' UGLY DESIGNED IT HERSELF!
THIS IS THE PRES-ENT!!

READ THIS WAY

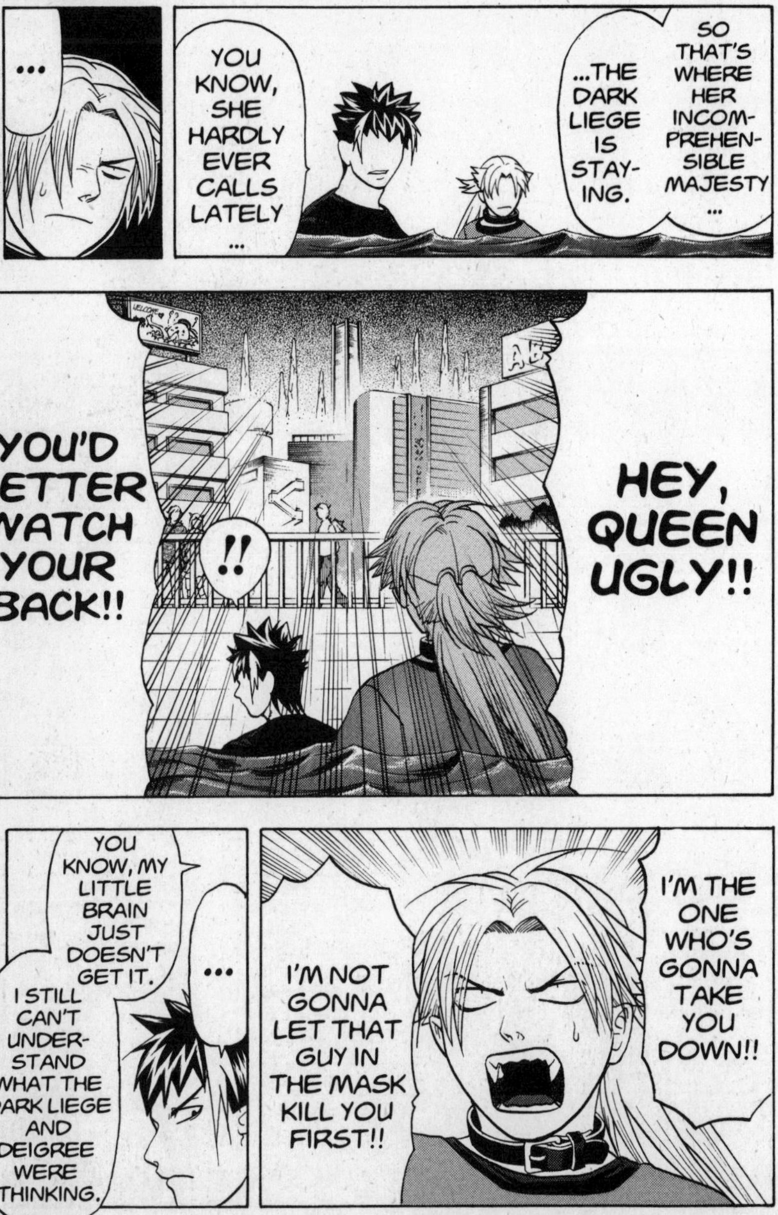
SO THAT'S WHERE HER INCOMPREHENSIBLE MAJESTY...
...THE DARK LIEGE IS STAYING.
YOU KNOW, SHE HARDLY EVER CALLS LATELY...
...
HEY, QUEEN UGLY!!
YOU'D BETTER WATCH YOUR BACK!!
!!
I'M THE ONE WHO'S GONNA TAKE YOU DOWN!!
I'M NOT GONNA LET THAT GUY IN THE MASK KILL YOU FIRST!!
...
YOU KNOW, MY LITTLE BRAIN JUST DOESN'T GET IT.
I STILL CAN'T UNDERSTAND WHAT THE DARK LIEGE AND DEIGREE WERE THINKING.

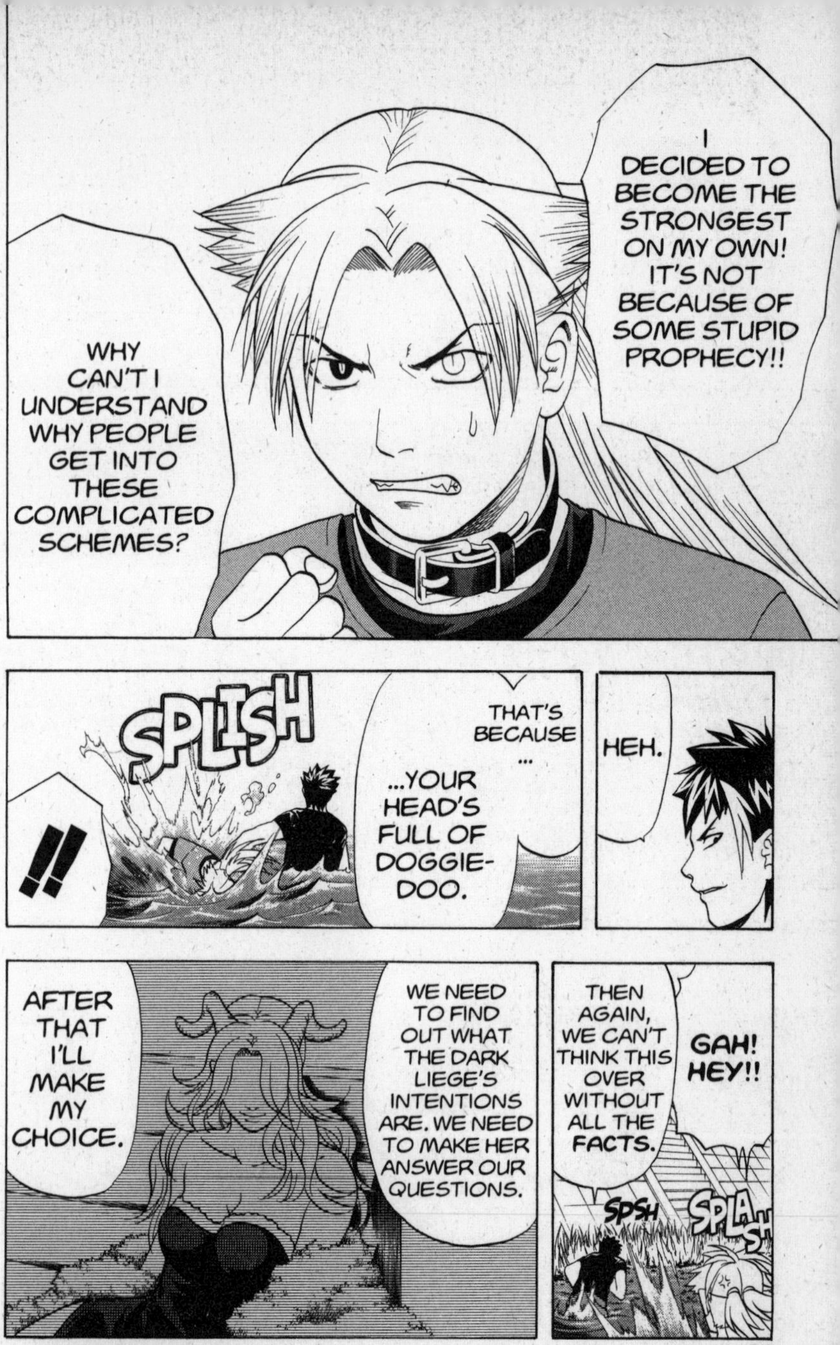
I DECIDED TO BECOME THE STRONGEST ON MY OWN! IT'S NOT BECAUSE OF SOME STUPID PROPHECY!!
WHY CAN'T I UNDERSTAND WHY PEOPLE GET INTO THESE COMPLICATED SCHEMES?
HEH.
THAT'S BECAUSE ...
...YOUR HEAD'S FULL OF DOGGIE-DOO.
SPLISH
!!
GAH! HEY!!
THEN AGAIN, WE CAN'T THINK THIS OVER WITHOUT ALL THE **FACTS.**
SPSH
SPLASH
WE NEED TO FIND OUT WHAT THE DARK LIEGE'S INTENTIONS ARE. WE NEED TO MAKE HER ANSWER OUR QUESTIONS.
AFTER THAT I'LL MAKE MY CHOICE.

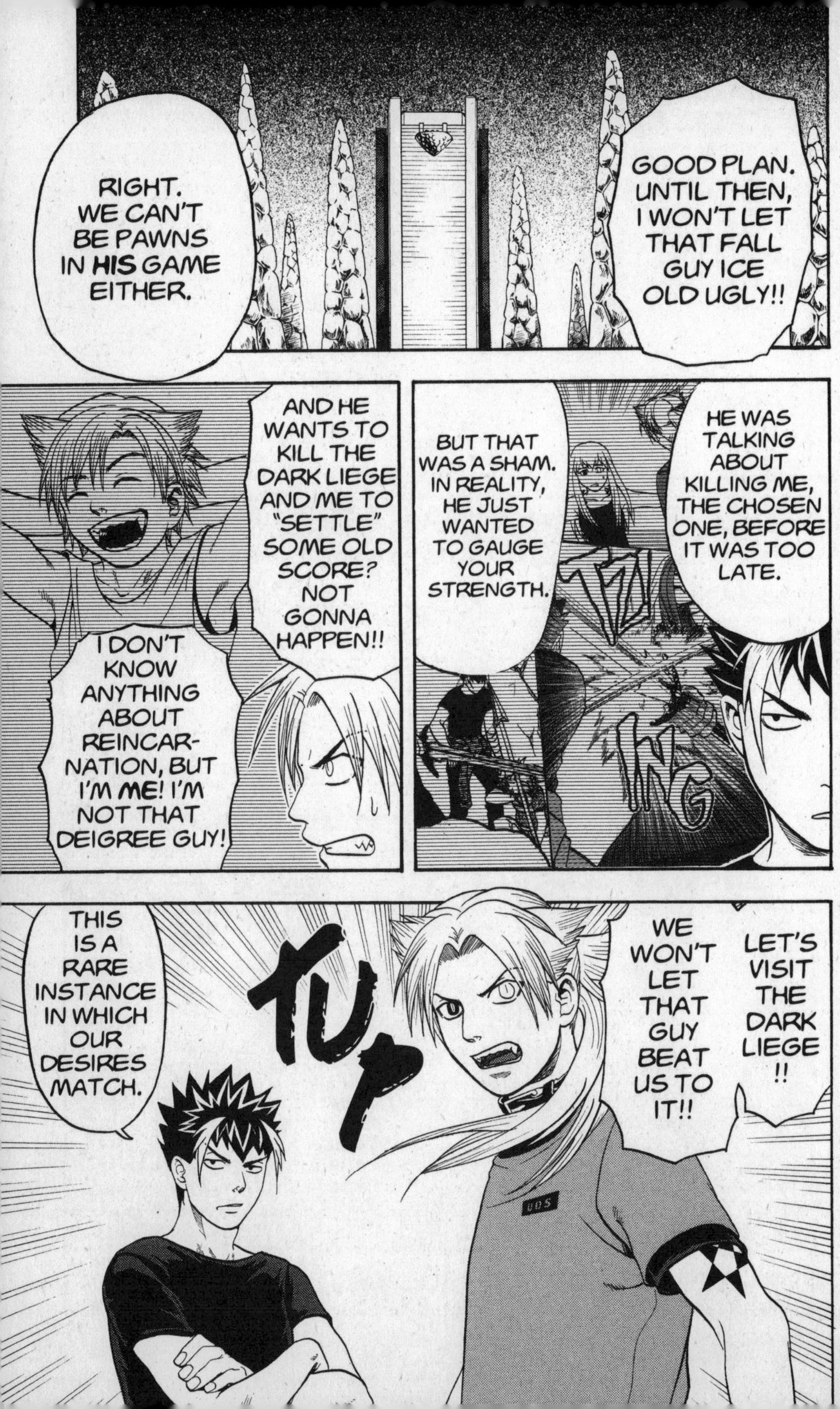
GOOD PLAN. UNTIL THEN, I WON'T LET THAT FALL GUY ICE OLD UGLY!!
RIGHT. WE CAN'T BE PAWNS IN **HIS** GAME EITHER.
HE WAS TALKING ABOUT KILLING ME, THE CHOSEN ONE, BEFORE IT WAS TOO LATE.
BUT THAT WAS A SHAM. IN REALITY, HE JUST WANTED TO GAUGE YOUR STRENGTH.
TZING
AND HE WANTS TO KILL THE DARK LIEGE AND ME TO "SETTLE" SOME OLD SCORE? NOT GONNA HAPPEN!!
I DON'T KNOW ANYTHING ABOUT REINCAR-NATION, BUT I'M **ME**! I'M NOT THAT DEIGREE GUY!
LET'S VISIT THE DARK LIEGE!!
WE WON'T LET THAT GUY BEAT US TO IT!!
THIS IS A RARE INSTANCE IN WHICH OUR DESIRES MATCH.

SO...
...HOW DO WE GET THERE?
IT LOOKS DISTANT.
I DON'T KNOW!!
CAN'T YOU TRANSPORT THERE LIKE THE OTHER DEMONS CAN?
TZZT
IT'S TOO FAR AWAY!
YOU SHOULD KNOW BY NOW THAT I SUCK AT COMPLICATED SUPPORT MAGIC LIKE THAT!
THAT'S RIGHT... YOU ALSO HAVE TROUBLE WITH HEALING MAGIC.
YOU REALLY ARE JUST A BIG DUMB ATTACK DOG.
GRR
THROB
LIKE MATH, HEALING MAGIC IS HARD!
POW
I CAN! I JUST CAN'T USE IT WELL!!
KICK
I THOUGHT A CERBERUS COULD USE EVERY TYPE OF MAGIC.
THEN YOU'RE JUST TOO IGNORANT TO DEVELOP YOUR SKILLS.
BIG WORDS FROM A HUMAN WITH NO POWER OF HIS OWN!!
PUNCH
Hey! My store!
CRACK
EEEK!
OVER HERE!! IT'S THEM!!
HEY, YOU TWO!!
You still want to fight, toy poodle?
You still wanna die? 'Cause keep up with the dog jokes and I swear I'll kill you!
STOMP STOMP
SALE

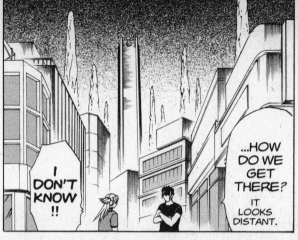

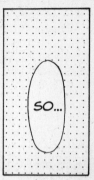

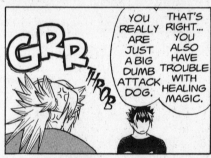

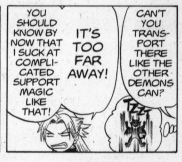

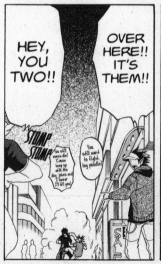

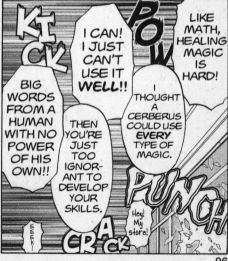

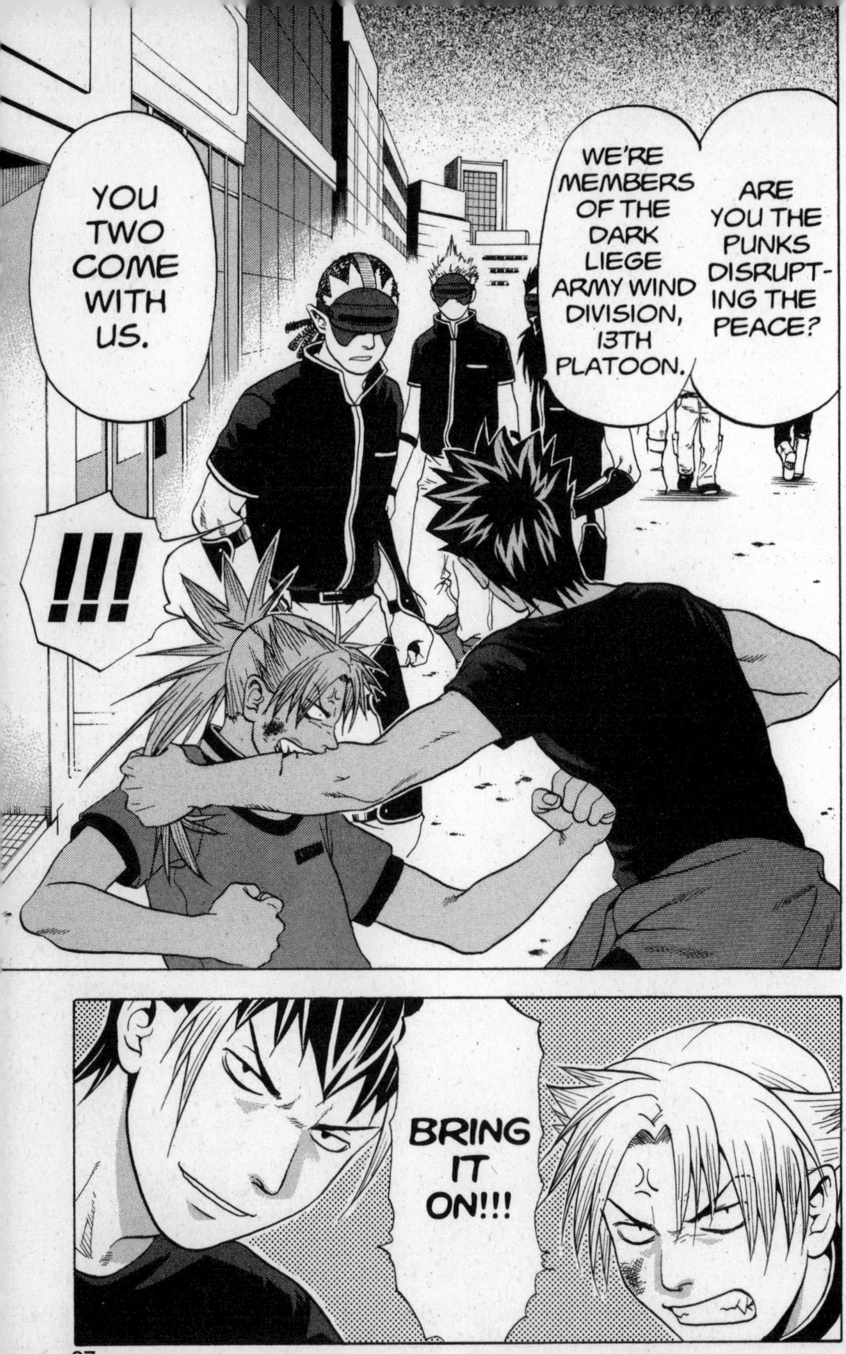
ARE YOU THE PUNKS DISRUPTING THE PEACE?
WE'RE MEMBERS OF THE DARK LIEGE ARMY WIND DIVISION, 13TH PLATOON.
YOU TWO COME WITH US.
!!!
BRING IT ON!!!

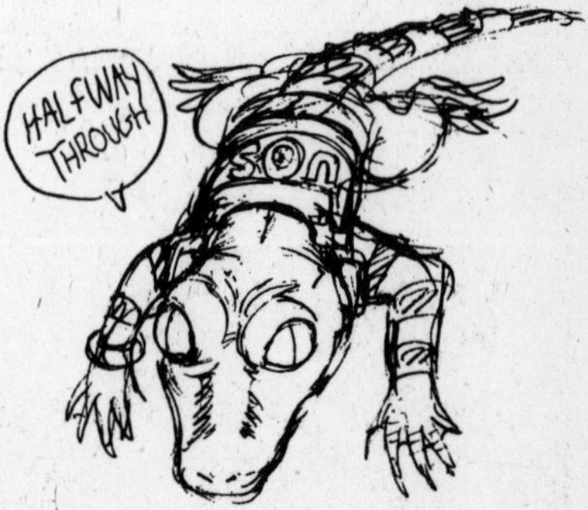
HALFWAY THROUGH

Story 23: The Ties That Bind

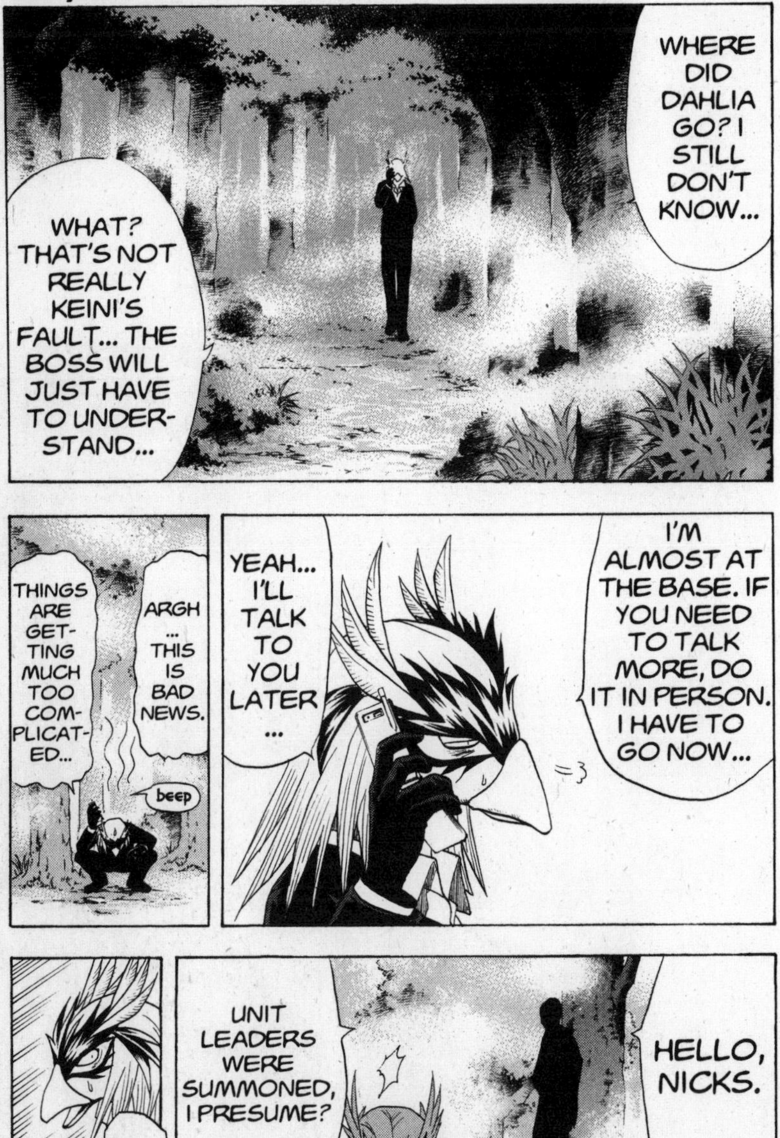
WHERE DID DAHLIA GO? I STILL DON'T KNOW...
WHAT? THAT'S NOT REALLY KEINI'S FAULT... THE BOSS WILL JUST HAVE TO UNDER-STAND...
I'M ALMOST AT THE BASE. IF YOU NEED TO TALK MORE, DO IT IN PERSON. I HAVE TO GO NOW...
YEAH... I'LL TALK TO YOU LATER...
ARGH ... THIS IS BAD NEWS.
THINGS ARE GET-TING MUCH TOO COM-PLICAT-ED...
beep
HELLO, NICKS.
UNIT LEADERS WERE SUMMONED, I PRESUME?
!!
YOU ...

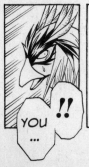

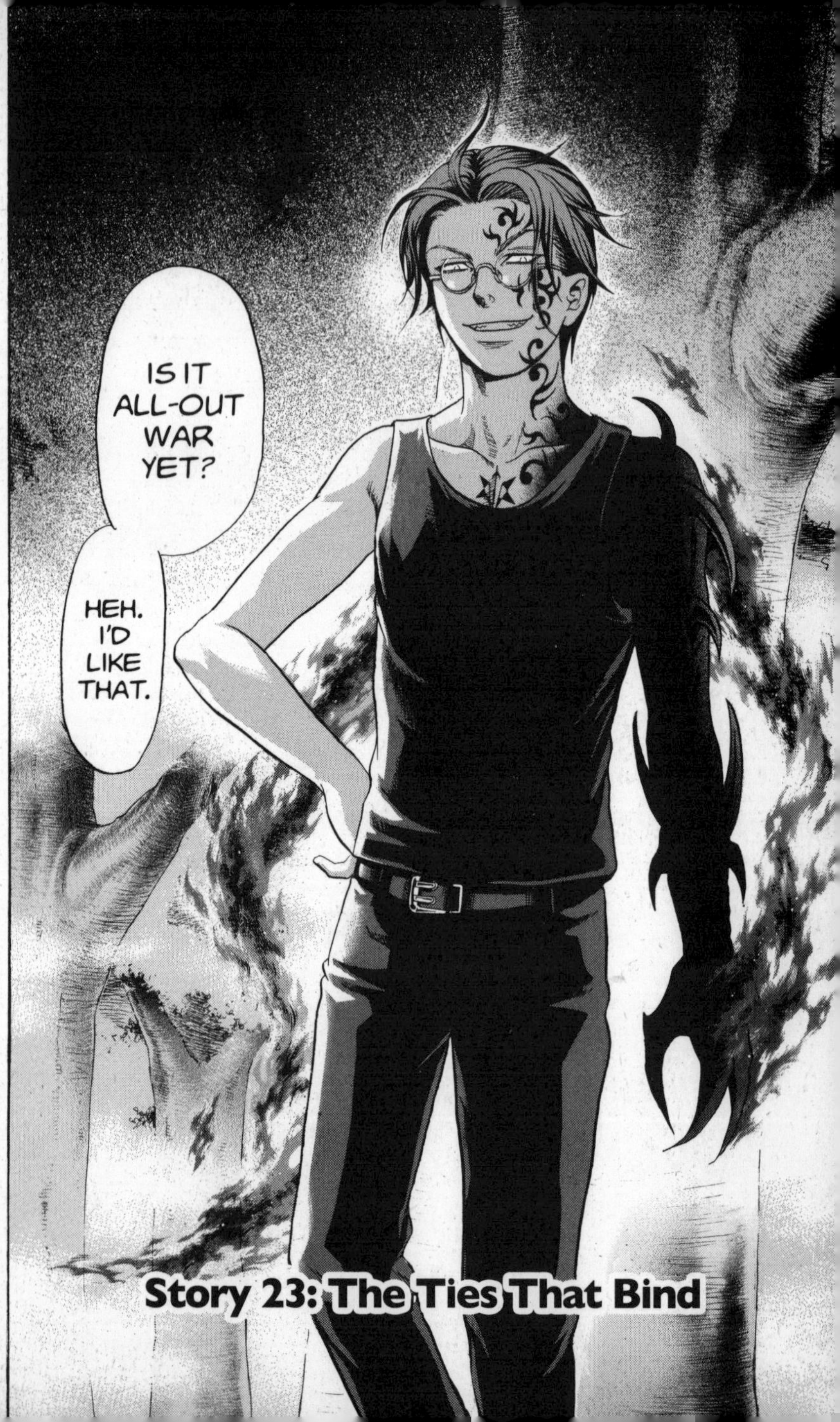
IS IT ALL-OUT WAR YET?
HEH. I'D LIKE THAT.
Story 23: The Ties That Bind

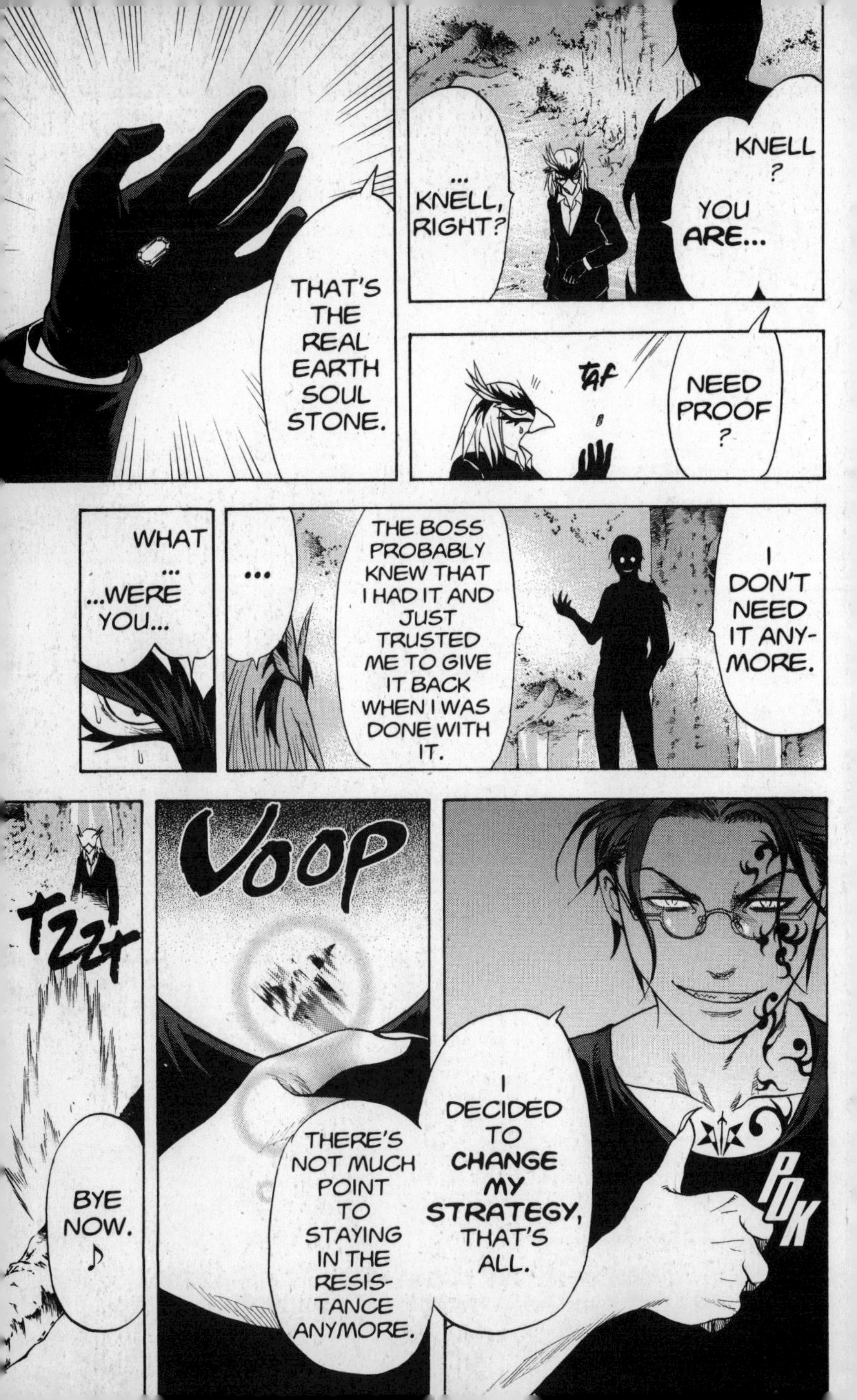
KNELL? YOU ARE...
...KNELL, RIGHT?
NEED PROOF?
TAF
THAT'S THE REAL EARTH SOUL STONE.
I DON'T NEED IT ANYMORE.
THE BOSS PROBABLY KNEW THAT I HAD IT AND JUST TRUSTED ME TO GIVE IT BACK WHEN I WAS DONE WITH IT.
...
WHAT... ...WERE YOU...
I DECIDED TO CHANGE MY STRATEGY, THAT'S ALL.
THERE'S NOT MUCH POINT TO STAYING IN THE RESISTANCE ANYMORE.
POK
VOOP
TZZT
BYE NOW. ♪

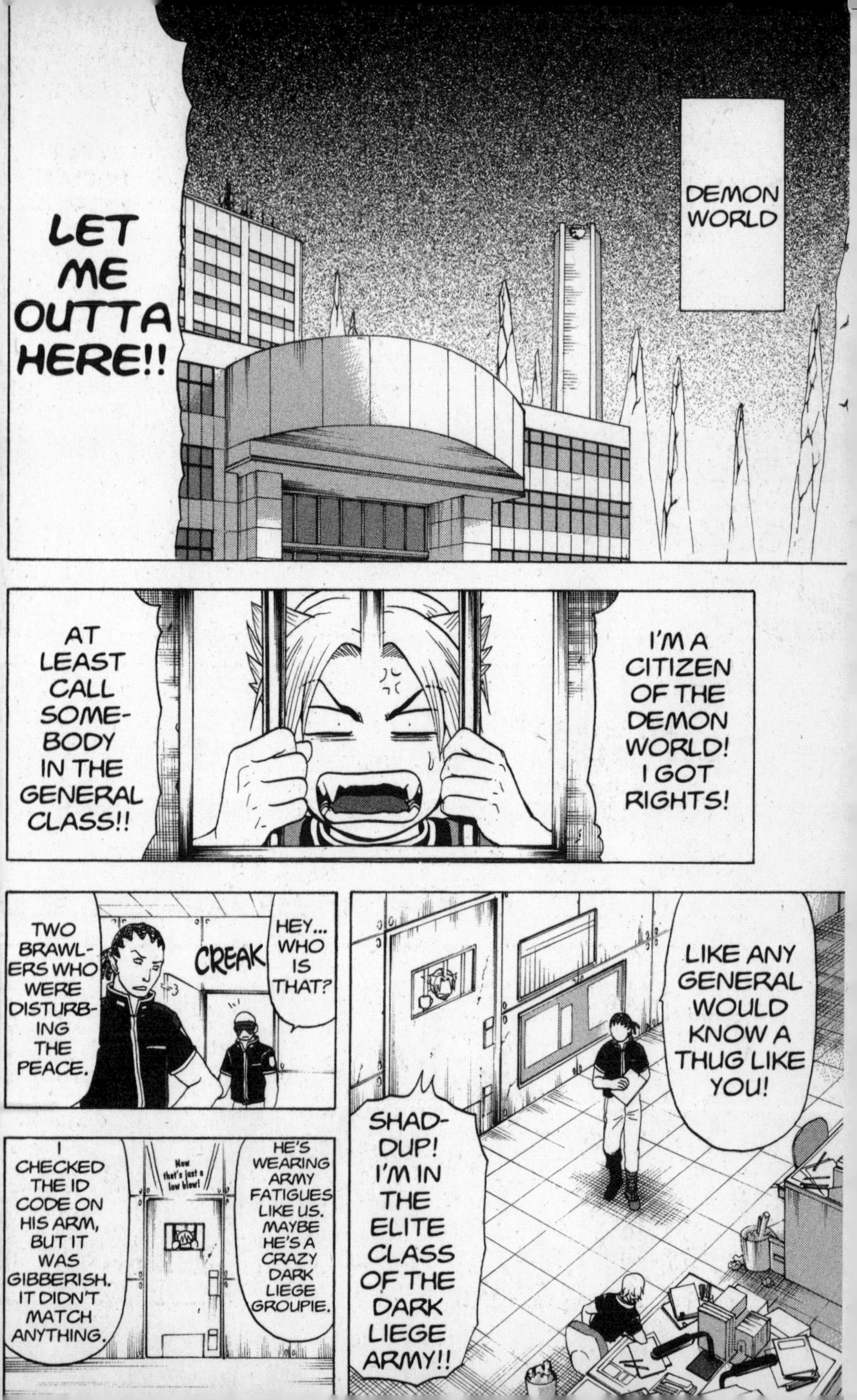
DEMON WORLD
LET ME OUTTA HERE!!
I'M A CITIZEN OF THE DEMON WORLD! I GOT RIGHTS!
AT LEAST CALL SOME-BODY IN THE GENERAL CLASS!!
LIKE ANY GENERAL WOULD KNOW A THUG LIKE YOU!
SHAD-DUP! I'M IN THE ELITE CLASS OF THE DARK LIEGE ARMY!!
HEY... WHO IS THAT?
CREAK
TWO BRAWL-ERS WHO WERE DISTURB-ING THE PEACE.
HE'S WEARING ARMY FATIGUES LIKE US. MAYBE HE'S A CRAZY DARK LIEGE GROUPIE.
Now that's just a low blow!
I CHECKED THE ID CODE ON HIS ARM, BUT IT WAS GIBBERISH. IT DIDN'T MATCH ANYTHING.

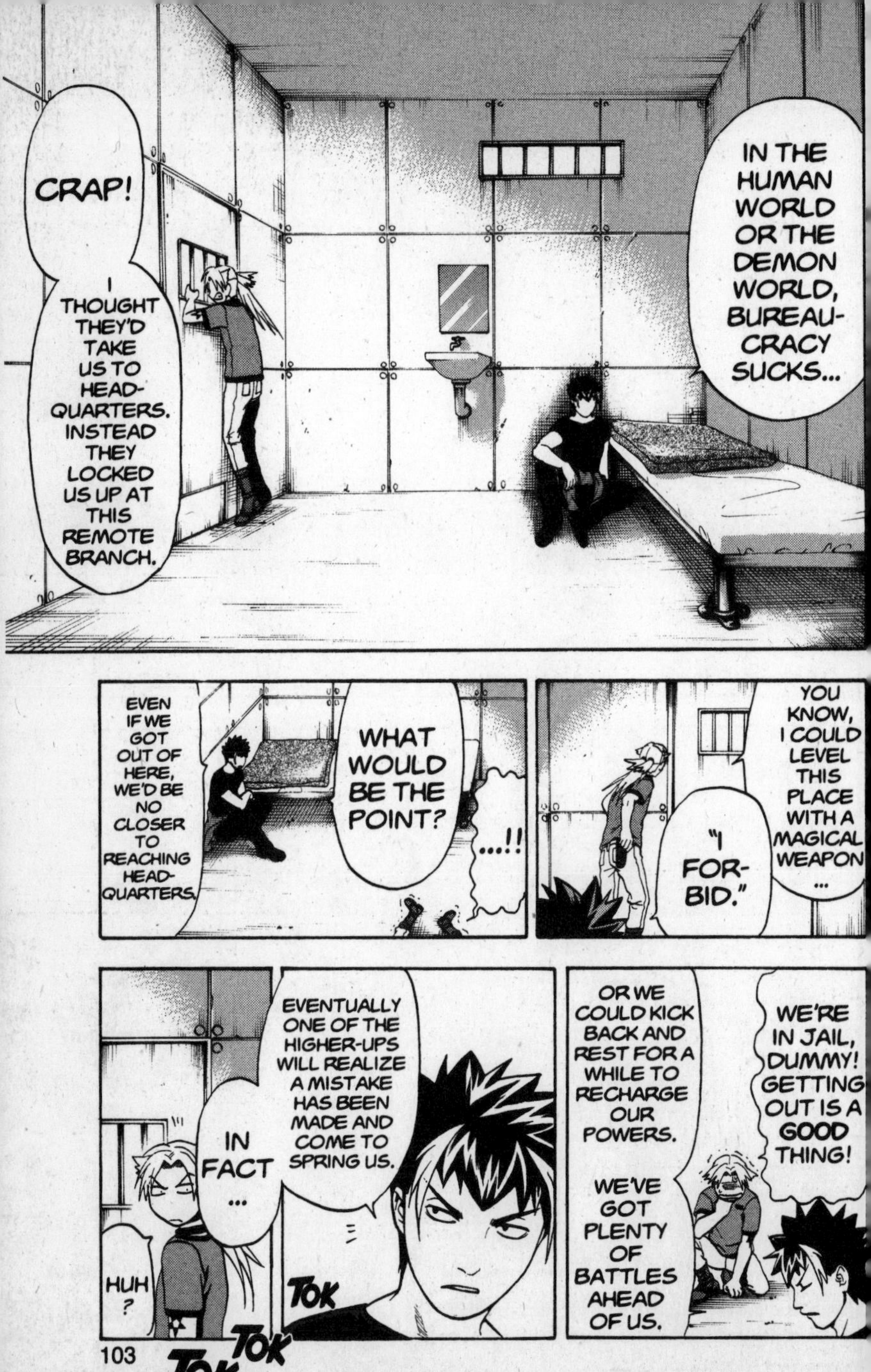
CRAP!
I THOUGHT THEY'D TAKE US TO HEAD-QUARTERS. INSTEAD THEY LOCKED US UP AT THIS REMOTE BRANCH.
IN THE HUMAN WORLD OR THE DEMON WORLD, BUREAU-CRACY SUCKS...
YOU KNOW, I COULD LEVEL THIS PLACE WITH A MAGICAL WEAPON...
"I FOR-BID."
WHAT WOULD BE THE POINT?
EVEN IF WE GOT OUT OF HERE, WE'D BE NO CLOSER TO REACHING HEAD-QUARTERS.
...!!
WE'RE IN JAIL, DUMMY! GETTING OUT IS A **GOOD** THING!
OR WE COULD KICK BACK AND REST FOR A WHILE TO RECHARGE OUR POWERS.
WE'VE GOT PLENTY OF BATTLES AHEAD OF US.
EVENTUALLY ONE OF THE HIGHER-UPS WILL REALIZE A MISTAKE HAS BEEN MADE AND COME TO SPRING US.
IN FACT...
TOK
HUH?
TOK
TOK

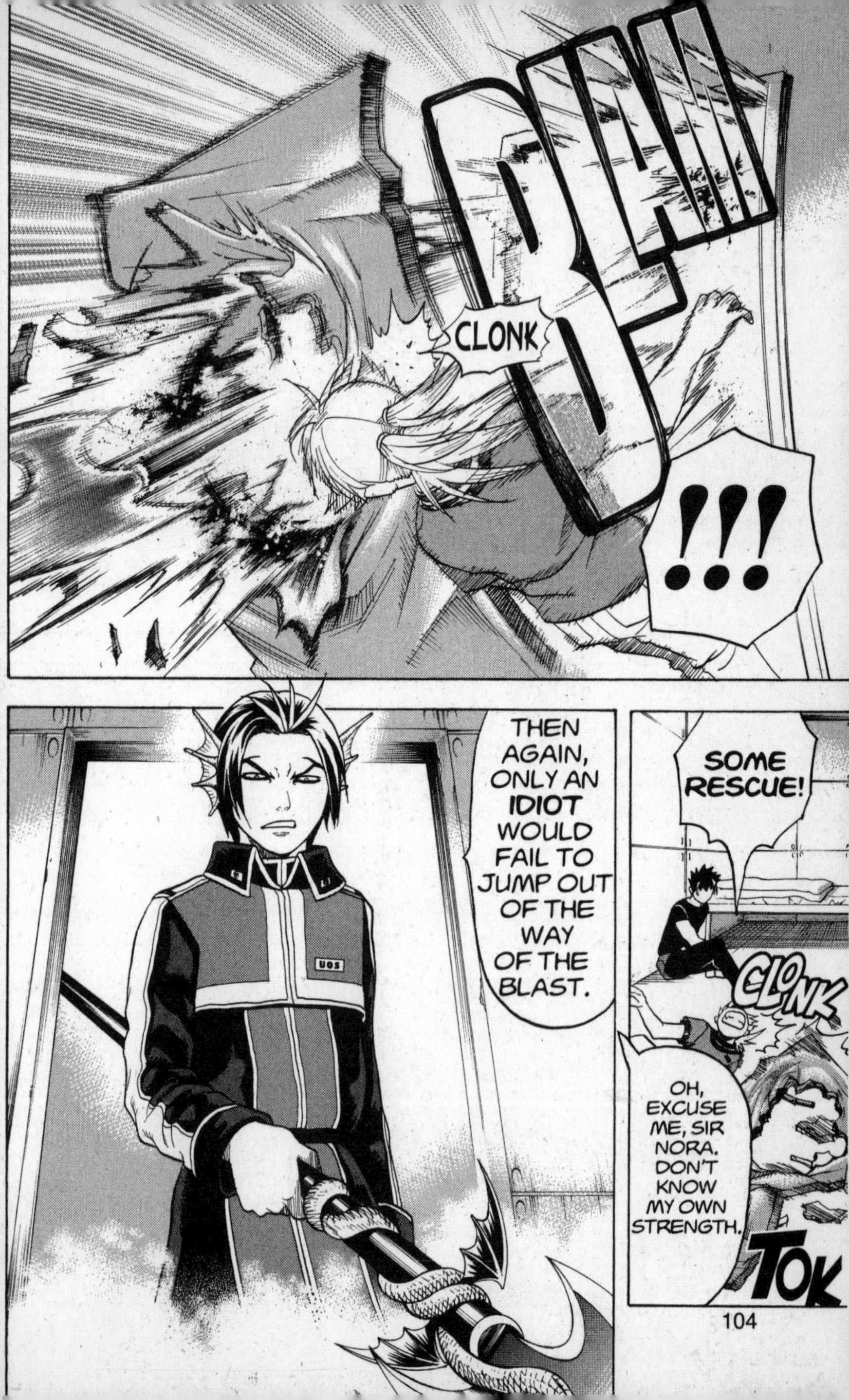
BLAM
CLONK
!!!
SOME RESCUE!
CLONK
OH, EXCUSE ME, SIR NORA. DON'T KNOW MY OWN STRENGTH.
TOK
THEN AGAIN, ONLY AN IDIOT WOULD FAIL TO JUMP OUT OF THE WAY OF THE BLAST.

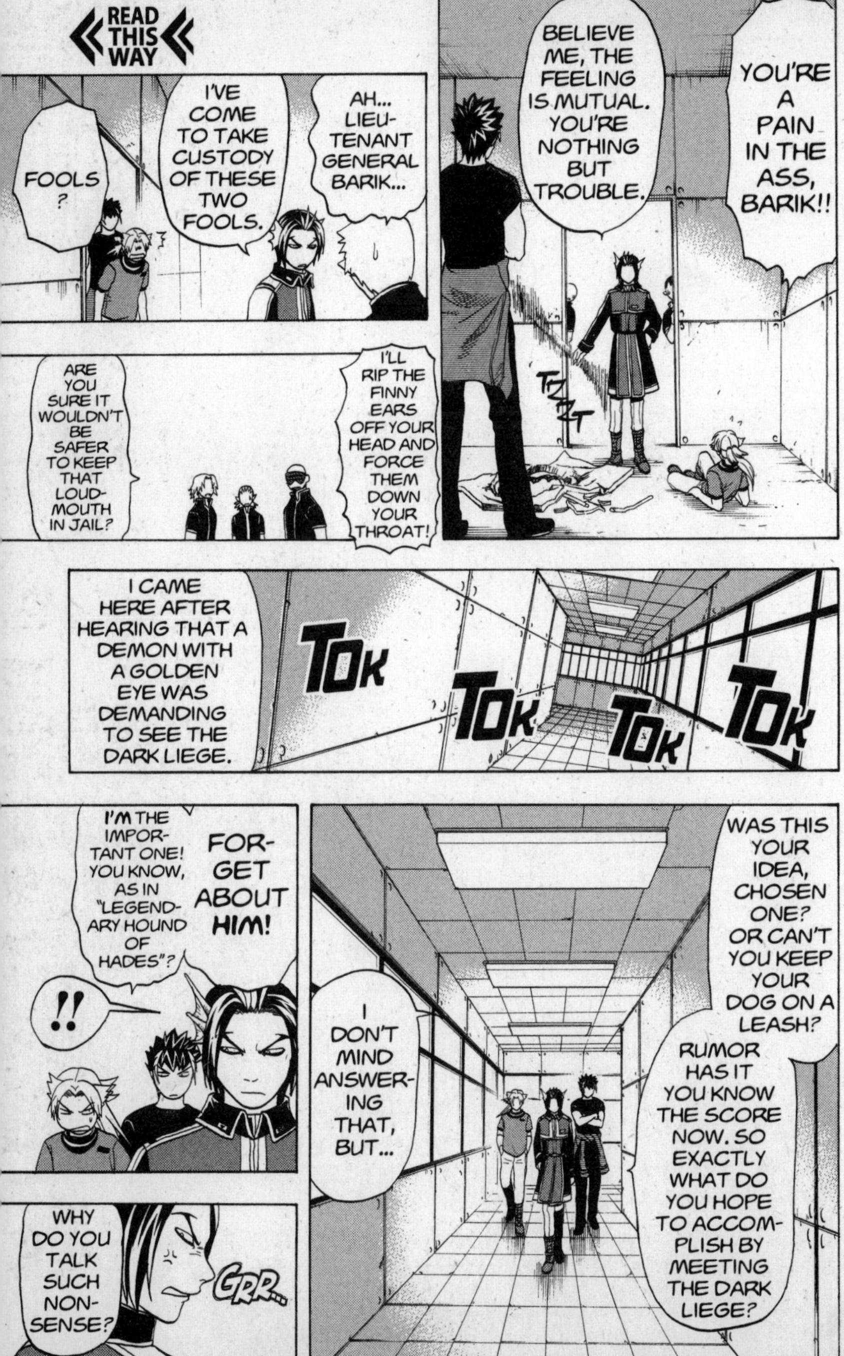
READ THIS WAY
YOU'RE A PAIN IN THE ASS, BARIK!!
BELIEVE ME, THE FEELING IS MUTUAL. YOU'RE NOTHING BUT TROUBLE.
TZZZT
AH... LIEU-TENANT GENERAL BARIK...
I'VE COME TO TAKE CUSTODY OF THESE TWO FOOLS.
FOOLS?
I'LL RIP THE FINNY EARS OFF YOUR HEAD AND FORCE THEM DOWN YOUR THROAT!
ARE YOU SURE IT WOULDN'T BE SAFER TO KEEP THAT LOUD-MOUTH IN JAIL?
TOK
TOK
TOK
TOK
I CAME HERE AFTER HEARING THAT A DEMON WITH A GOLDEN EYE WAS DEMANDING TO SEE THE DARK LIEGE.
WAS THIS YOUR IDEA, CHOSEN ONE? OR CAN'T YOU KEEP YOUR DOG ON A LEASH?
RUMOR HAS IT YOU KNOW THE SCORE NOW. SO EXACTLY WHAT DO YOU HOPE TO ACCOM-PLISH BY MEETING THE DARK LIEGE?
I DON'T MIND ANSWER-ING THAT, BUT...
FOR-GET ABOUT HIM!
I'M THE IMPOR-TANT ONE! YOU KNOW, AS IN "LEGEND-ARY HOUND OF HADES"?
!!
GRR...
WHY DO YOU TALK SUCH NON-SENSE?

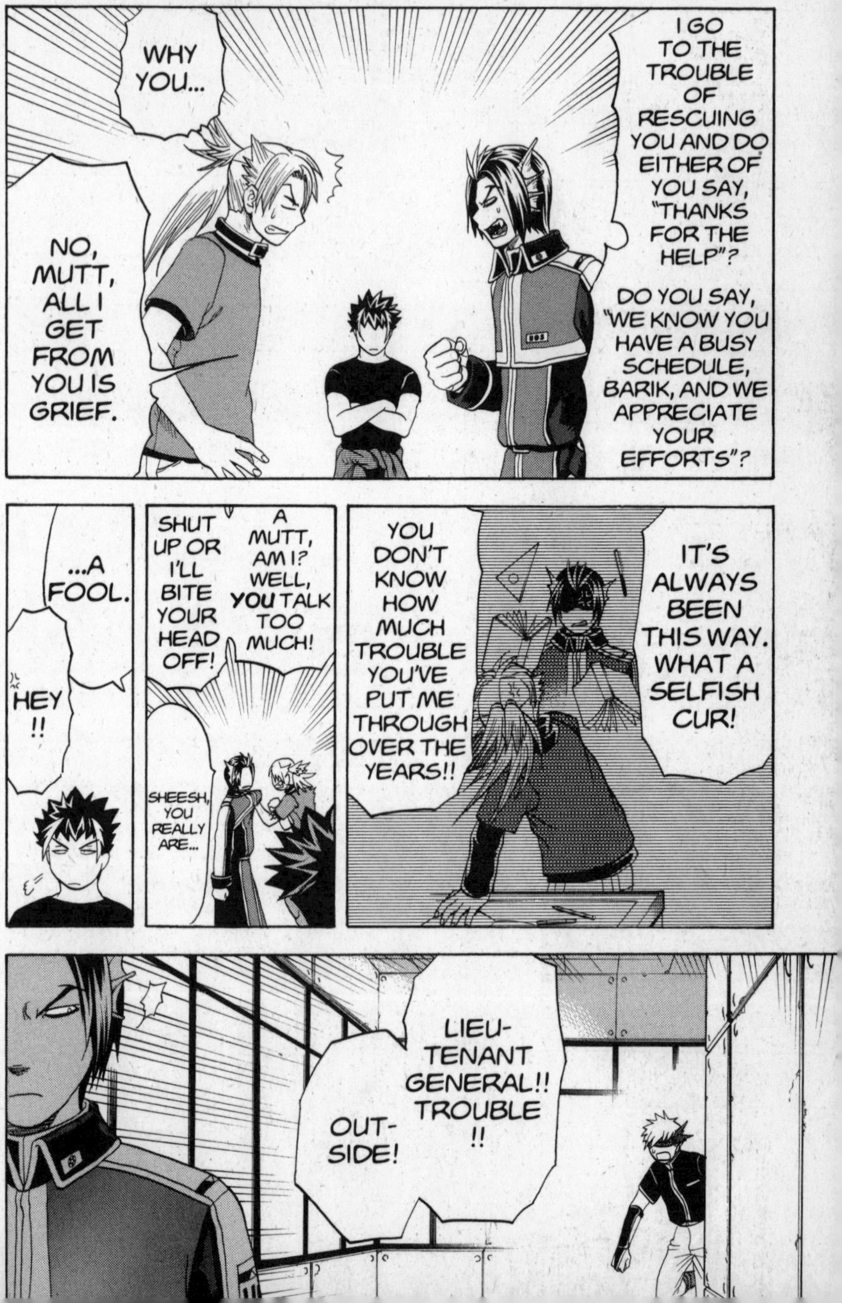
I GO TO THE TROUBLE OF RESCUING YOU AND DO EITHER OF YOU SAY, "THANKS FOR THE HELP"?
DO YOU SAY, "WE KNOW YOU HAVE A BUSY SCHEDULE, BARIK, AND WE APPRECIATE YOUR EFFORTS"?
WHY YOU...
NO, MUTT, ALL I GET FROM YOU IS GRIEF.
IT'S ALWAYS BEEN THIS WAY. WHAT A SELFISH CUR!
YOU DON'T KNOW HOW MUCH TROUBLE YOU'VE PUT ME THROUGH OVER THE YEARS!!
A MUTT, AM I? WELL, YOU TALK TOO MUCH!
SHUT UP OR I'LL BITE YOUR HEAD OFF!
SHEESH, YOU REALLY ARE...
...A FOOL.
HEY !!
LIEU-TENANT GENERAL!! TROUBLE !!
OUT-SIDE!

READ THIS WAY

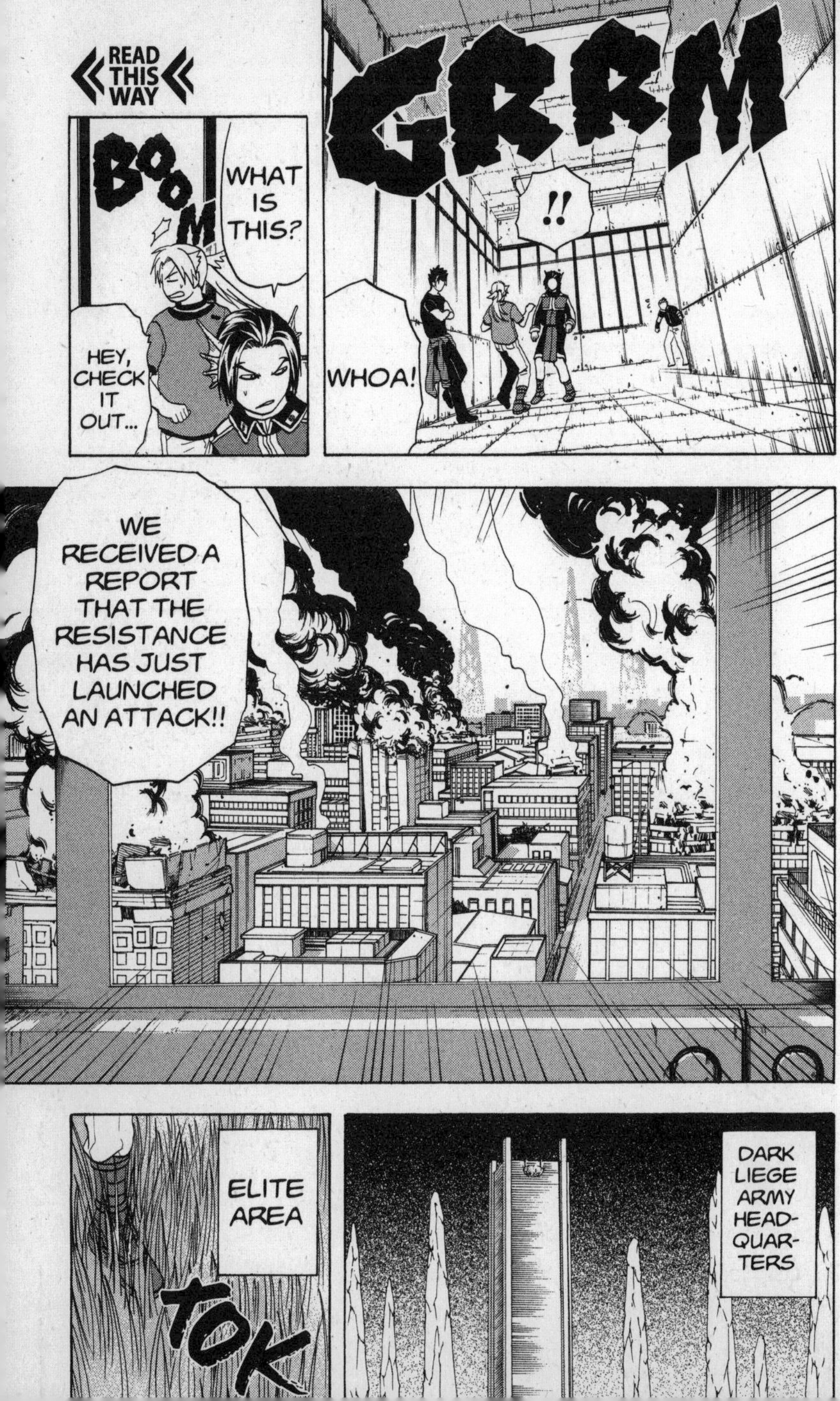
GRRM
!!
WHOA!
BOOM
WHAT IS THIS?
HEY, CHECK IT OUT...
WE RECEIVED A REPORT THAT THE RESISTANCE HAS JUST LAUNCHED AN ATTACK!!
DARK LIEGE ARMY HEAD-QUAR-TERS
ELITE AREA
TOK

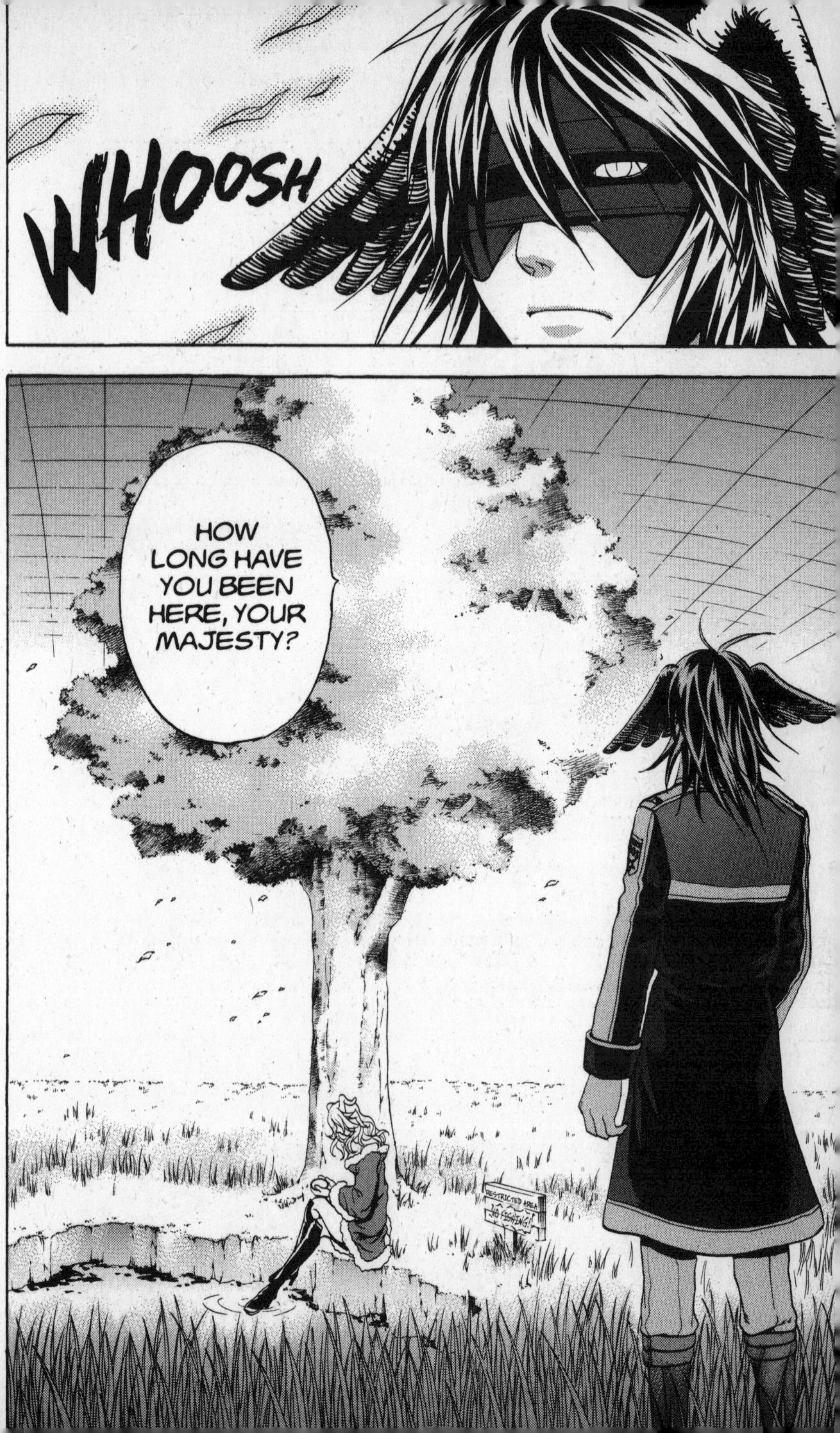
WHOOSH
HOW LONG HAVE YOU BEEN HERE, YOUR MAJESTY?
RESTRICTED AREA
NO FISHING!

READ THIS WAY

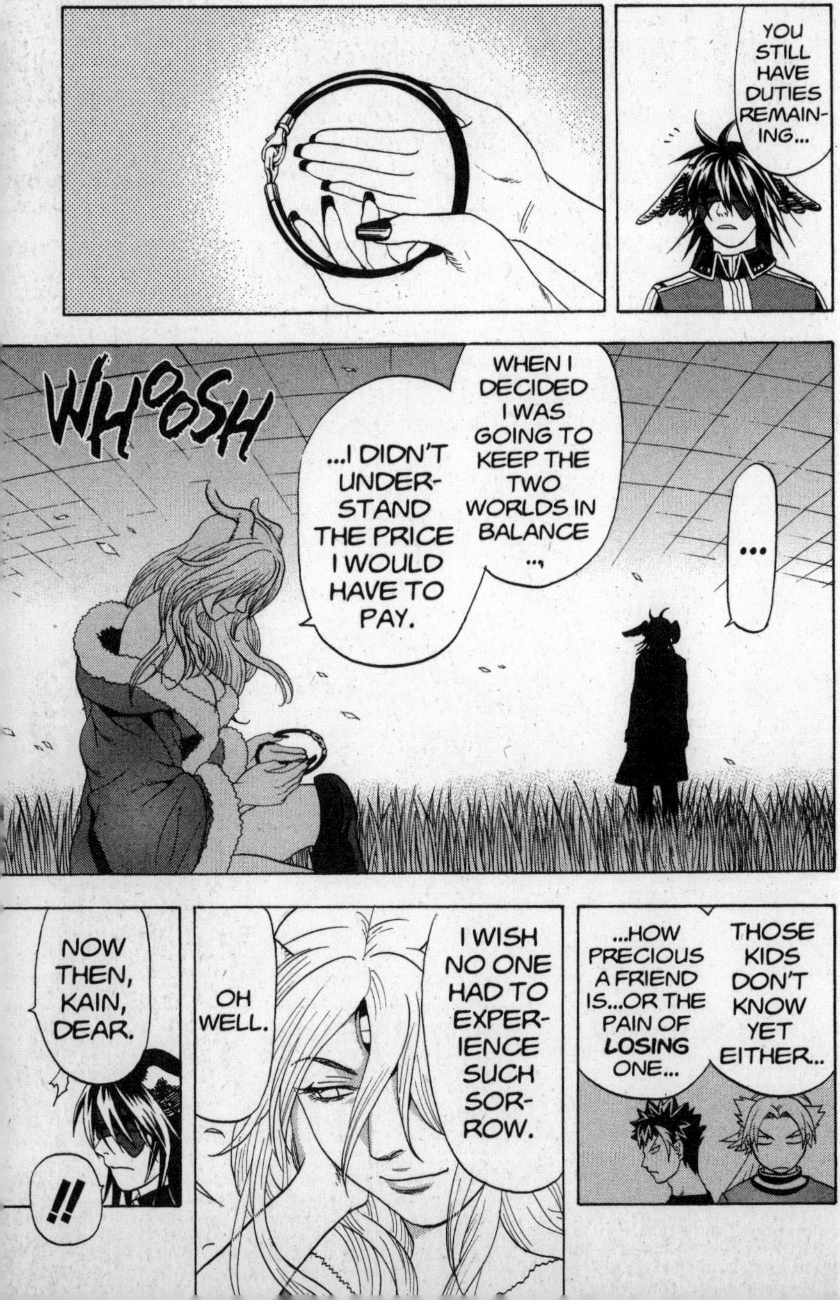
YOU STILL HAVE DUTIES REMAINING...
...
WHEN I DECIDED I WAS GOING TO KEEP THE TWO WORLDS IN BALANCE...,
...I DIDN'T UNDERSTAND THE PRICE I WOULD HAVE TO PAY.
WHOOSH
THOSE KIDS DON'T KNOW YET EITHER...
...HOW PRECIOUS A FRIEND IS...OR THE PAIN OF **LOSING** ONE...
I WISH NO ONE HAD TO EXPERIENCE SUCH SORROW.
OH WELL.
NOW THEN, KAIN, DEAR.
!!

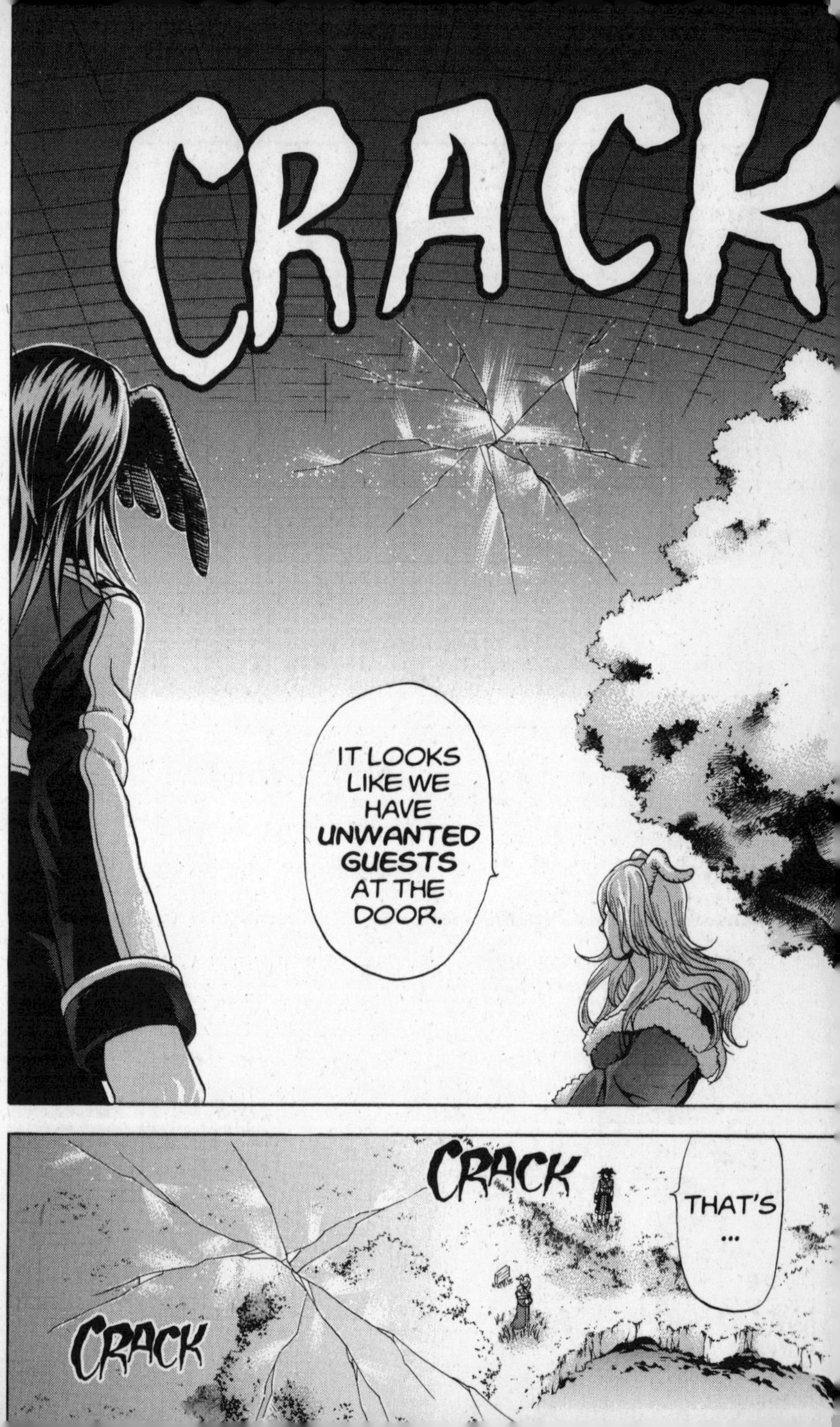
CRACK
IT LOOKS LIKE WE HAVE UNWANTED GUESTS AT THE DOOR.
THAT'S ...
CRACK
CRACK

READ THIS WAY

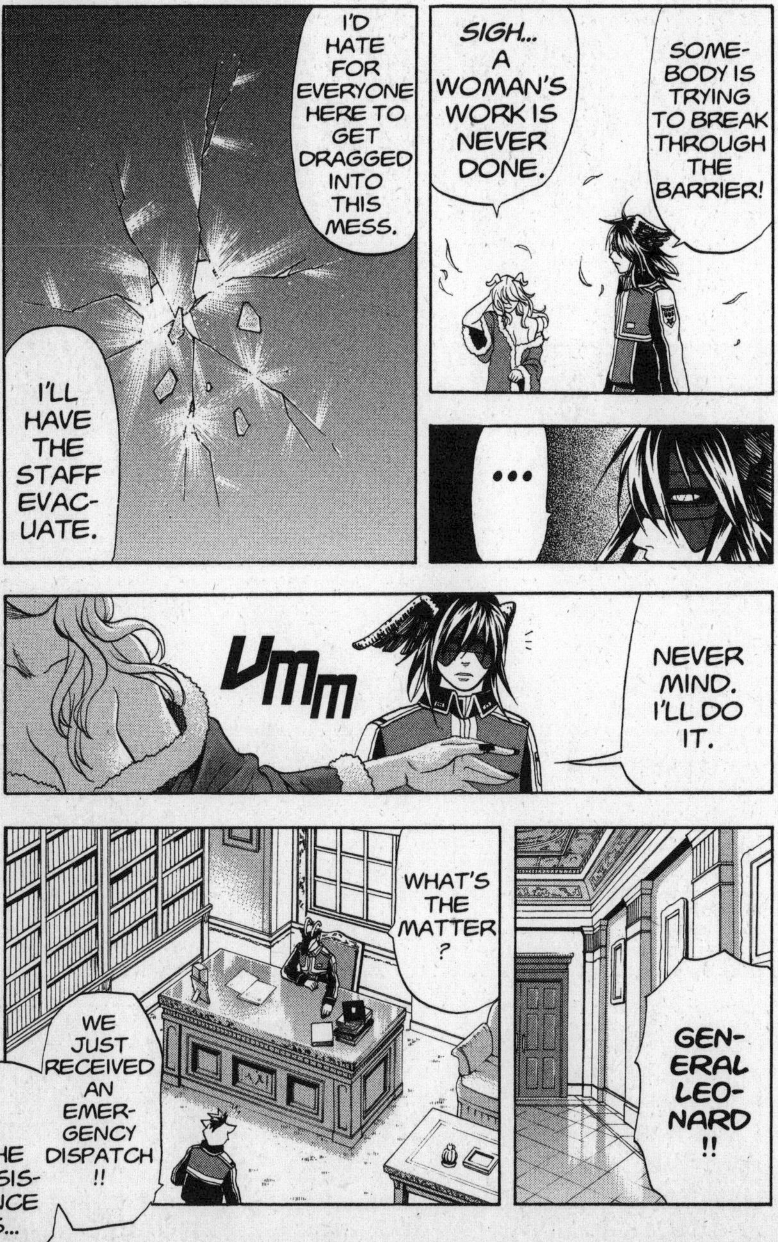
SOMEBODY IS TRYING TO BREAK THROUGH THE BARRIER!
SIGH... A WOMAN'S WORK IS NEVER DONE.
...
I'D HATE FOR EVERYONE HERE TO GET DRAGGED INTO THIS MESS.
I'LL HAVE THE STAFF EVACUATE.
NEVER MIND. I'LL DO IT.
UMM
GENERAL LEONARD!!
WHAT'S THE MATTER?
WE JUST RECEIVED AN EMERGENCY DISPATCH!!
THE RESISTANCE IS...

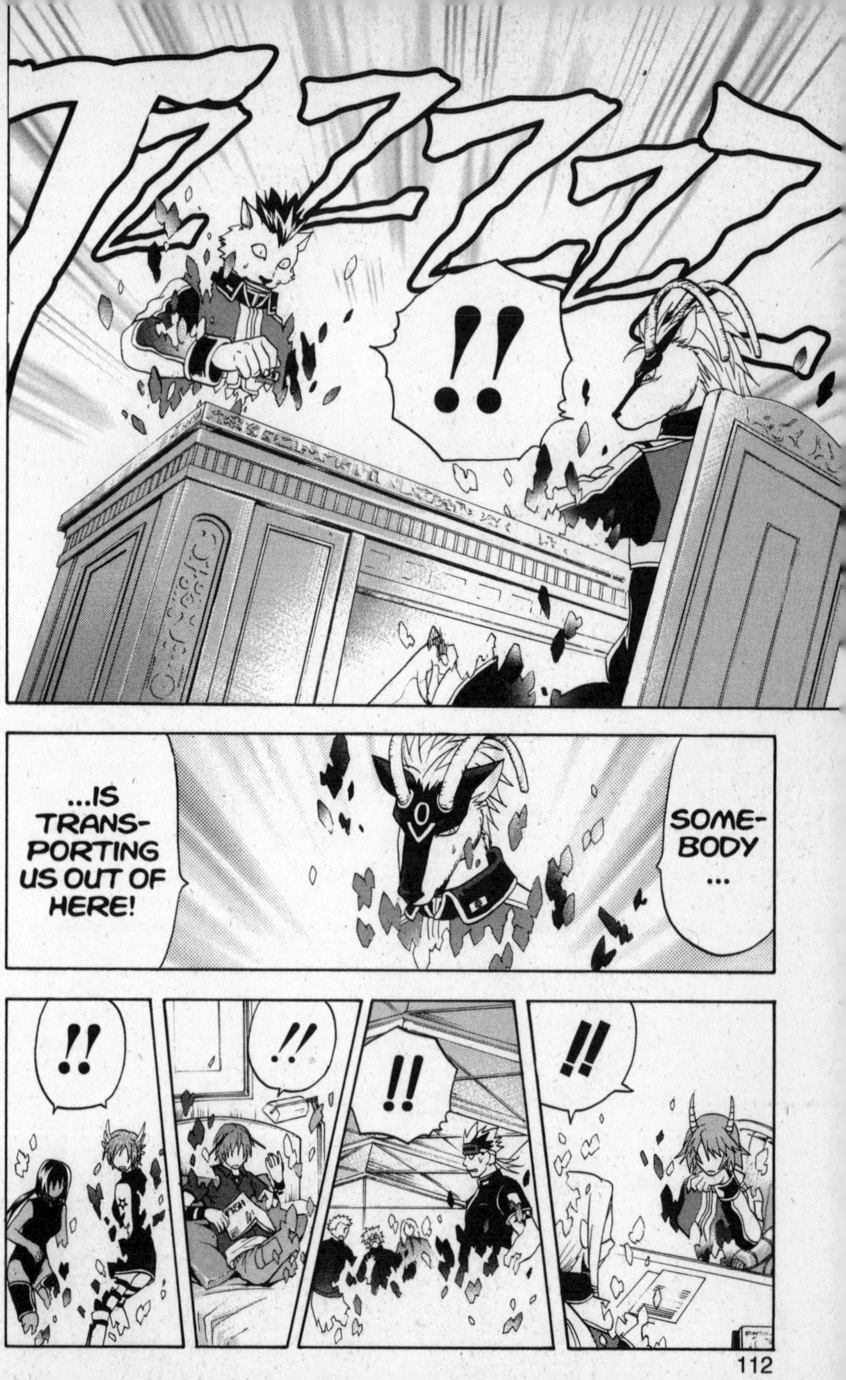
!!
SOME-BODY ...
...IS TRANS-PORTING US OUT OF HERE!
!!
!!
!!
!!

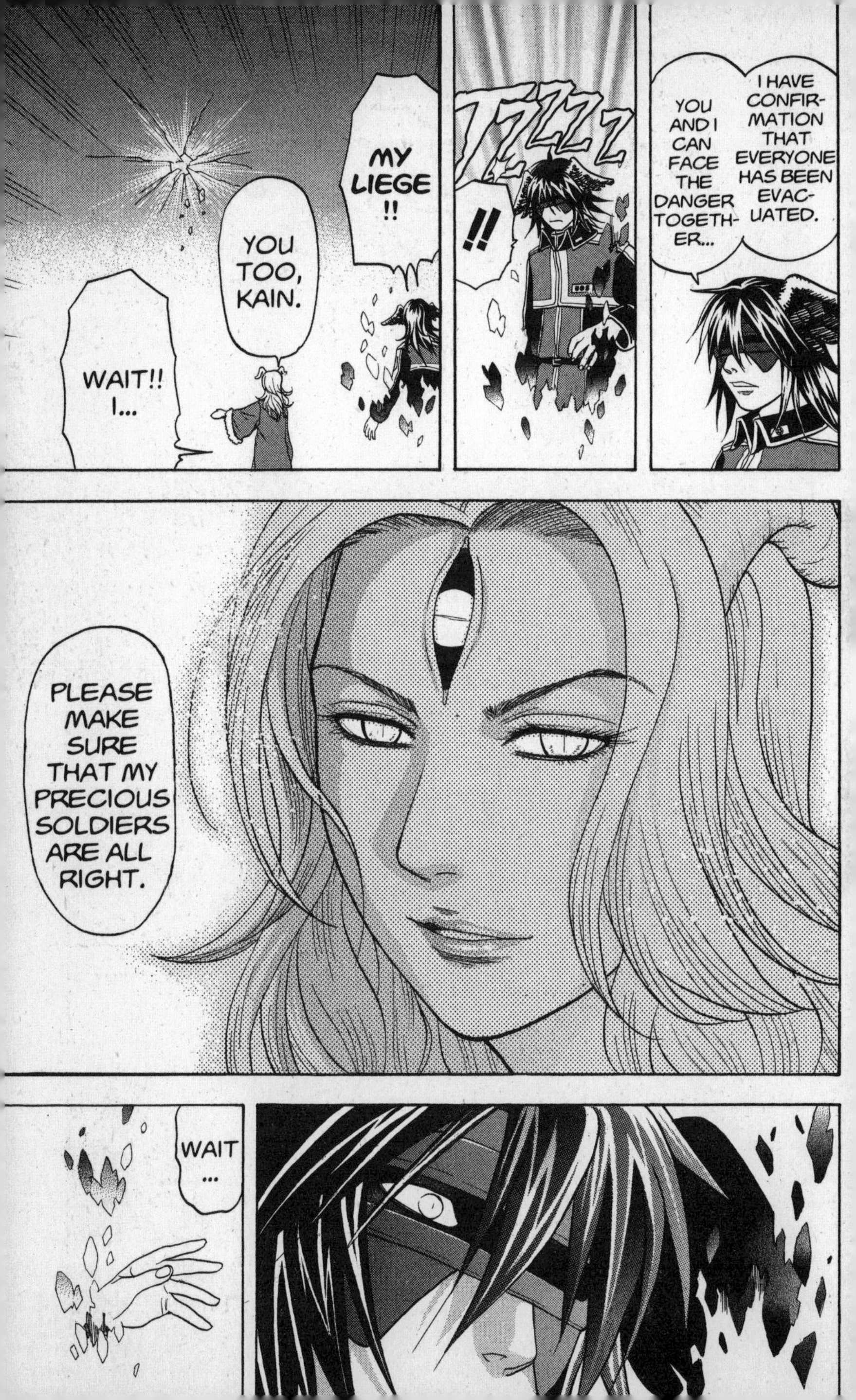
I HAVE CONFIRMATION THAT EVERYONE HAS BEEN EVACUATED.
YOU AND I CAN FACE THE DANGER TOGETHER...
TZZZZ
!!
MY LIEGE!!
YOU TOO, KAIN.
WAIT!! I...
PLEASE MAKE SURE THAT MY PRECIOUS SOLDIERS ARE ALL RIGHT.
WAIT ...

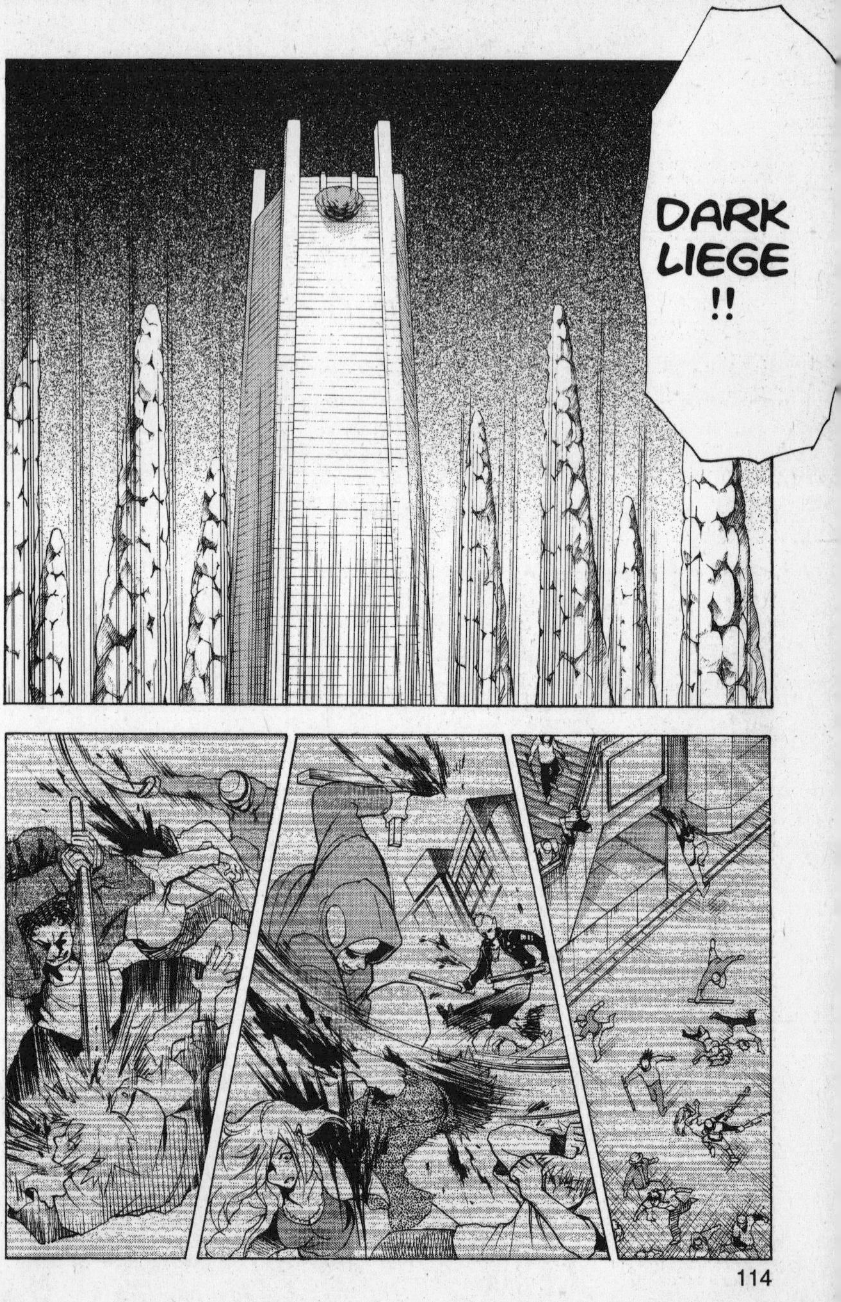
DARK LIEGE !!

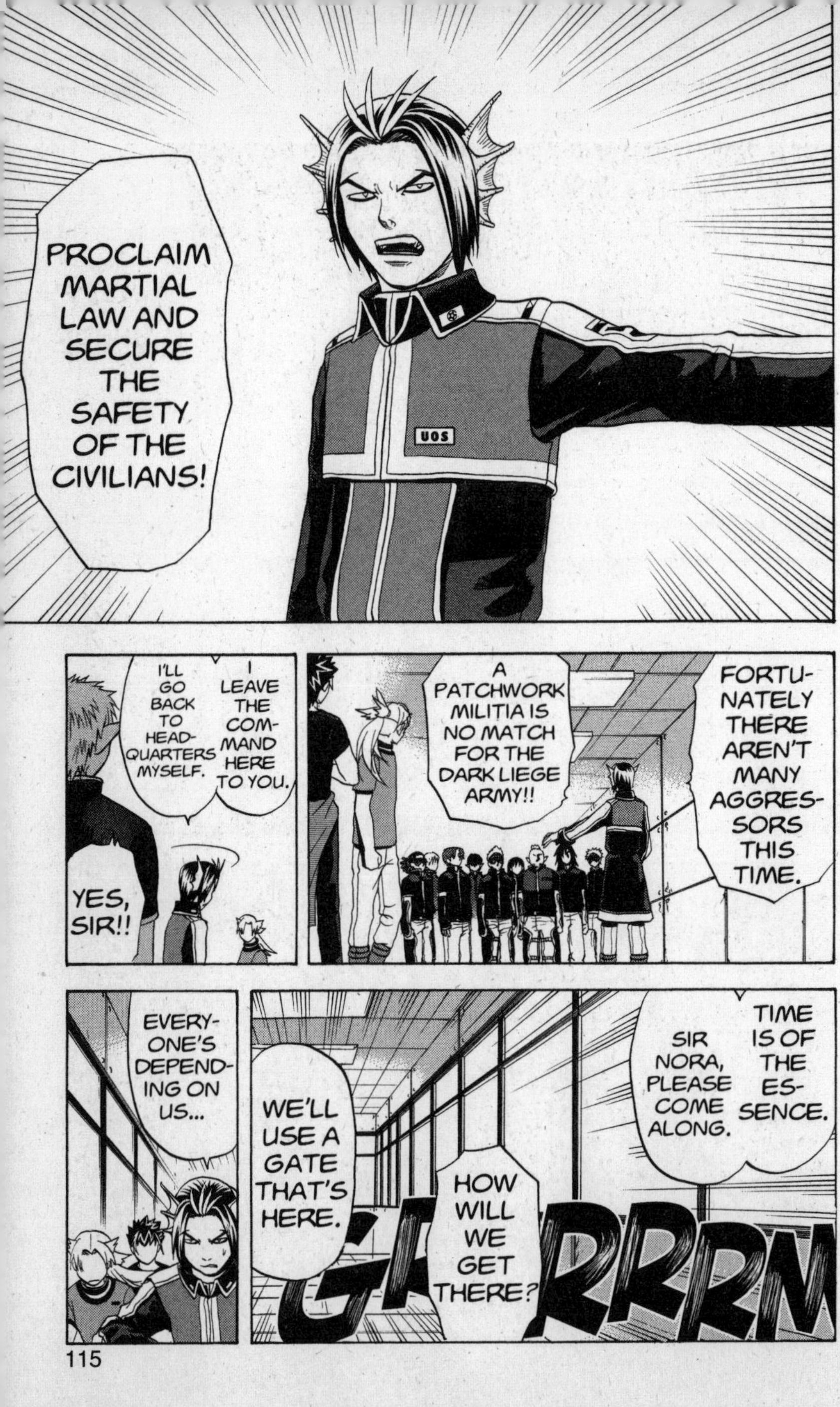
PROCLAIM MARTIAL LAW AND SECURE THE SAFETY OF THE CIVILIANS!
FORTUNATELY THERE AREN'T MANY AGGRESSORS THIS TIME.
A PATCHWORK MILITIA IS NO MATCH FOR THE DARK LIEGE ARMY!!
I LEAVE THE COMMAND HERE TO YOU.
I'LL GO BACK TO HEADQUARTERS MYSELF.
YES, SIR!!
TIME IS OF THE ESSENCE.
SIR NORA, PLEASE COME ALONG.
HOW WILL WE GET THERE?
WE'LL USE A GATE THAT'S HERE.
EVERYONE'S DEPENDING ON US...

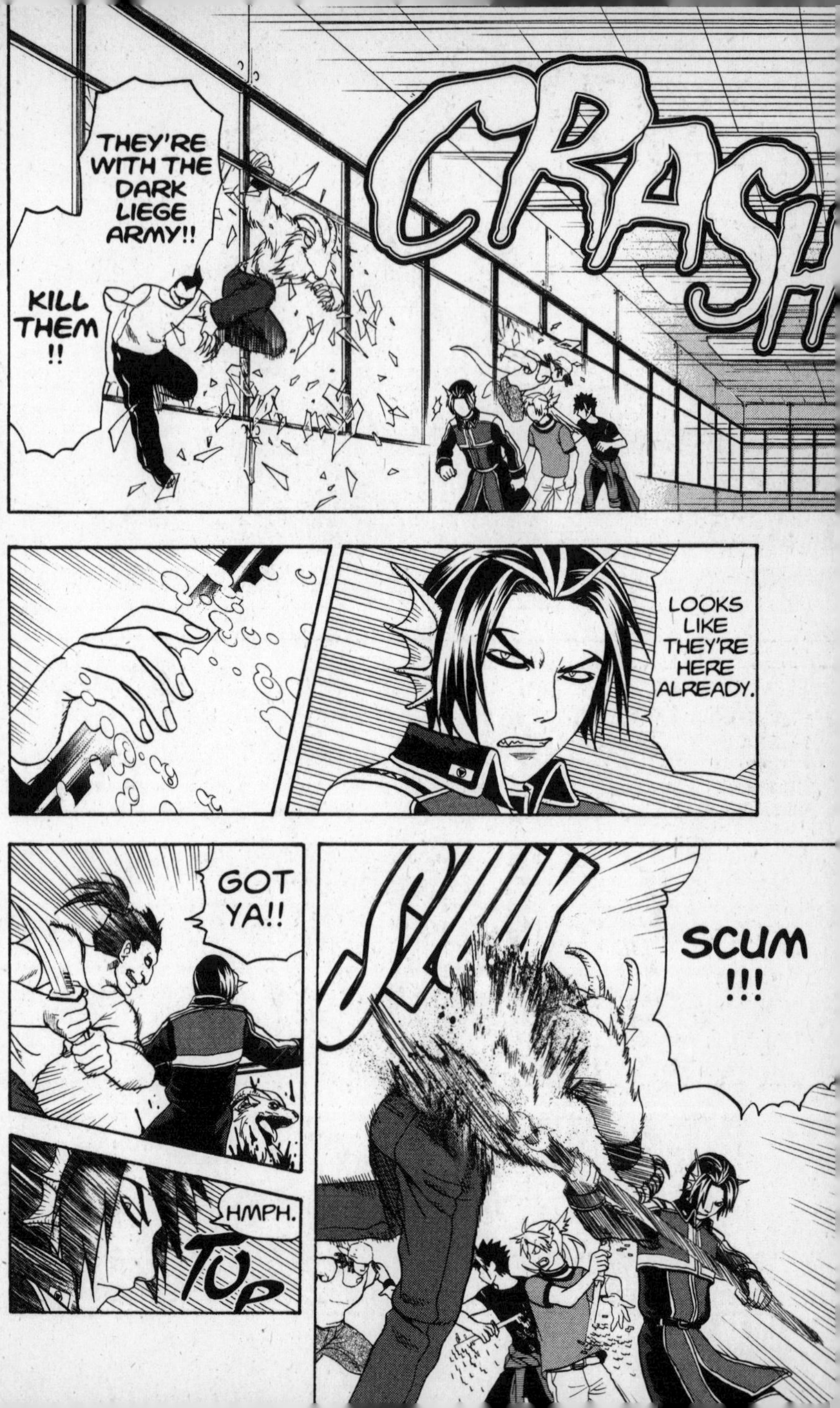
CRASH
THEY'RE WITH THE DARK LIEGE ARMY!!
KILL THEM!!
LOOKS LIKE THEY'RE HERE ALREADY.
SCUM!!!
GOT YA!!
HMPH.
TUP

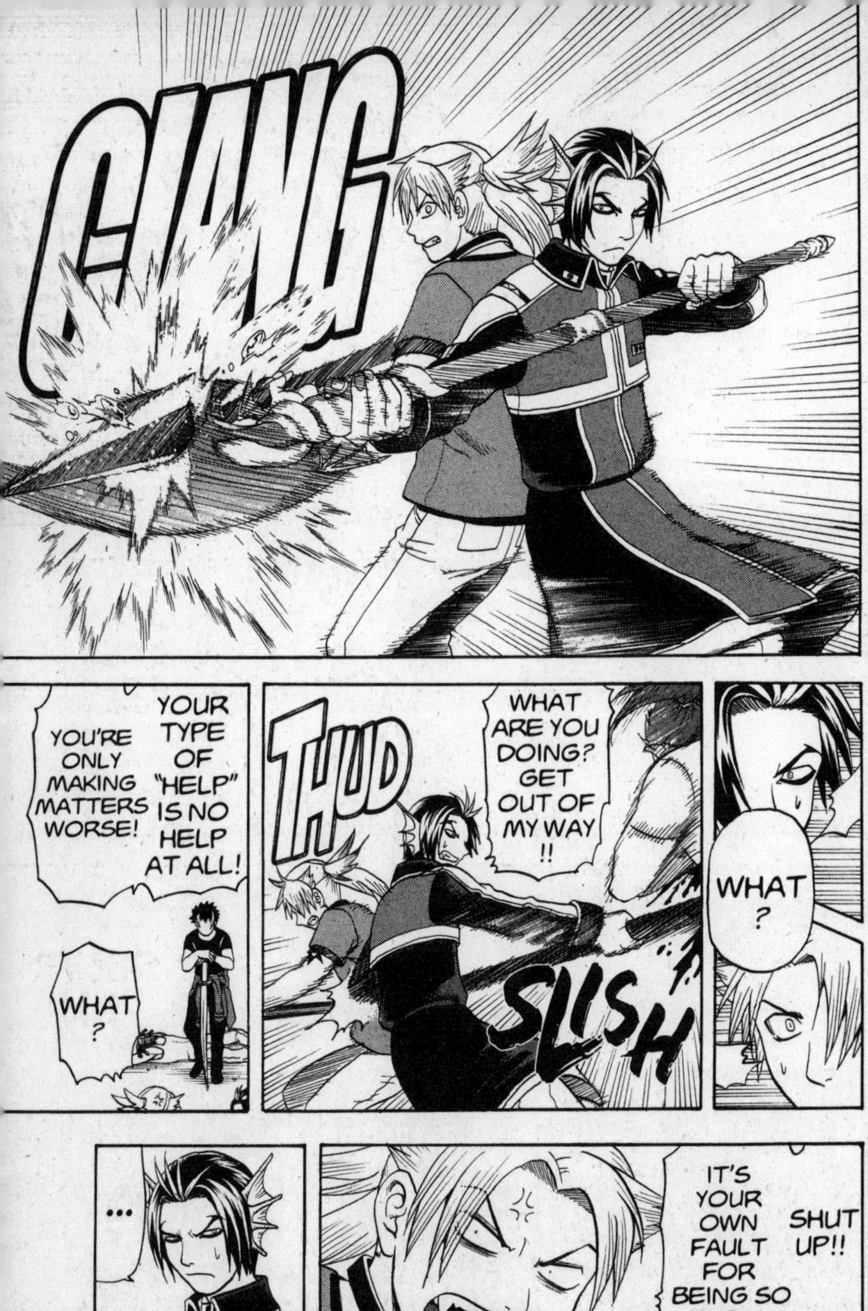
CLANG
WHAT?
WHAT ARE YOU DOING? GET OUT OF MY WAY!!
THUD
SLISH
YOUR TYPE OF "HELP" IS NO HELP AT ALL!
YOU'RE ONLY MAKING MATTERS WORSE!
WHAT?
SHUT UP!!
IT'S YOUR OWN FAULT FOR BEING SO SLOW.
...

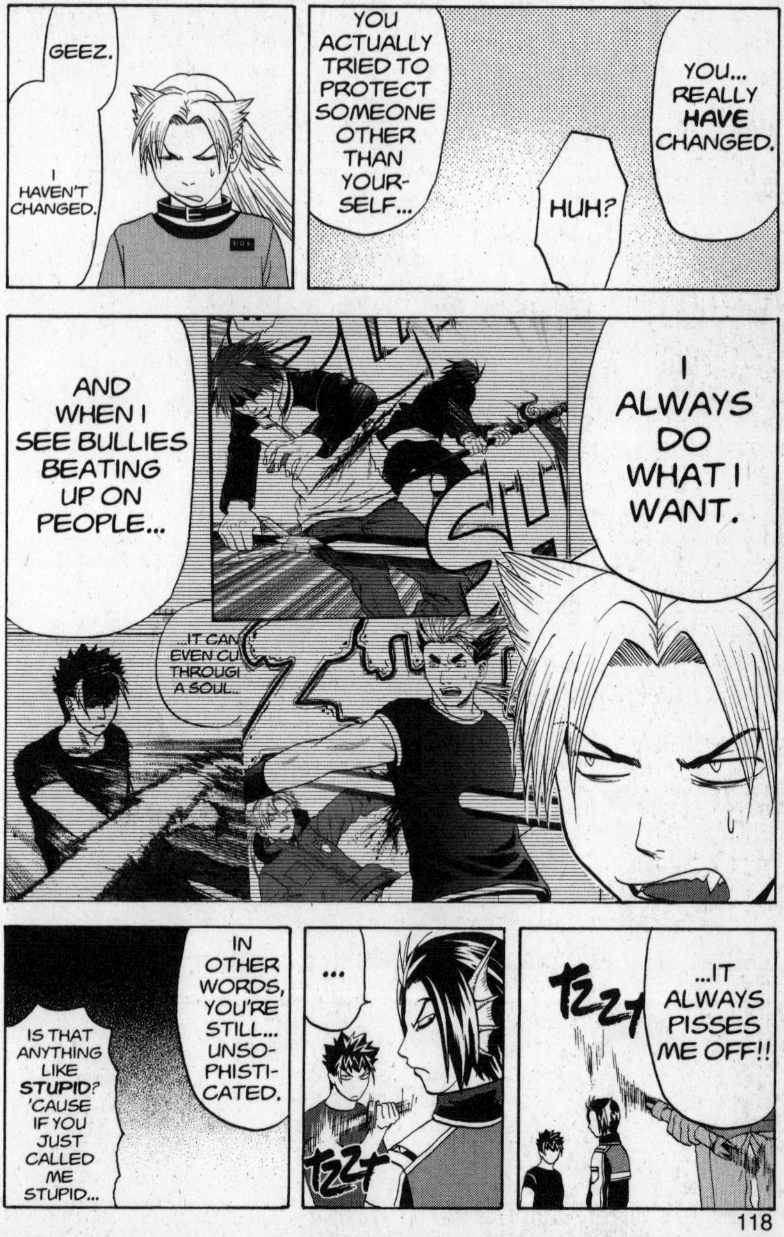
YOU... REALLY HAVE CHANGED.
HUH?
YOU ACTUALLY TRIED TO PROTECT SOMEONE OTHER THAN YOURSELF...
GEEZ.
I HAVEN'T CHANGED.
I ALWAYS DO WHAT I WANT.
AND WHEN I SEE BULLIES BEATING UP ON PEOPLE...
...IT CAN EVEN CU THROUGI A SOUL...
TZZT
...IT ALWAYS PISSES ME OFF!!
...
TZZT
IN OTHER WORDS, YOU'RE STILL... UNSOPHISTICATED.
IS THAT ANYTHING LIKE STUPID? 'CAUSE IF YOU JUST CALLED ME STUPID...

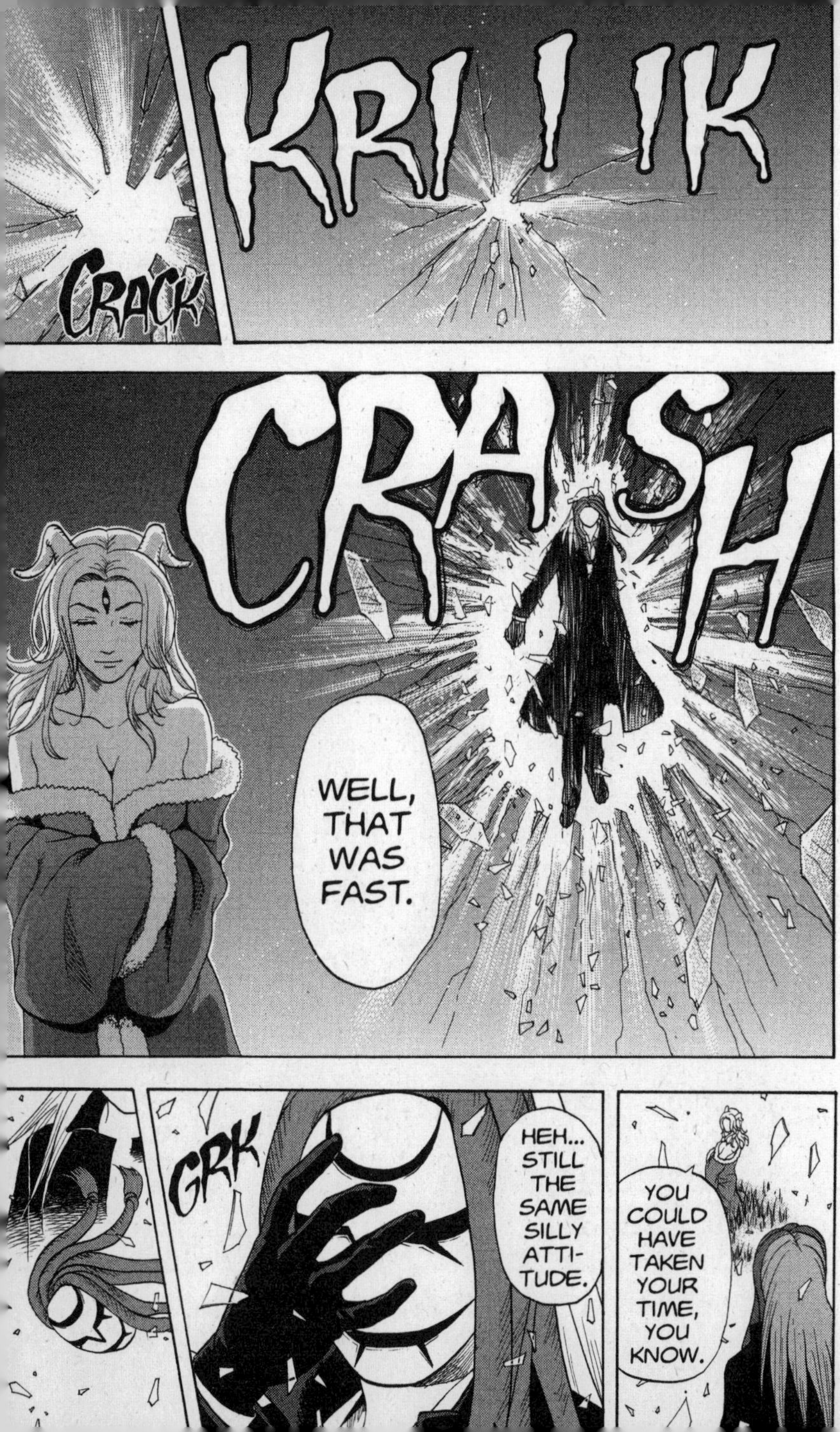
KRI I IK
CRACK
CRASH
WELL, THAT WAS FAST.
YOU COULD HAVE TAKEN YOUR TIME, YOU KNOW.
HEH... STILL THE SAME SILLY ATTI-TUDE.
GRK

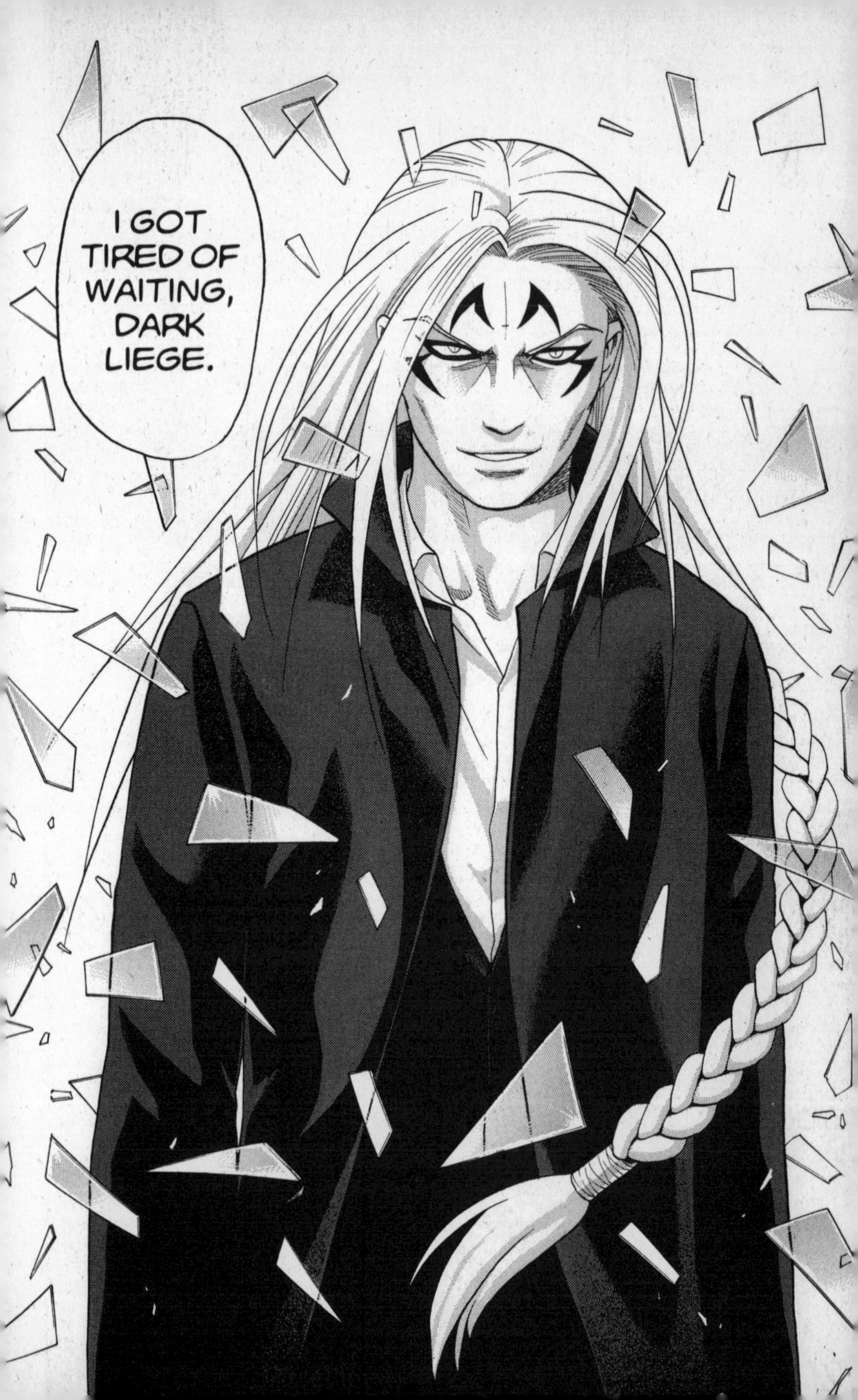
I GOT TIRED OF WAITING, DARK LIEGE.

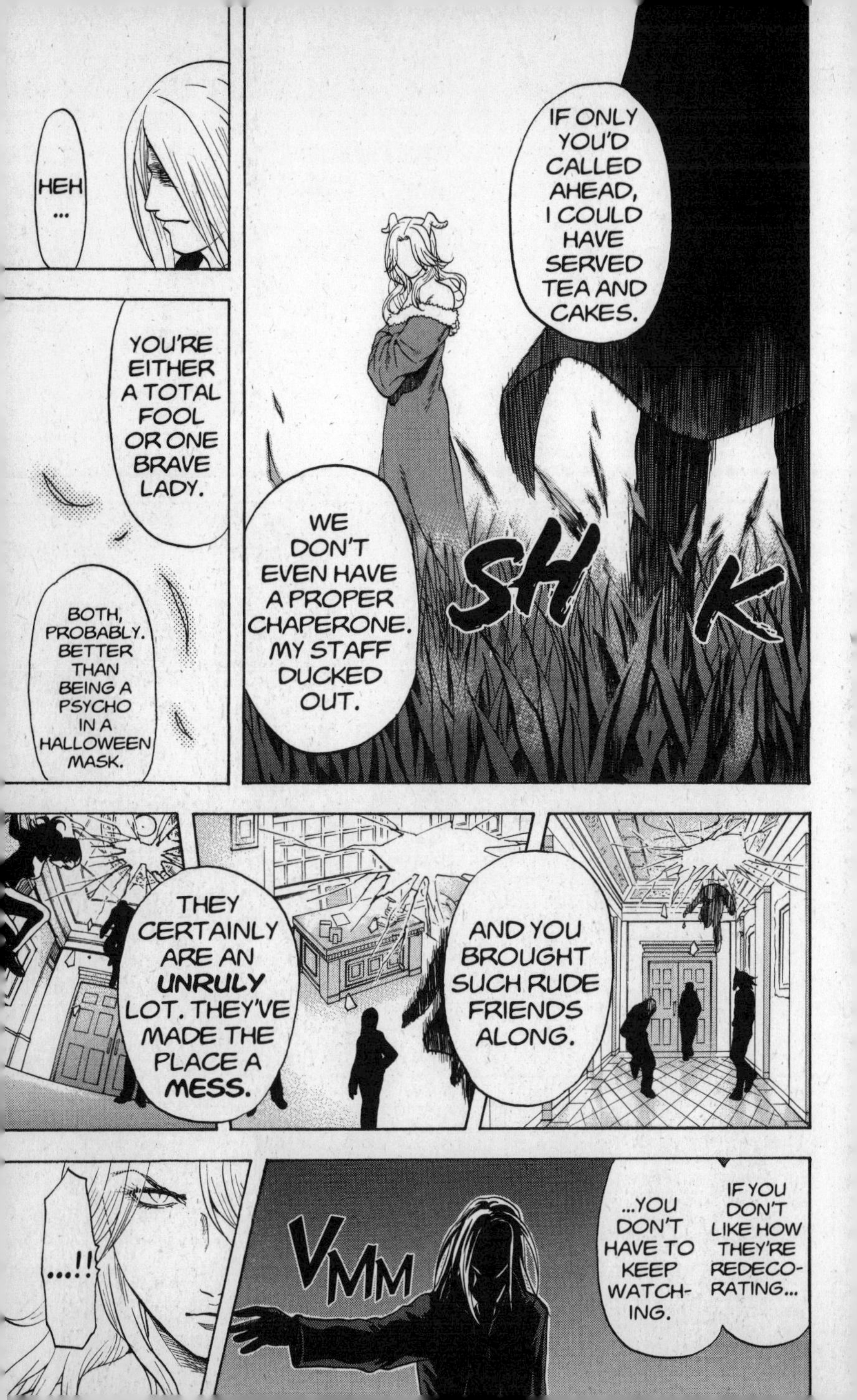
IF ONLY YOU'D CALLED AHEAD, I COULD HAVE SERVED TEA AND CAKES.
WE DON'T EVEN HAVE A PROPER CHAPERONE. MY STAFF DUCKED OUT.
SHK
HEH...
YOU'RE EITHER A TOTAL FOOL OR ONE BRAVE LADY.
BOTH, PROBABLY. BETTER THAN BEING A PSYCHO IN A HALLOWEEN MASK.
AND YOU BROUGHT SUCH RUDE FRIENDS ALONG.
THEY CERTAINLY ARE AN UNRULY LOT. THEY'VE MADE THE PLACE A MESS.
IF YOU DON'T LIKE HOW THEY'RE REDECO-RATING...
...YOU DON'T HAVE TO KEEP WATCH-ING.
VMM
...!!

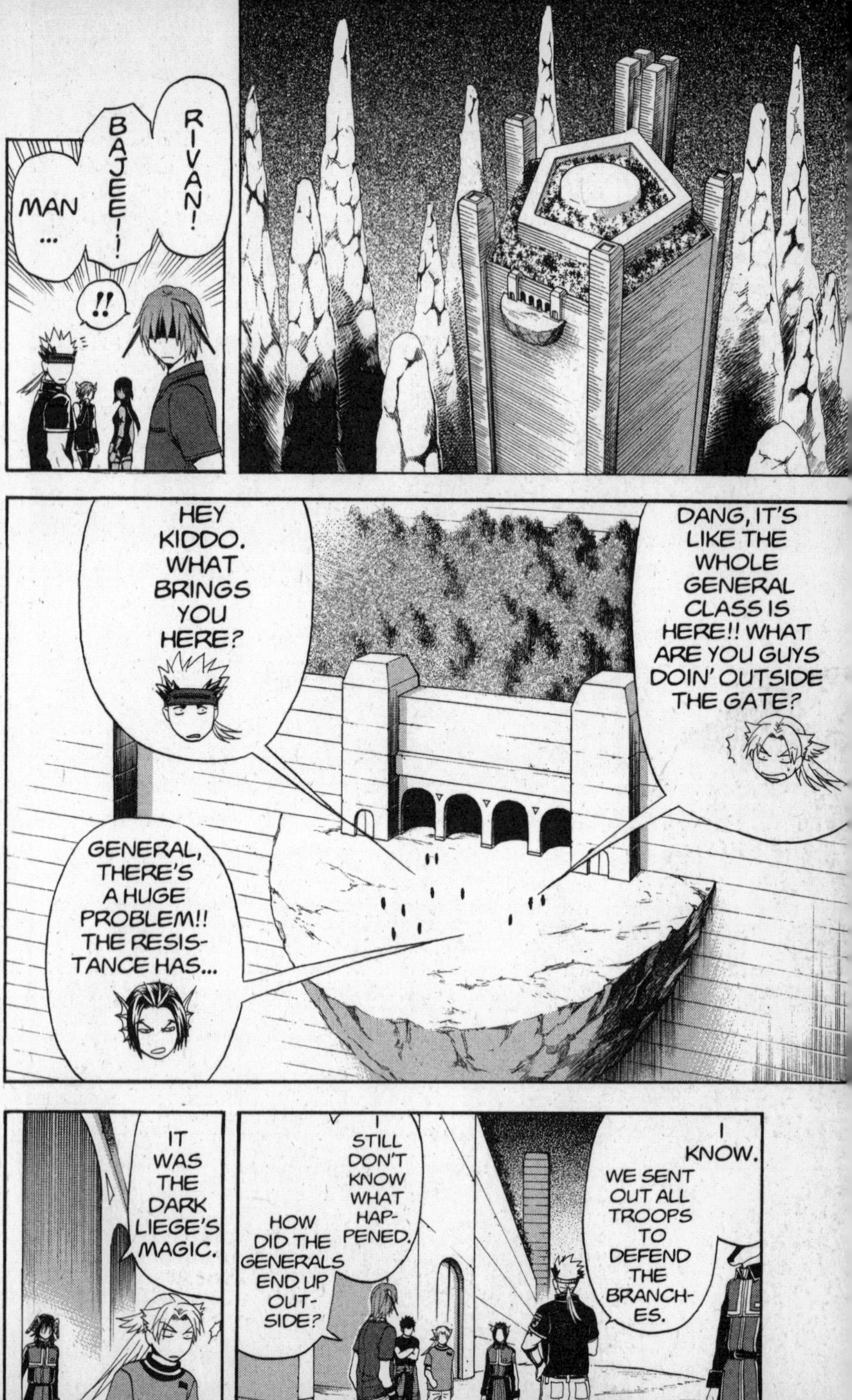
RIVAN!
BAJEE!!
MAN...
!!
DANG, IT'S LIKE THE WHOLE GENERAL CLASS IS HERE!! WHAT ARE YOU GUYS DOIN' OUTSIDE THE GATE?
HEY KIDDO. WHAT BRINGS YOU HERE?
GENERAL, THERE'S A HUGE PROBLEM!! THE RESIS-TANCE HAS...
I KNOW.
WE SENT OUT ALL TROOPS TO DEFEND THE BRANCH-ES.
I STILL DON'T KNOW WHAT HAP-PENED.
HOW DID THE GENERALS END UP OUT-SIDE?
IT WAS THE DARK LIEGE'S MAGIC.

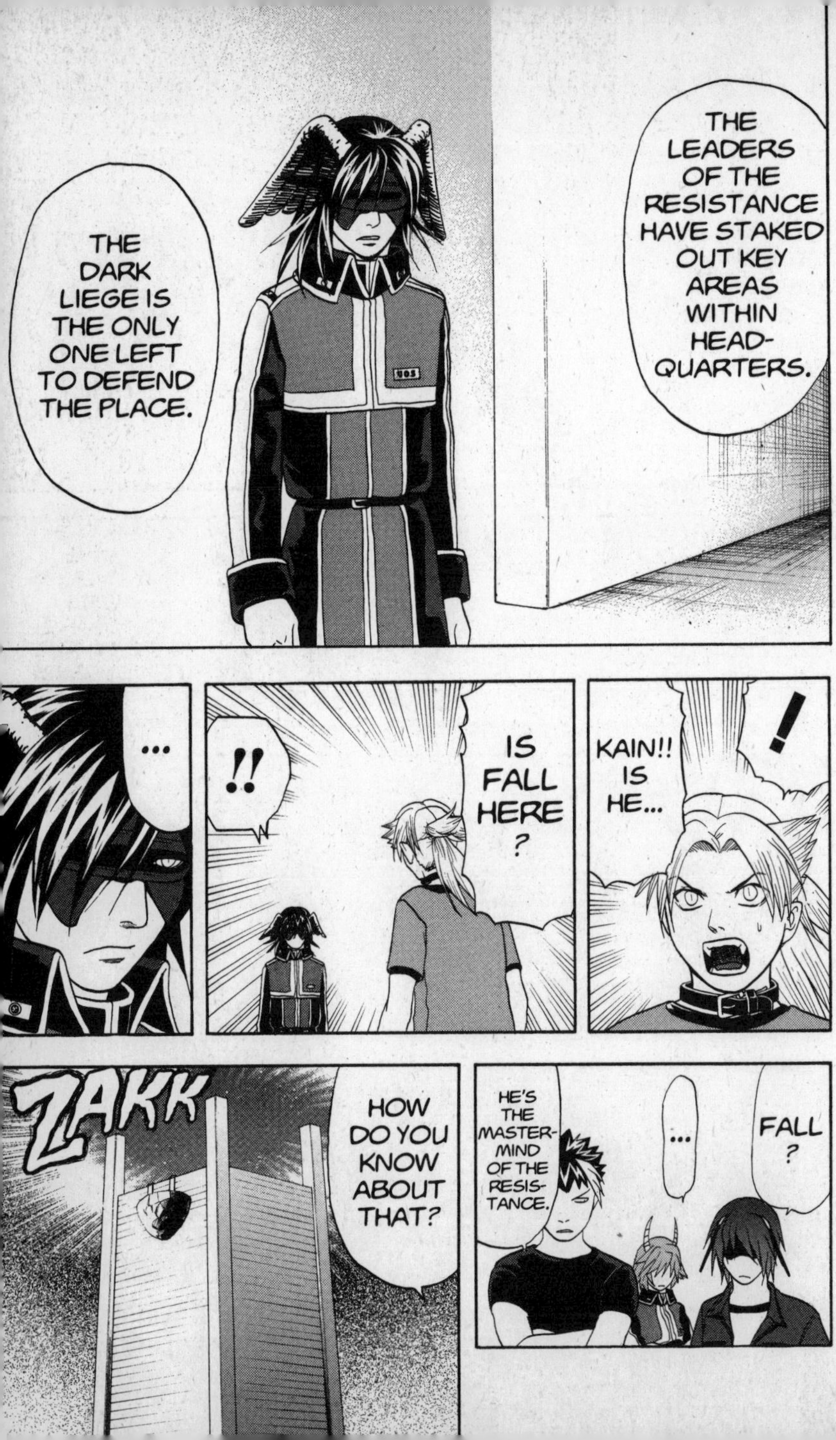
THE LEADERS OF THE RESISTANCE HAVE STAKED OUT KEY AREAS WITHIN HEAD-QUARTERS.
THE DARK LIEGE IS THE ONLY ONE LEFT TO DEFEND THE PLACE.
!
KAIN!! IS HE...
IS FALL HERE?
!!
...
FALL?
...
HE'S THE MASTER-MIND OF THE RESIS-TANCE.
HOW DO YOU KNOW ABOUT THAT?
ZAKK

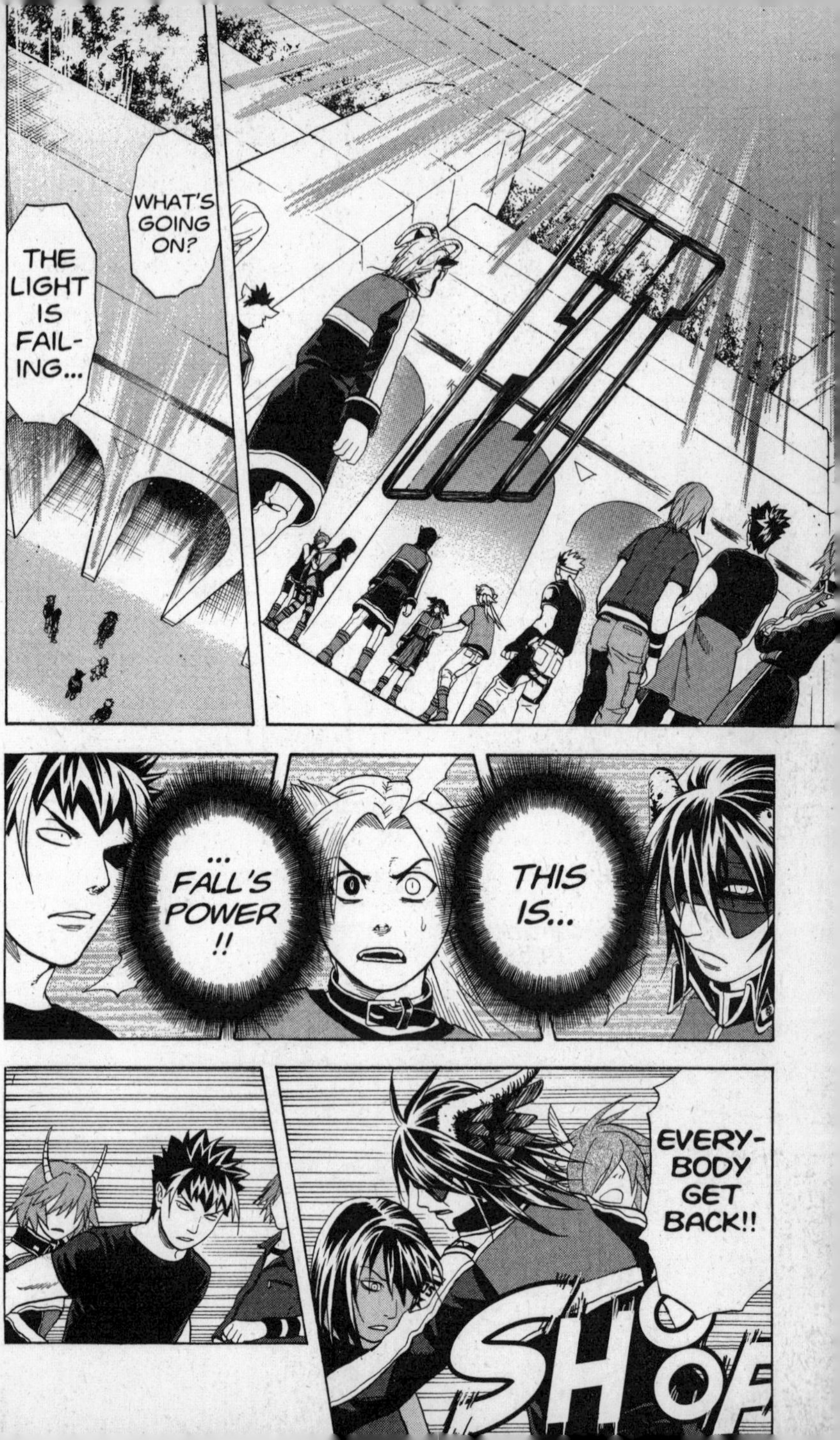

WHAT'S GOING ON?
THE LIGHT IS FAIL-ING...
THIS IS...
...FALL'S POWER!!
EVERY-BODY GET BACK!!
SHOOF

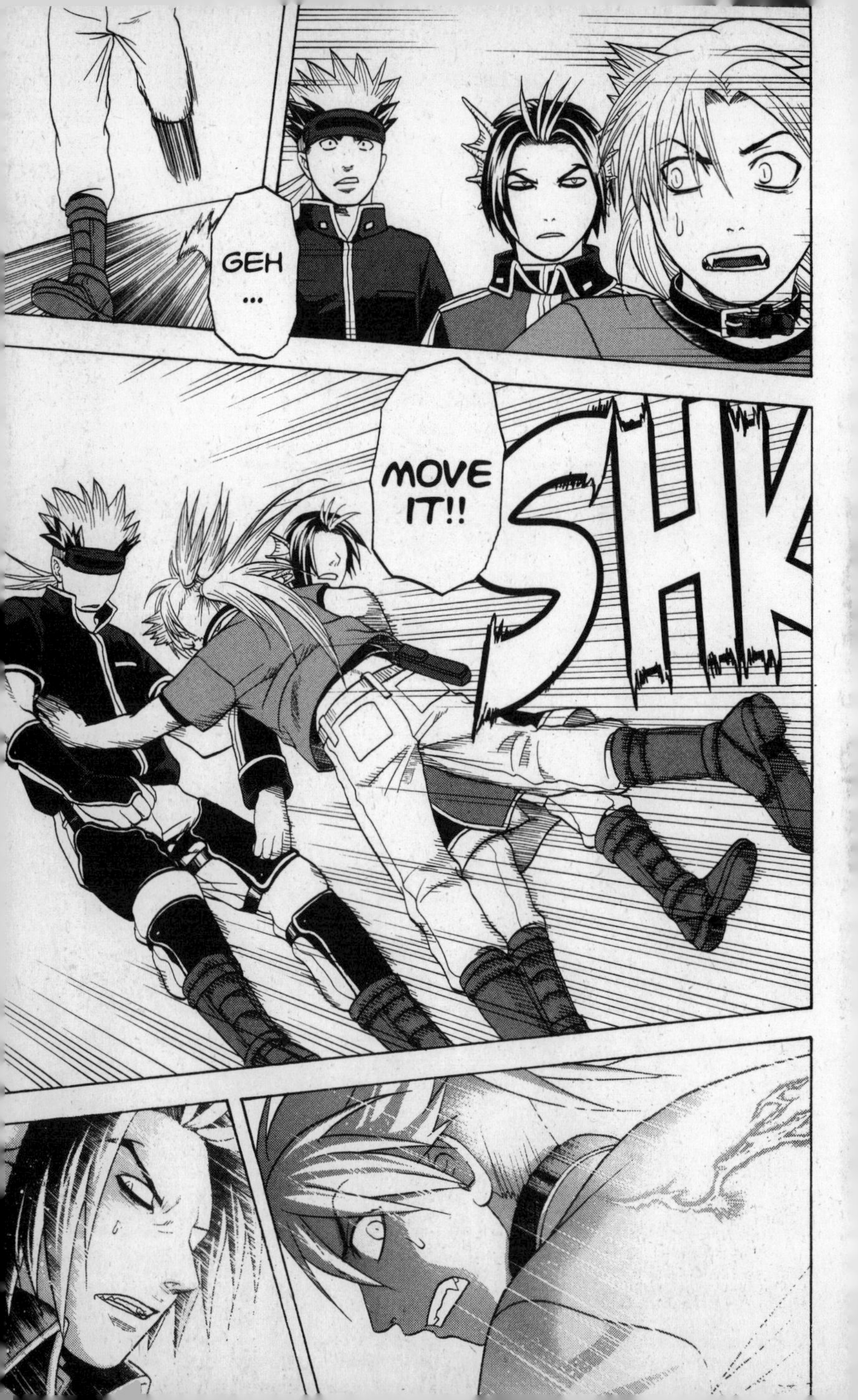
GEH ...
SHK
MOVE IT!!

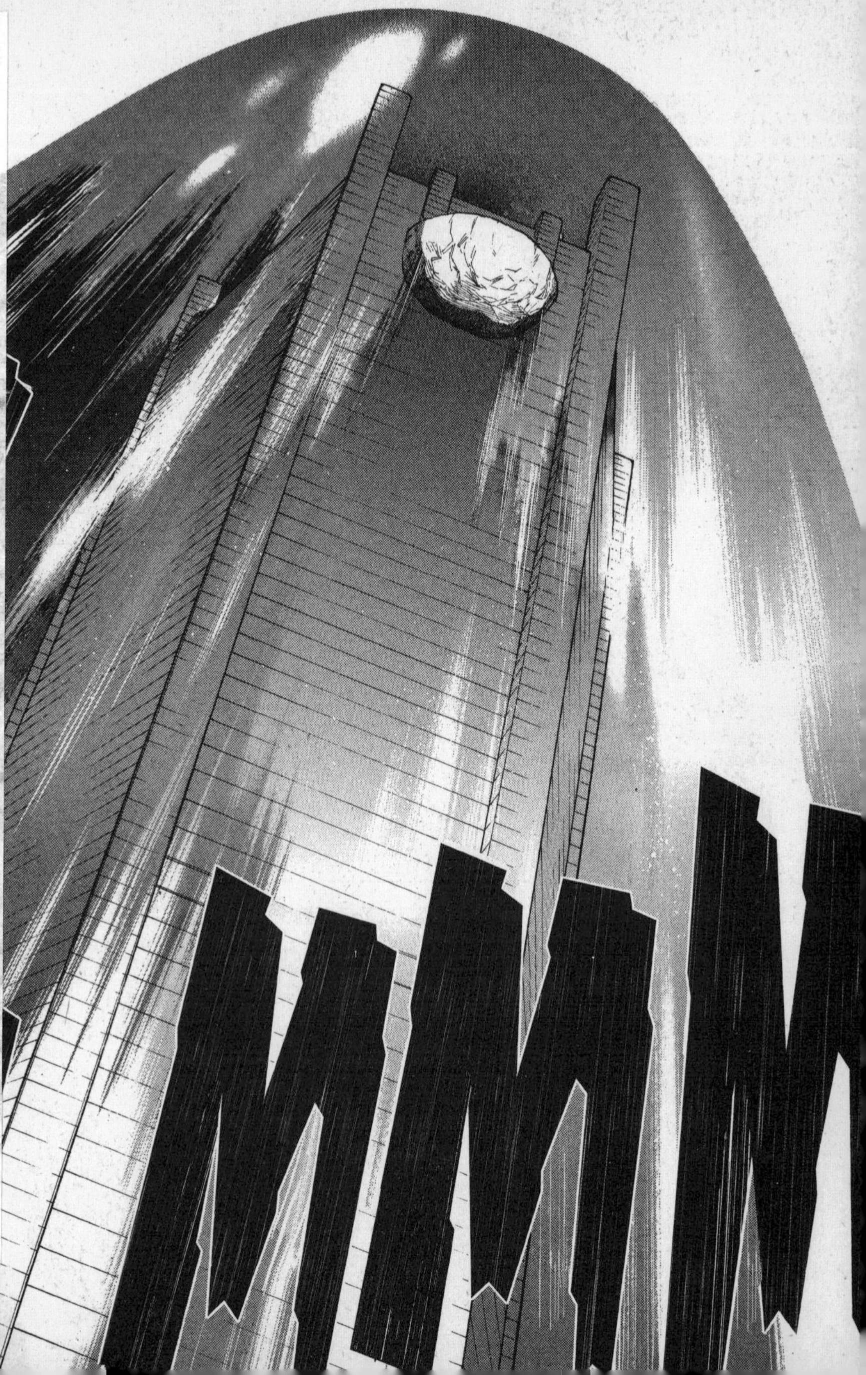
MMM

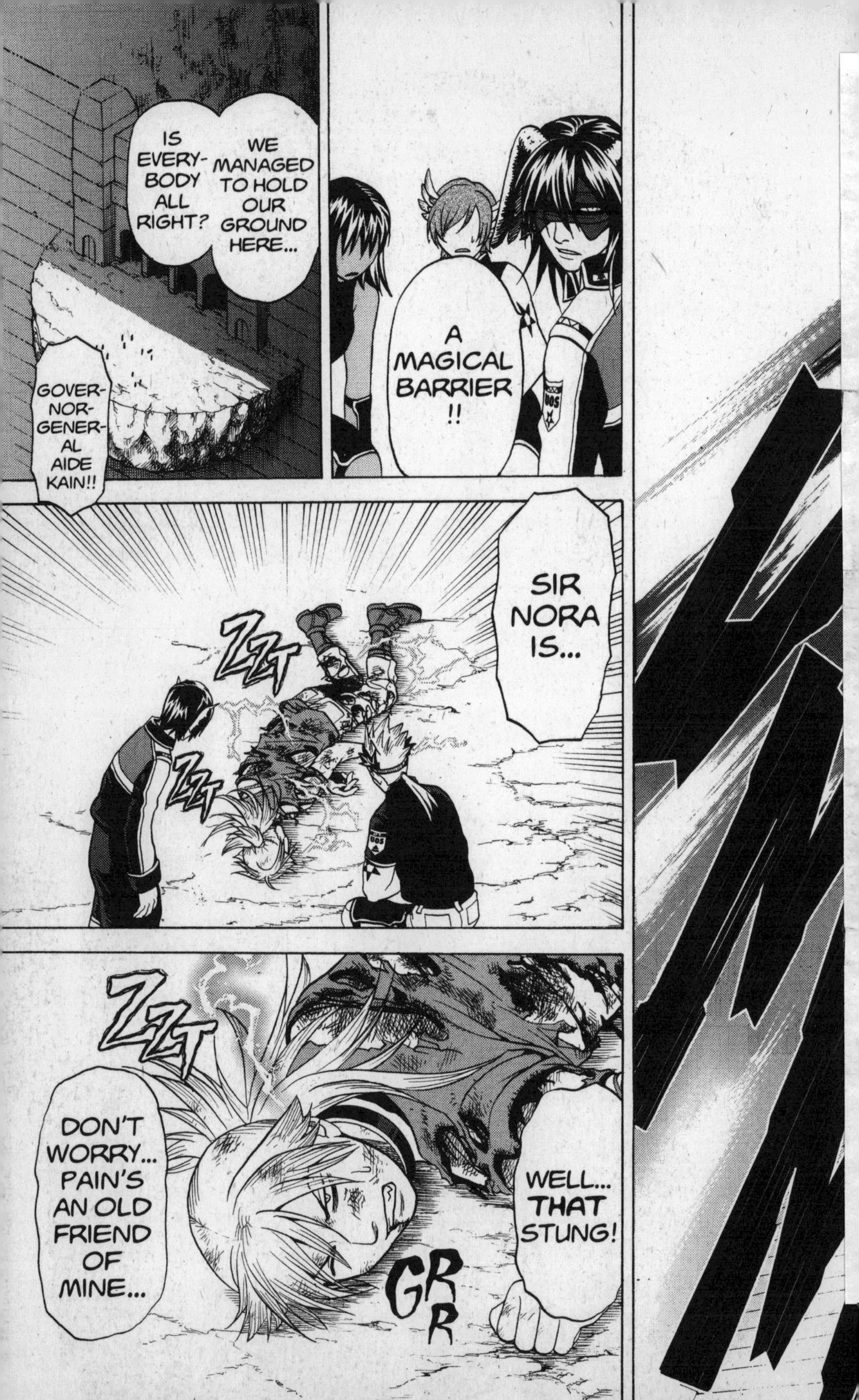
A MAGICAL BARRIER!!
WE MANAGED TO HOLD OUR GROUND HERE...
IS EVERYBODY ALL RIGHT?
GOVER-NOR-GENER-AL AIDE KAIN!!
SIR NORA IS...
ZZZT
ZZT
WELL... THAT STUNG!
ZZZT
DON'T WORRY... PAIN'S AN OLD FRIEND OF MINE...
GRR

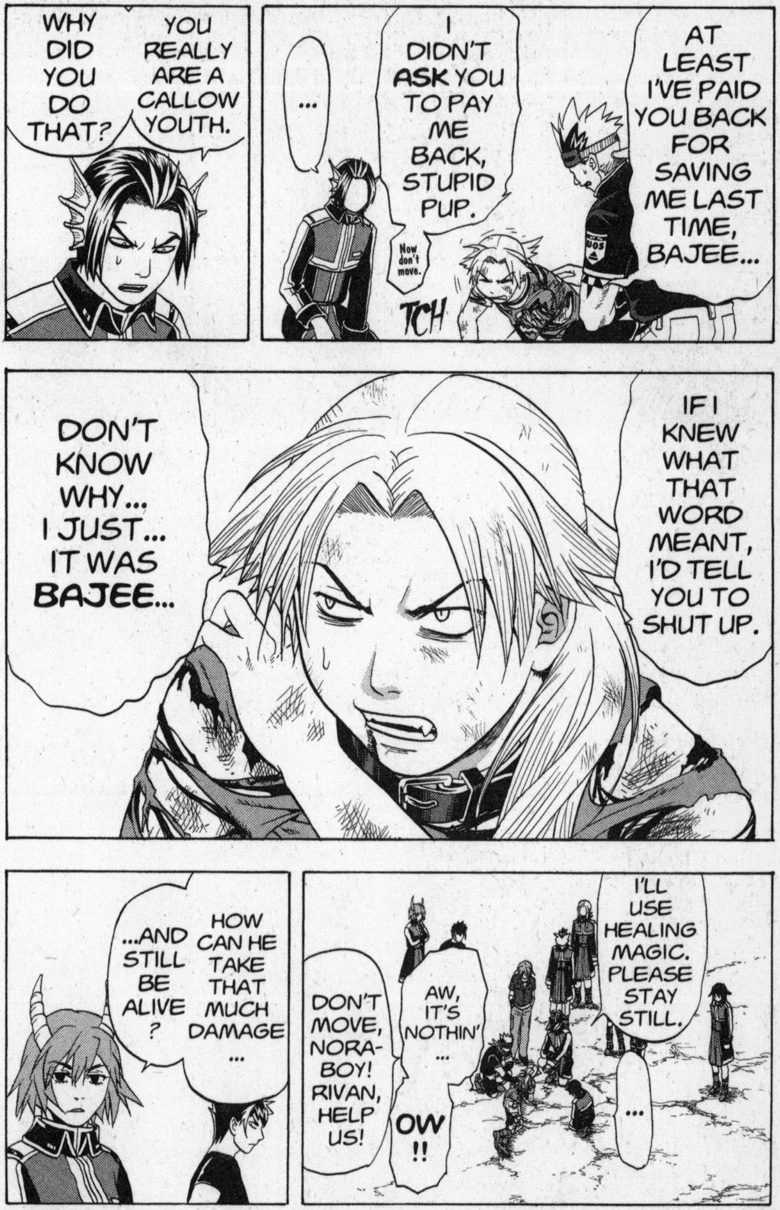
AT LEAST I'VE PAID YOU BACK FOR SAVING ME LAST TIME, BAJEE...
I DIDN'T **ASK** YOU TO PAY ME BACK, STUPID PUP.
...
Now don't move.
TCH
YOU REALLY ARE A CALLOW YOUTH.
WHY DID YOU DO THAT?
IF I KNEW WHAT THAT WORD MEANT, I'D TELL YOU TO SHUT UP.
DON'T KNOW WHY... I JUST... IT WAS **BAJEE**...
I'LL USE HEALING MAGIC. PLEASE STAY STILL.
AW, IT'S NOTHIN'... OW!!
...
DON'T MOVE, NORA-BOY! RIVAN, HELP US!
HOW CAN HE TAKE THAT MUCH DAMAGE...
...AND STILL BE ALIVE?

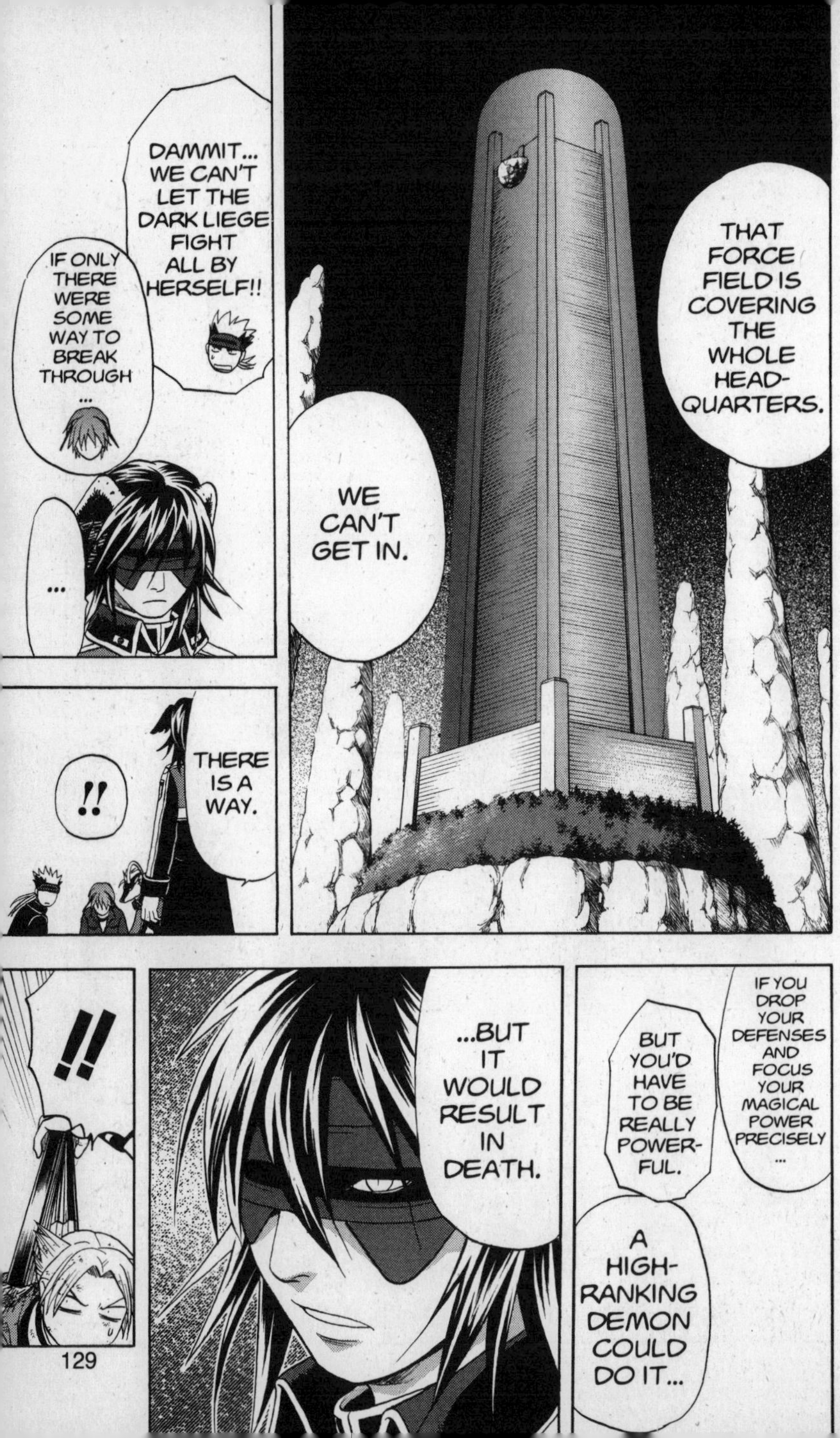
THAT FORCE FIELD IS COVERING THE WHOLE HEAD-QUARTERS.
WE CAN'T GET IN.
DAMMIT... WE CAN'T LET THE DARK LIEGE FIGHT ALL BY HERSELF!!
IF ONLY THERE WERE SOME WAY TO BREAK THROUGH...
...
THERE IS A WAY.
!!
IF YOU DROP YOUR DEFENSES AND FOCUS YOUR MAGICAL POWER PRECISELY...
BUT YOU'D HAVE TO BE REALLY POWER-FUL.
A HIGH-RANKING DEMON COULD DO IT...
...BUT IT WOULD RESULT IN DEATH.
!!

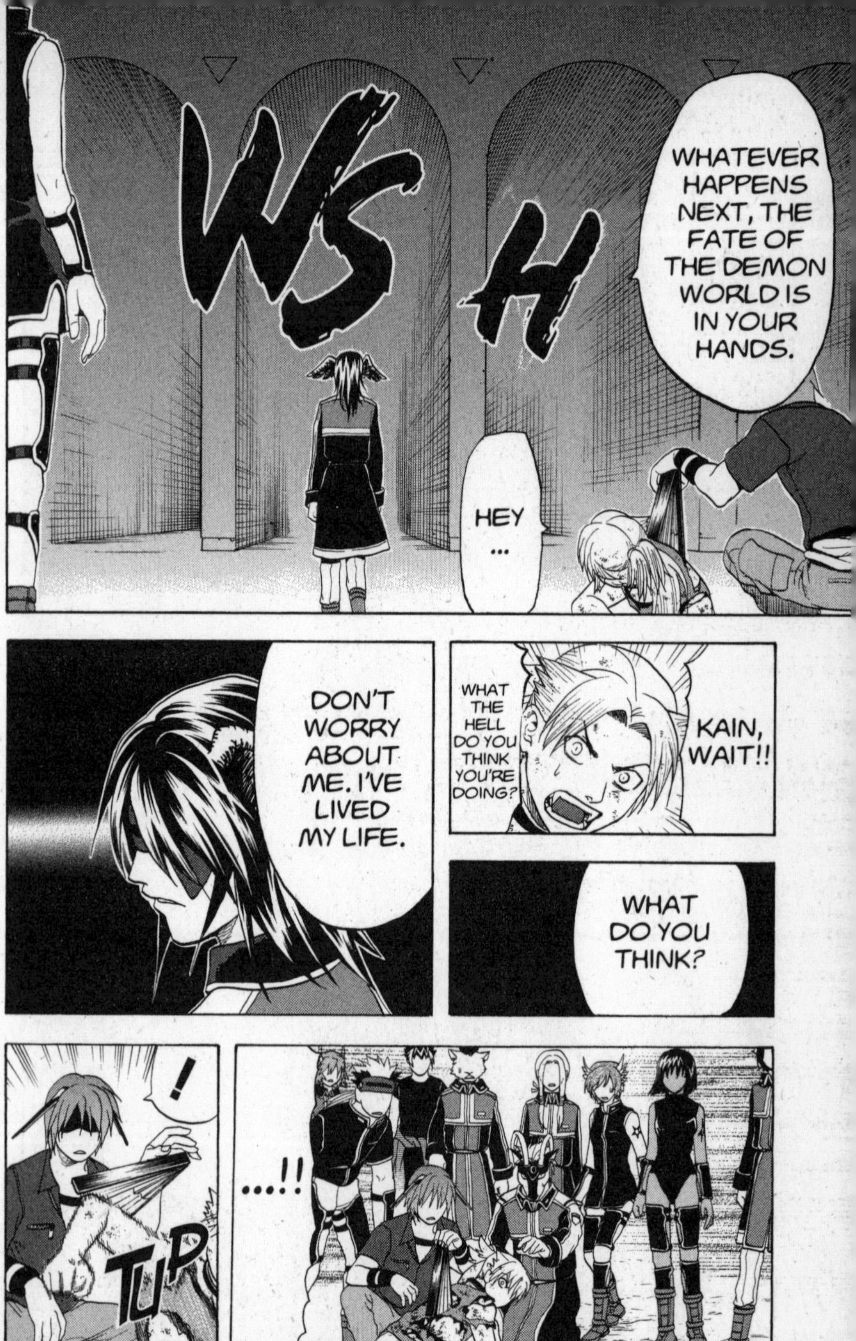
WSH
WHATEVER HAPPENS NEXT, THE FATE OF THE DEMON WORLD IS IN YOUR HANDS.
HEY ...
KAIN, WAIT!!
WHAT THE HELL DO YOU THINK YOU'RE DOING?
WHAT DO YOU THINK?
DON'T WORRY ABOUT ME. I'VE LIVED MY LIFE.
...!!
!
TUP

READ THIS WAY

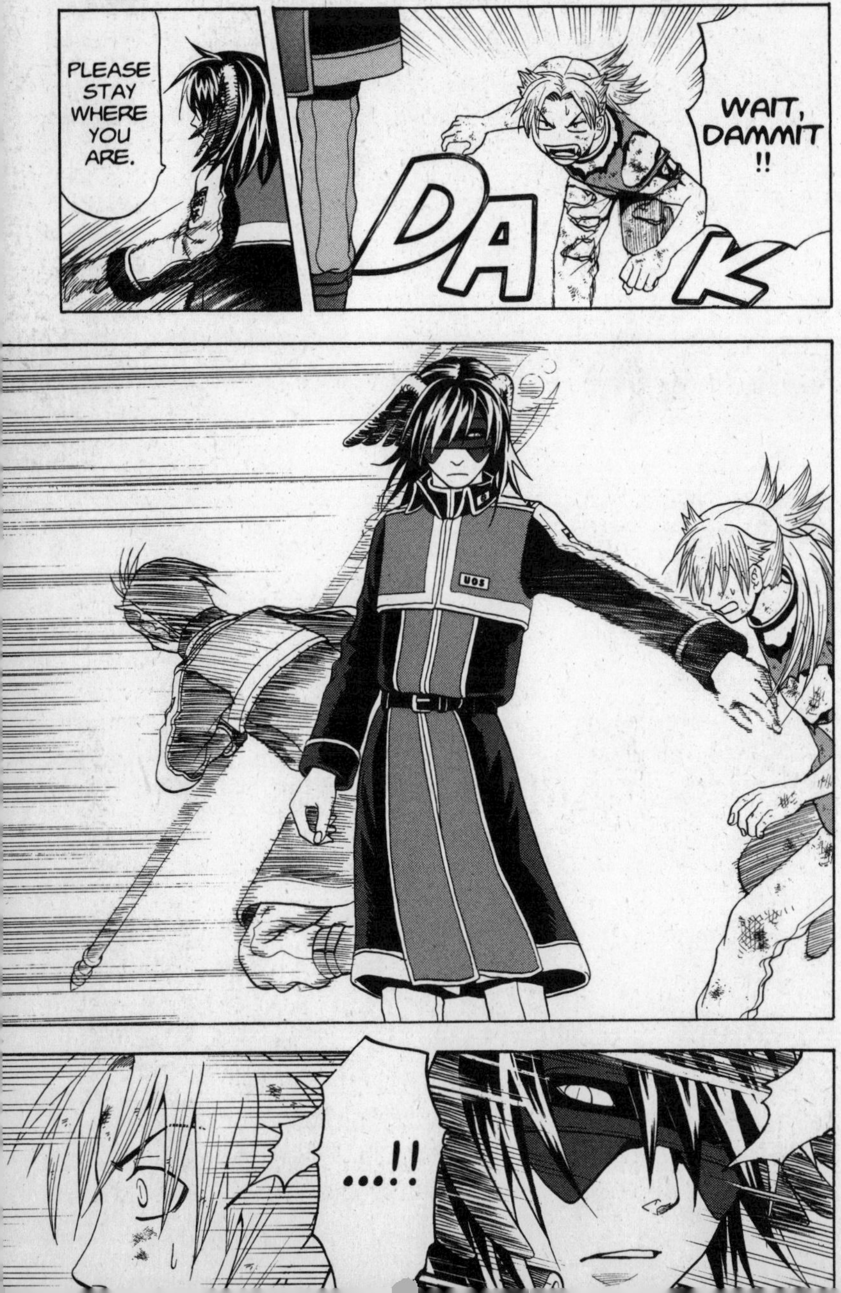
WAIT, DAMMIT!!
DAK
PLEASE STAY WHERE YOU ARE.
UOS
...!!

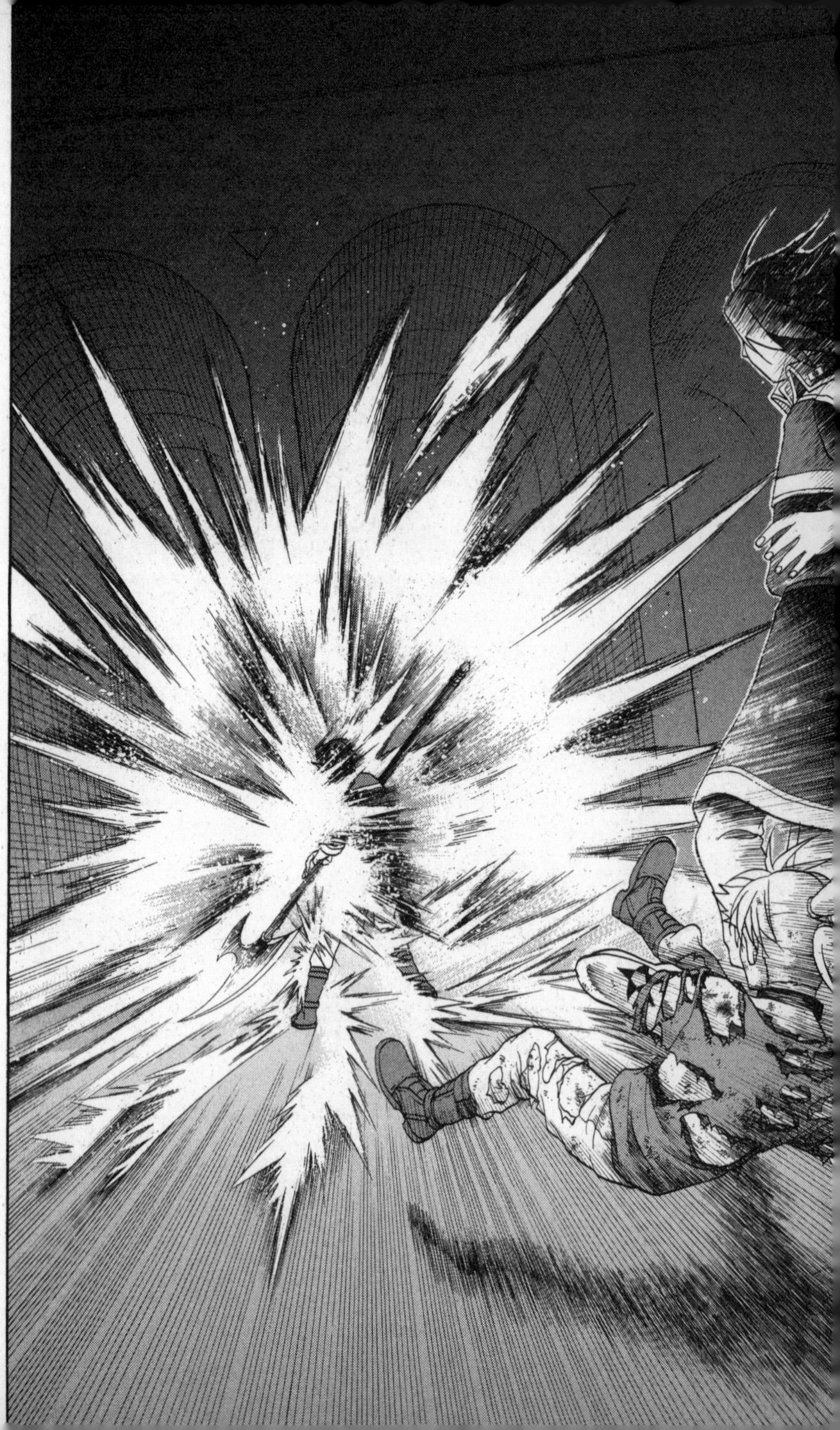

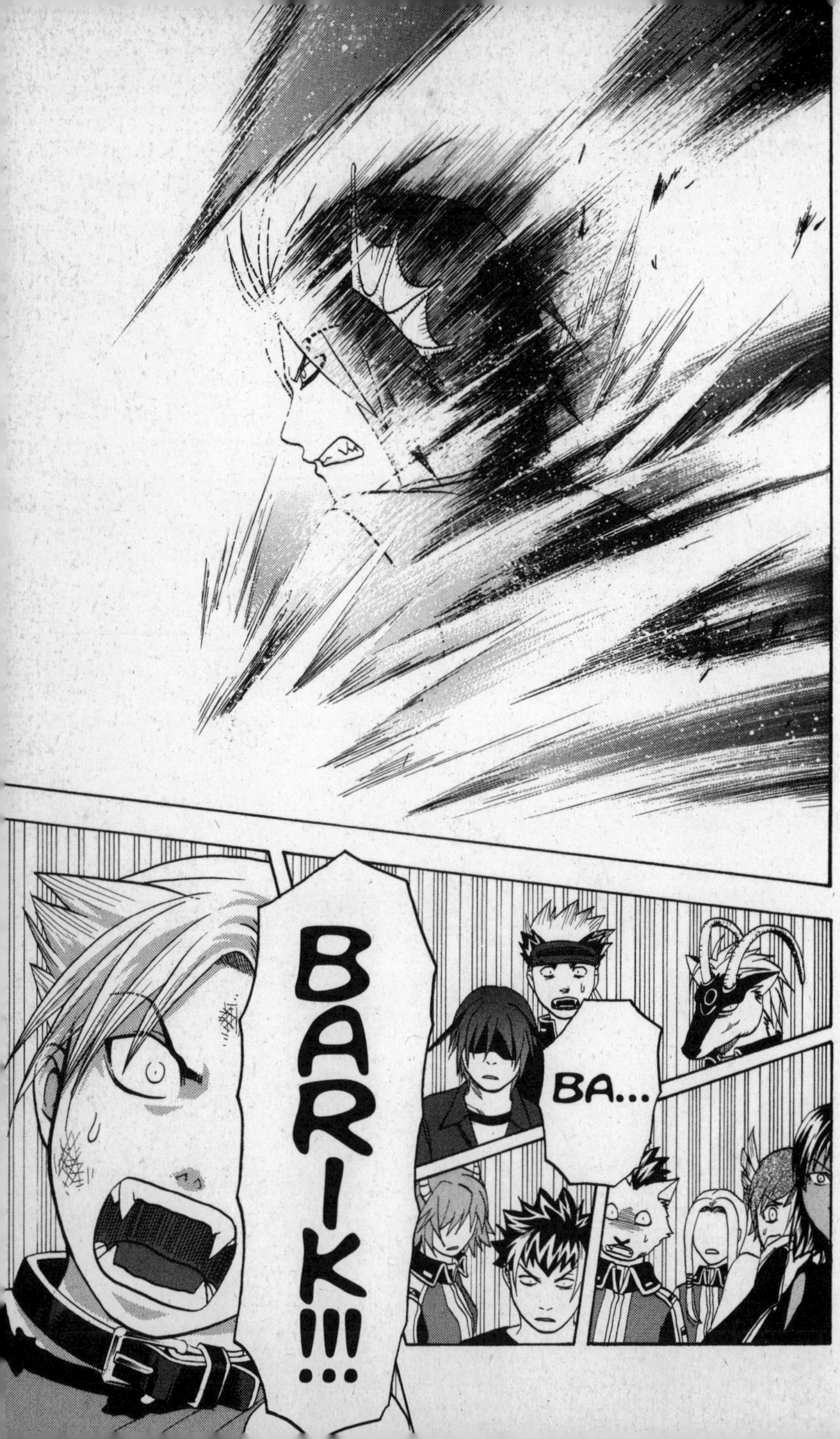
BA...
BARIK!!!

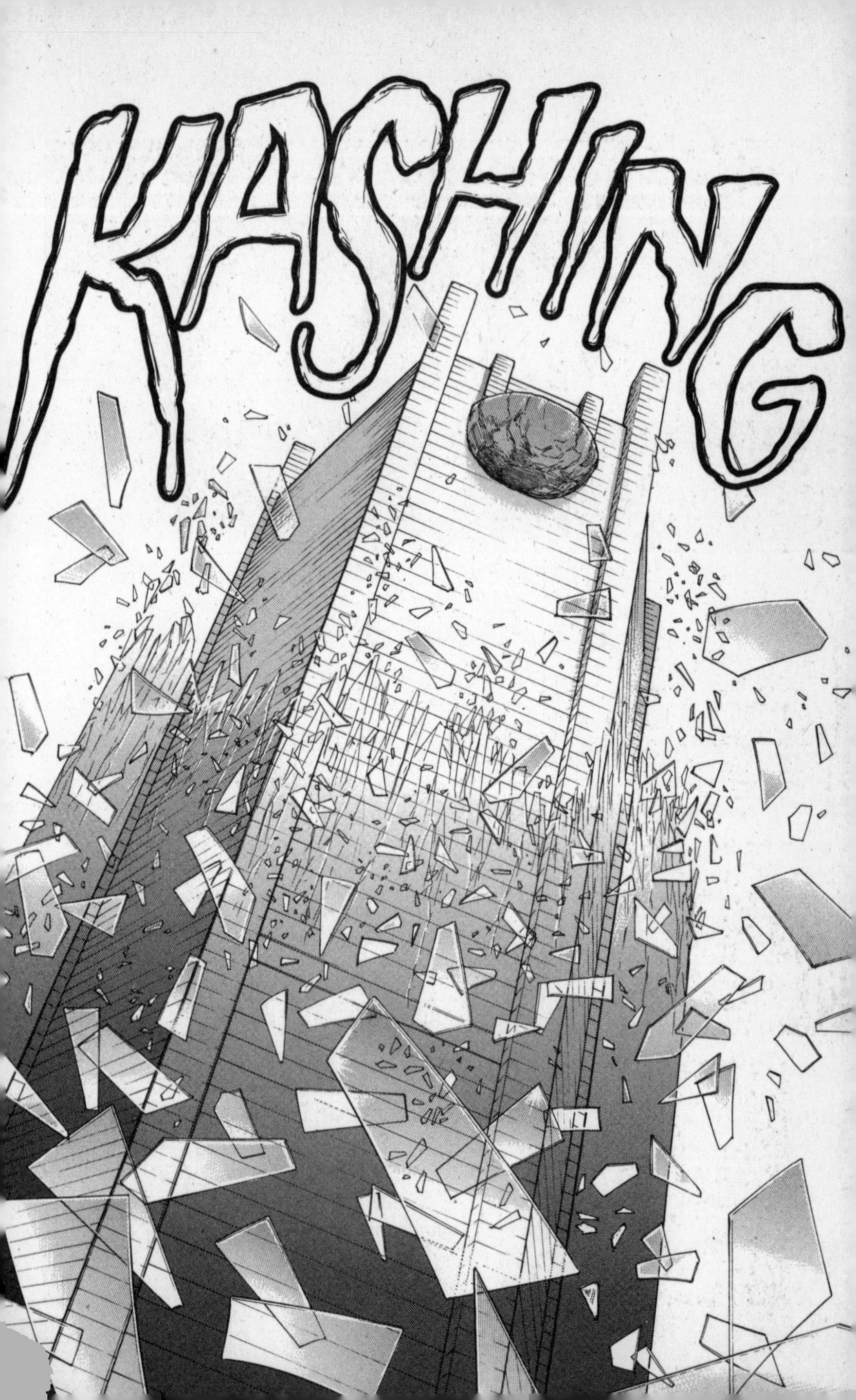
KASHING

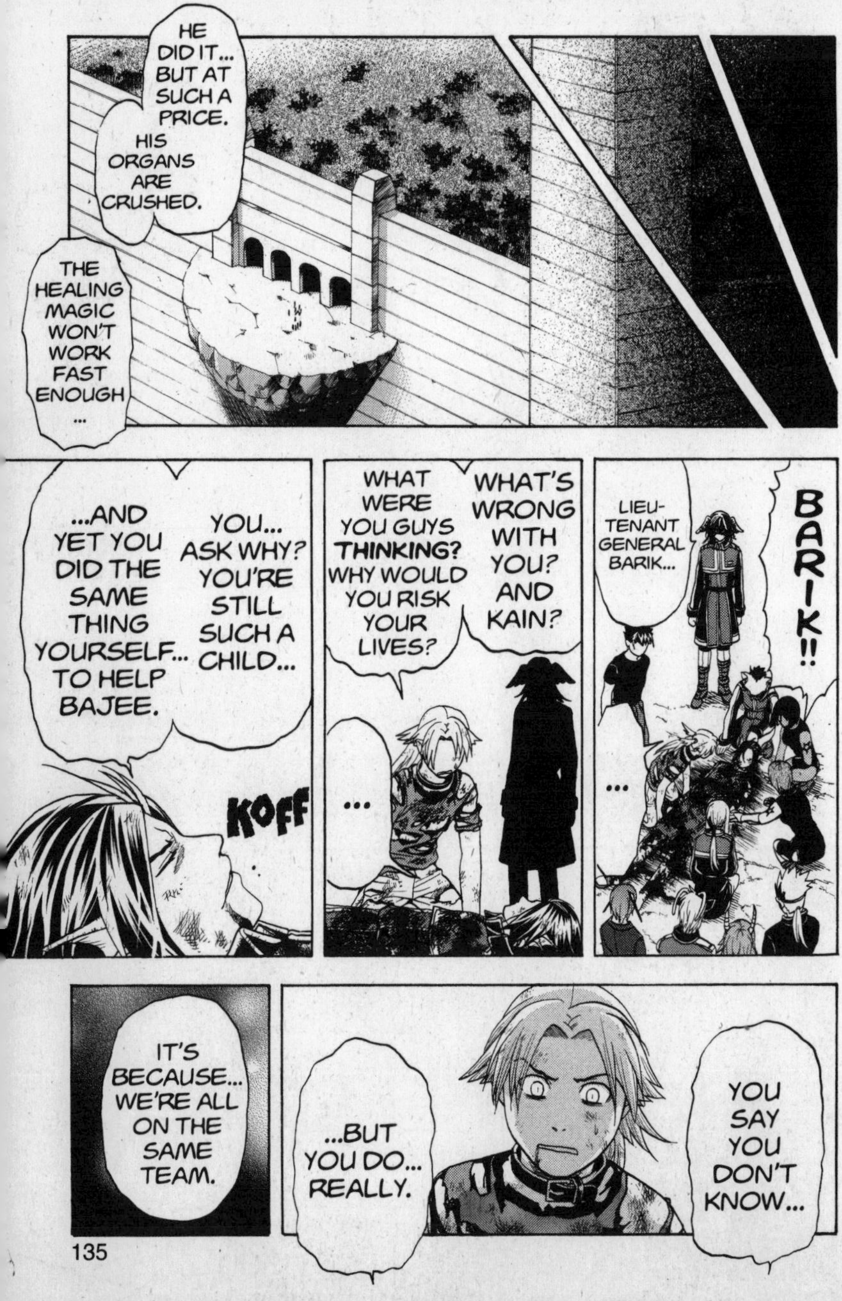
HE DID IT... BUT AT SUCH A PRICE.
HIS ORGANS ARE CRUSHED.
THE HEALING MAGIC WON'T WORK FAST ENOUGH...
BARIK!!
LIEU-TENANT GENERAL BARIK...
...
WHAT'S WRONG WITH YOU? AND KAIN?
WHAT WERE YOU GUYS **THINKING?** WHY WOULD YOU RISK YOUR LIVES?
...
YOU... ASK WHY? YOU'RE STILL SUCH A CHILD...
...AND YET YOU DID THE SAME THING YOURSELF... TO HELP BAJEE.
KOFF
YOU SAY YOU DON'T KNOW...
...BUT YOU DO... REALLY.
IT'S BECAUSE... WE'RE ALL ON THE SAME TEAM.

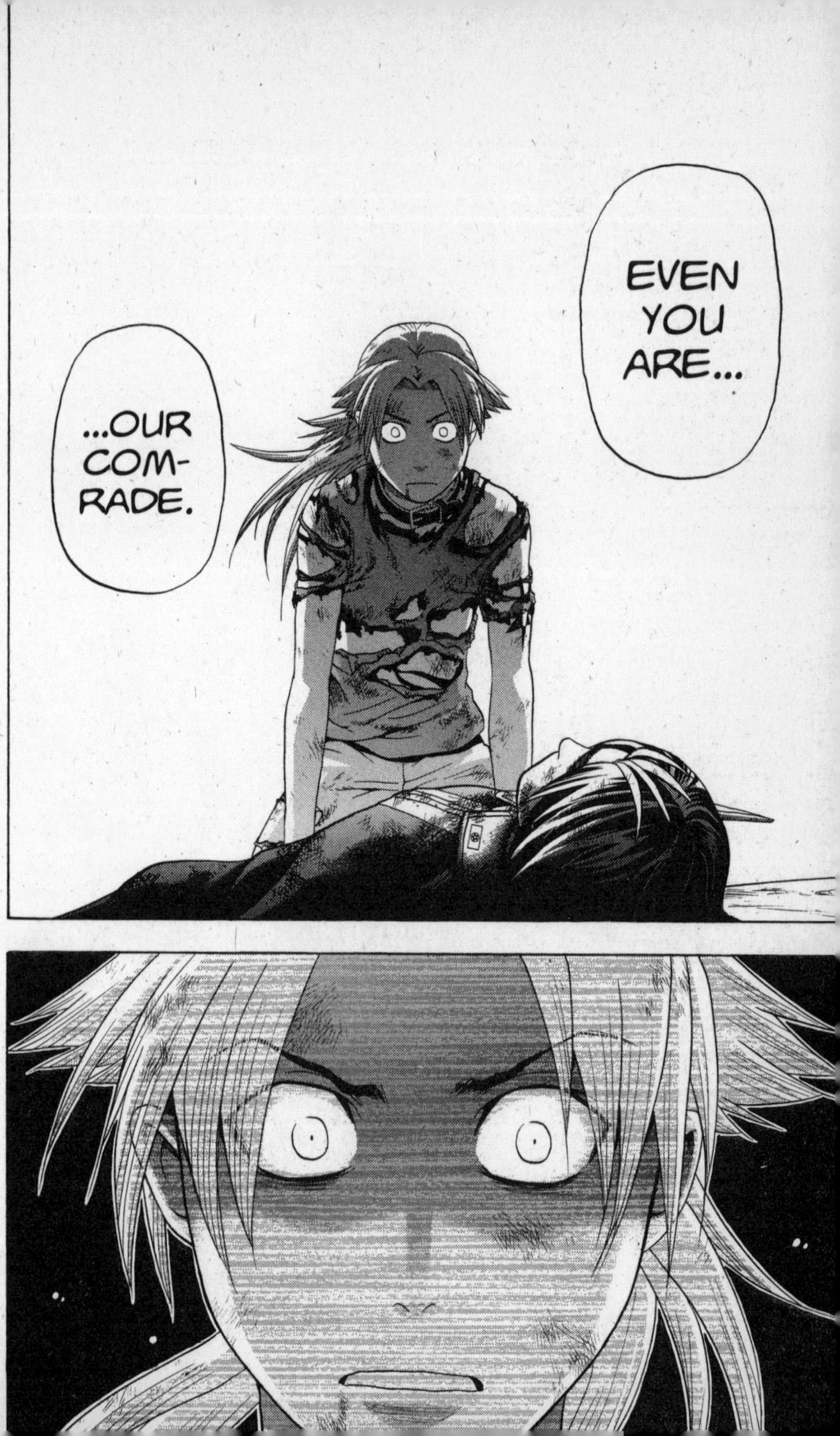
EVEN YOU ARE...
...OUR COM-RADE.

READ THIS WAY

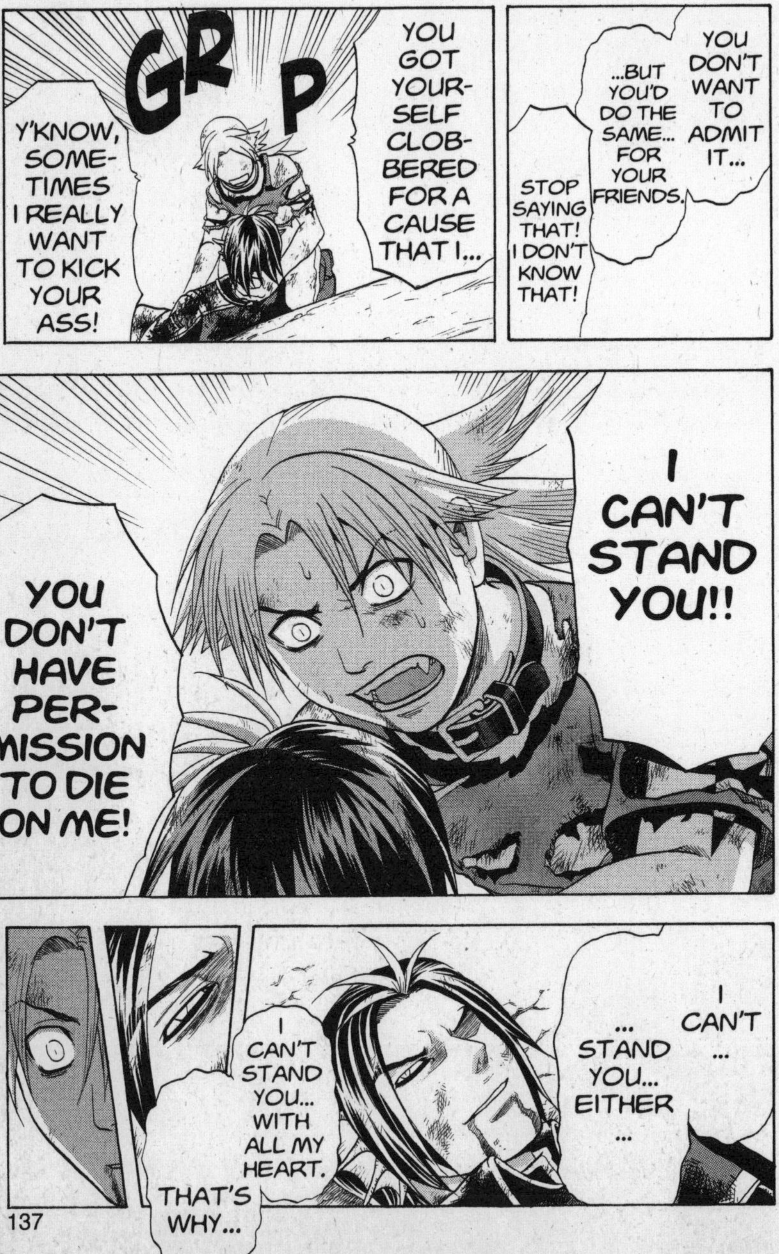
YOU DON'T WANT TO ADMIT IT...
...BUT YOU'D DO THE SAME... FOR YOUR FRIENDS.
STOP SAYING THAT! I DON'T KNOW THAT!
YOU GOT YOURSELF CLOBBERED FOR A CAUSE THAT I...
GRP
Y'KNOW, SOMETIMES I REALLY WANT TO KICK YOUR ASS!
I CAN'T STAND YOU!!
YOU DON'T HAVE PERMISSION TO DIE ON ME!
I CAN'T...
...STAND YOU... EITHER...
I CAN'T STAND YOU... WITH ALL MY HEART.
THAT'S WHY...

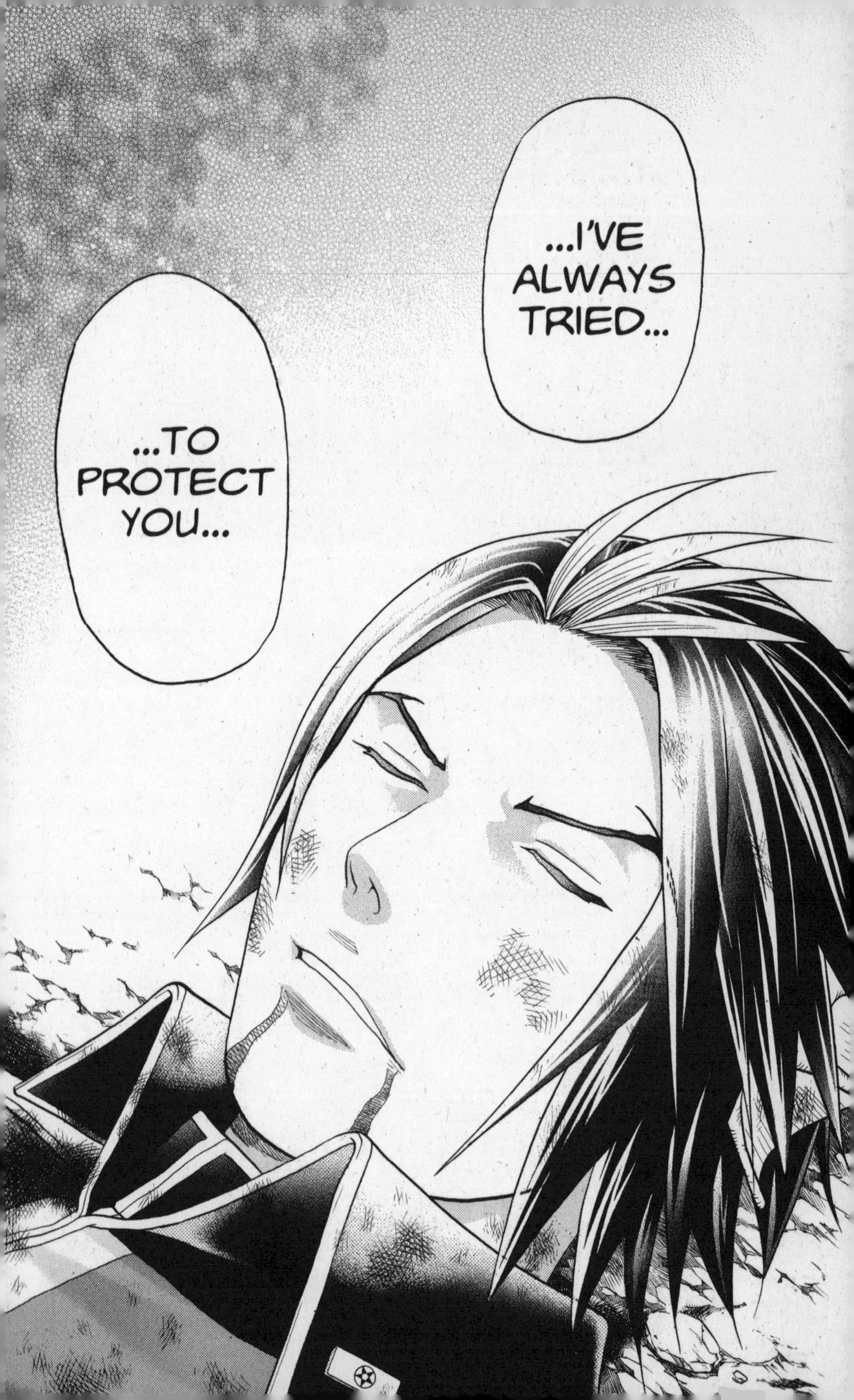
...I'VE ALWAYS TRIED...
...TO PROTECT YOU...

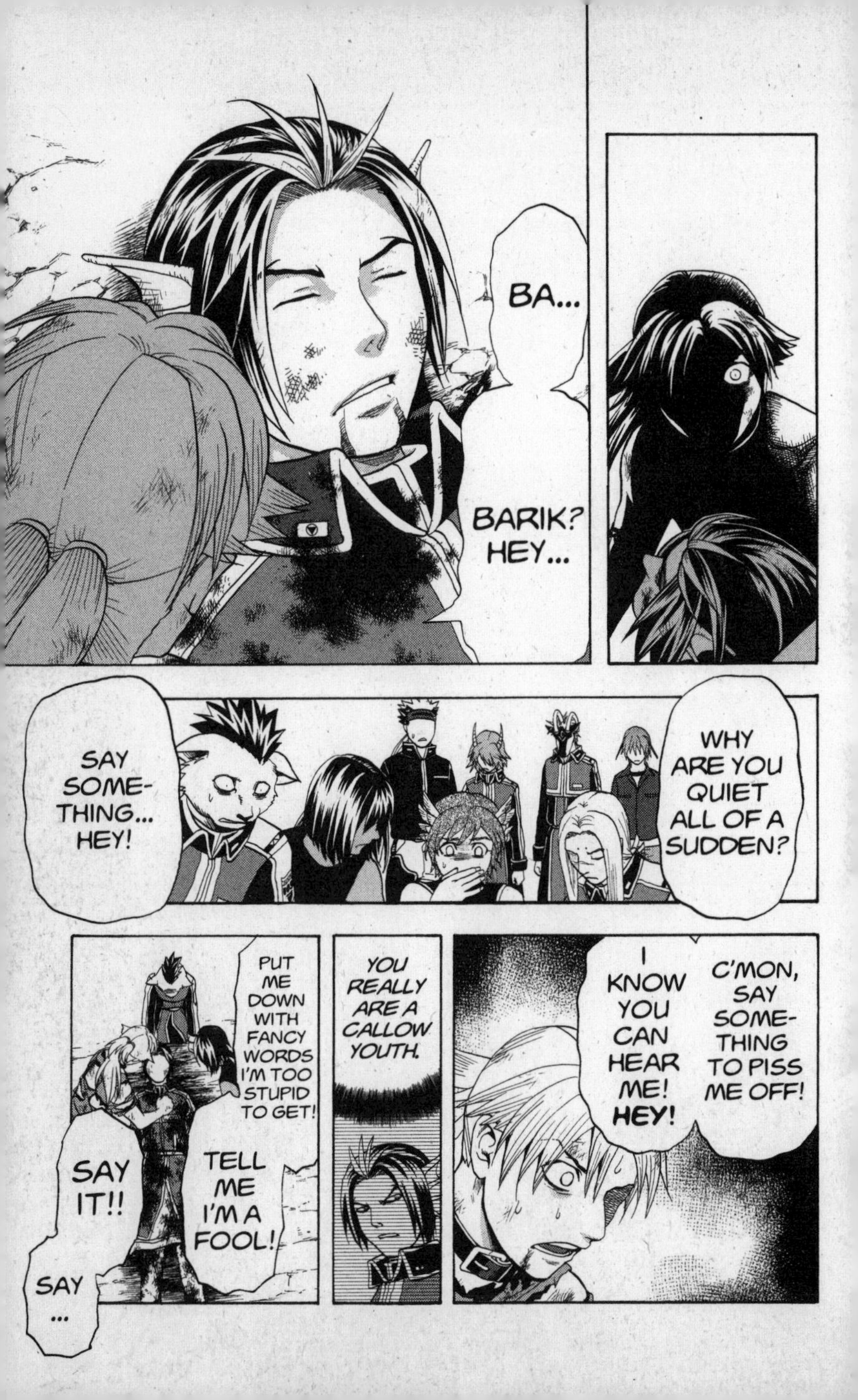
BA...
BARIK? HEY...
WHY ARE YOU QUIET ALL OF A SUDDEN?
SAY SOME-THING... HEY!
C'MON, SAY SOME-THING TO PISS ME OFF!
I KNOW YOU CAN HEAR ME! HEY!
YOU REALLY ARE A CALLOW YOUTH.
PUT ME DOWN WITH FANCY WORDS I'M TOO STUPID TO GET!
TELL ME I'M A FOOL!
SAY IT!!
SAY ...

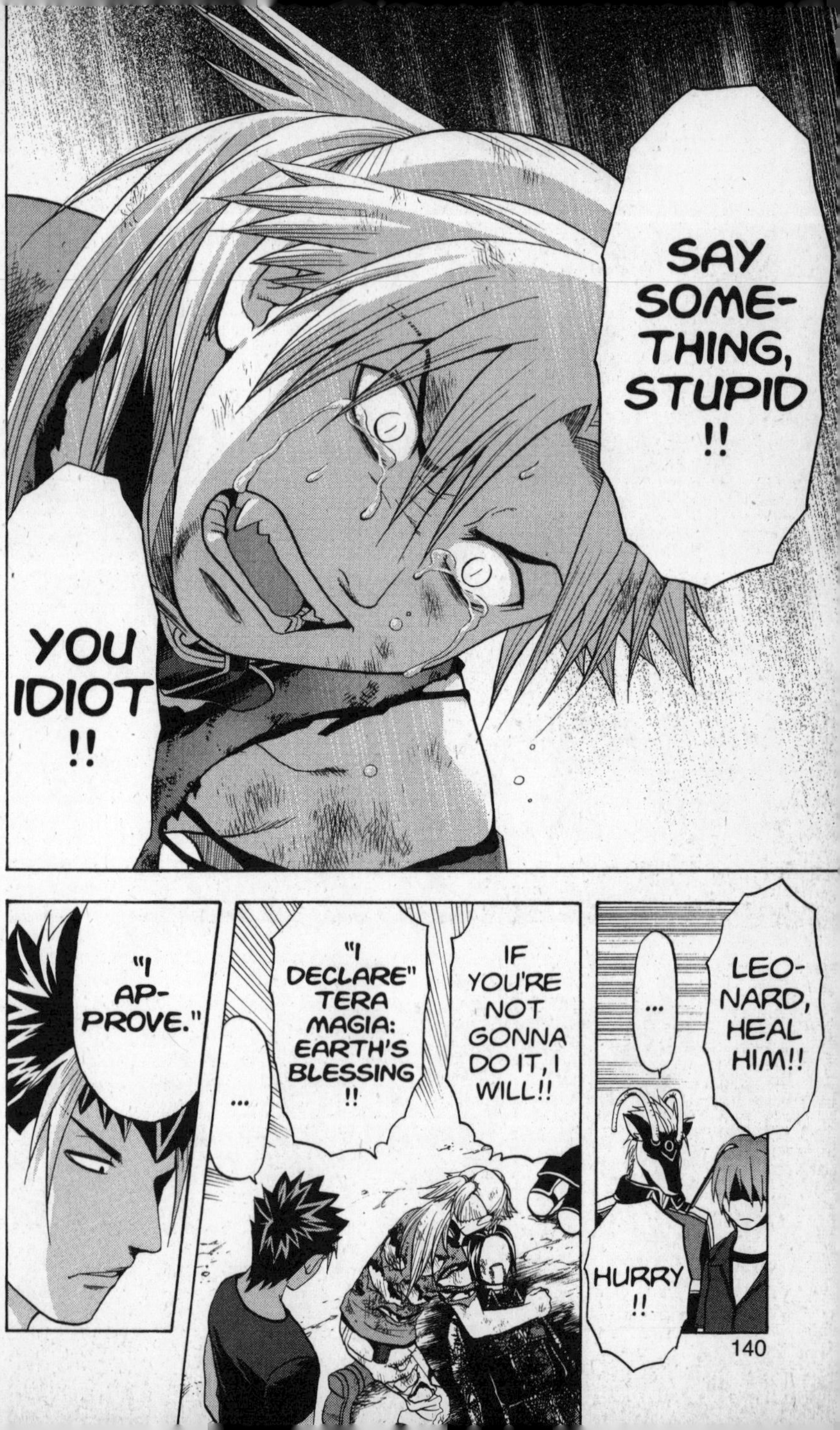
SAY SOME-THING, STUPID!!
YOU IDIOT!!
LEO-NARD, HEAL HIM!!
...
HURRY!!
IF YOU'RE NOT GONNA DO IT, I WILL!!
"I DECLARE" TERA MAGIA: EARTH'S BLESSING!!
...
"I AP-PROVE."

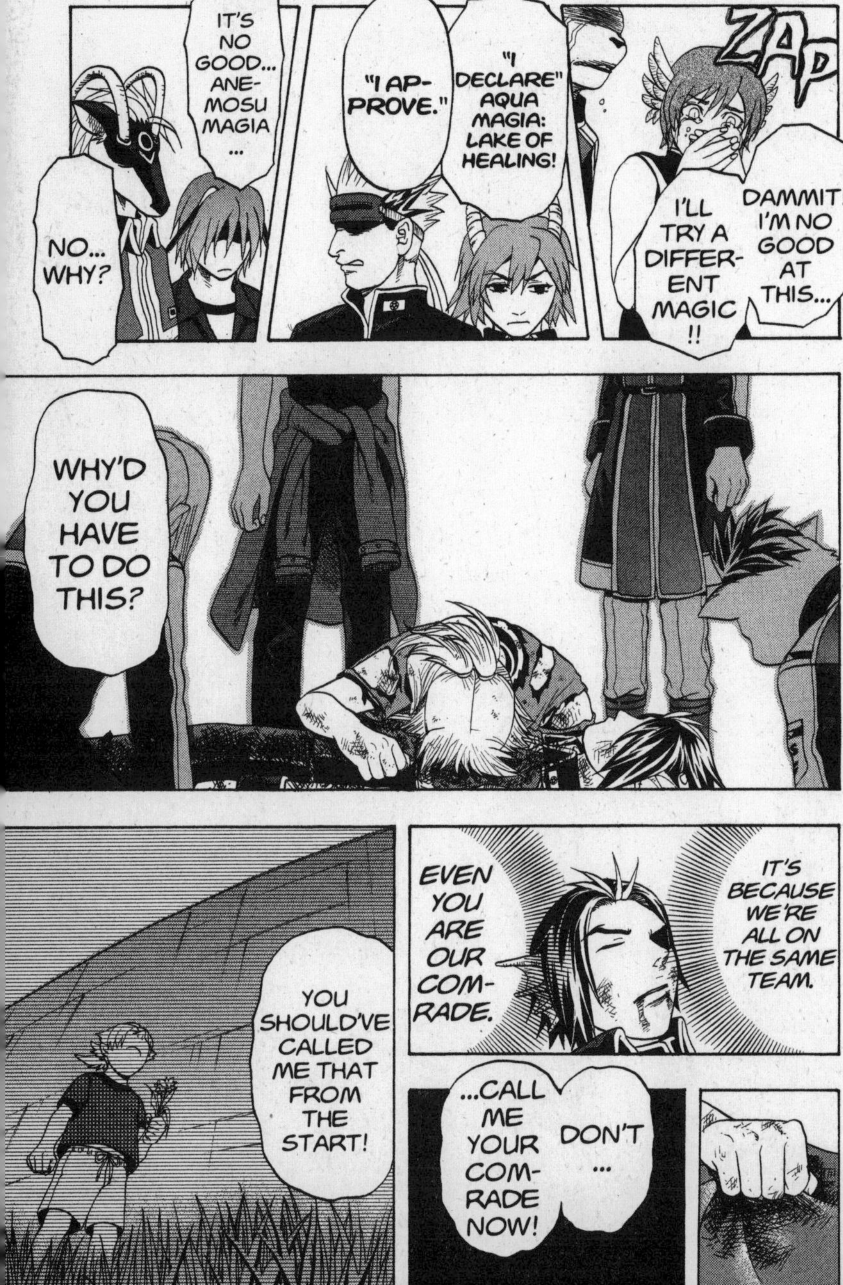
ZAP
DAMMIT! I'M NO GOOD AT THIS...
I'LL TRY A DIFFERENT MAGIC!!
"I DECLARE" AQUA MAGIA: LAKE OF HEALING!
"I APPROVE."
IT'S NO GOOD... ANEMOSU MAGIA...
NO... WHY?
WHY'D YOU HAVE TO DO THIS?
IT'S BECAUSE WE'RE ALL ON THE SAME TEAM.
EVEN YOU ARE OUR COMRADE.
DON'T...
...CALL ME YOUR COMRADE NOW!
YOU SHOULD'VE CALLED ME THAT FROM THE START!

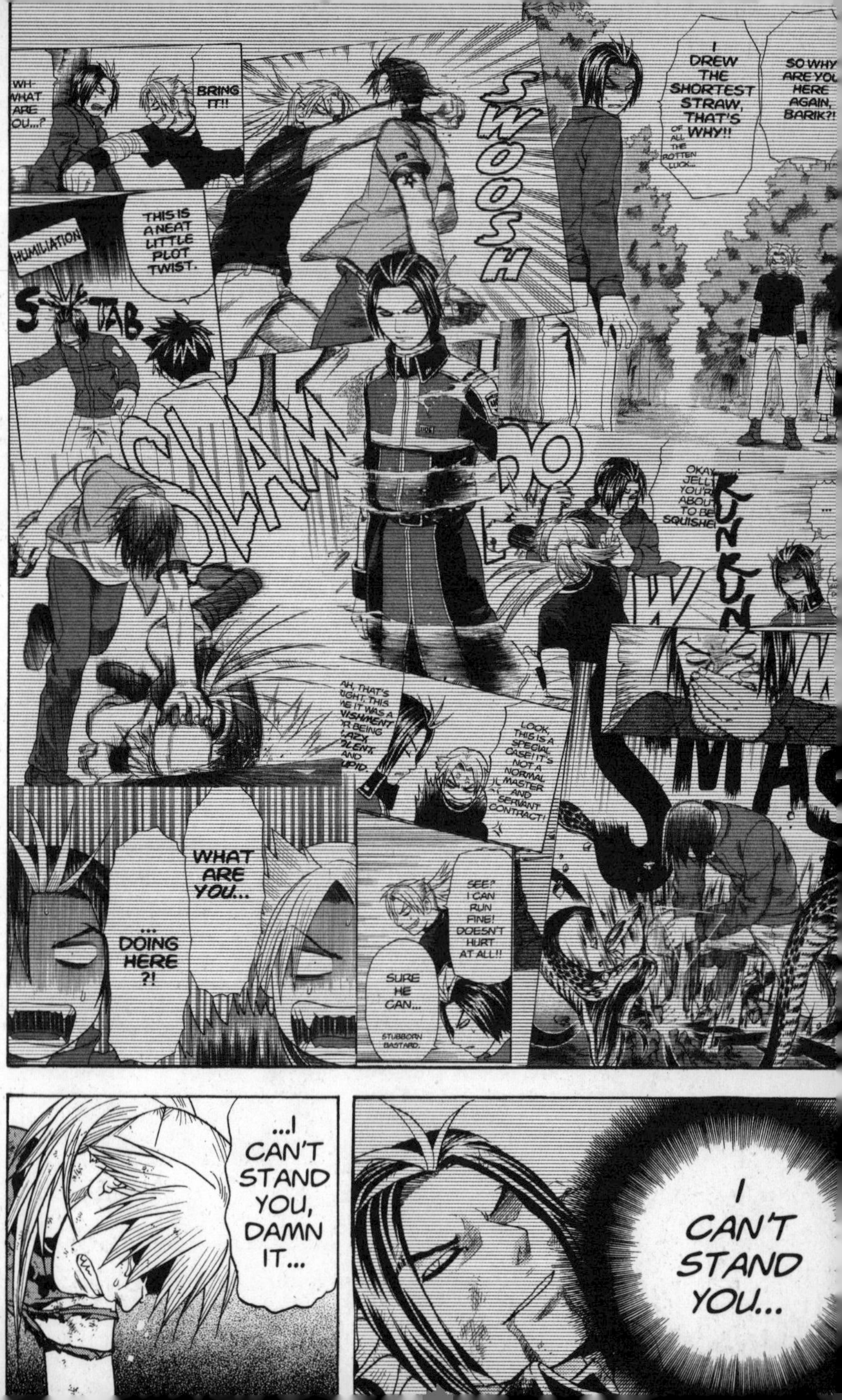
SO WHY ARE YOU HERE AGAIN, BARIK?!
I DREW THE SHORTEST STRAW, THAT'S WHY!!
OF ALL THE ROTTEN LUCK...
SWOOSH
BRING IT!!
WH-WHAT ARE OU...?
THIS IS A NEAT LITTLE PLOT TWIST.
HUMILIATION
S-TAB
SLAM
...
KUNKUN
SMAS
LOOK, THIS IS A SPECIAL CASE!! IT'S NOT A NORMAL MASTER AND SERVANT CONTRACT!
SEE? I CAN RUN FINE! DOESN'T HURT AT ALL!!
SURE HE CAN...
STUBBORN BASTARD.
WHAT ARE YOU...
... DOING HERE ?!
I CAN'T STAND YOU...
...I CAN'T STAND YOU, DAMN IT...

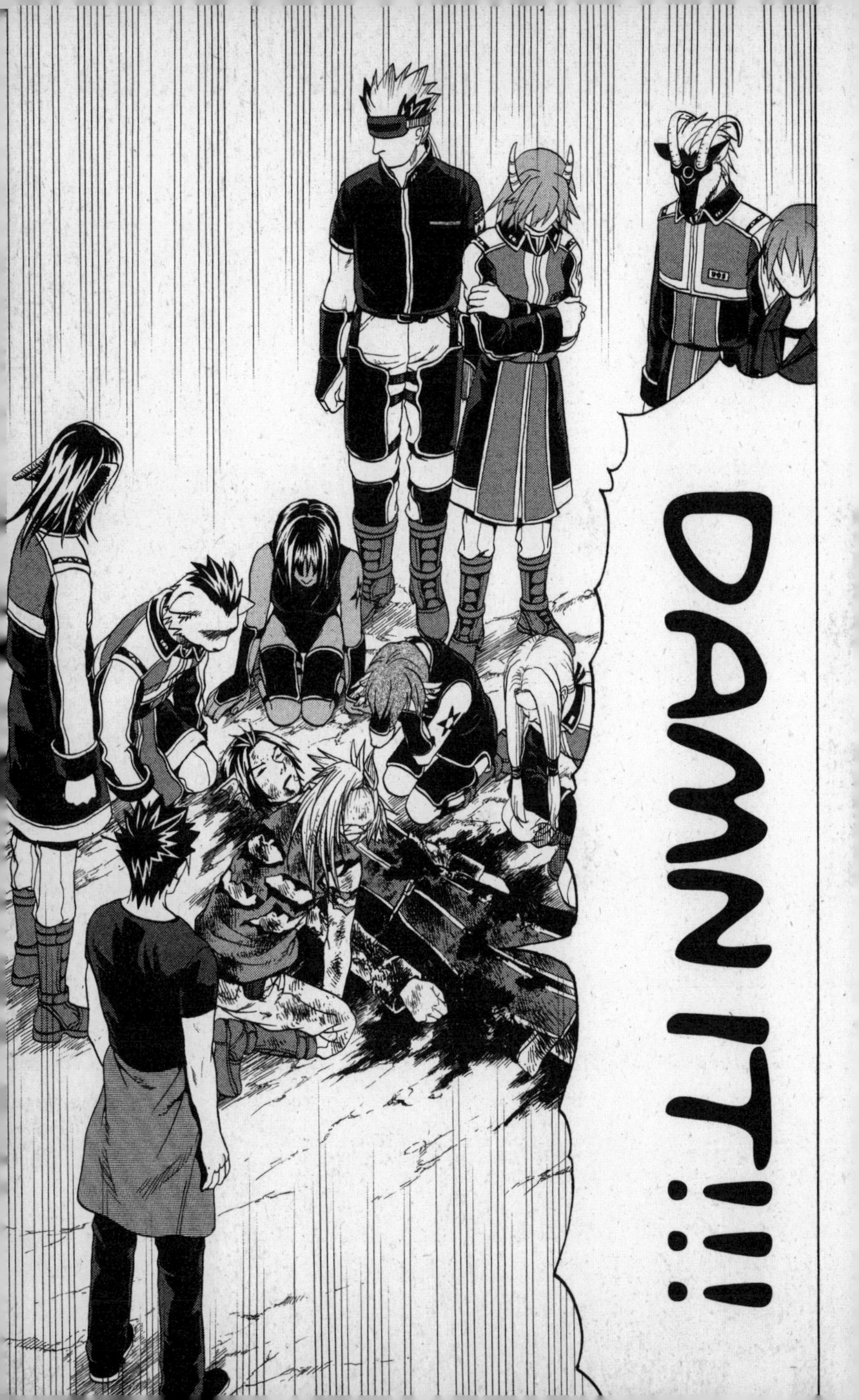
DAMN IT!!!

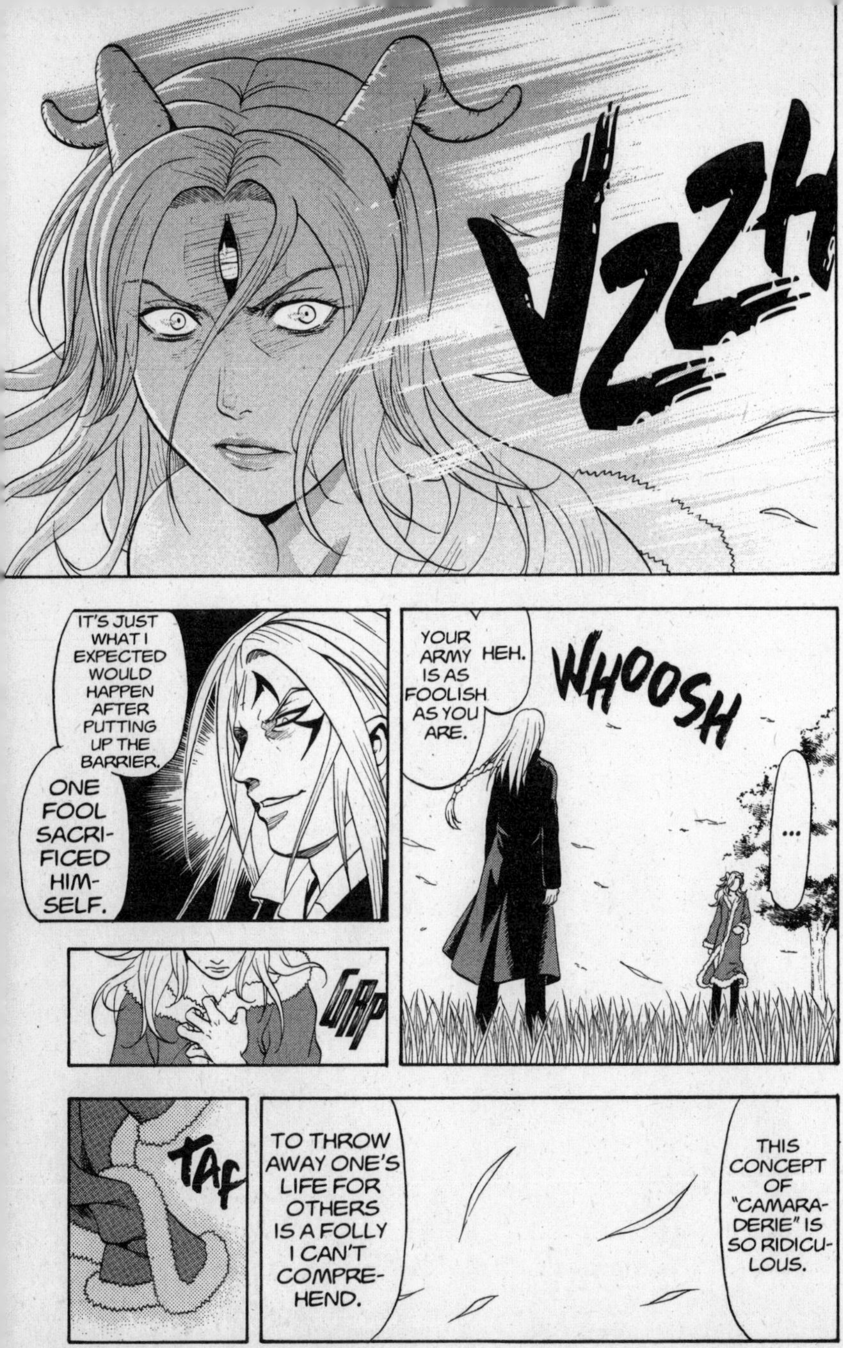
VZZH
WHOOSH
HEH.
YOUR ARMY IS AS FOOLISH AS YOU ARE.
...
IT'S JUST WHAT I EXPECTED WOULD HAPPEN AFTER PUTTING UP THE BARRIER.
ONE FOOL SACRIFICED HIMSELF.
GRIP
THIS CONCEPT OF "CAMARADERIE" IS SO RIDICULOUS.
TO THROW AWAY ONE'S LIFE FOR OTHERS IS A FOLLY I CAN'T COMPREHEND.
TAF

Story 24: Memories

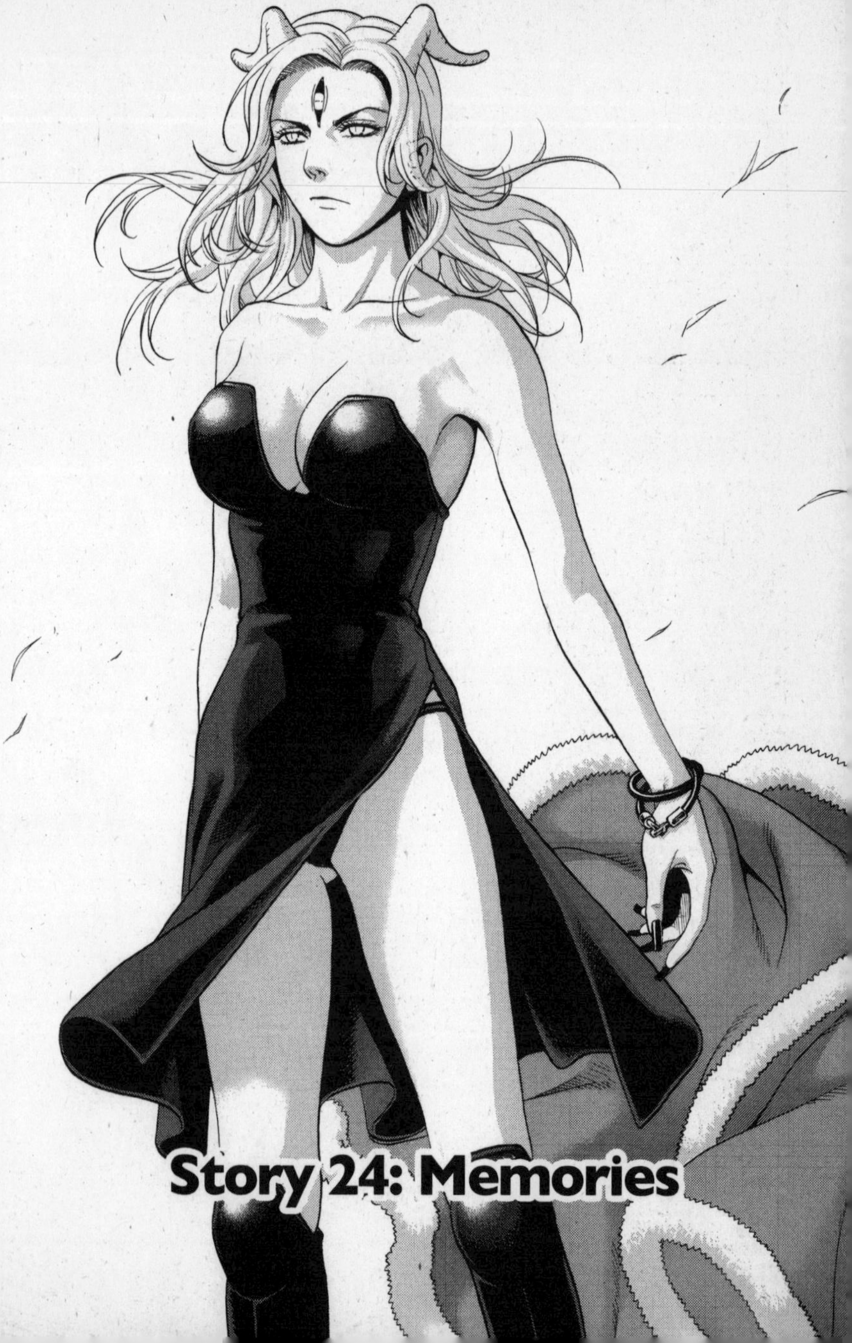

Story 24: Memories

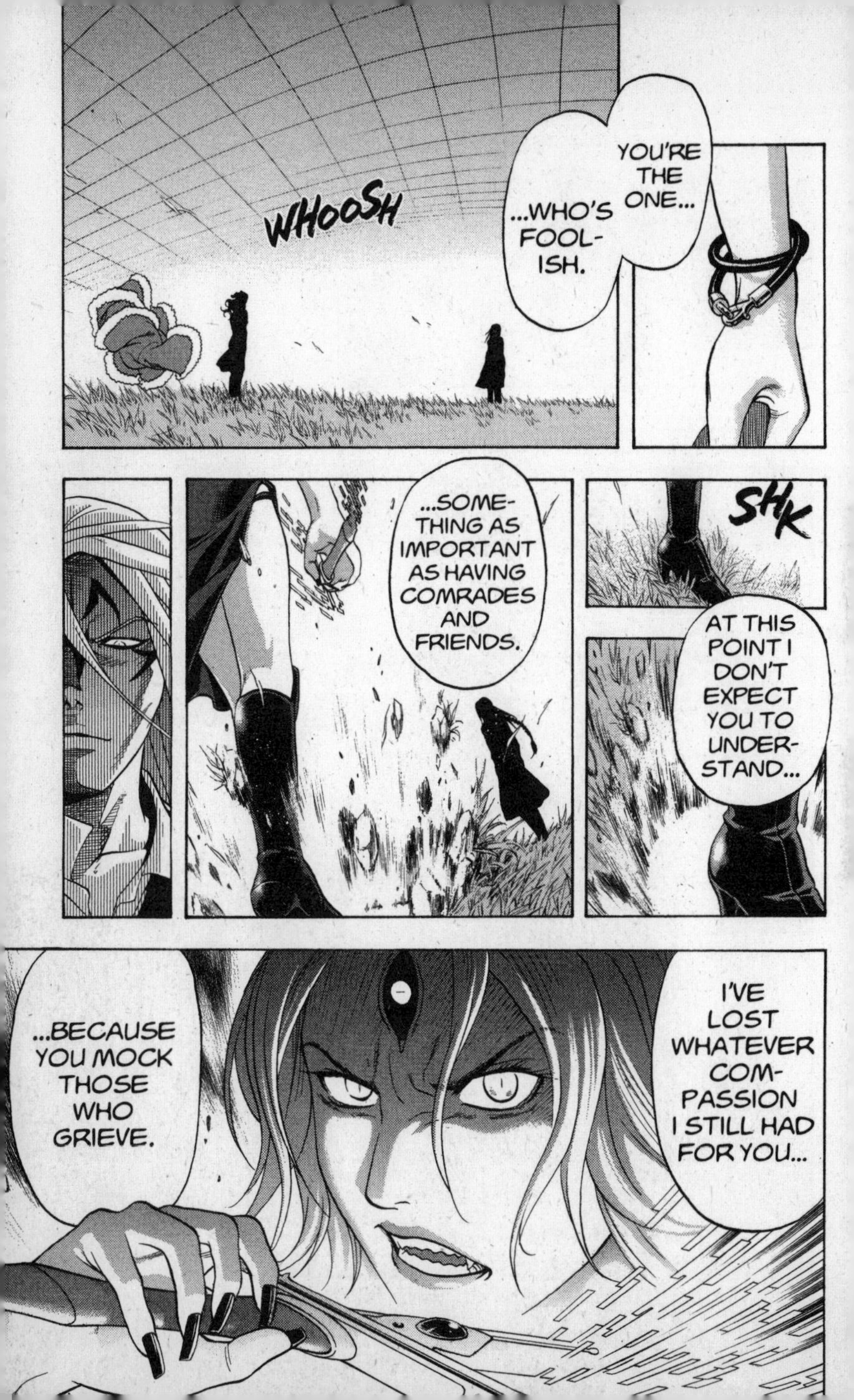

YOU'RE THE ONE... ...WHO'S FOOL-ISH.
WHOOSH
SHK
AT THIS POINT I DON'T EXPECT YOU TO UNDER-STAND...
...SOME-THING AS IMPORTANT AS HAVING COMRADES AND FRIENDS.
I'VE LOST WHATEVER COM-PASSION I STILL HAD FOR YOU...
...BECAUSE YOU MOCK THOSE WHO GRIEVE.

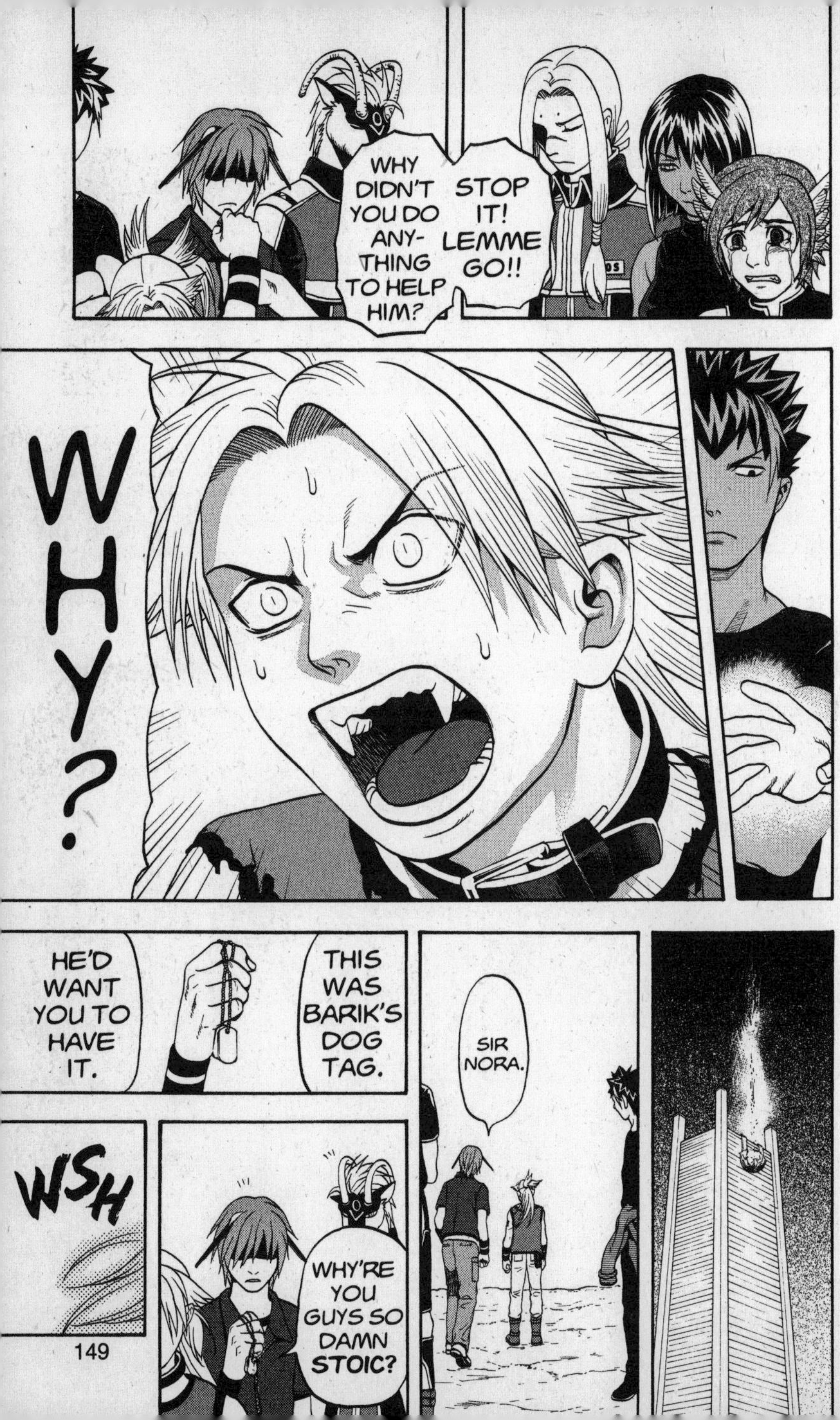
STOP IT! LEMME GO!!
WHY DIDN'T YOU DO ANYTHING TO HELP HIM?
WHY?
SIR NORA.
THIS WAS BARIK'S DOG TAG.
HE'D WANT YOU TO HAVE IT.
WHY'RE YOU GUYS SO DAMN STOIC?
WSH

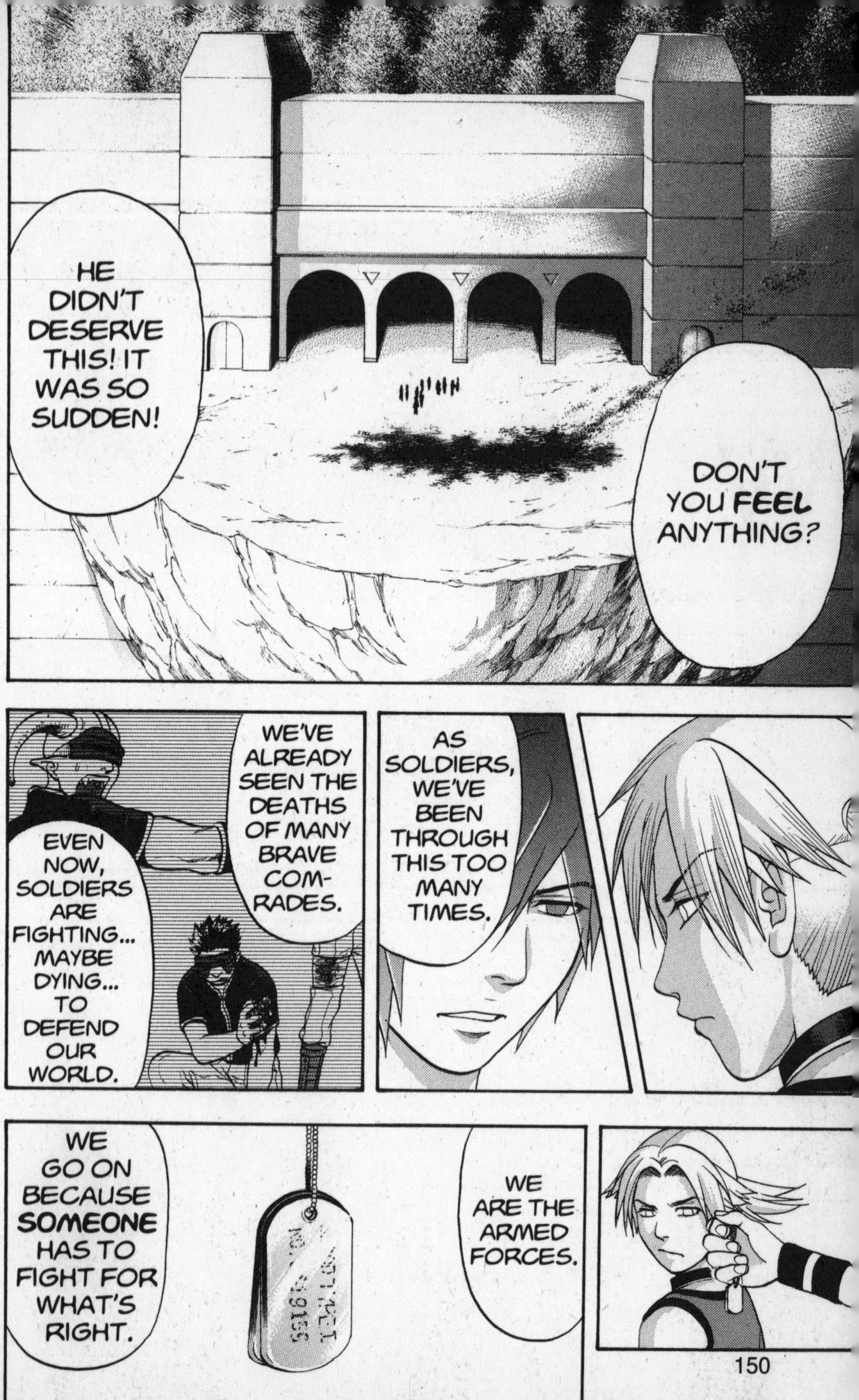
HE DIDN'T DESERVE THIS! IT WAS SO SUDDEN!
DON'T YOU **FEEL** ANYTHING?
AS SOLDIERS, WE'VE BEEN THROUGH THIS TOO MANY TIMES.
WE'VE ALREADY SEEN THE DEATHS OF MANY BRAVE COM-RADES.
EVEN NOW, SOLDIERS ARE FIGHTING... MAYBE DYING... TO DEFEND OUR WORLD.
WE ARE THE ARMED FORCES.
WE GO ON BECAUSE **SOMEONE** HAS TO FIGHT FOR WHAT'S RIGHT.

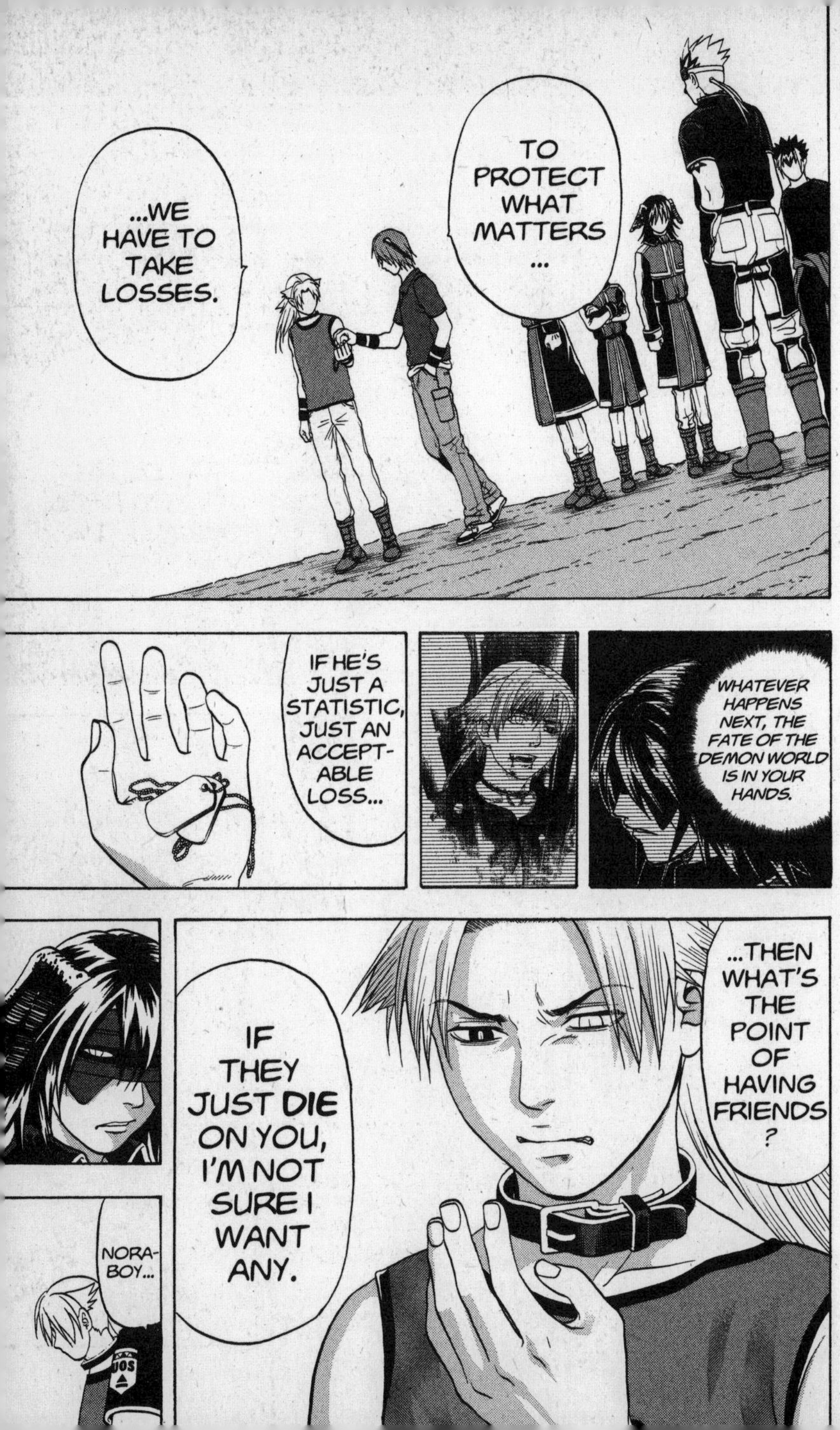
TO PROTECT WHAT MATTERS...
...WE HAVE TO TAKE LOSSES.
WHATEVER HAPPENS NEXT, THE FATE OF THE DEMON WORLD IS IN YOUR HANDS.
IF HE'S JUST A STATISTIC, JUST AN ACCEPT-ABLE LOSS...
...THEN WHAT'S THE POINT OF HAVING FRIENDS?
IF THEY JUST DIE ON YOU, I'M NOT SURE I WANT ANY.
NORA-BOY...
UOS

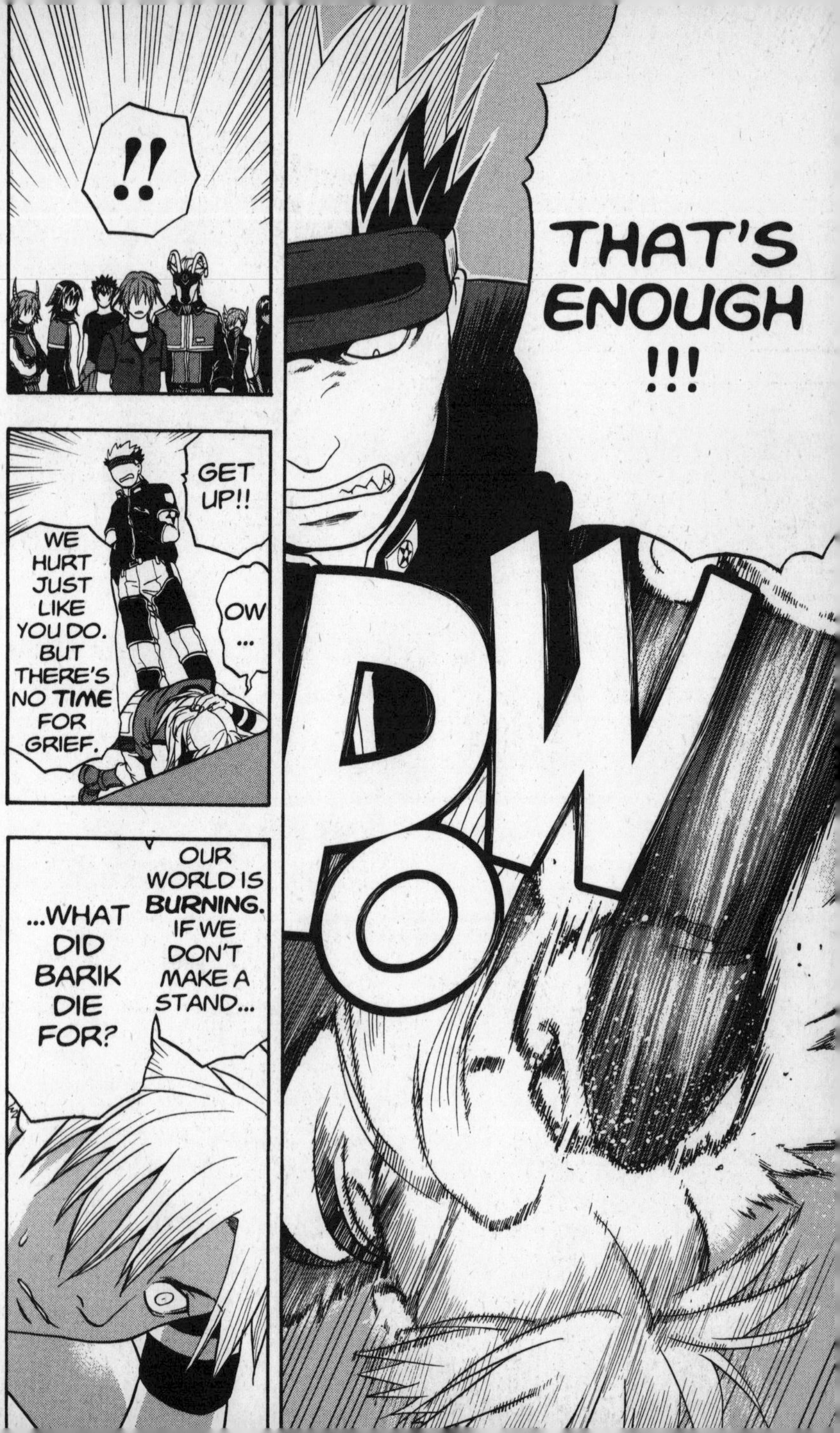
THAT'S ENOUGH!!!
POW
!!
GET UP!!
OW...
WE HURT JUST LIKE YOU DO. BUT THERE'S NO TIME FOR GRIEF.
OUR WORLD IS BURNING. IF WE DON'T MAKE A STAND...
...WHAT DID BARIK DIE FOR?

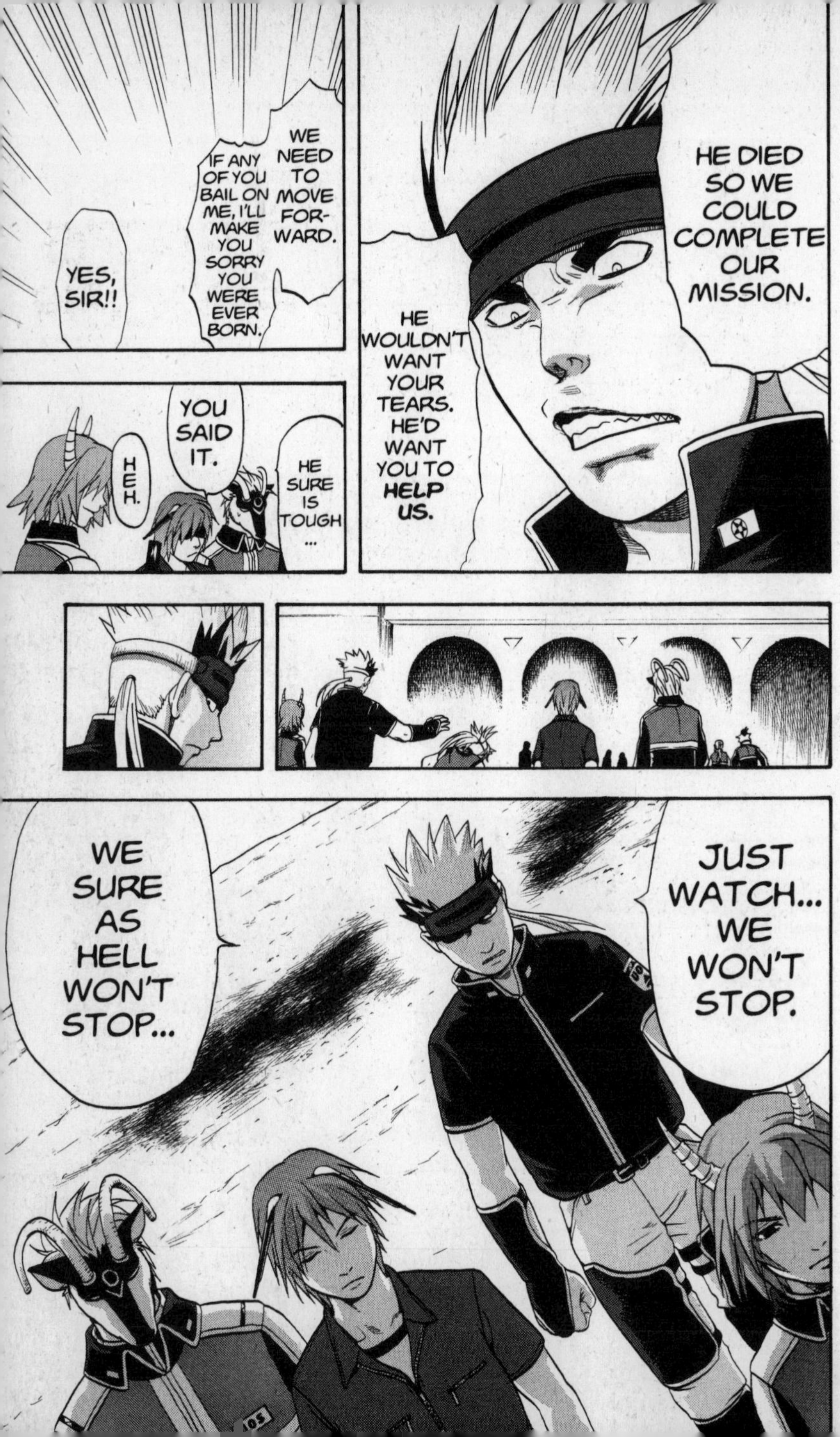
HE DIED SO WE COULD COMPLETE OUR MISSION.
HE WOULDN'T WANT YOUR TEARS. HE'D WANT YOU TO **HELP US.**
WE NEED TO MOVE FOR-WARD.
IF ANY OF YOU BAIL ON ME, I'LL MAKE YOU SORRY YOU WERE EVER BORN.
YES, SIR!!
HE SURE IS TOUGH...
YOU SAID IT.
HEH.
JUST WATCH... WE WON'T STOP.
WE SURE AS HELL WON'T STOP...

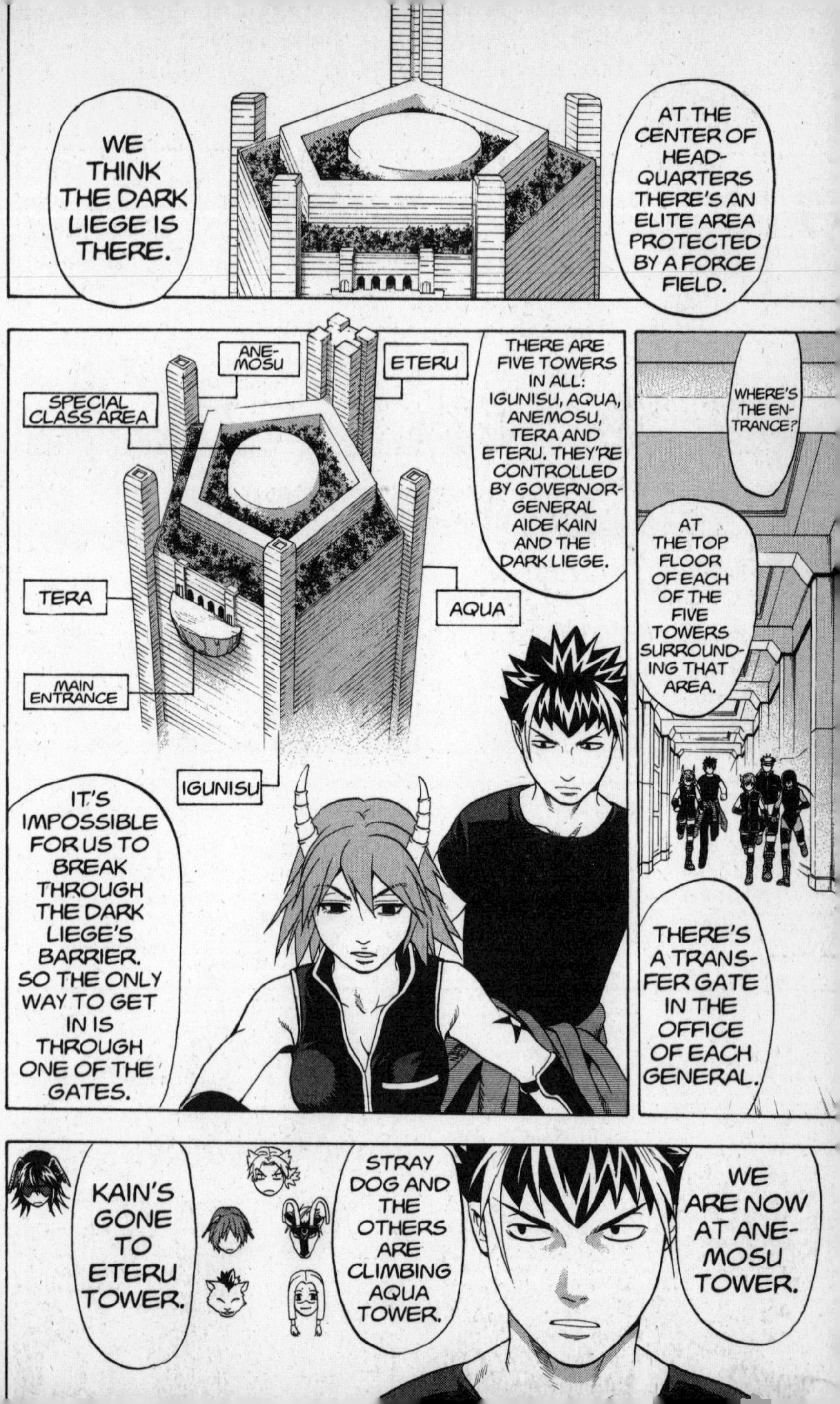

AT THE CENTER OF HEAD-QUARTERS THERE'S AN ELITE AREA PROTECTED BY A FORCE FIELD.
WE THINK THE DARK LIEGE IS THERE.
WHERE'S THE EN-TRANCE?
AT THE TOP FLOOR OF EACH OF THE FIVE TOWERS SURROUND-ING THAT AREA.
THERE'S A TRANS-FER GATE IN THE OFFICE OF EACH GENERAL.
THERE ARE FIVE TOWERS IN ALL: IGUNISU, AQUA, ANEMOSU, TERA AND ETERU. THEY'RE CONTROLLED BY GOVERNOR-GENERAL AIDE KAIN AND THE DARK LIEGE.
ETERU
ANE-MOSU
SPECIAL CLASS AREA
TERA
AQUA
MAIN ENTRANCE
IGUNISU
IT'S IMPOSSIBLE FOR US TO BREAK THROUGH THE DARK LIEGE'S BARRIER. SO THE ONLY WAY TO GET IN IS THROUGH ONE OF THE GATES.
WE ARE NOW AT ANE-MOSU TOWER.
STRAY DOG AND THE OTHERS ARE CLIMBING AQUA TOWER.
KAIN'S GONE TO ETERU TOWER.

READ THIS WAY

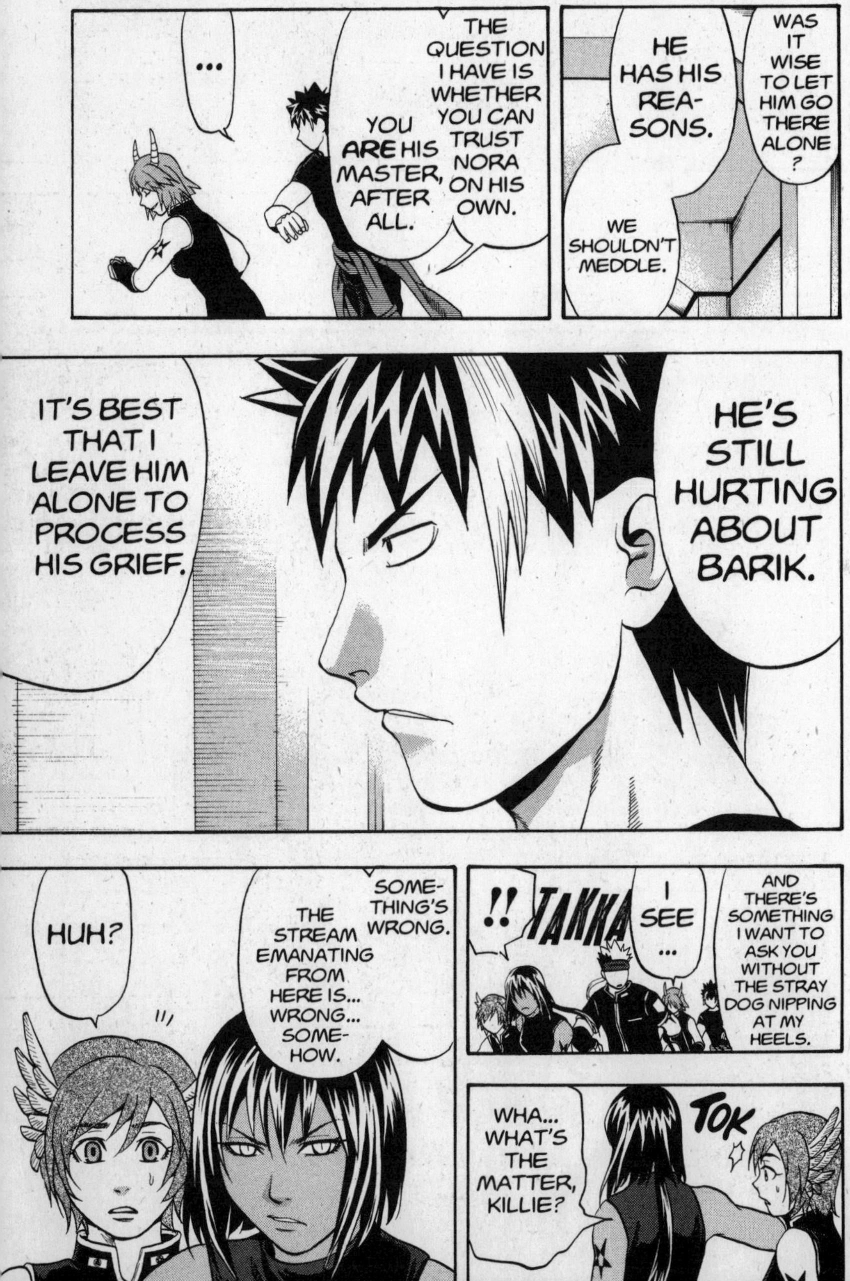
WAS IT WISE TO LET HIM GO THERE ALONE?
HE HAS HIS REASONS.
WE SHOULDN'T MEDDLE.
THE QUESTION I HAVE IS WHETHER YOU CAN TRUST NORA ON HIS OWN.
YOU ARE HIS MASTER, AFTER ALL.
...
HE'S STILL HURTING ABOUT BARIK.
IT'S BEST THAT I LEAVE HIM ALONE TO PROCESS HIS GRIEF.
AND THERE'S SOMETHING I WANT TO ASK YOU WITHOUT THE STRAY DOG NIPPING AT MY HEELS.
I SEE...
TAKKA
!!
TOK
WHA... WHAT'S THE MATTER, KILLIE?
SOME-THING'S WRONG.
THE STREAM EMANATING FROM HERE IS... WRONG... SOME-HOW.
HUH?

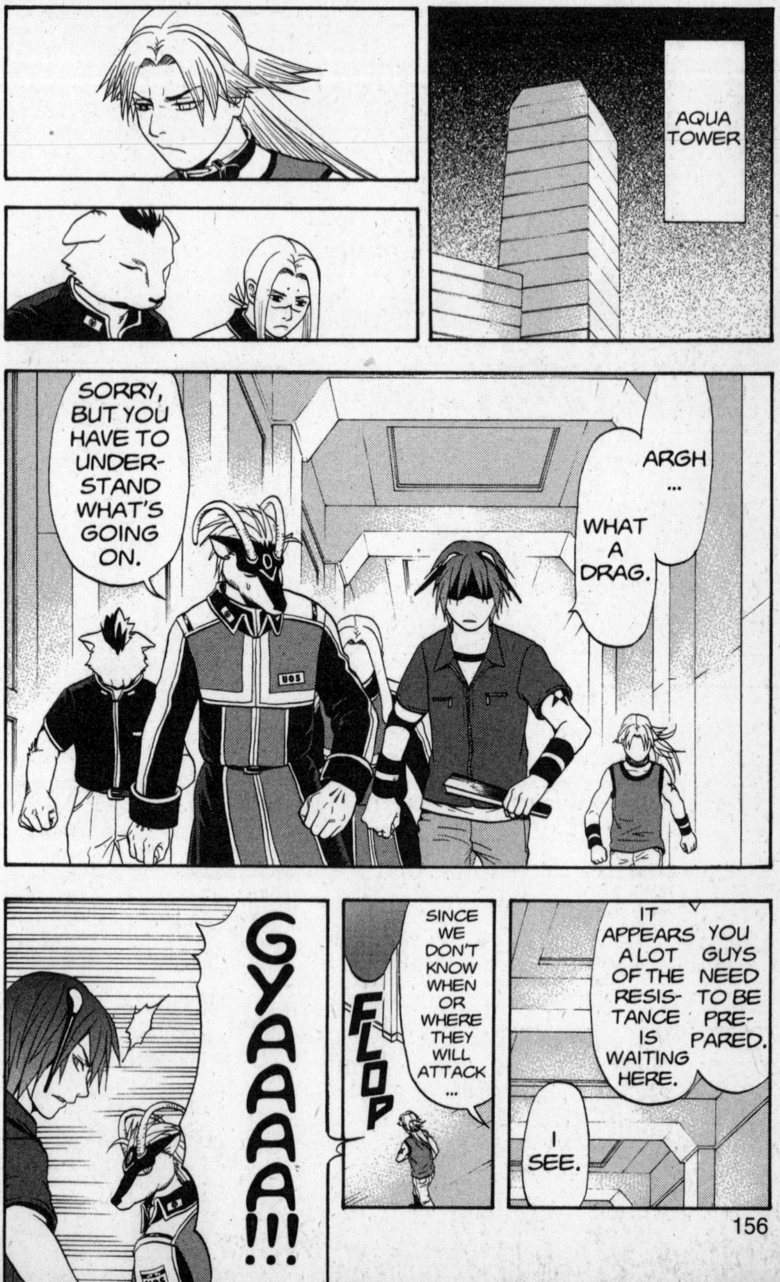
AQUA TOWER
ARGH ... WHAT A DRAG.
SORRY, BUT YOU HAVE TO UNDERSTAND WHAT'S GOING ON.
IT APPEARS A LOT OF THE RESISTANCE IS WAITING HERE. YOU GUYS NEED TO BE PREPARED.
I SEE.
SINCE WE DON'T KNOW WHEN OR WHERE THEY WILL ATTACK ...
FLOP
GYAAAA!!!

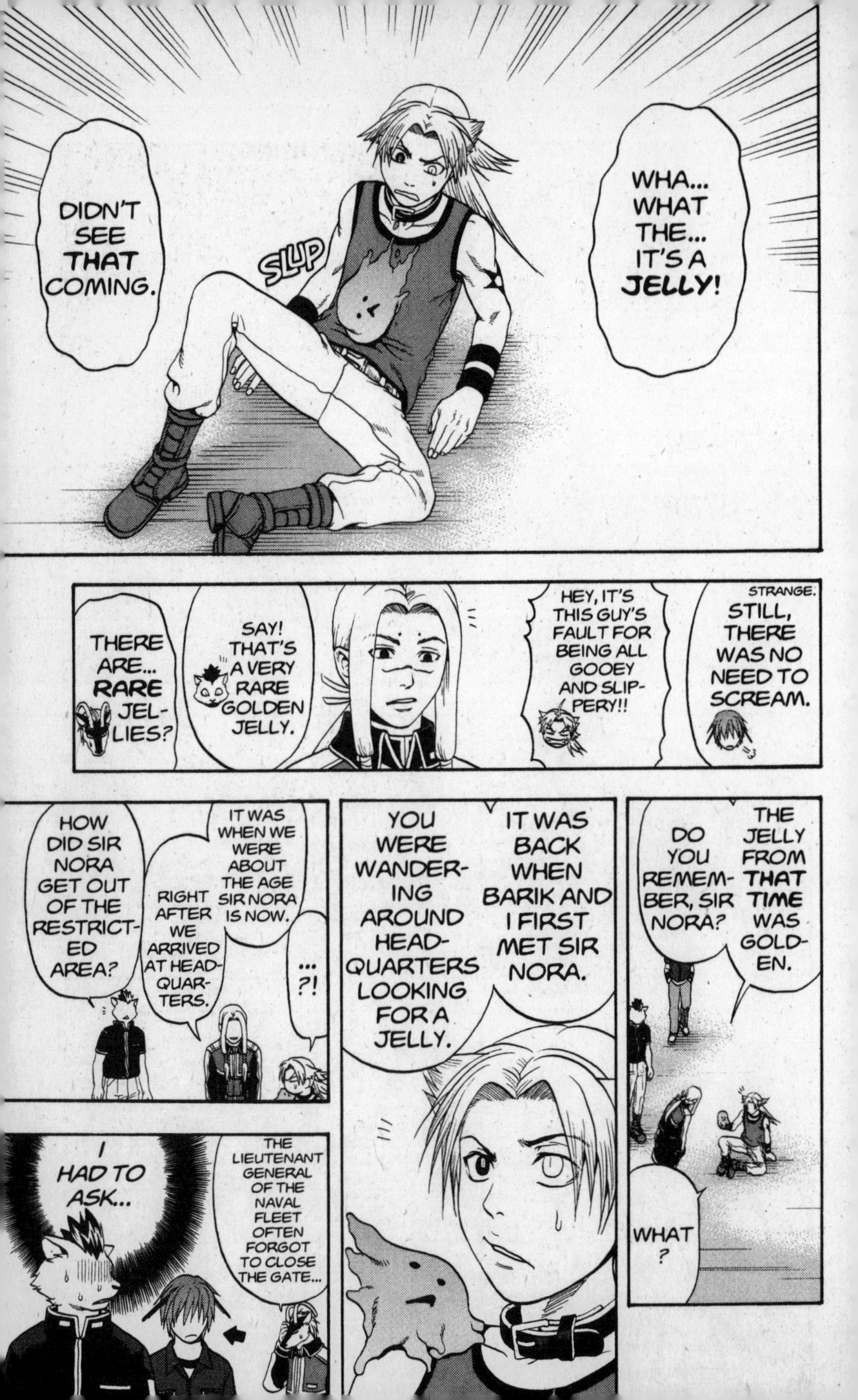
WHA... WHAT THE... IT'S A JELLY!
SLIP
DIDN'T SEE THAT COMING.
STRANGE.
STILL, THERE WAS NO NEED TO SCREAM.
HEY, IT'S THIS GUY'S FAULT FOR BEING ALL GOOEY AND SLIP-PERY!!
SAY! THAT'S A VERY RARE GOLDEN JELLY.
THERE ARE... RARE JEL-LIES?
THE JELLY FROM THAT TIME WAS GOLD-EN.
DO YOU REMEM-BER, SIR NORA?
WHAT?
IT WAS BACK WHEN BARIK AND I FIRST MET SIR NORA.
YOU WERE WANDER-ING AROUND HEAD-QUARTERS LOOKING FOR A JELLY.
IT WAS WHEN WE WERE ABOUT THE AGE SIR NORA IS NOW.
RIGHT AFTER WE ARRIVED AT HEAD-QUAR-TERS.
...?!
HOW DID SIR NORA GET OUT OF THE RESTRICT-ED AREA?
THE LIEUTENANT GENERAL OF THE NAVAL FLEET OFTEN FORGOT TO CLOSE THE GATE...
I HAD TO ASK...

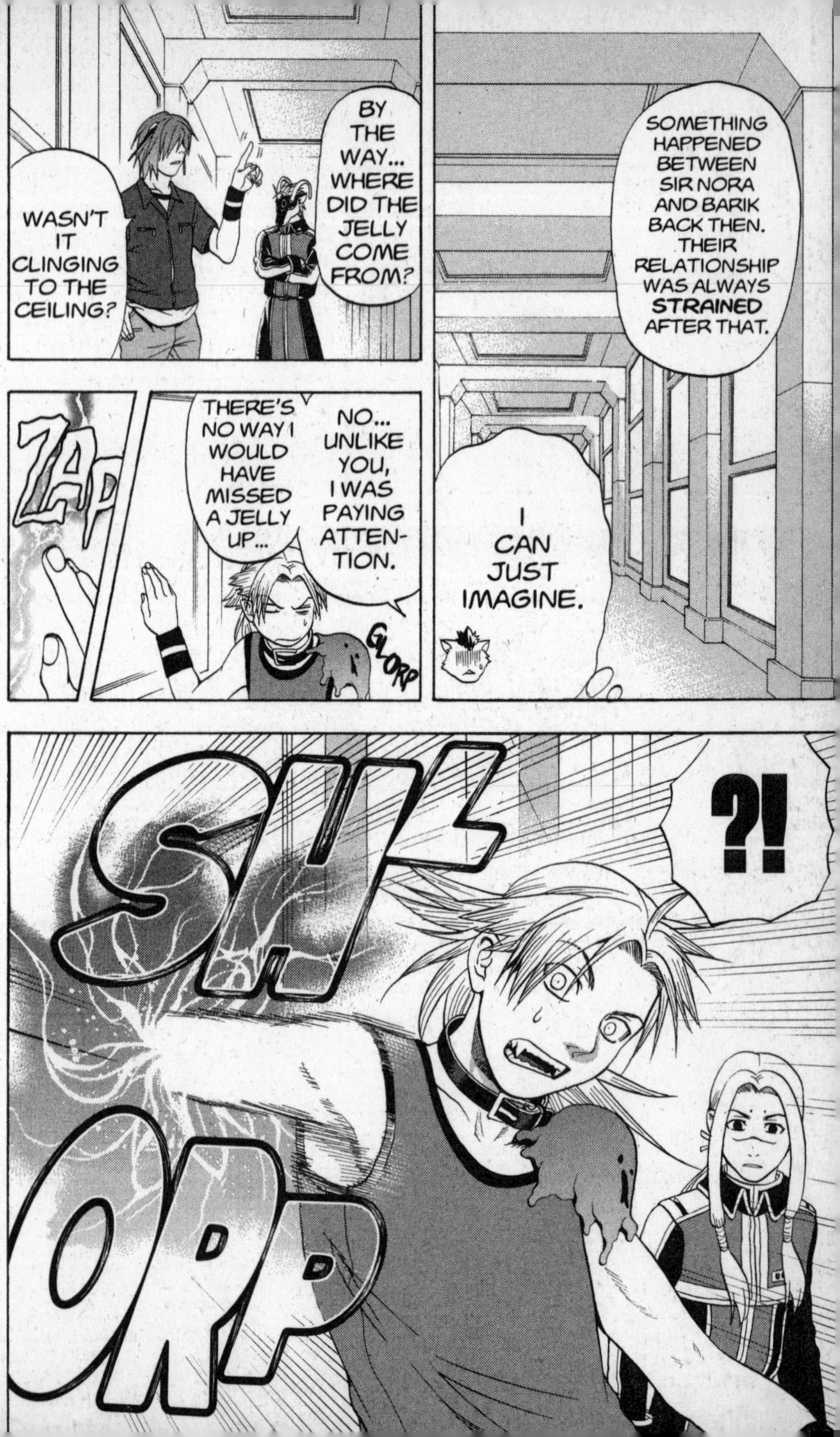
SOMETHING HAPPENED BETWEEN SIR NORA AND BARIK BACK THEN. THEIR RELATIONSHIP WAS ALWAYS **STRAINED** AFTER THAT.
I CAN JUST IMAGINE.
BY THE WAY... WHERE DID THE JELLY COME FROM?
WASN'T IT CLINGING TO THE CEILING?
NO... UNLIKE YOU, I WAS PAYING ATTEN-TION.
THERE'S NO WAY I WOULD HAVE MISSED A JELLY UP...
ZAP
GLORP
?!
SHLORP

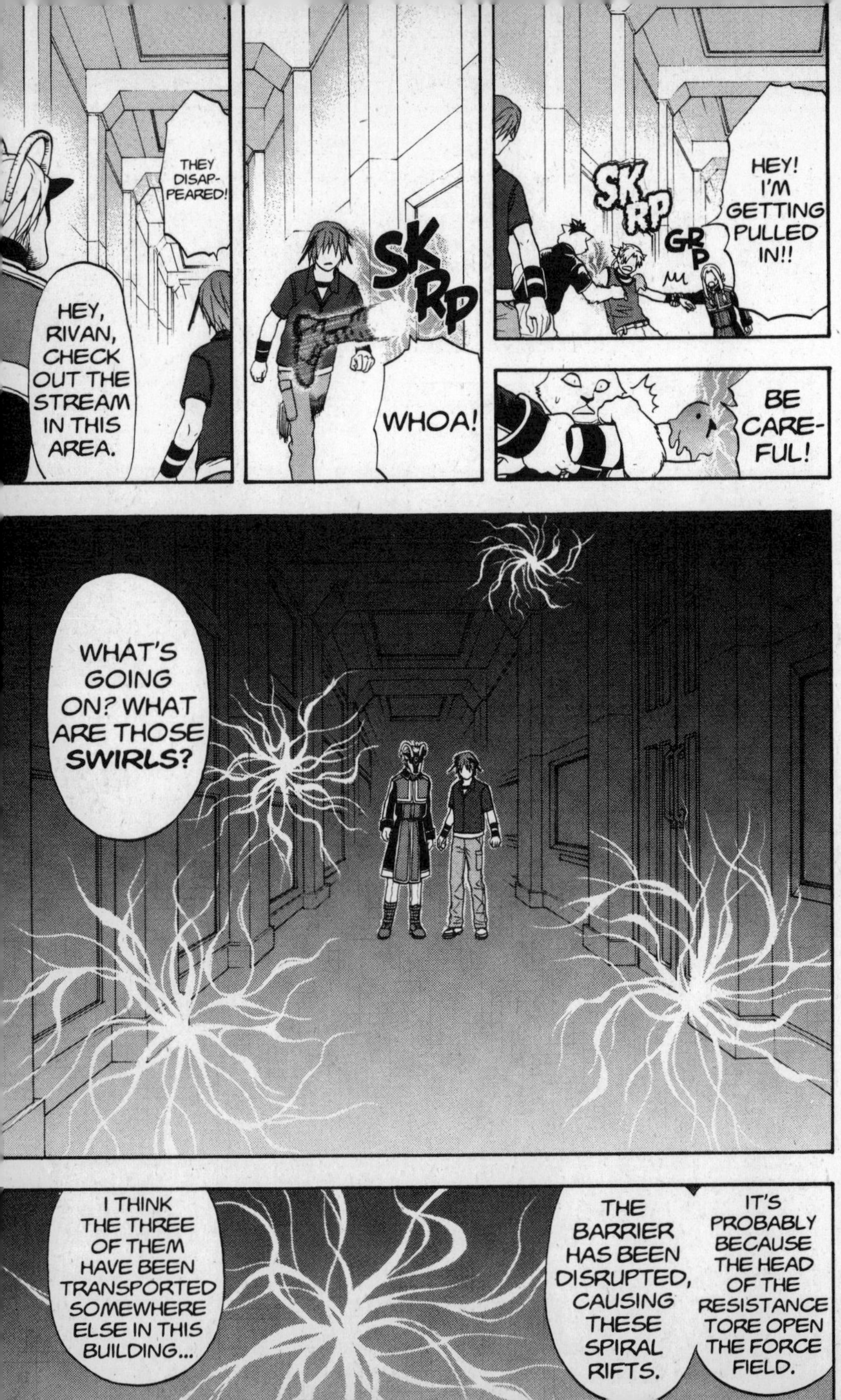
HEY! I'M GETTING PULLED IN!!
GRP
SKRP
BE CARE-FUL!
SKRP
WHOA!
THEY DISAP-PEARED!
HEY, RIVAN, CHECK OUT THE STREAM IN THIS AREA.
WHAT'S GOING ON? WHAT ARE THOSE SWIRLS?
IT'S PROBABLY BECAUSE THE HEAD OF THE RESISTANCE TORE OPEN THE FORCE FIELD.
THE BARRIER HAS BEEN DISRUPTED, CAUSING THESE SPIRAL RIFTS.
I THINK THE THREE OF THEM HAVE BEEN TRANSPORTED SOMEWHERE ELSE IN THIS BUILDING...

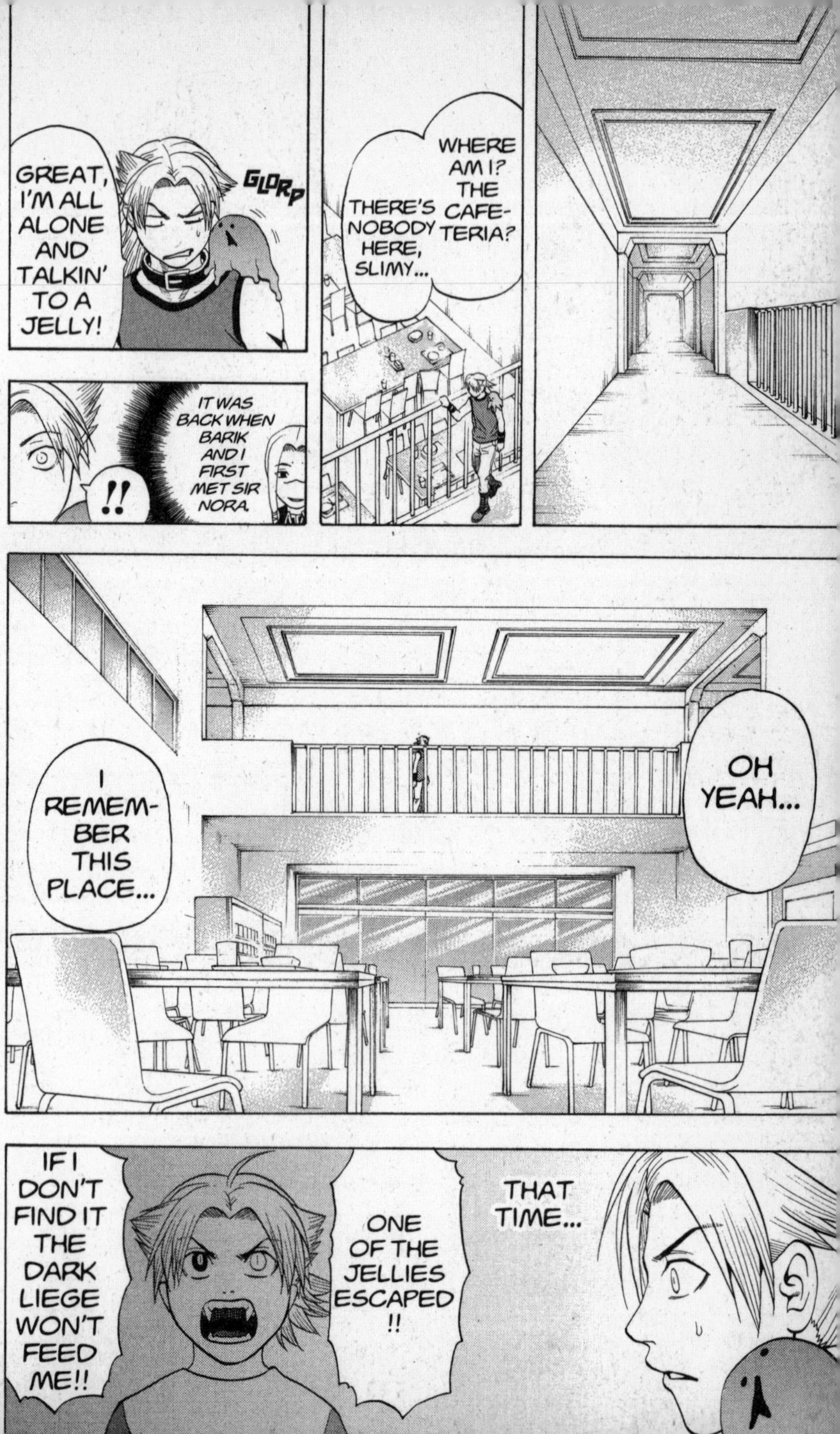
WHERE AM I? THE CAFETERIA?
THERE'S NOBODY HERE, SLIMY...
GREAT, I'M ALL ALONE AND TALKIN' TO A JELLY!
GLORP
IT WAS BACK WHEN BARIK AND I FIRST MET SIR NORA.
!!
OH YEAH...
I REMEMBER THIS PLACE...
THAT TIME...
ONE OF THE JELLIES ESCAPED!!
IF I DON'T FIND IT THE DARK LIEGE WON'T FEED ME!!

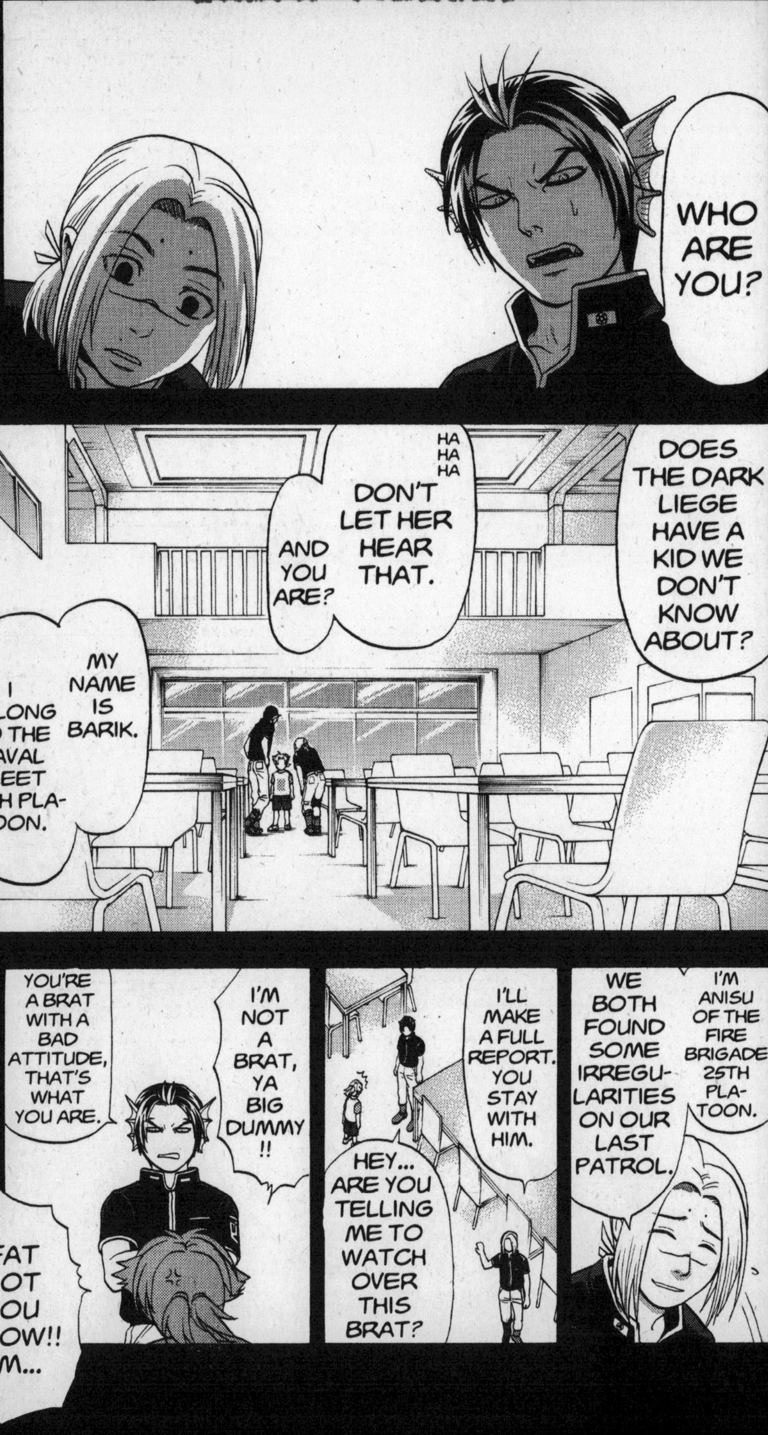
WHO ARE YOU?
DOES THE DARK LIEGE HAVE A KID WE DON'T KNOW ABOUT?
HA HA HA
DON'T LET HER HEAR THAT.
AND YOU ARE?
MY NAME IS BARIK.
I BELONG TO THE NAVAL FLEET 49TH PLATOON.
I'M ANISU OF THE FIRE BRIGADE 25TH PLATOON.
WE BOTH FOUND SOME IRREGULARITIES ON OUR LAST PATROL.
I'LL MAKE A FULL REPORT. YOU STAY WITH HIM.
HEY... ARE YOU TELLING ME TO WATCH OVER THIS BRAT?
I'M NOT A BRAT, YA BIG DUMMY!!
YOU'RE A BRAT WITH A BAD ATTITUDE, THAT'S WHAT YOU ARE.
FAT LOT YOU KNOW!! I'M...

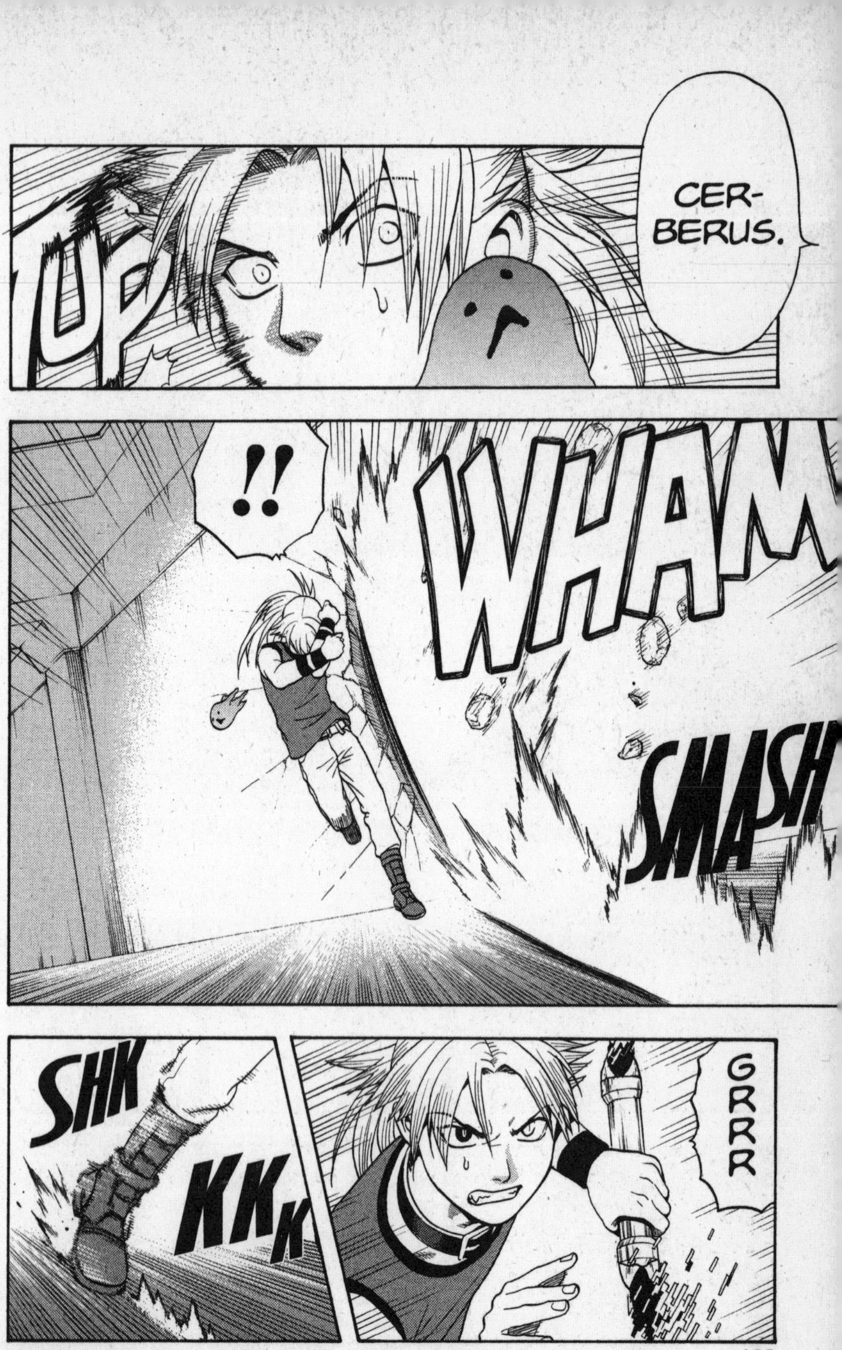
CER-
BERUS.
TUP
WHAM
SMASH
!!
GRRR
SHK
KKK

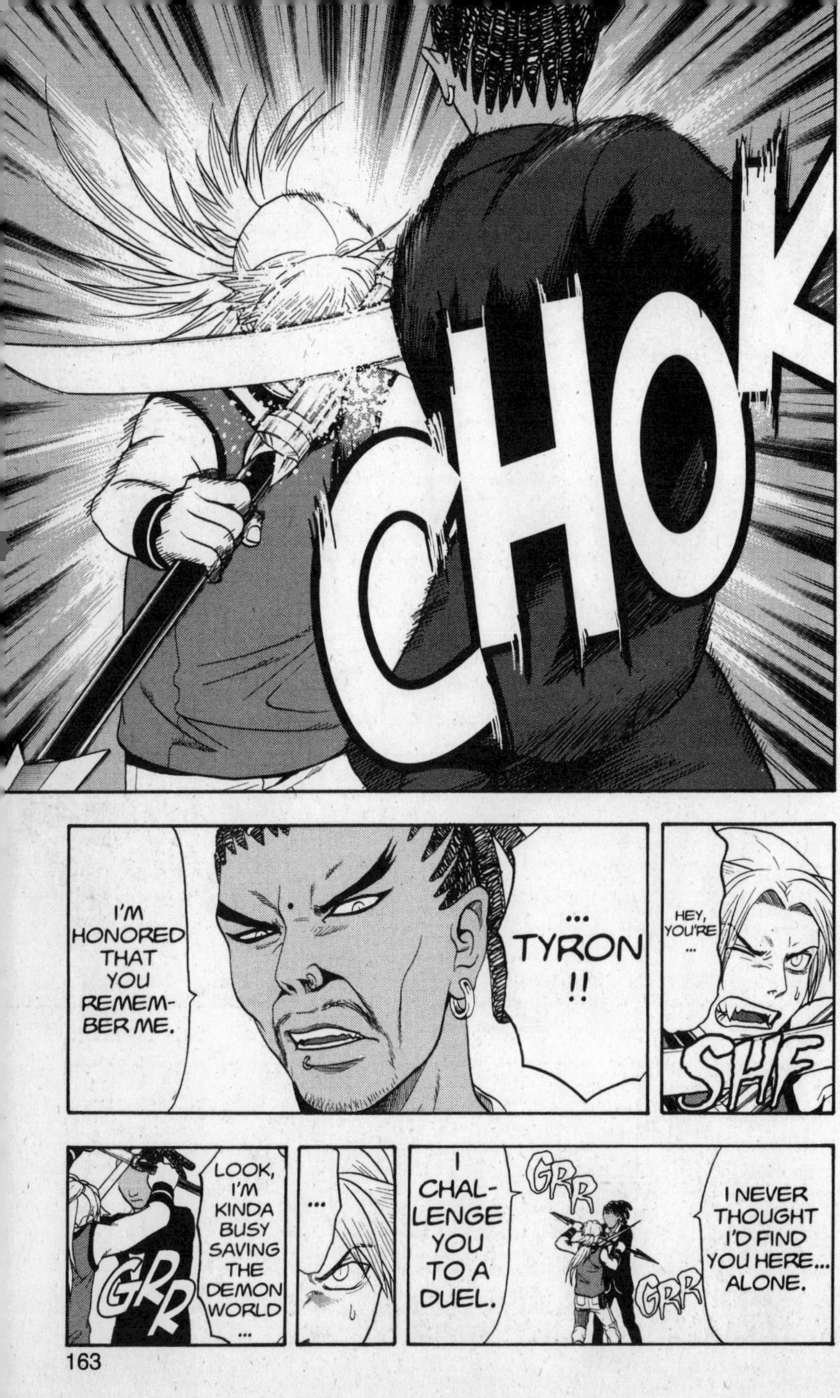
CHOK
HEY, YOU'RE ...
SHF
... TYRON !!
I'M HONORED THAT YOU REMEMBER ME.
I NEVER THOUGHT I'D FIND YOU HERE... ALONE.
GRR
GRR
I CHALLENGE YOU TO A DUEL.
...
LOOK, I'M KINDA BUSY SAVING THE DEMON WORLD ...
GRR

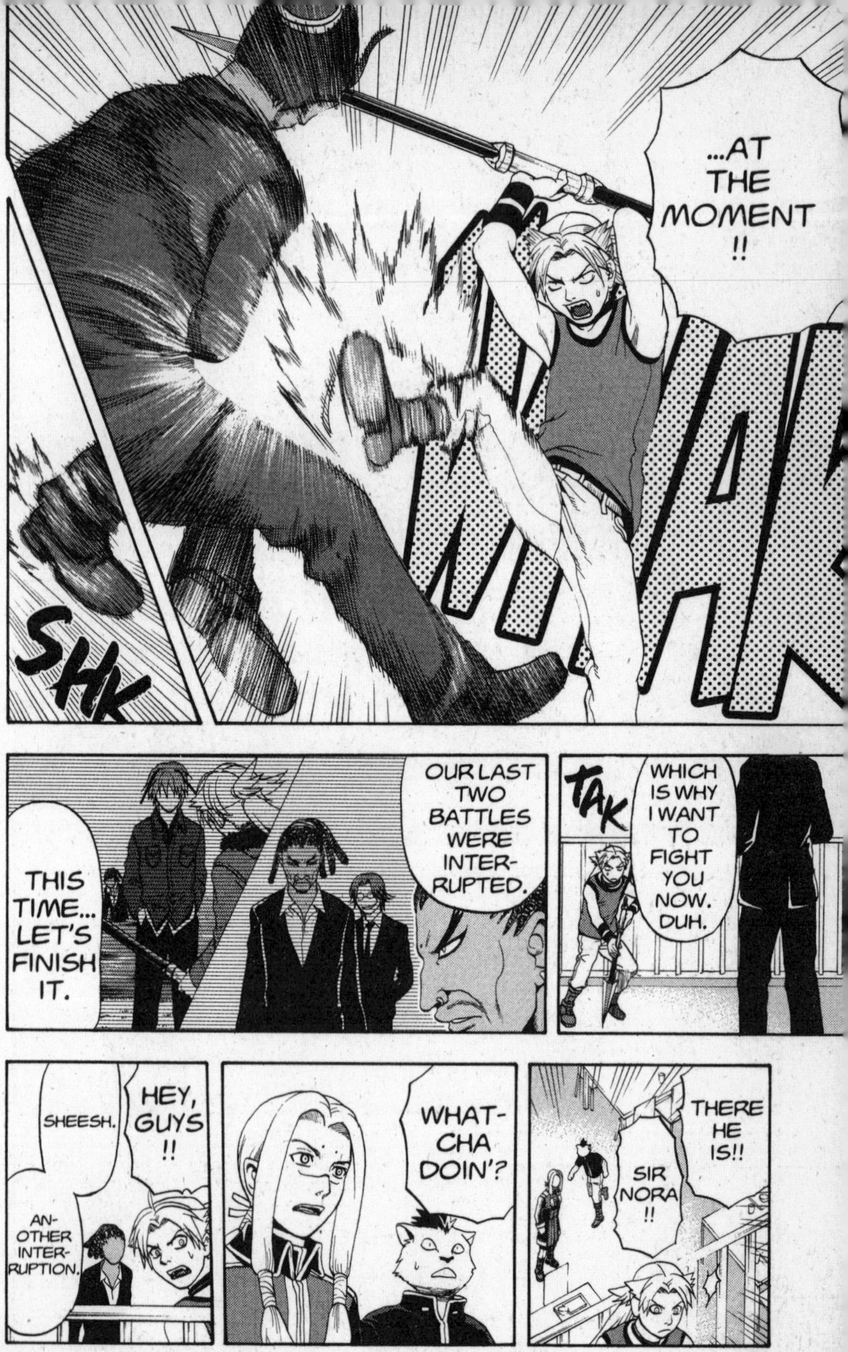
...AT THE MOMENT !!
WHAK
SHK
TAK
WHICH IS WHY I WANT TO FIGHT YOU NOW. DUH.
OUR LAST TWO BATTLES WERE INTER-RUPTED.
THIS TIME... LET'S FINISH IT.
THERE HE IS!!
SIR NORA !!
WHAT-CHA DOIN'?
HEY, GUYS !!
SHEESH.
AN-OTHER INTER-RUPTION.

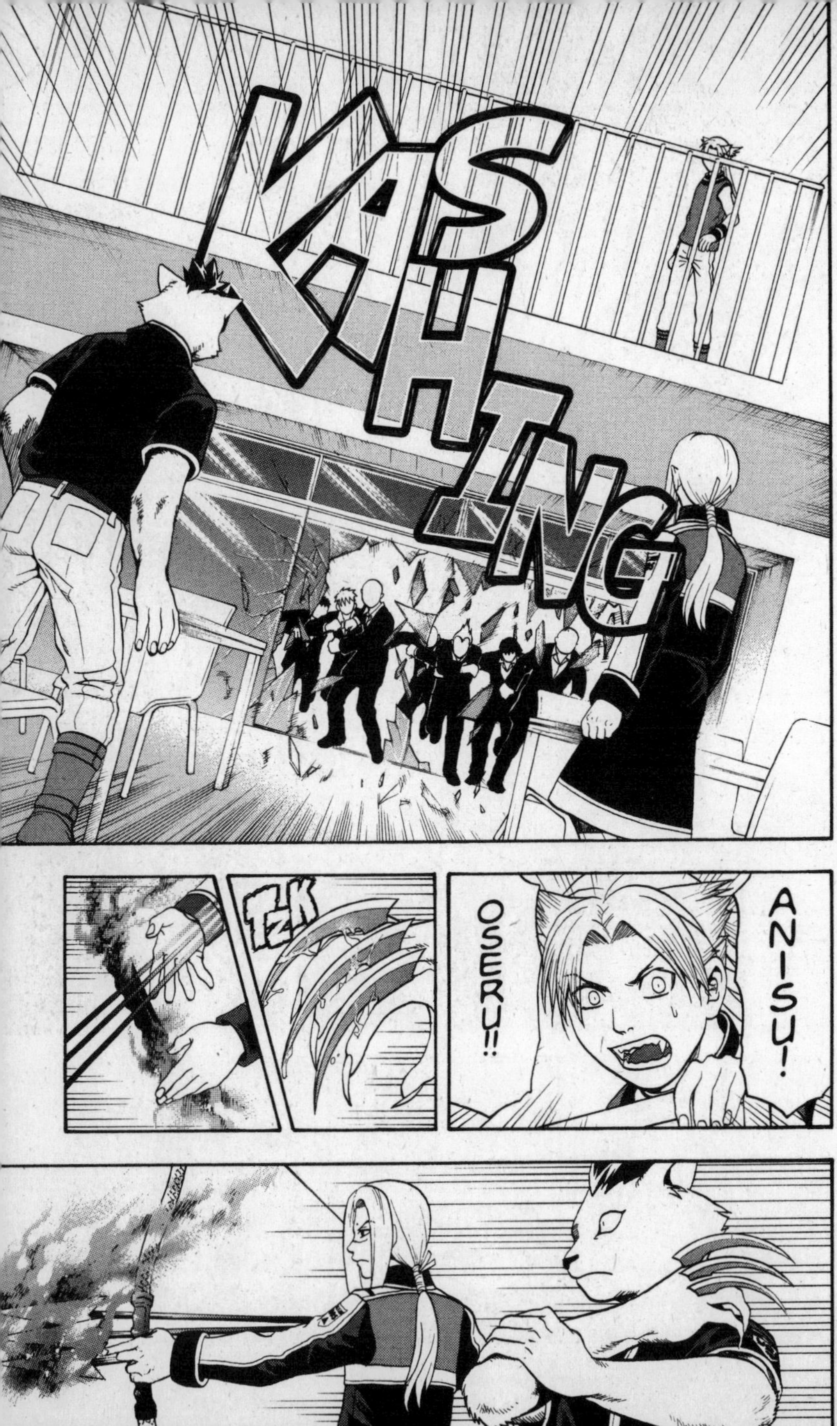

WASHHHING
ANISU!
OSERU!!
TZK

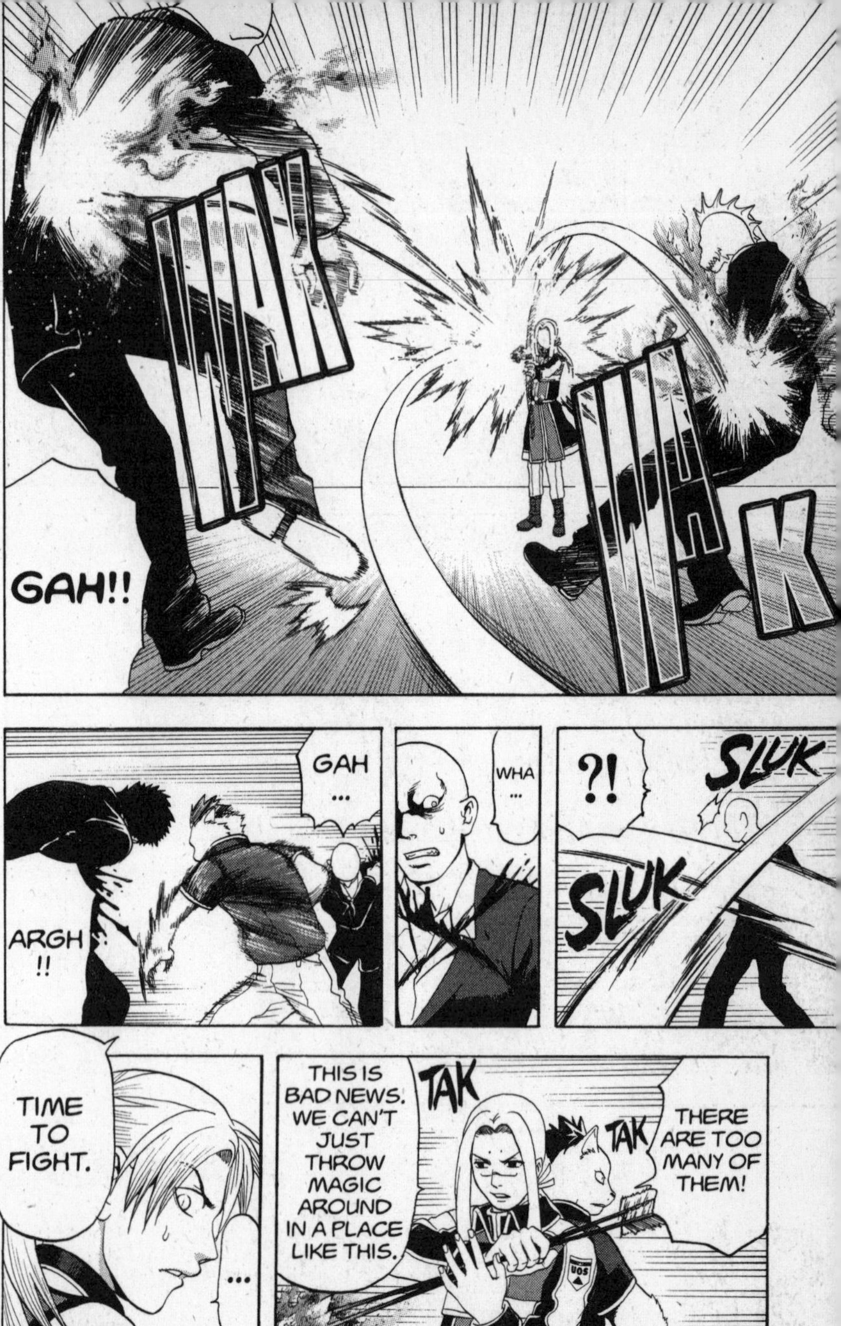
WHAK
WHAK
GAH!!
?!
SLUK
SLUK
WHA ...
GAH ...
ARGH !!
THERE ARE TOO MANY OF THEM!
TAK
TAK
THIS IS BAD NEWS. WE CAN'T JUST THROW MAGIC AROUND IN A PLACE LIKE THIS.
TIME TO FIGHT.
...

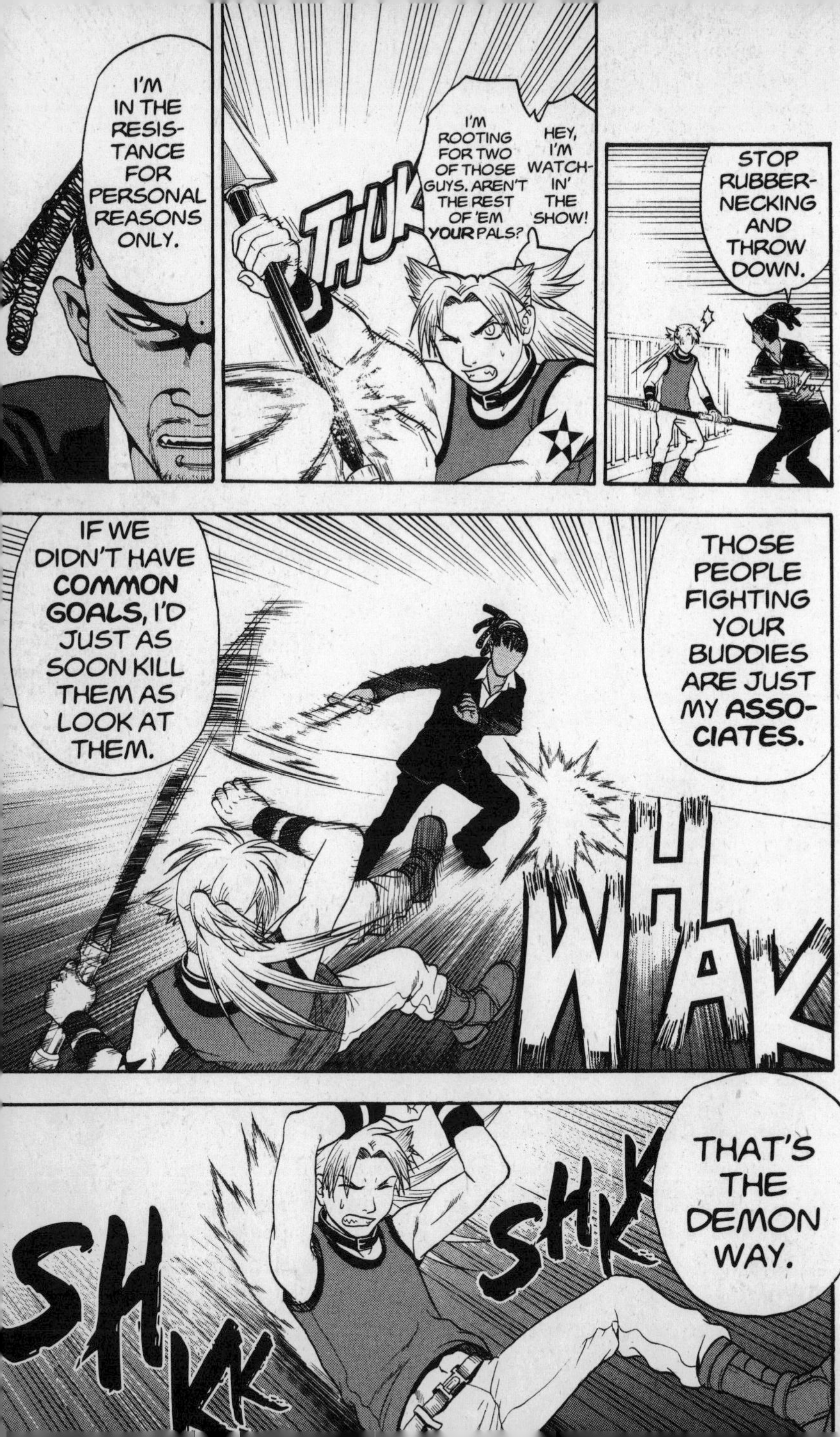
STOP RUBBER-NECKING AND THROW DOWN.
HEY, I'M WATCHIN' THE SHOW!
I'M ROOTING FOR TWO OF THOSE GUYS. AREN'T THE REST OF 'EM **YOUR** PALS?
THUK
I'M IN THE RESIS-TANCE FOR PERSONAL REASONS ONLY.
THOSE PEOPLE FIGHTING YOUR BUDDIES ARE JUST MY **ASSO-CIATES.**
IF WE DIDN'T HAVE **COMMON GOALS,** I'D JUST AS SOON KILL THEM AS LOOK AT THEM.
WHAK
THAT'S THE DEMON WAY.
SHK
SHKK

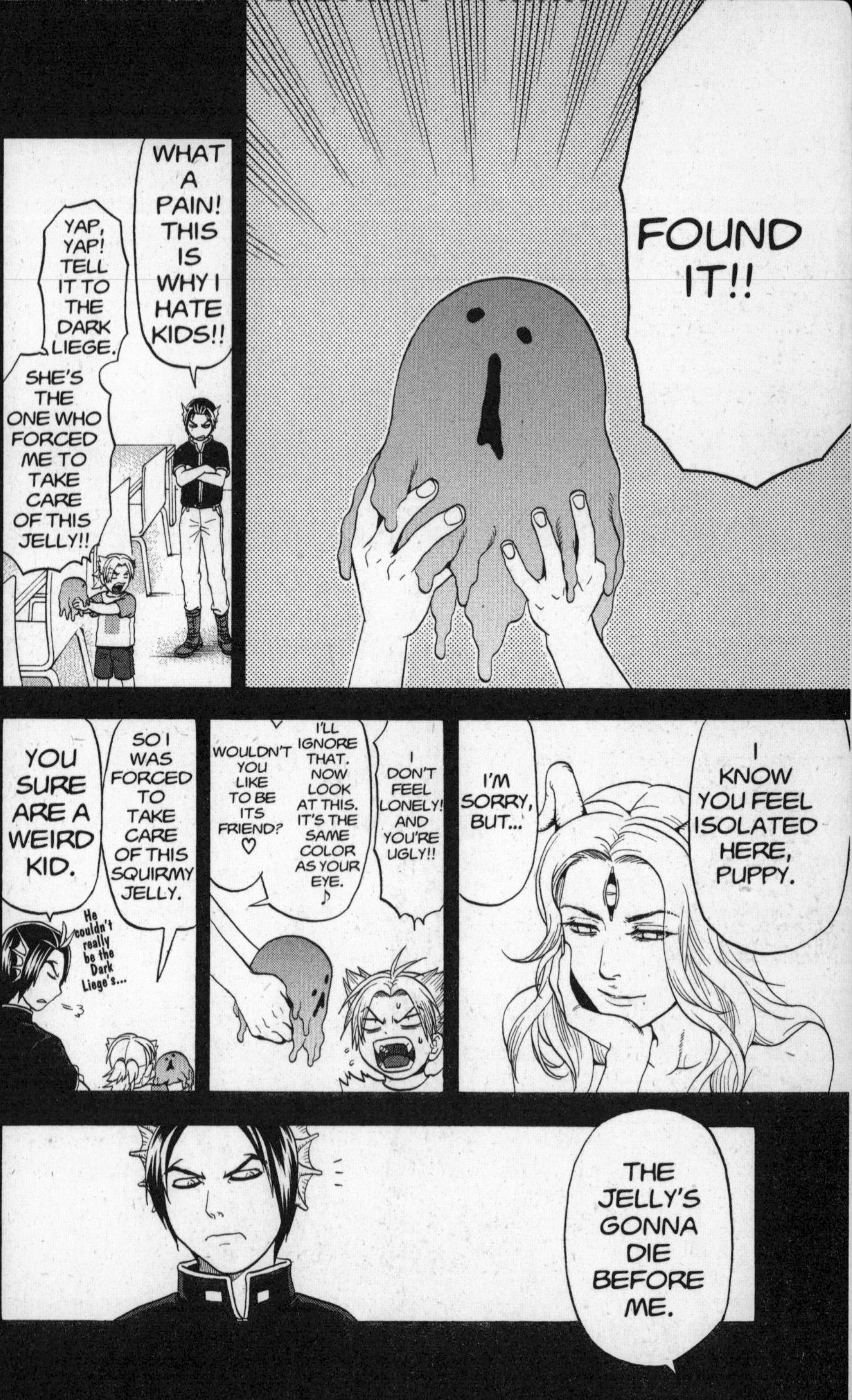
FOUND IT!!
WHAT A PAIN! THIS IS WHY I HATE KIDS!!
YAP, YAP! TELL IT TO THE DARK LIEGE.
SHE'S THE ONE WHO FORCED ME TO TAKE CARE OF THIS JELLY!!
I KNOW YOU FEEL ISOLATED HERE, PUPPY.
I'M SORRY, BUT...
I DON'T FEEL LONELY! AND YOU'RE UGLY!!
I'LL IGNORE THAT. NOW LOOK AT THIS. IT'S THE SAME COLOR AS YOUR EYE. ♪
WOULDN'T YOU LIKE TO BE ITS FRIEND? ♡
SO I WAS FORCED TO TAKE CARE OF THIS SQUIRMY JELLY.
YOU SURE ARE A WEIRD KID.
He couldn't really be the Dark Liege's...
THE JELLY'S GONNA DIE BEFORE ME.

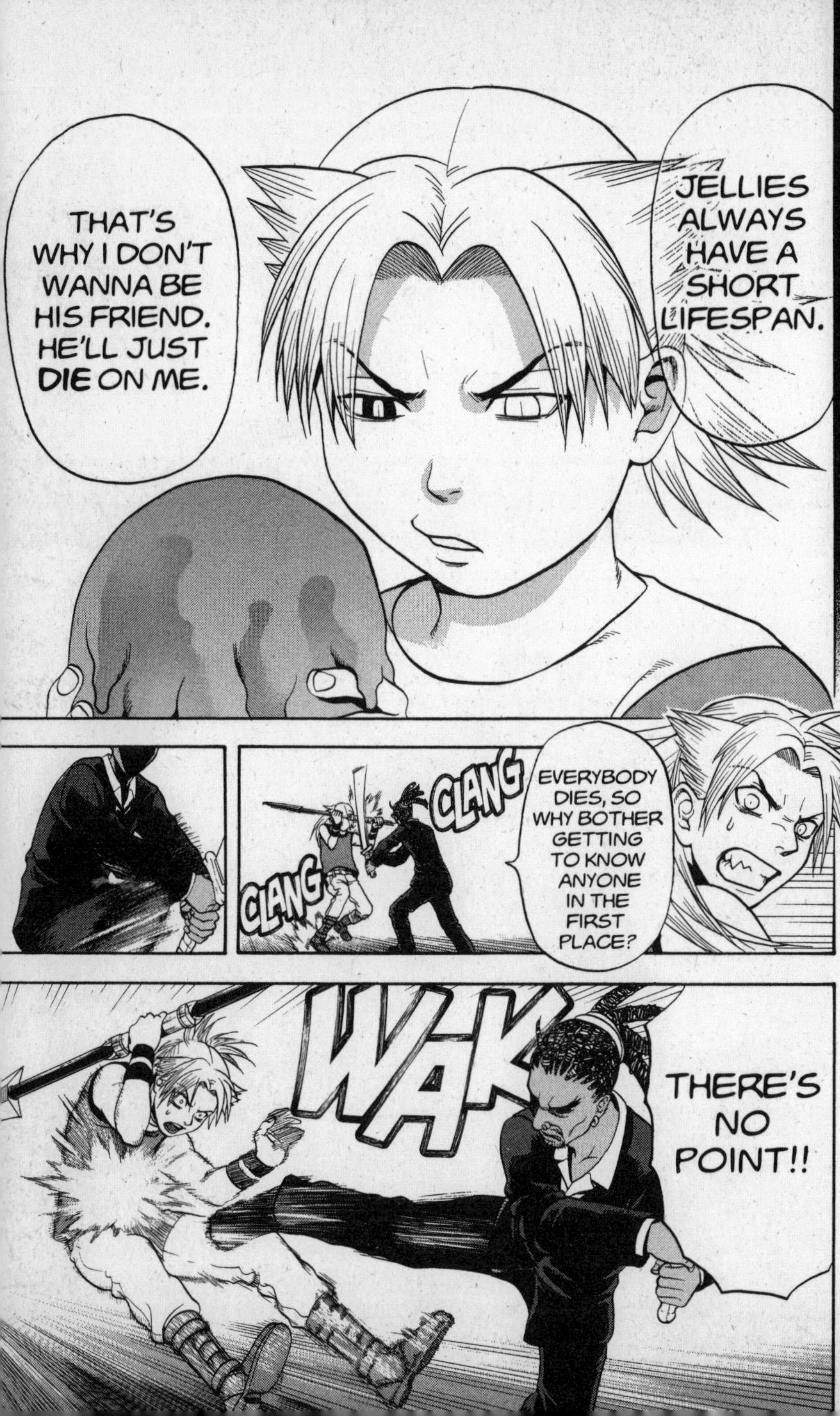
JELLIES ALWAYS HAVE A SHORT LIFESPAN.
THAT'S WHY I DON'T WANNA BE HIS FRIEND. HE'LL JUST **DIE** ON ME.
EVERYBODY DIES, SO WHY BOTHER GETTING TO KNOW ANYONE IN THE FIRST PLACE?
CLANG
CLANG
WAK
THERE'S NO POINT!!

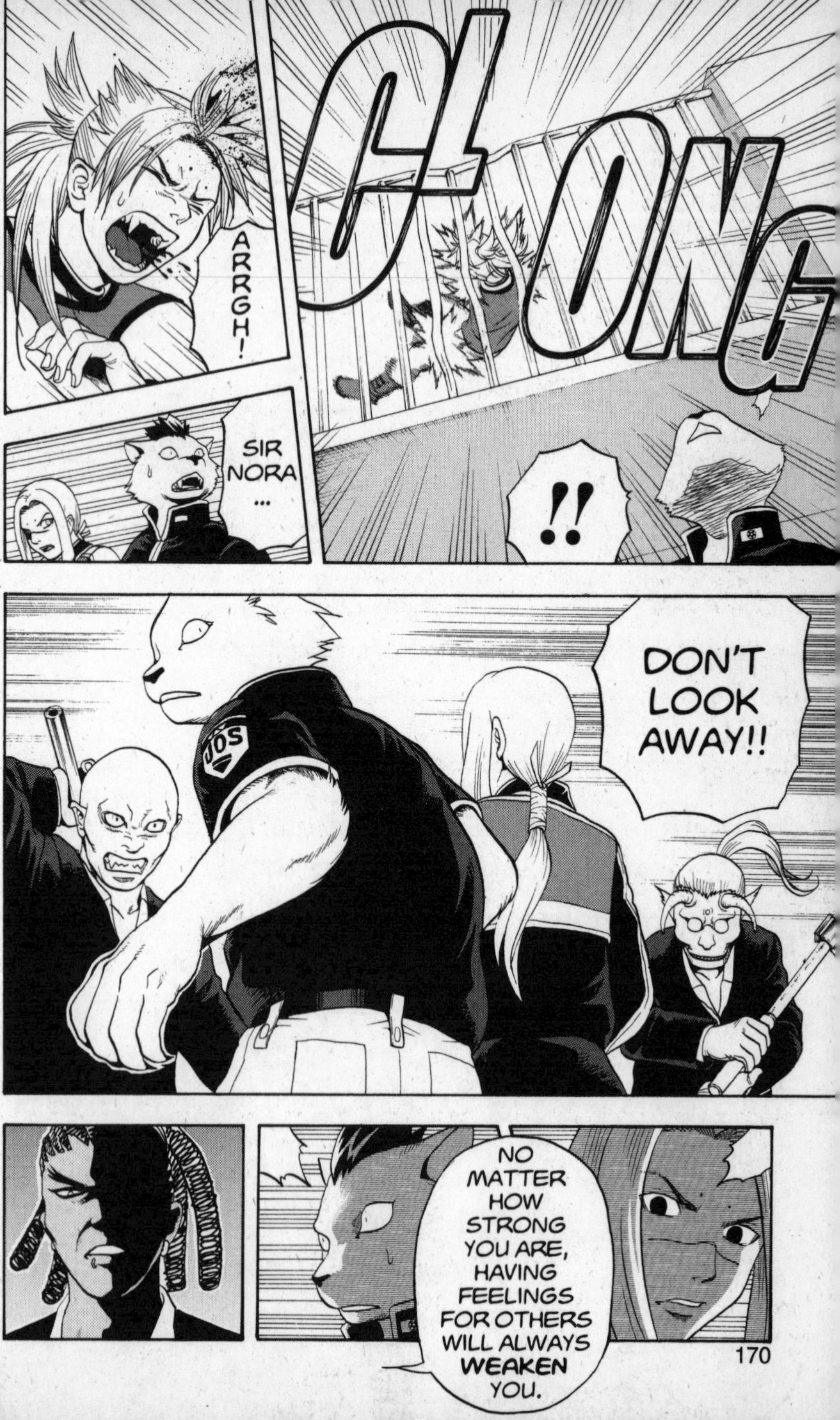
CLONG
!!
ARRGH!
SIR NORA ...
DON'T LOOK AWAY!!
NO MATTER HOW STRONG YOU ARE, HAVING FEELINGS FOR OTHERS WILL ALWAYS WEAKEN YOU.

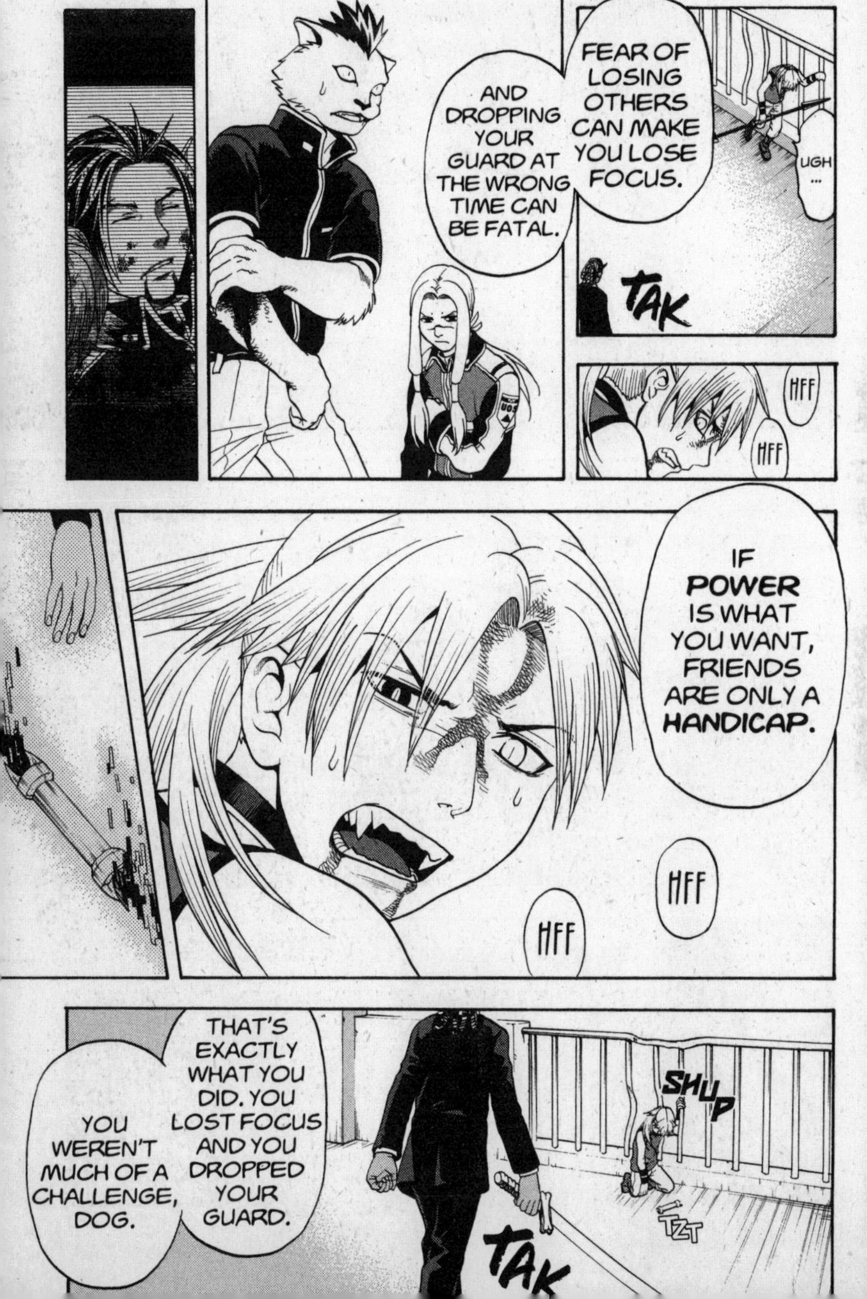
FEAR OF LOSING OTHERS CAN MAKE YOU LOSE FOCUS.
UGH ...
TAK
HFF
HFF
AND DROPPING YOUR GUARD AT THE WRONG TIME CAN BE FATAL.
IF **POWER** IS WHAT YOU WANT, FRIENDS ARE ONLY A **HANDICAP.**
HFF
HFF
SHUP
THAT'S EXACTLY WHAT YOU DID. YOU LOST FOCUS AND YOU DROPPED YOUR GUARD.
YOU WEREN'T MUCH OF A CHALLENGE, DOG.
TZT
TAK

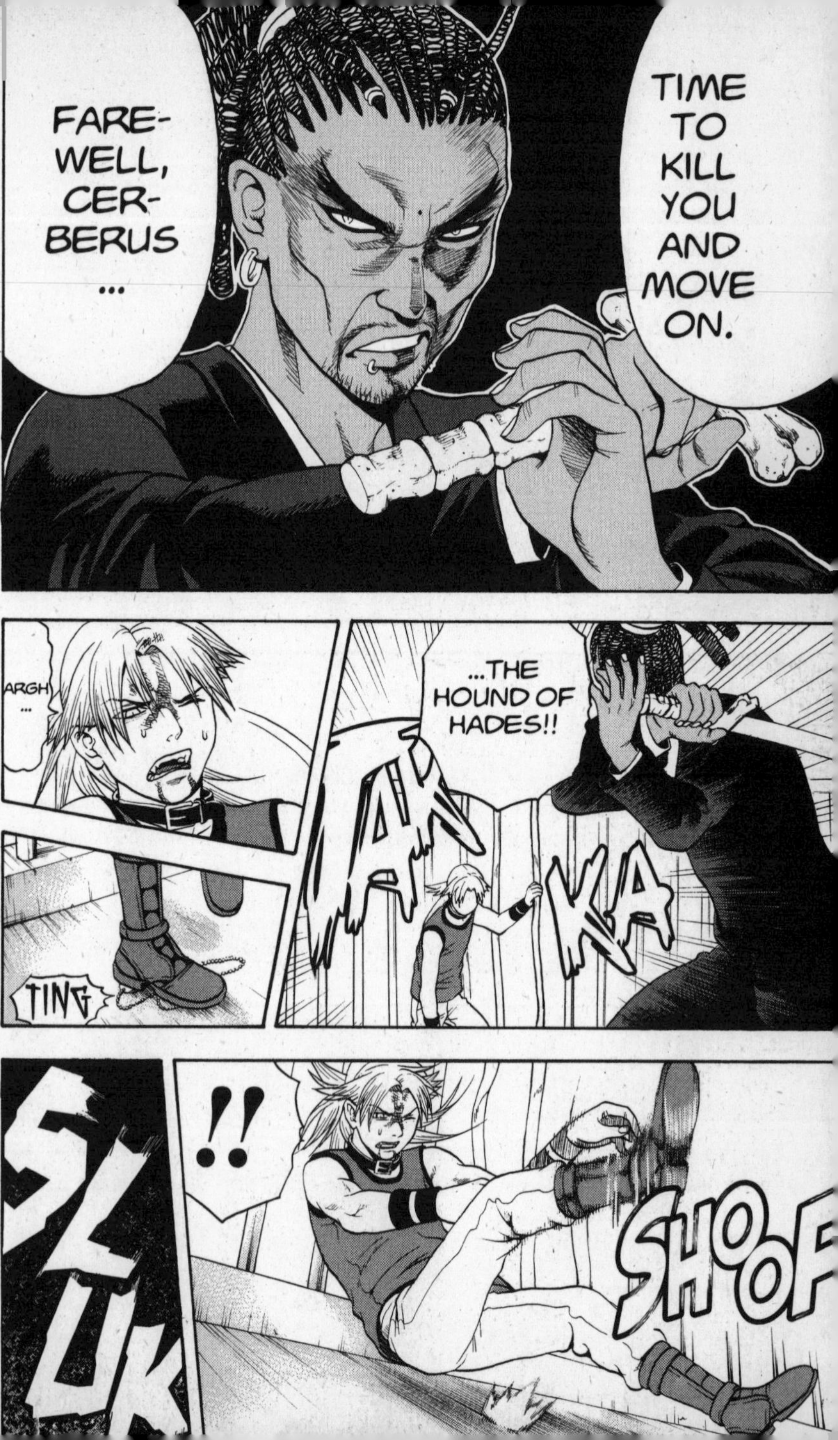
TIME TO KILL YOU AND MOVE ON.
FAREWELL, CERBERUS...
...THE HOUND OF HADES!!
KA
AK
ARGH...
TING
SHOOF
!!
SLUK

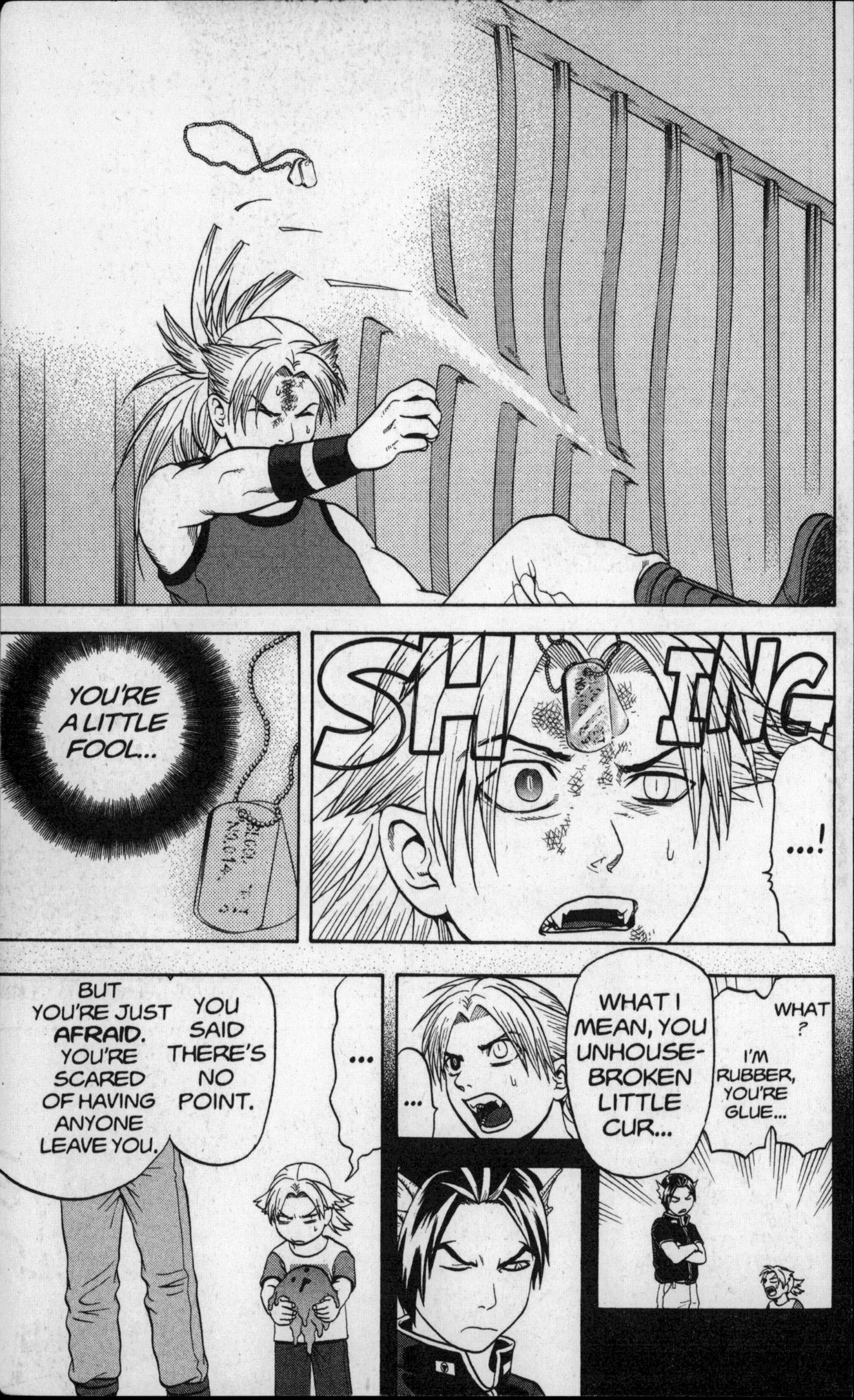
SH ING
...!
YOU'RE A LITTLE FOOL...
WHAT ?
I'M RUBBER, YOU'RE GLUE...
WHAT I MEAN, YOU UNHOUSE-BROKEN LITTLE CUR...
...
...
YOU SAID THERE'S NO POINT.
BUT YOU'RE JUST **AFRAID**. YOU'RE SCARED OF HAVING ANYONE LEAVE YOU.

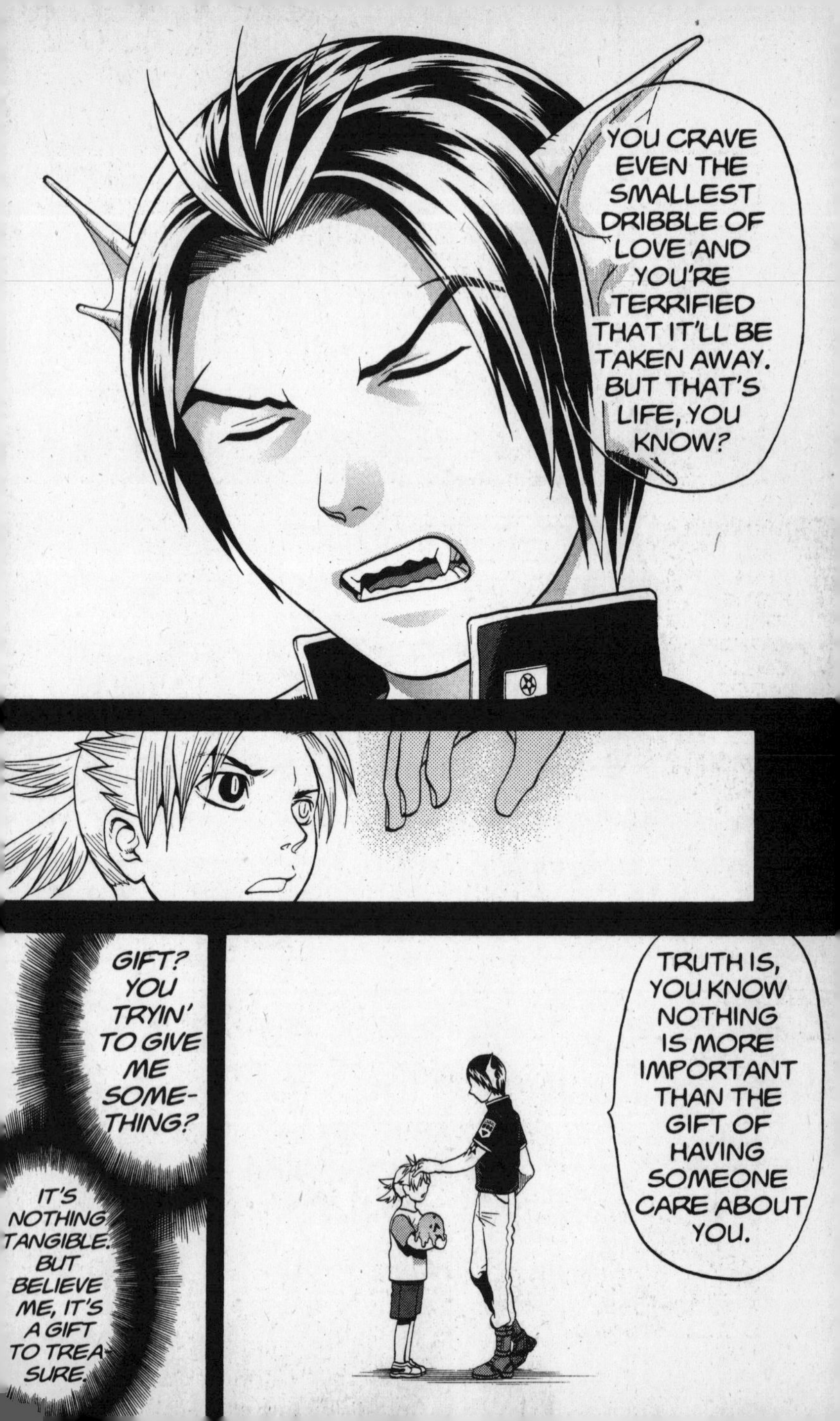
YOU CRAVE EVEN THE SMALLEST DRIBBLE OF LOVE AND YOU'RE TERRIFIED THAT IT'LL BE TAKEN AWAY. BUT THAT'S LIFE, YOU KNOW?
TRUTH IS, YOU KNOW NOTHING IS MORE IMPORTANT THAN THE GIFT OF HAVING SOMEONE CARE ABOUT YOU.
GIFT? YOU TRYIN' TO GIVE ME SOME-THING?
IT'S NOTHING TANGIBLE. BUT BELIEVE ME, IT'S A GIFT TO TREA-SURE.

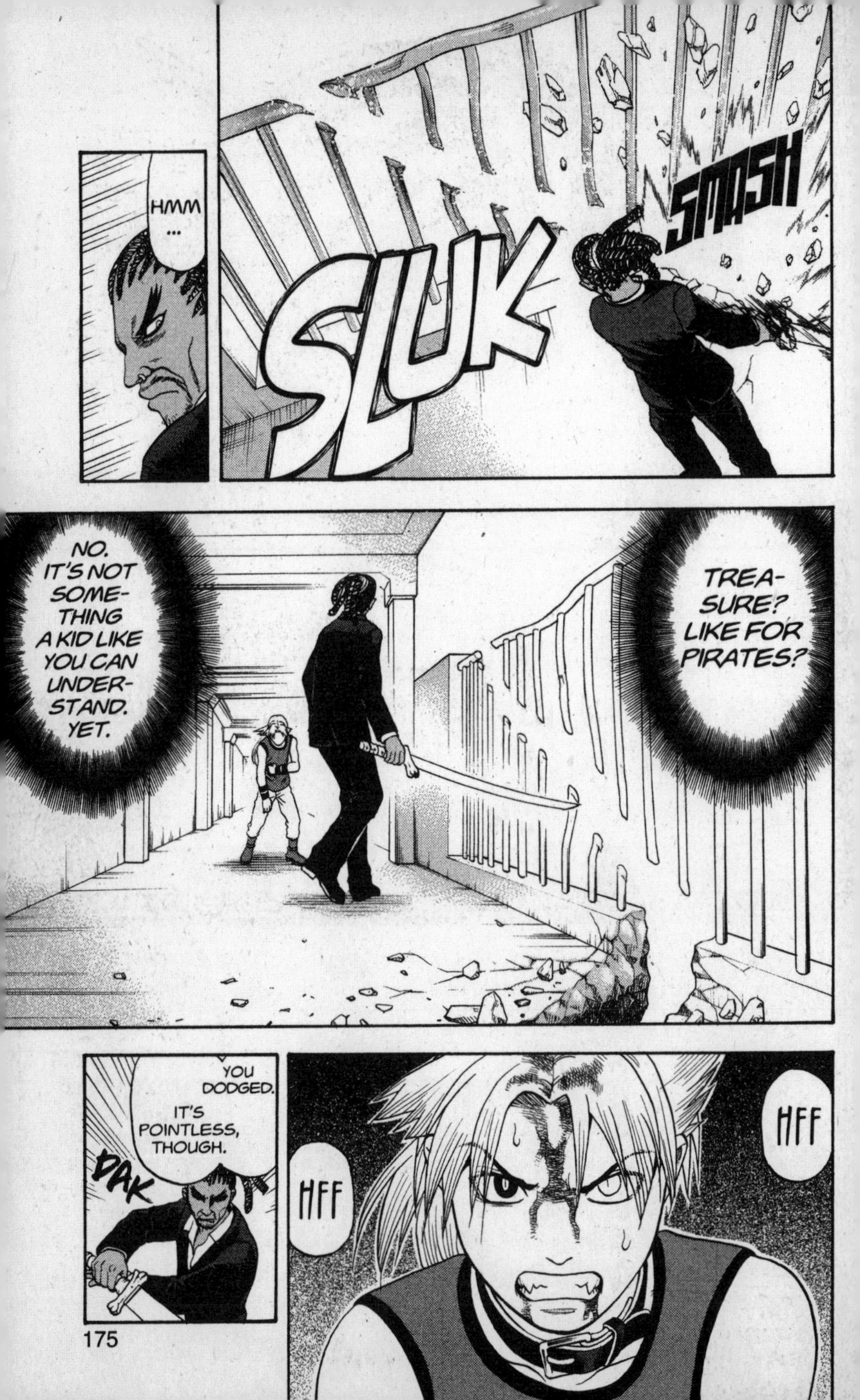
SMASH
SLUK
HMM ...
TREA-SURE? LIKE FOR PIRATES?
NO. IT'S NOT SOME-THING A KID LIKE YOU CAN UNDER-STAND. YET.
HFF
HFF
YOU DODGED.
IT'S POINTLESS, THOUGH.
DAK

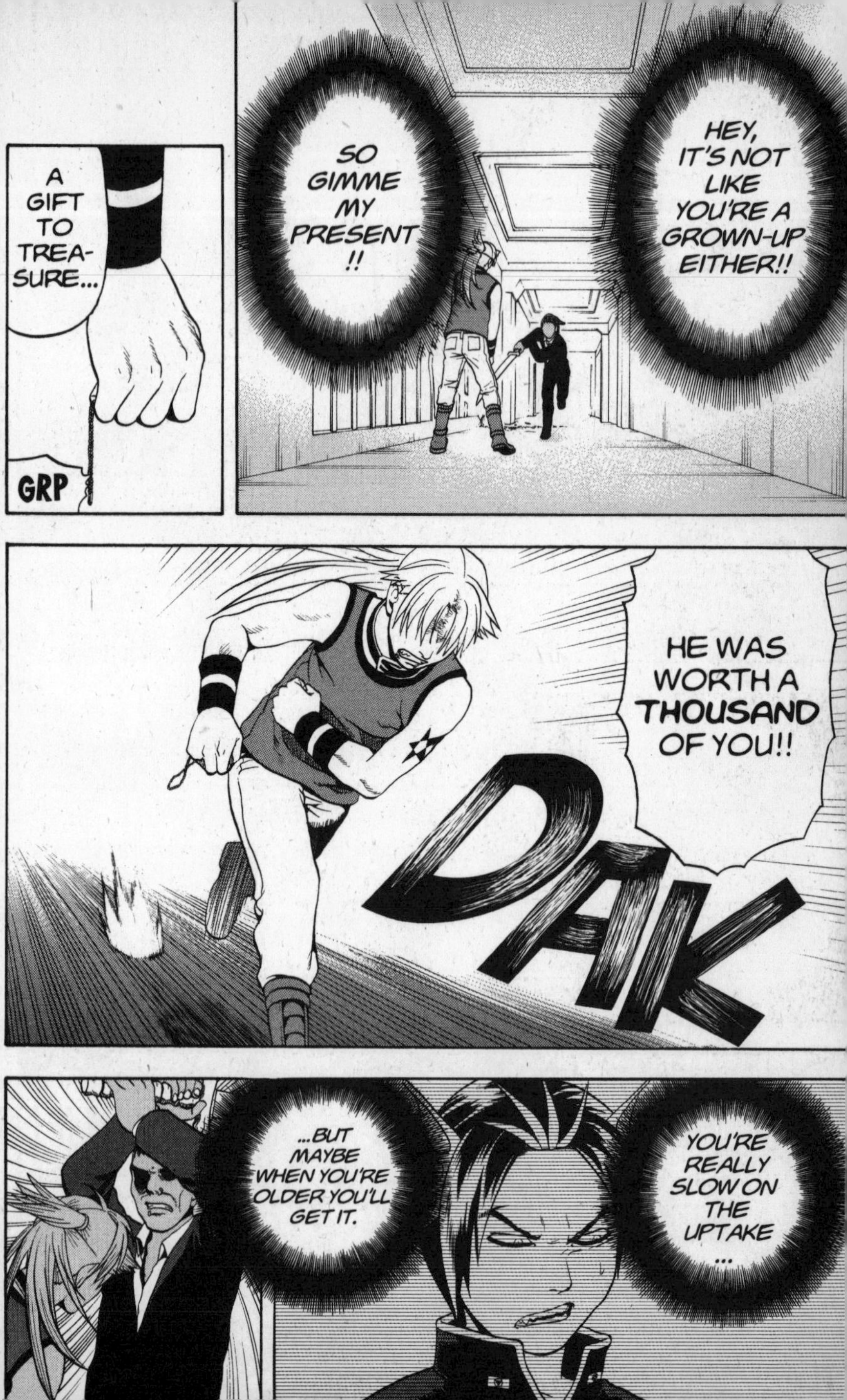
HEY, IT'S NOT LIKE YOU'RE A GROWN-UP EITHER!!
SO GIMME MY PRESENT!!
A GIFT TO TREASURE...
GRP
HE WAS WORTH A THOUSAND OF YOU!!
DAK
YOU'RE REALLY SLOW ON THE UPTAKE...
...BUT MAYBE WHEN YOU'RE OLDER YOU'LL GET IT.

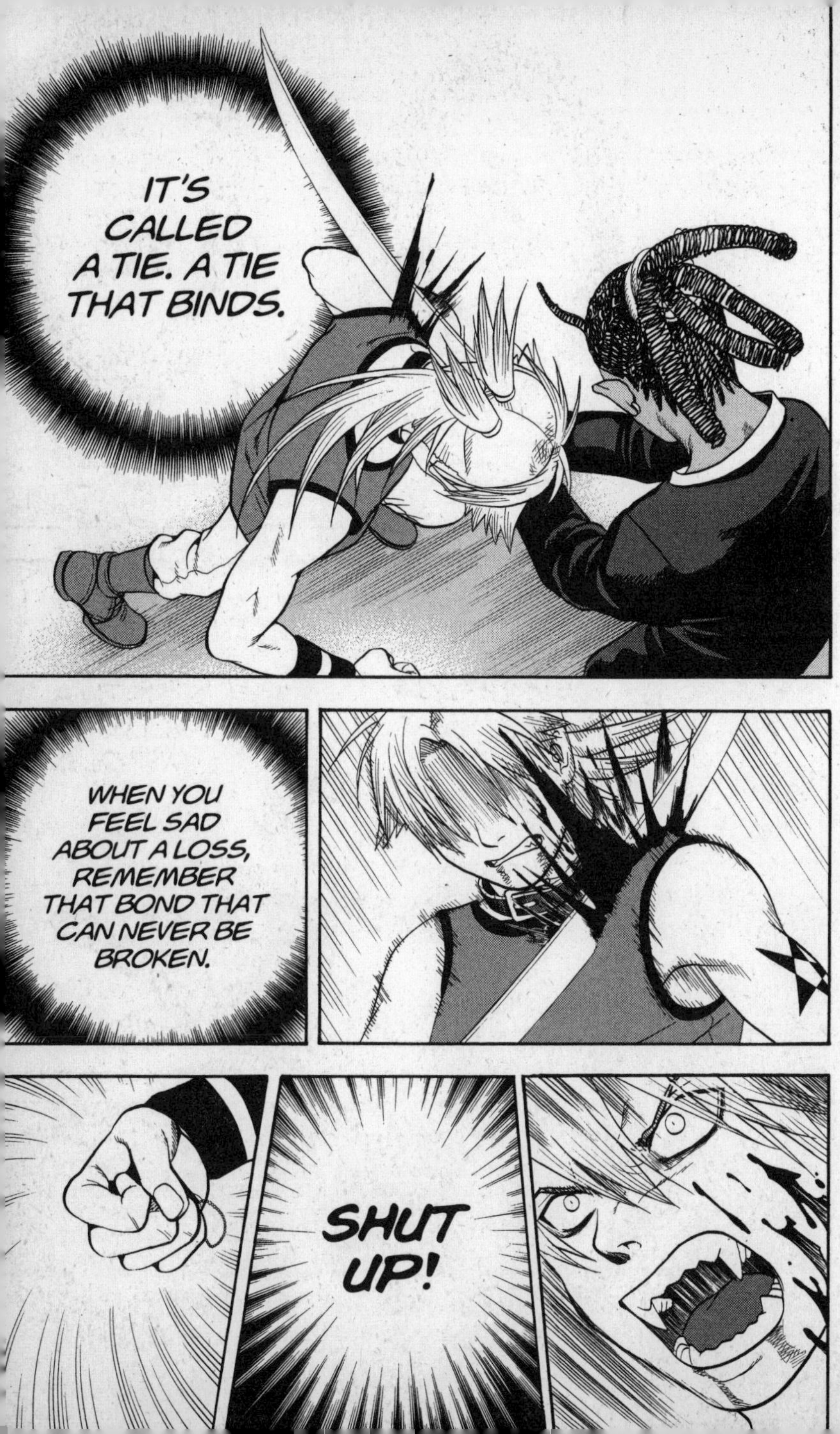
IT'S CALLED A TIE. A TIE THAT BINDS.
WHEN YOU FEEL SAD ABOUT A LOSS, REMEMBER THAT BOND THAT CAN NEVER BE BROKEN.
SHUT UP!

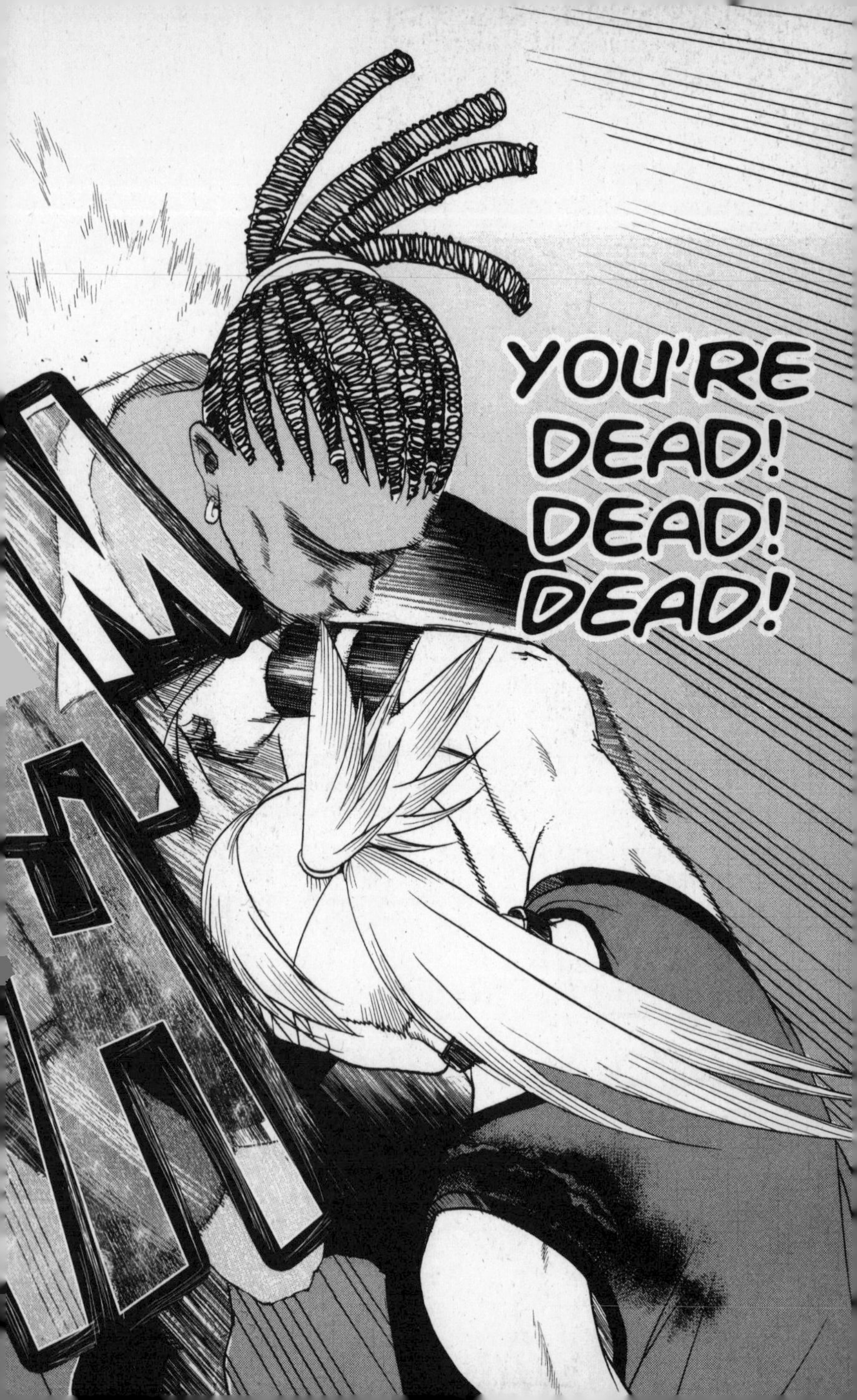
YOU'RE DEAD! DEAD! DEAD!

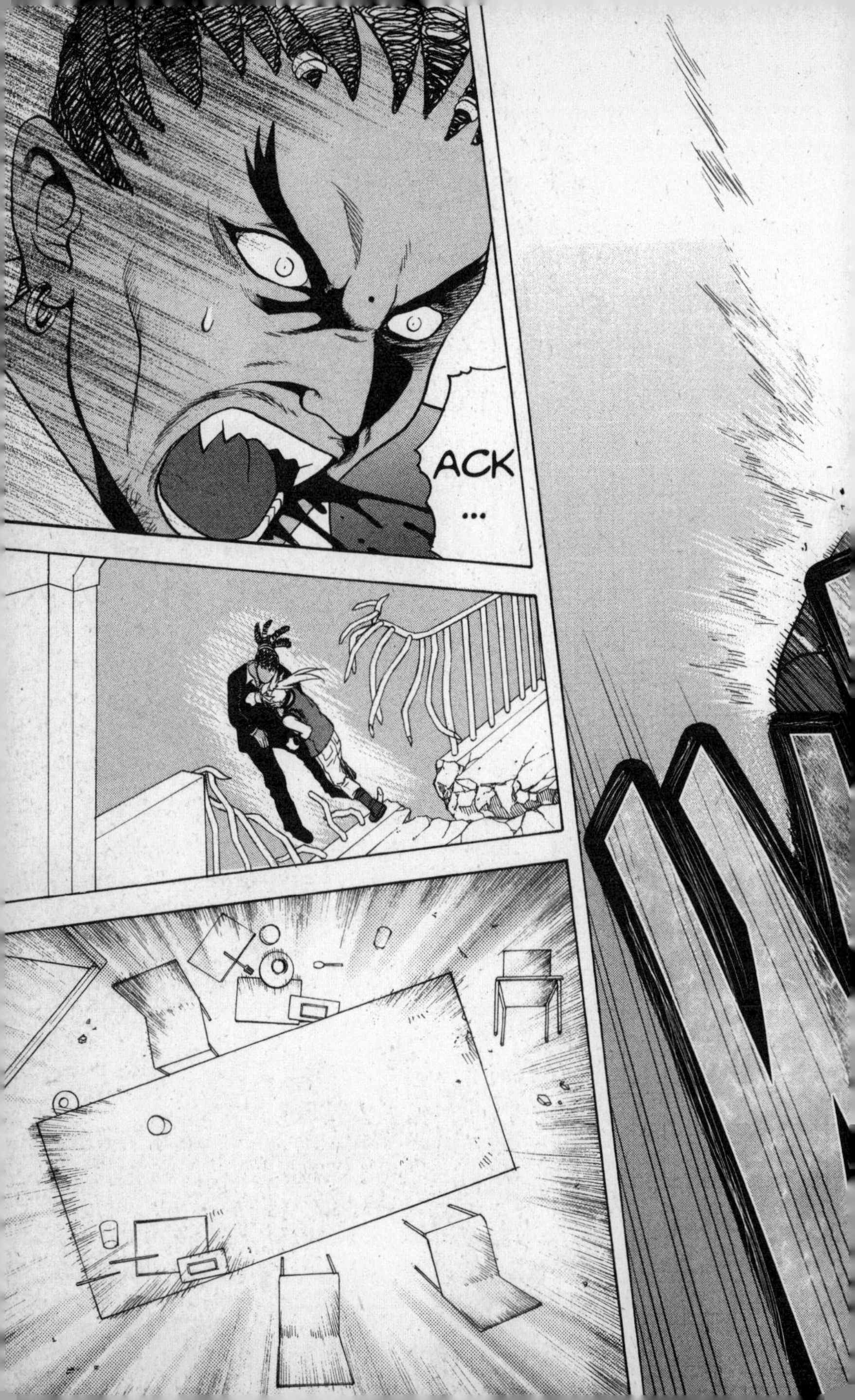
ACK
...

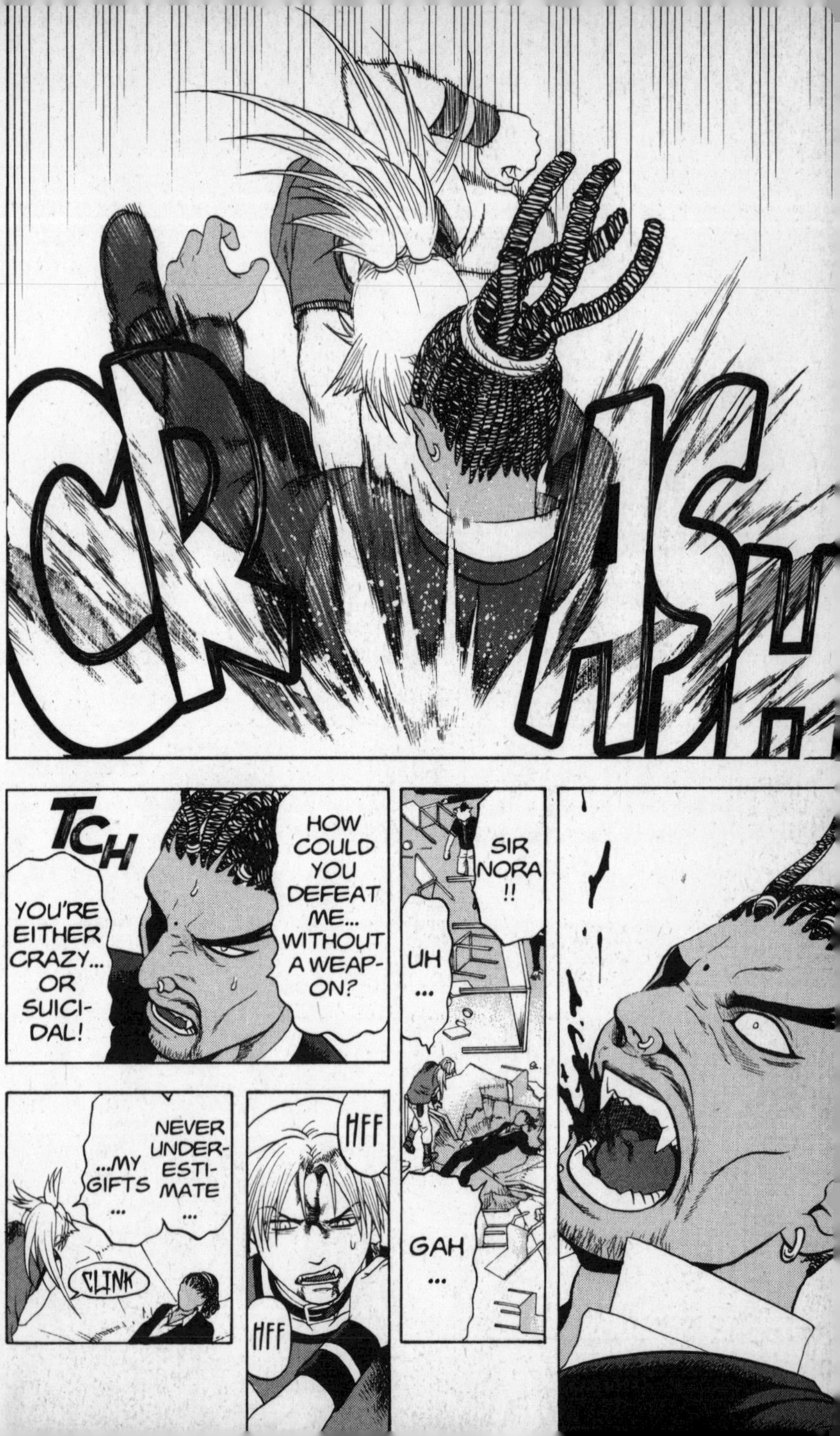
CRASH!!
SIR NORA !!
UH ...
GAH ...
TCH
HOW COULD YOU DEFEAT ME... WITHOUT A WEAPON?
YOU'RE EITHER CRAZY... OR SUICIDAL!
HFF
HFF
NEVER UNDERESTIMATE ...
...MY GIFTS ...
CLINK

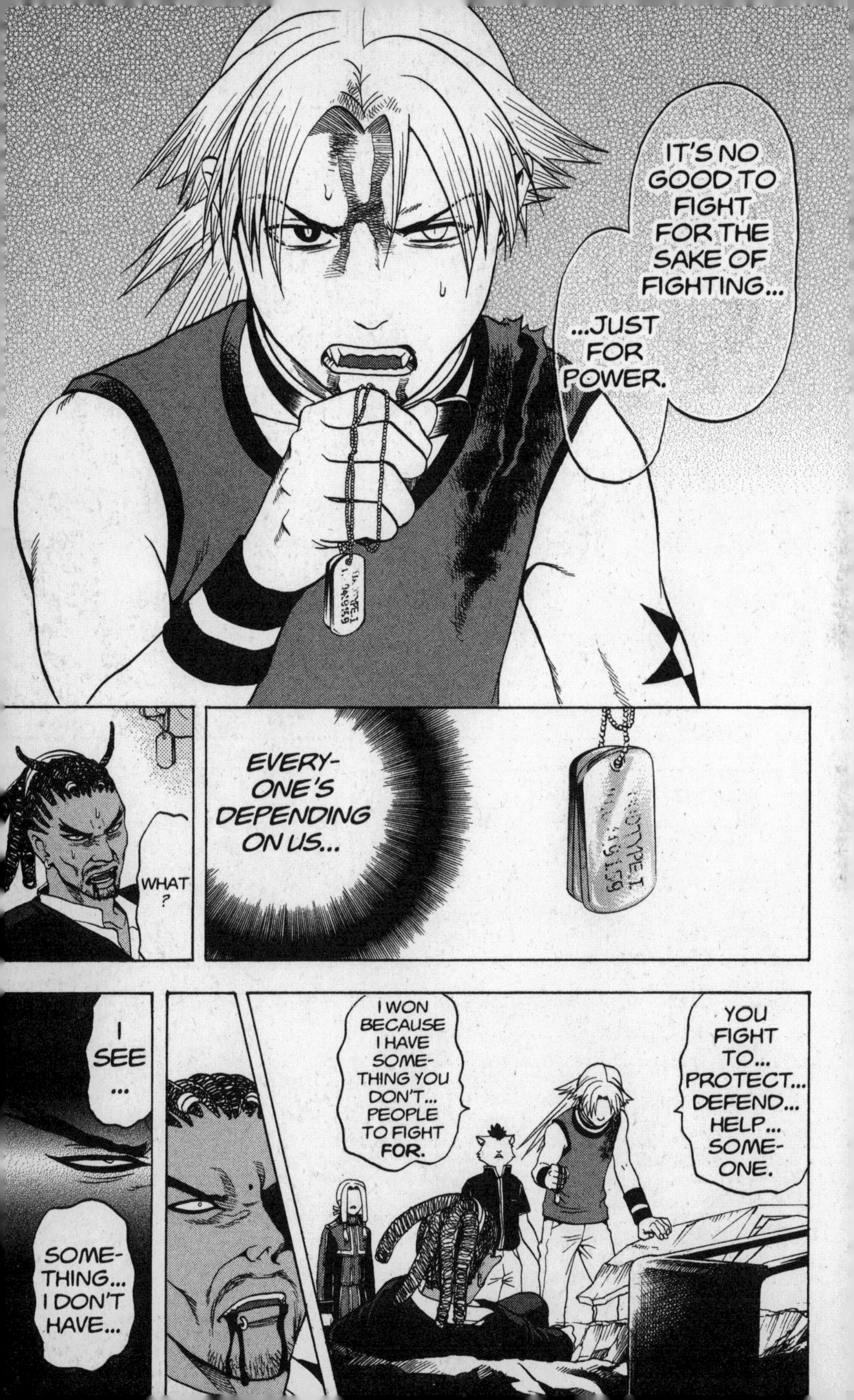
IT'S NO GOOD TO FIGHT FOR THE SAKE OF FIGHTING...
...JUST FOR POWER.
EVERYONE'S DEPENDING ON US...
WHAT?
YOU FIGHT TO... PROTECT... DEFEND... HELP... SOMEONE.
I WON BECAUSE I HAVE SOMETHING YOU DON'T... PEOPLE TO FIGHT FOR.
I SEE...
SOMETHING... I DON'T HAVE...

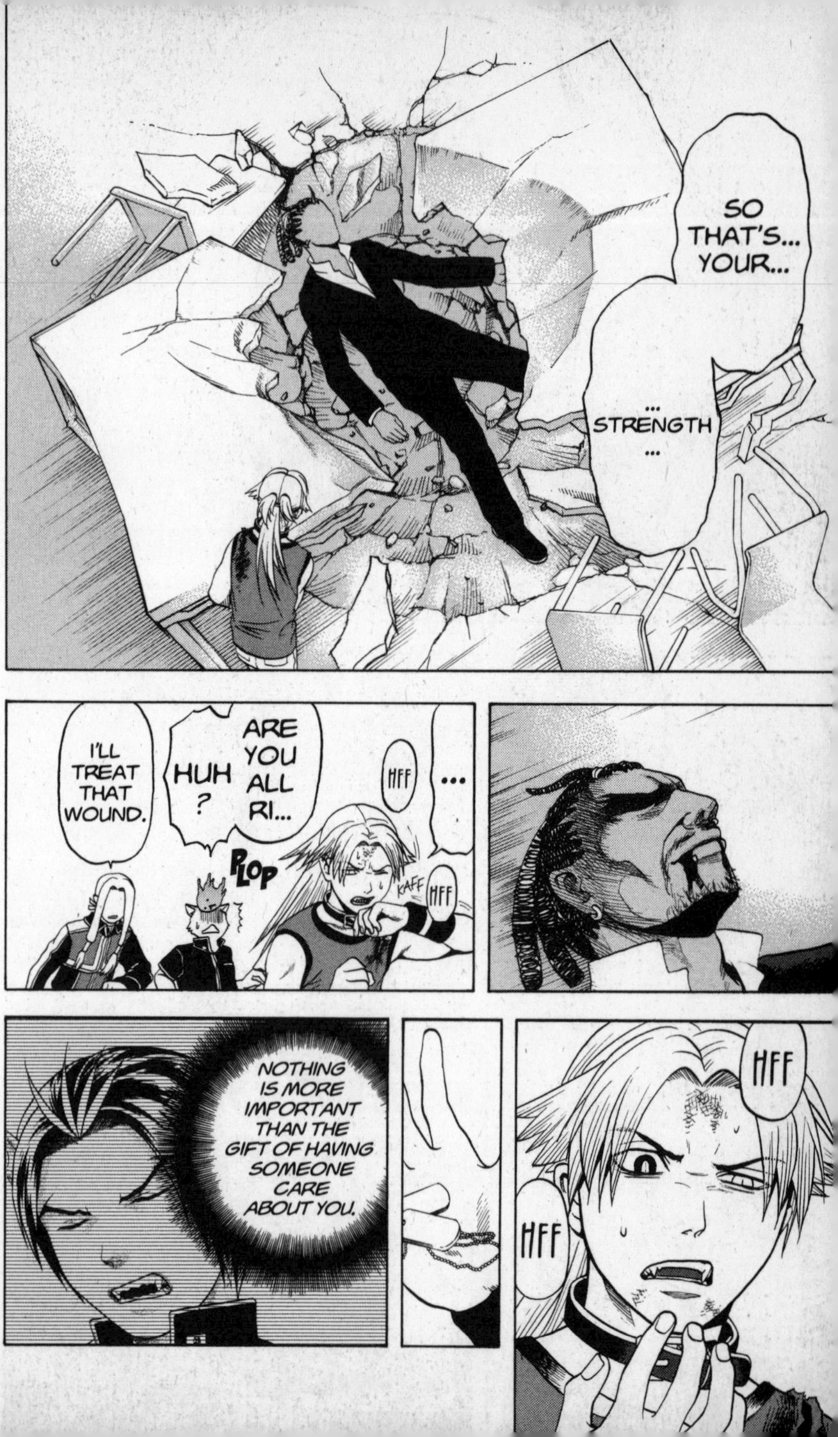
SO THAT'S... YOUR...
... STRENGTH ...
...
HFF
KAFF
HFF
ARE YOU ALL RI...
HUH ?
PLOP
I'LL TREAT THAT WOUND.
HFF
HFF
NOTHING IS MORE IMPORTANT THAN THE GIFT OF HAVING SOMEONE CARE ABOUT YOU.

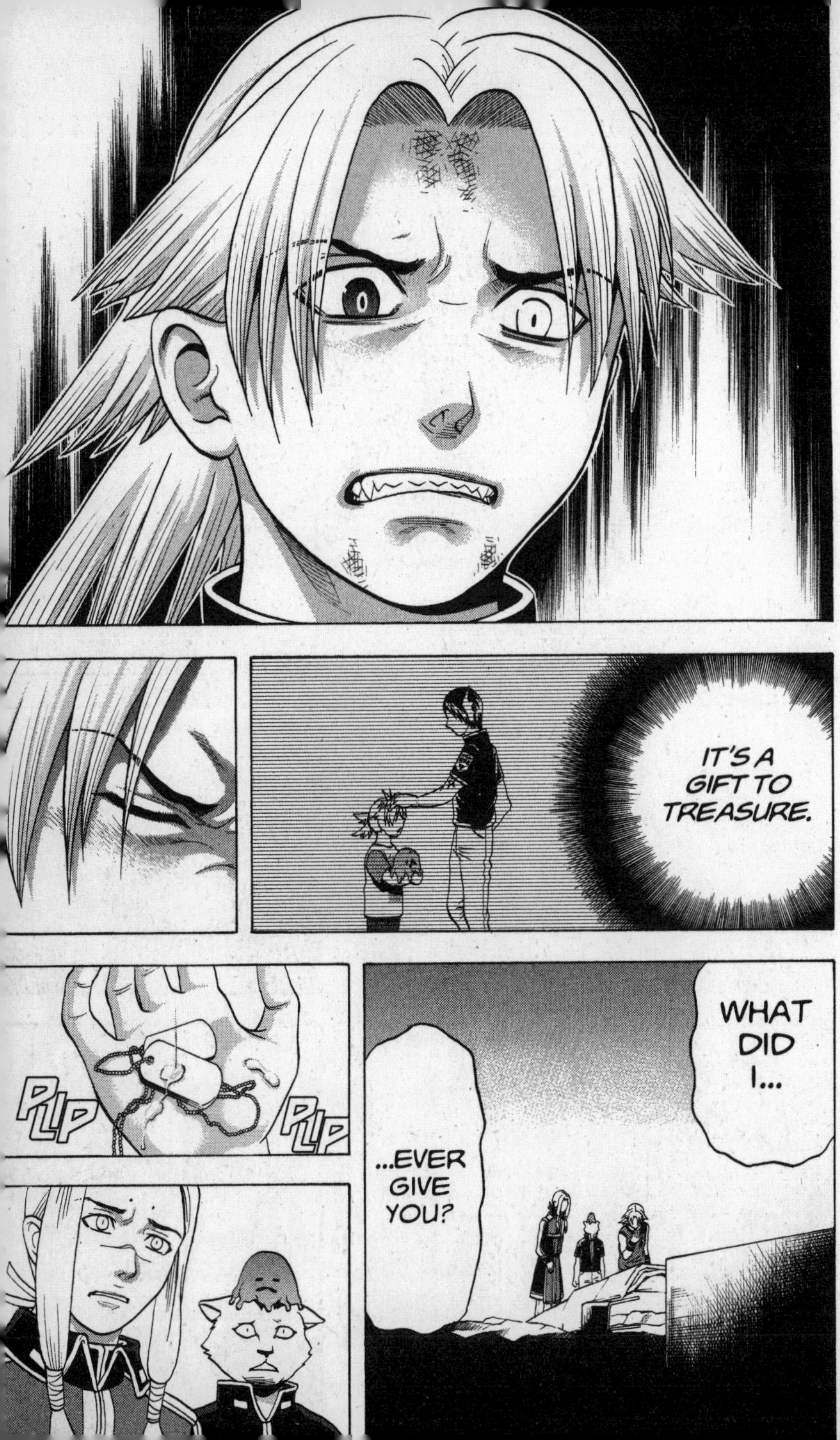
IT'S A GIFT TO TREASURE.
WHAT DID I...
...EVER GIVE YOU?
PLIP
PLIP

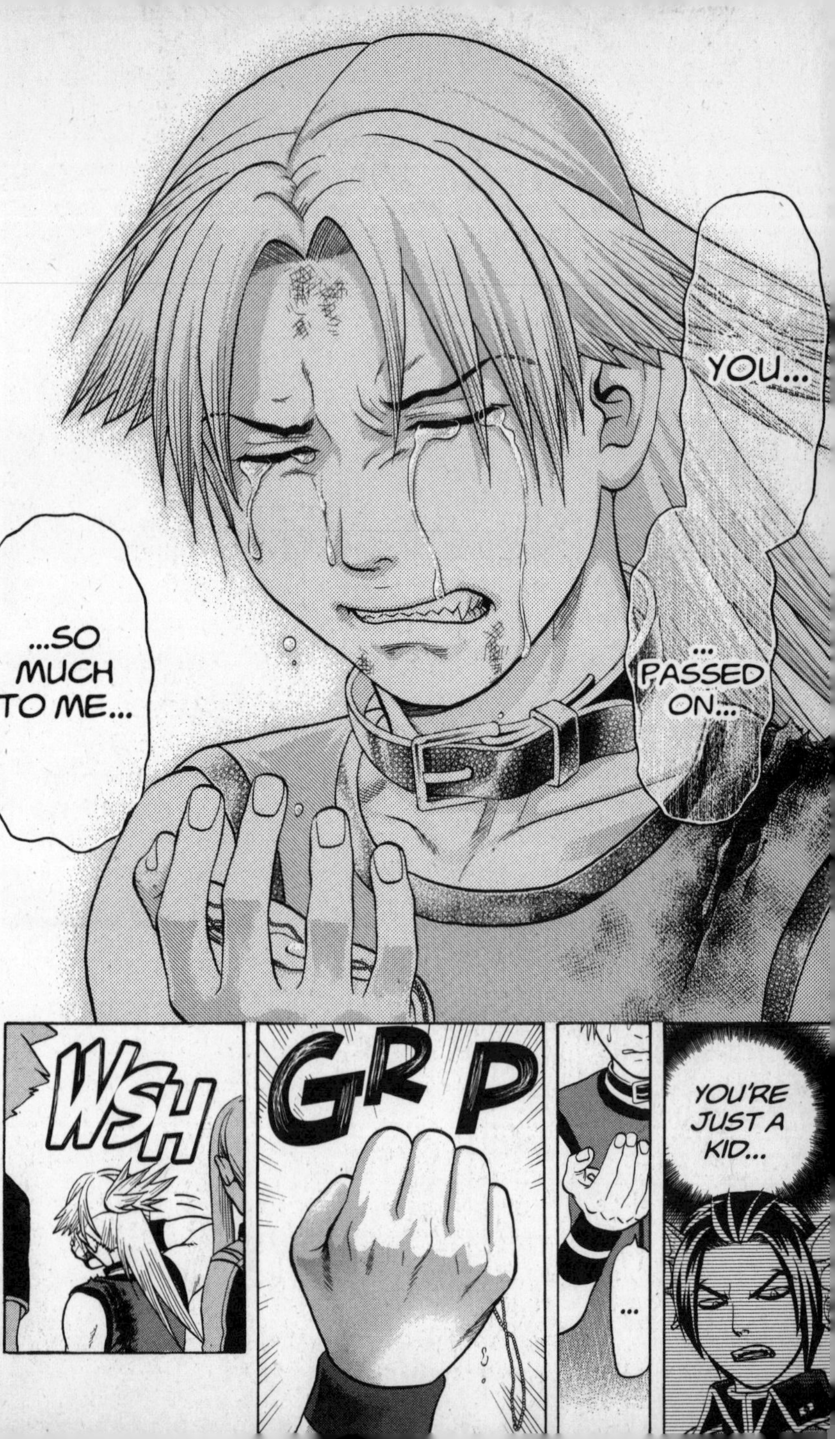
YOU...
...PASSED ON...
...SO MUCH TO ME...
YOU'RE JUST A KID...
...
GRP
WSH

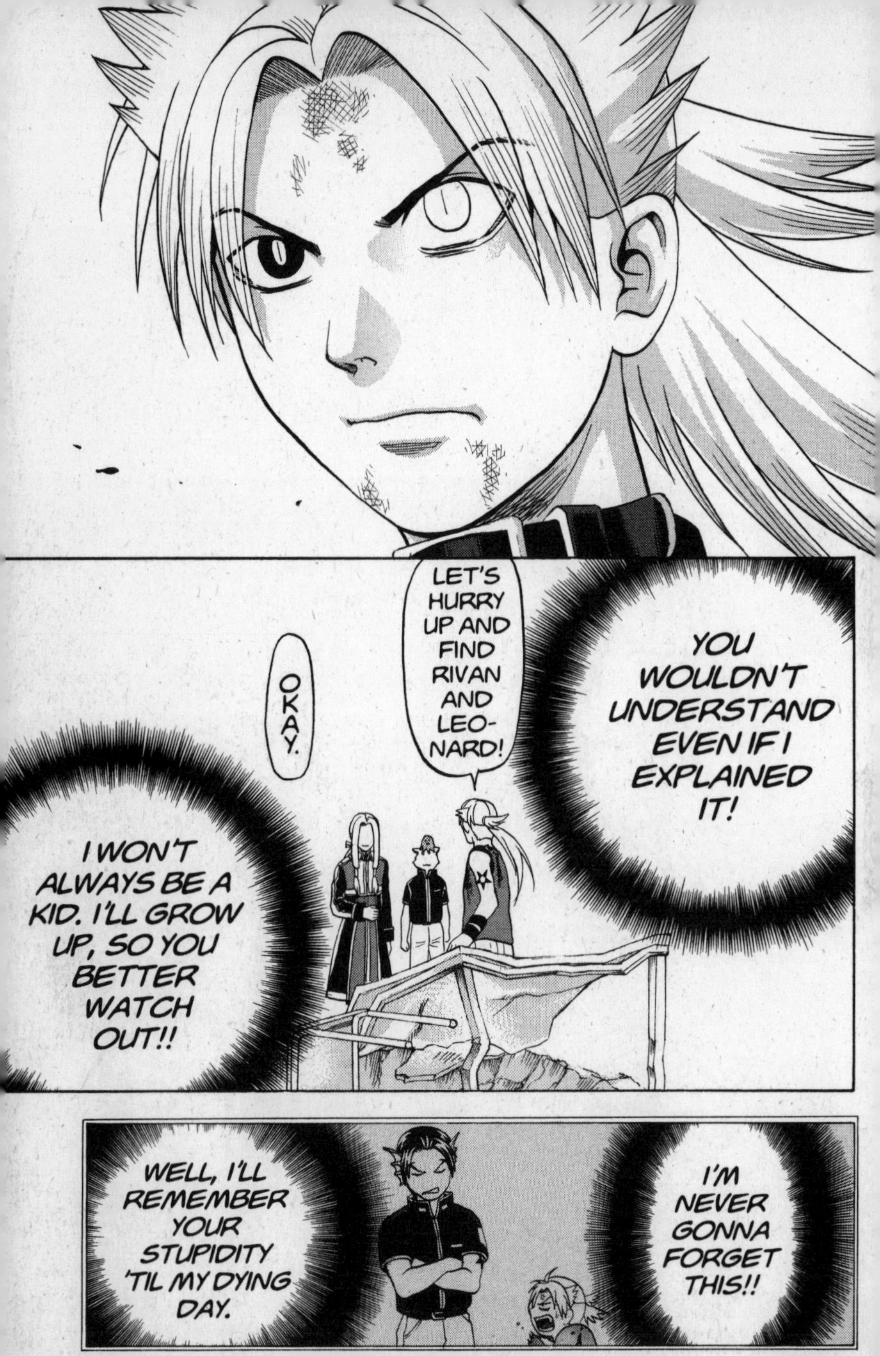
YOU WOULDN'T UNDERSTAND EVEN IF I EXPLAINED IT!
LET'S HURRY UP AND FIND RIVAN AND LEO-NARD!
OKAY.
I WON'T ALWAYS BE A KID. I'LL GROW UP, SO YOU BETTER WATCH OUT!!
I'M NEVER GONNA FORGET THIS!!
WELL, I'LL REMEMBER YOUR STUPIDITY 'TIL MY DYING DAY.

Volume 6: Cerberus and the Dark Liege—End

ROUGH SKETCHES I DREW
BEFORE I STARTED *NORA.*

NORA MAILBAG

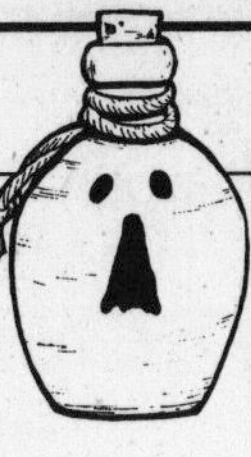

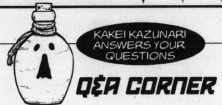

KAKEI KAZUNARI ANSWERS YOUR QUESTIONS

Q&A CORNER

Q: I WOULD LIKE TO ASK KAKEI SENSEI A QUESTION. HUMANS HAVE BLOOD TYPES AND BIRTHDAYS, BUT DO DEMONS HAVE THEM TOO? ENLIGHTEN ME! (AMI HOJO, SAITAMA PREFECTURE)

A: THEY DO HAVE BLOOD TYPES, BUT THEY'RE DIFFERENT FROM HUMAN BLOOD TYPES (TYPE A, TYPE B, ETC.). DEMONS BEGAN CELEBRATING BIRTHDAYS AFTER THE CURRENT DARK LIEGE STARTED USING THE HUMAN CALENDAR IN THE DEMON WORLD.

Q: HOW LONG AGO DID THE PREVIOUS CERBERUS, DEIGREE, LIVE? (NUMBER 2 REAR GUARD, IWATE PREFECTURE)

A: IT WAS ABOUT 2,000 TO 3,000 YEARS AGO.

Q: HOW DID RIVAN BECOME SO LAZY? (JIN AKIKAZE , HOKKAIDO)

A: HE WAS BORN LAZY.

← CONTINUED ON THE NEXT PAGE...

NORA MAILBAG

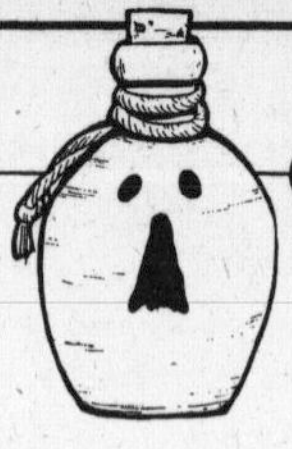

KAKEI KAZUNARI ANSWERS YOUR QUESTIONS

Q&A CORNER

Q: HOW DO YOU COME UP WITH NAMES FOR YOUR CHARACTERS? (FENRISULFR, HOKKAIDO)

A: I GET THIS QUESTION A LOT. SETTING ASIDE CERTAIN CHARACTERS LIKE NORA AND DEIGREE, MANY OF MY DEMONS' NAMES ARE BASED ON THE NAMES OF DEVILS THAT APPEAR IN FOLKLORE AND LITERATURE FROM DIFFERENT CULTURES. I GET LETTERS GUESSING WHERE I GOT CERTAIN NAMES, BUT I PREFER TO LET THE FANS WONDER. IT'S MORE FUN THAT WAY.

CALL FOR LETTERS

SEND LETTERS AND FAN ART TO:

VIZ MEDIA, LLC
NORA EDITOR
P.O. BOX 77010
SAN FRANCISCO, CA 94107

☆IF YOU SEND IN FAN ART, PLEASE DRAW CLEARLY WITH BLACK INK. (PENCILS AND MECHANICAL PENCILS WILL NOT REPRODUCE.) BE SURE TO INCLUDE YOUR NAME AND ADDRESS.

☆WE CANNOT RETURN ANYTHING YOU SEND US. IF YOU WANT TO KEEP THE ORIGINAL, JUST SEND IN A COPY.

☆ALL DRAWINGS BECOME THE PROPERTY OF *SHONEN JUMP*. HOWEVER, IF THEY ARE EVER REPRINTED WE WILL CONTACT THE APPLICANT AGAIN FOR CONSENT.

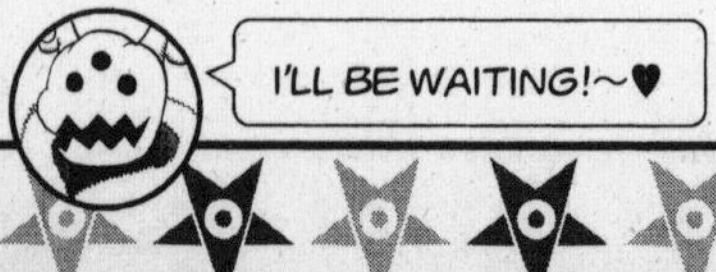
I'LL BE WAITING!~♥

↑JOHN HIRASAKA(♂)

WORKING HARD OR HARDLY WORKING, PART ONE

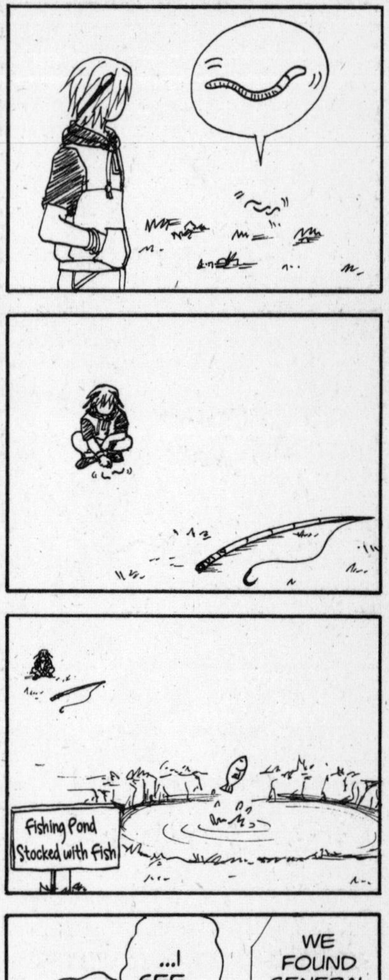
Fishing Pond
Stocked with Fish
WE FOUND GENERAL RIVAN!!
HE WAS RIGHT WHERE YOU THOUGHT HE WAS.
...I SEE... THAT'S GOOD...
I'M STARTING TO GET A HEADACHE...

WORKING HARD OR HARDLY WORKING, PART TWO

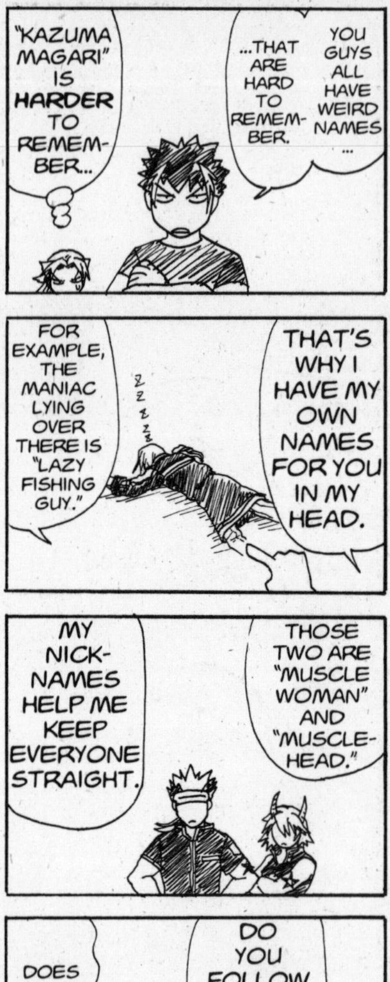
YOU GUYS ALL HAVE WEIRD NAMES...
...THAT ARE HARD TO REMEMBER.
“KAZUMA MAGARI” IS **HARDER** TO REMEMBER...
THAT'S WHY I HAVE MY OWN NAMES FOR YOU IN MY HEAD.
FOR EXAMPLE, THE MANIAC LYING OVER THERE IS “LAZY FISHING GUY.”
THOSE TWO ARE “MUSCLE WOMAN” AND “MUSCLE-HEAD.”
MY NICKNAMES HELP ME KEEP EVERYONE STRAIGHT.
DO YOU FOLLOW ME, “NURSE GOATY”?
DOES INSANITY RUN IN YOUR FAMILY?

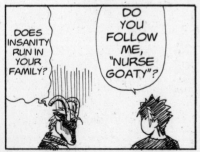

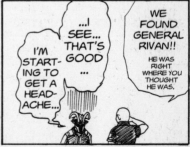

FOCUS ON JELLY

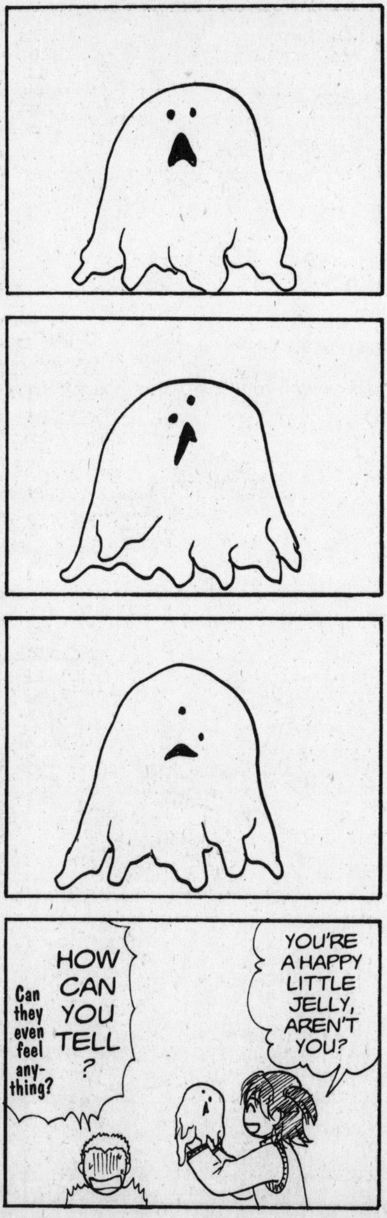
YOU'RE A HAPPY LITTLE JELLY, AREN'T YOU?
HOW CAN YOU TELL?
Can they even feel any-thing?

FOCUS ON JELLY, PART TWO

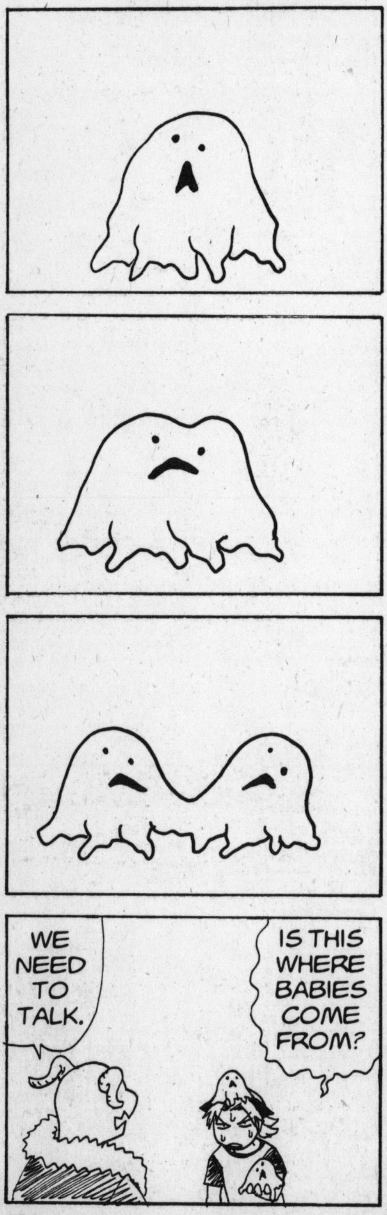
IS THIS WHERE BABIES COME FROM?
WE NEED TO TALK.

STAFF PAGE

THE FIENDISH STAFF THAT WORKED ON VOLUME 6 (IN NO PARTICULAR ORDER):

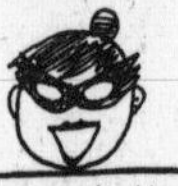

Empress Yoshinon

HER SHARP TONGUE IS A DEADLY WEAPON. RECENTLY, WHILE SHE WAS LOOKING OUT THE WINDOW AND DAYDREAMING, SHE SAID, "IF ONLY REAL-LIFE GUYS WERE AS INTERESTING AS MANGA CHARACTERS." WE ARE AFRAID TO ASK WHAT HAD HAPPENED IN HER CLOUDED PAST TO MAKE HER THINK THAT WAY.

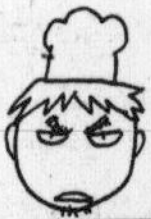

Chef Hitouji

BRILLIANT ILLUSTRATOR AND COOK, ALBEIT AN ECCENTRIC ONE. HIS DIRTY LITTLE SECRET: HE'S A SCAREDY-CAT WHO CAN'T SLEEP AFTER SEEING SCARY SHOWS ON TELEVISION.

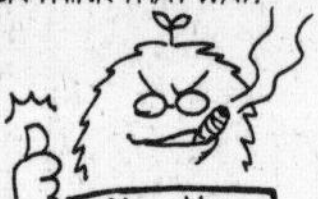

Ohga-king

THE MASTER OF BUTTING-IN, OFTEN COMPARED TO A CARTOON CHARACTER. HE'S ALSO A GOOD COOK, ALTHOUGH HE COMPLAINS THAT NOW HE HAS TO WATCH COOKING PROGRAMS EVERY DAY TO FEED OUR STAFF.

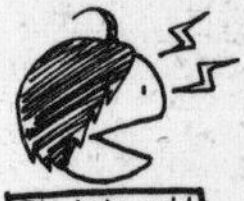

Dr. Kobayashi

THE KING OF 3-D DRAWING AND THE ARTIST WITH THE HANDS OF GOD. FOR SOME REASON KOBAYASHI OWNS LOTS OF RARE AND UNUSUAL DVDS AND MAGAZINES. HIS PRIVATE LIFE IS FILLED WITH MYSTERY. FOR INSTANCE, NOBODY KNOWS WHEN HE SLEEPS (IF HE EVER DOES).

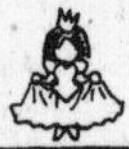

Princess Shibayan

DON'T LET HER SWEET FACE FOOL YOU: SHE'S A BORN SCHEMER. BEFORE WE KNEW IT SHE HAD A CANDY MACHINE INSTALLED IN THE STUDIO. ALTHOUGH SHE'S YOUNG, SHE'S VERY FAMILIAR WITH CLASSIC NINTENDO GAMES.

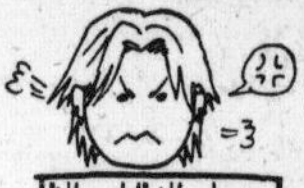

"Hirachi" Hirakawa

A DECENT GUY WHO JUST HAPPENS TO LOOK LIKE A HOODLUM, CAUSING HIM A LOT OF TROUBLE. ALTHOUGH HE WORKS FAST, HE'S KIND OF SLOW ON THE UPTAKE.

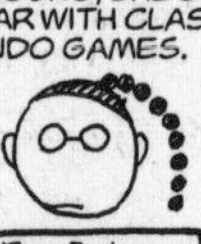

Ryu Fujiwara

A HONG KONG MOVIE FAN WHO IS TRYING TO GROW HIS HAIR INTO A CHINESE PIGTAIL. HE DRAWS WITH A CHOPSTICK PEN HE MADE HIMSELF. YOU CAN'T GET ANYTHING OUT OF HIM WHILE THE HANSHIN TIGERS ARE PLAYING YOKOHAMA ON TELEVISION.

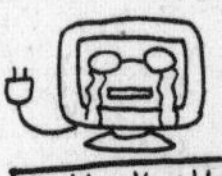

Machine Yunokichi

THE BRAVE IT MASTER WHO CAN'T ALWAYS MIND HIS OWN BUSINESS. BECAUSE HE HAS SUCH BEAUTIFUL AND ABUNDANT HAIR, HE IS THE ENEMY OF ALL BALDING MEN!

BIRTHDAY PRESENT

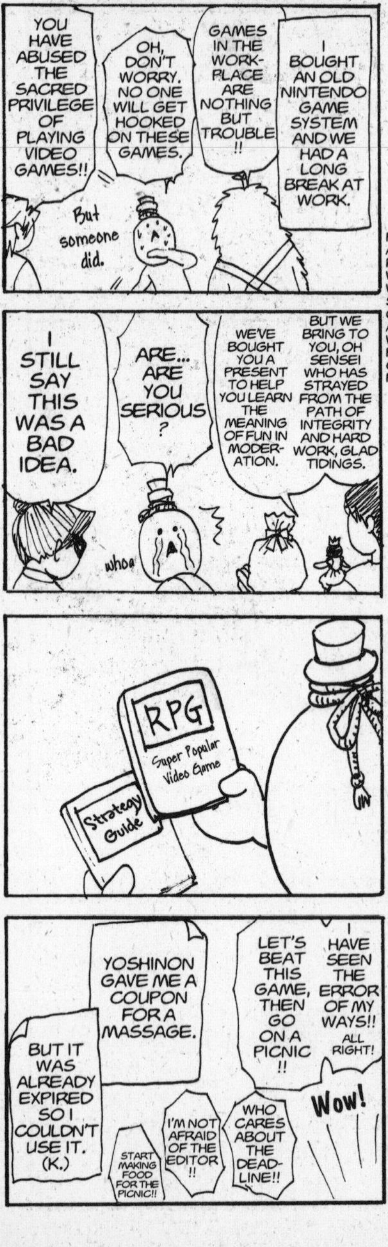
I BOUGHT AN OLD NINTENDO GAME SYSTEM AND WE HAD A LONG BREAK AT WORK.
GAMES IN THE WORKPLACE ARE NOTHING BUT TROUBLE!!
OH, DON'T WORRY. NO ONE WILL GET HOOKED ON THESE GAMES.
YOU HAVE ABUSED THE SACRED PRIVILEGE OF PLAYING VIDEO GAMES!!
But someone did.
BUT WE BRING TO YOU, OH SENSEI WHO HAS STRAYED FROM THE PATH OF INTEGRITY AND HARD WORK, GLAD TIDINGS.
WE'VE BOUGHT YOU A PRESENT TO HELP YOU LEARN THE MEANING OF FUN IN MODERATION.
ARE... ARE YOU SERIOUS?
I STILL SAY THIS WAS A BAD IDEA.
whoa
RPG
Super Popular Video Game
Strategy Guide
I HAVE SEEN THE ERROR OF MY WAYS!!
ALL RIGHT!
LET'S BEAT THIS GAME, THEN GO ON A PICNIC!!
Wow!
WHO CARES ABOUT THE DEADLINE!!
YOSHINON GAVE ME A COUPON FOR A MASSAGE.
I'M NOT AFRAID OF THE EDITOR!!
START MAKING FOOD FOR THE PICNIC!!
BUT IT WAS ALREADY EXPIRED SO I COULDN'T USE IT. (K.)

COOKING WITH TAKESHI HITOUJI

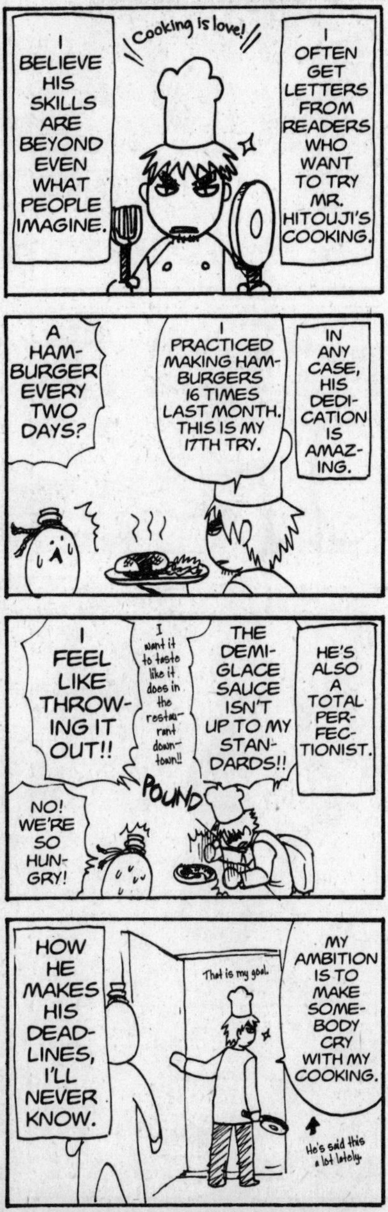
I OFTEN GET LETTERS FROM READERS WHO WANT TO TRY MR. HITOUJI'S COOKING.
Cooking is love!
I BELIEVE HIS SKILLS ARE BEYOND EVEN WHAT PEOPLE IMAGINE.
IN ANY CASE, HIS DEDICATION IS AMAZING.
I PRACTICED MAKING HAMBURGERS 16 TIMES LAST MONTH. THIS IS MY 17TH TRY.
A HAMBURGER EVERY TWO DAYS?
HE'S ALSO A TOTAL PERFECTIONIST.
THE DEMI-GLACE SAUCE ISN'T UP TO MY STANDARDS!!
I want it to taste like it does in the restaurant downtown!!
I FEEL LIKE THROWING IT OUT!!
POUND
NO! WE'RE SO HUNGRY!
MY AMBITION IS TO MAKE SOMEBODY CRY WITH MY COOKING.
He's said this a lot lately.
That is my goal.
HOW HE MAKES HIS DEADLINES, I'LL NEVER KNOW.

INGRATITUDE

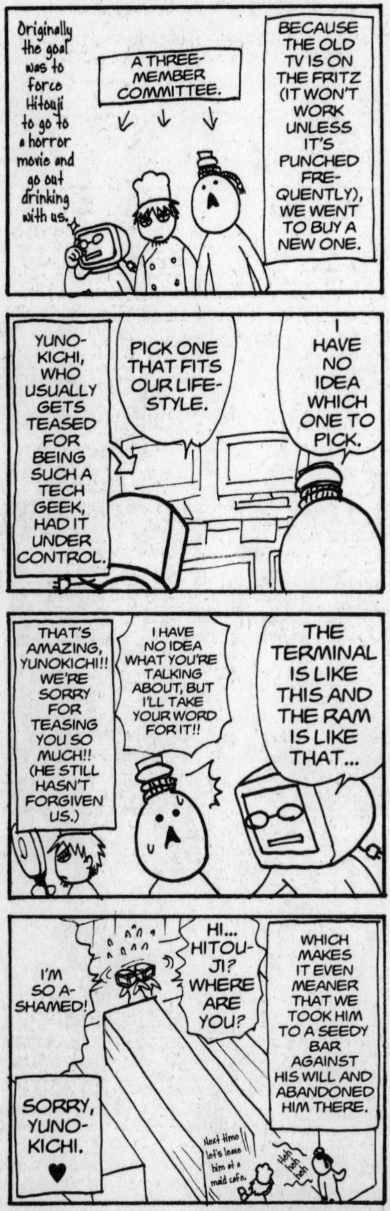
BECAUSE THE OLD TV IS ON THE FRITZ (IT WON'T WORK UNLESS IT'S PUNCHED FREQUENTLY), WE WENT TO BUY A NEW ONE.
A THREE-MEMBER COMMITTEE.
Originally the goal was to force Hitouji to go to a horror movie and go out drinking with us.
I HAVE NO IDEA WHICH ONE TO PICK.
PICK ONE THAT FITS OUR LIFESTYLE.
YUNOKICHI, WHO USUALLY GETS TEASED FOR BEING SUCH A TECH GEEK, HAD IT UNDER CONTROL.
THE TERMINAL IS LIKE THIS AND THE RAM IS LIKE THAT...
I HAVE NO IDEA WHAT YOU'RE TALKING ABOUT, BUT I'LL TAKE YOUR WORD FOR IT!!
THAT'S AMAZING, YUNOKICHI!! WE'RE SORRY FOR TEASING YOU SO MUCH!! (HE STILL HASN'T FORGIVEN US.)
WHICH MAKES IT EVEN MEANER THAT WE TOOK HIM TO A SEEDY BAR AGAINST HIS WILL AND ABANDONED HIM THERE.
HI... HITOUJI? WHERE ARE YOU?
I'M SO ASHAMED!
SORRY, YUNOKICHI. ♥
Heh heh heh
Next time let's leave him at a maid cafe.

↑ DRAWN BY KAZUNARI KAKEI, WHO ISN'T IN THE BEST OF HEALTH (WHICH IS HIS OWN FAULT).

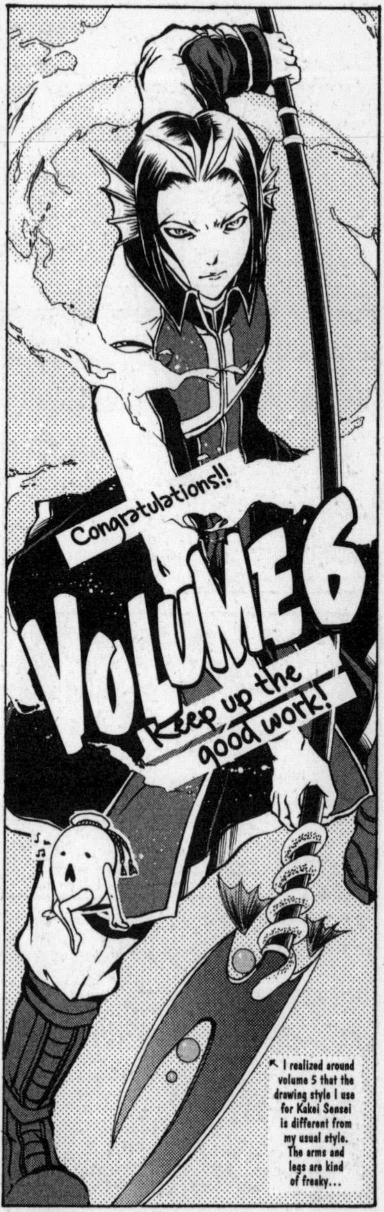
Congratulations!!
VOLUME 6
Keep up the good work!
I realized around volume 5 that the drawing style I use for Kakei Sensei is different from my usual style. The arms and legs are kind of freaky...

↑ DRAWN BY SHIBAYAN, THE LITTLE PATISSIER

■ I SEE LONDON, I SEE FRANCE...

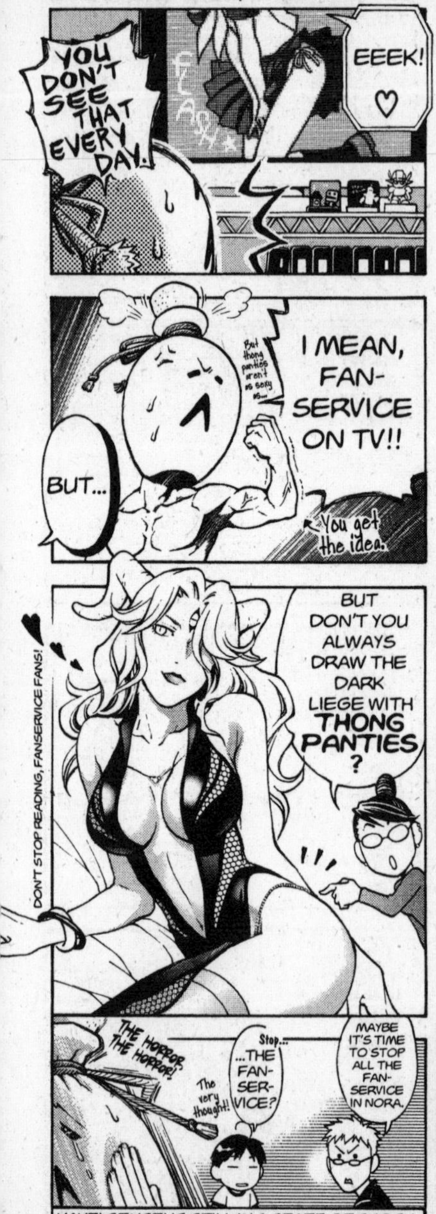
EEEK! ♡
FLASH ★
YOU DON'T SEE THAT EVERY DAY.
I MEAN, FAN-SERVICE ON TV!!
But thong panties aren't as sexy as...
BUT...
You get the idea.
BUT DON'T YOU ALWAYS DRAW THE DARK LIEGE WITH THONG PANTIES?
DON'T STOP READING, FANSERVICE FANS!
MAYBE IT'S TIME TO STOP ALL THE FAN-SERVICE IN NORA.
Stop... ...THE FAN-SERVICE?
The very thought!!
THE HORROR THE HORROR!
KAKEI SENSEI IS STILL IN A STATE OF SHOCK.

↑ DRAWN BY DR. KOBAYASHI, THE MAD SCIENTIST

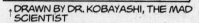

A BALANCED DIET?

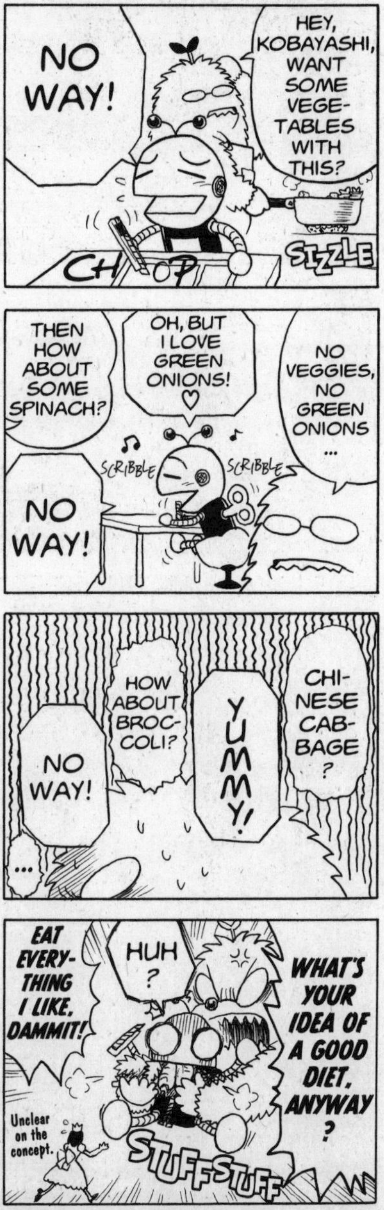
HEY, KOBAYASHI, WANT SOME VEGETABLES WITH THIS?
NO WAY!
SIZZLE
CHOP
NO VEGGIES, NO GREEN ONIONS ...
OH, BUT I LOVE GREEN ONIONS! ♡
THEN HOW ABOUT SOME SPINACH?
SCRIBBLE
SCRIBBLE
NO WAY!
CHINESE CABBAGE?
YUMMY!
HOW ABOUT BROCCOLI?
NO WAY!
...
WHAT'S YOUR IDEA OF A GOOD DIET, ANYWAY?
HUH?
EAT EVERYTHING I LIKE, DAMMIT!
STUFFSTUFF
Unclear on the concept.

DON'T UNDERESTIMATE SHIBAYAN

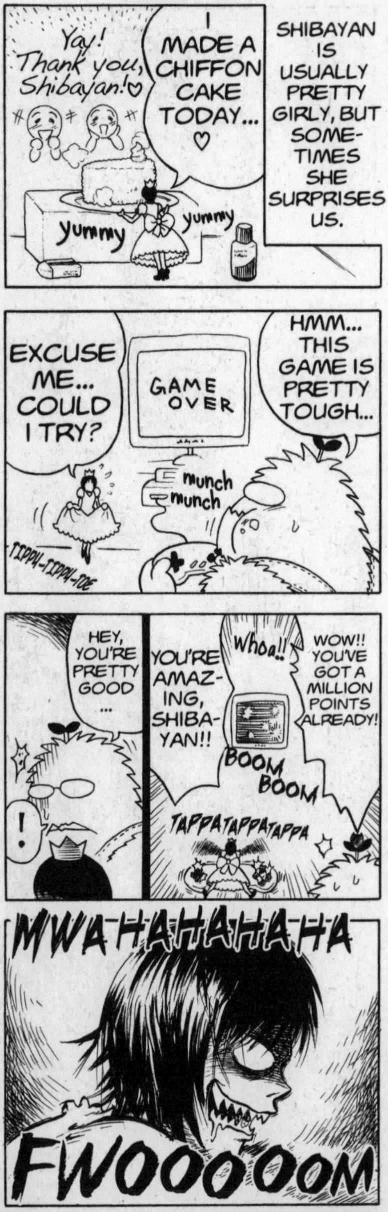
SHIBAYAN IS USUALLY PRETTY GIRLY, BUT SOMETIMES SHE SURPRISES US.
I MADE A CHIFFON CAKE TODAY... ♡
Yay! Thank you, Shibayan!♡
yummy
yummy
HMM... THIS GAME IS PRETTY TOUGH...
GAME OVER
munch munch
EXCUSE ME... COULD I TRY?
TIPPY-TIPPY-TOE
WOW!! YOU'VE GOT A MILLION POINTS ALREADY!
Whoa!!
YOU'RE AMAZING, SHIBAYAN!!
BOOM BOOM
TAPPATAPPATAPPA
HEY, YOU'RE PRETTY GOOD ...
!
MWAHAHAHAHA
FWOOOOOM

↑ DRAWN BY COSTUMED CHARACTER AND MASTER CHEF OHGA-KING

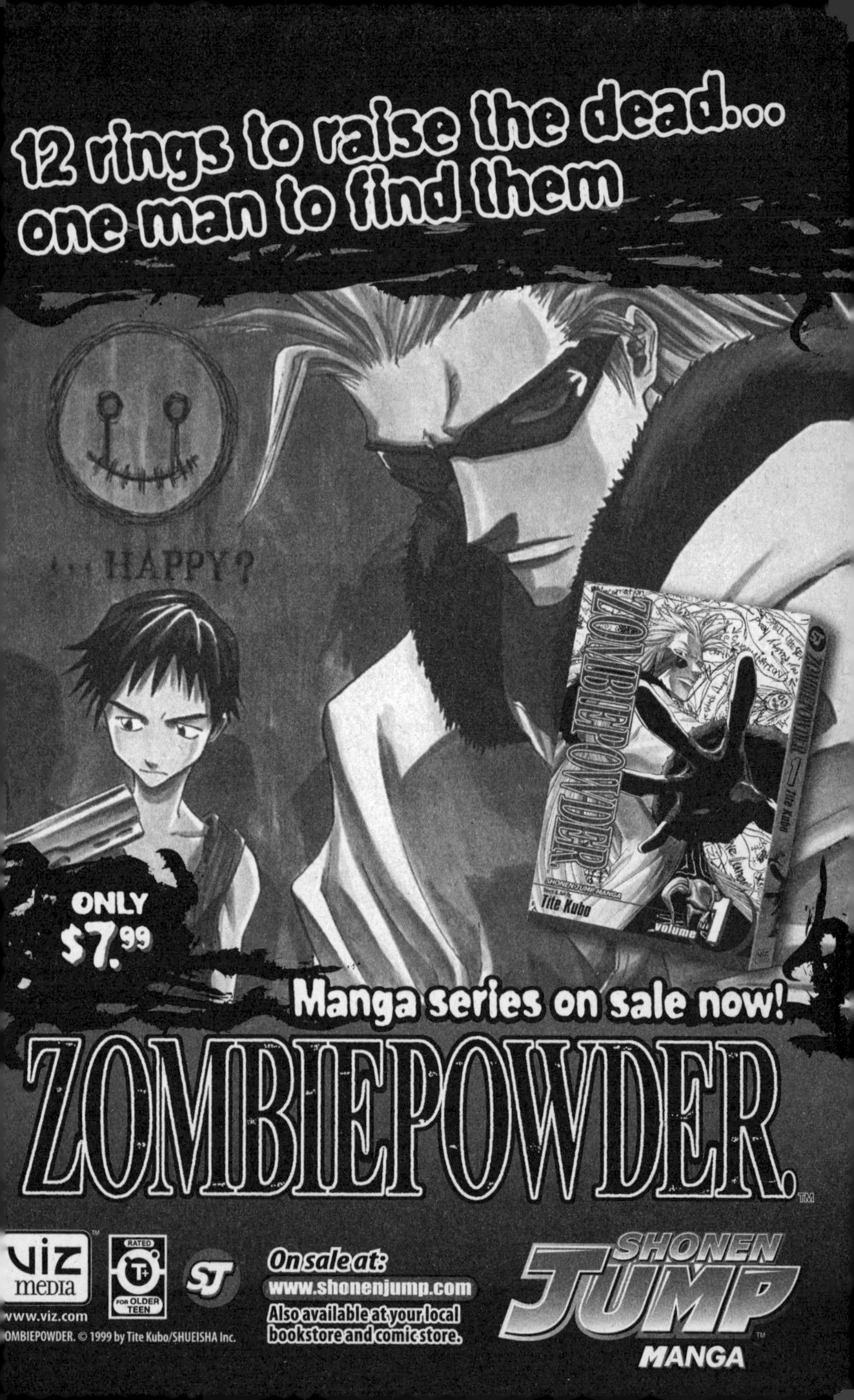
12 rings to raise the dead...
one man to find them
...HAPPY?
ONLY $7.99
Manga series on sale now!
ZOMBIEPOWDER.
viz media
www.viz.com
ZOMBIEPOWDER. © 1999 by Tite Kubo/SHUEISHA Inc.
RATED T+ FOR OLDER TEEN
On sale at:
www.shonenjump.com
Also available at your local bookstore and comic store.
SHONEN JUMP MANGA

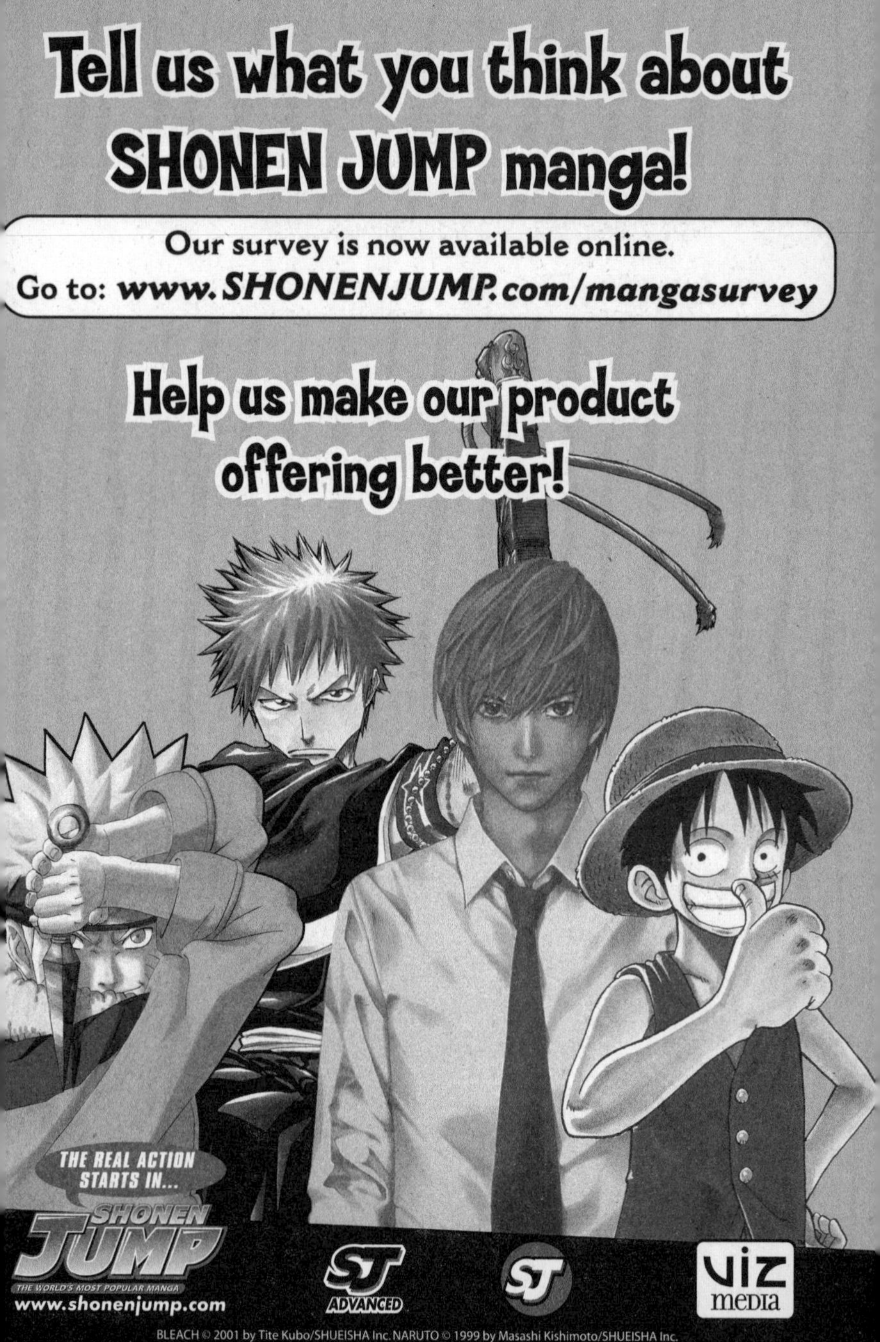
Tell us what you think about
SHONEN JUMP manga!
Our survey is now available online.
Go to: www.SHONENJUMP.com/mangasurvey
Help us make our product
offering better!
THE REAL ACTION STARTS IN...
SHONEN JUMP
THE WORLD'S MOST POPULAR MANGA
www.shonenjump.com
SJ ADVANCED
SJ
viz media